T
DUBLIN

Donated to

**Visual Art Degree
Sherkin Island**

the sixties decade of design revolution by lesley jackson

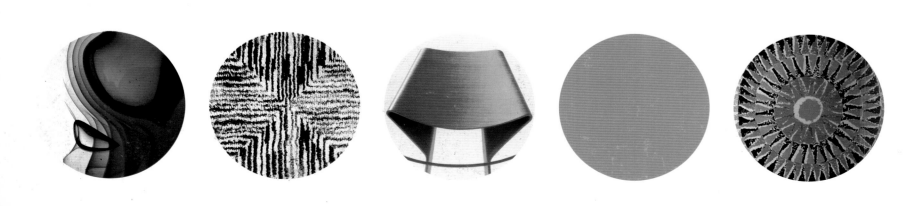

decade of design revolution

the sixties

lesley jackson

Φ

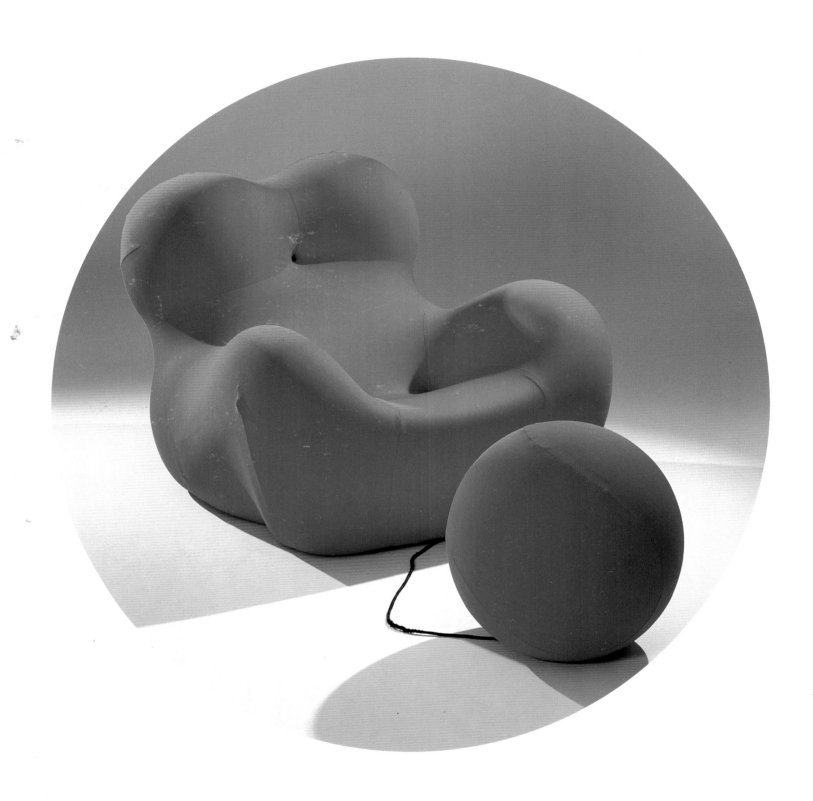

contents

In the spring of 1947 the French couturier Christian Dior electrified the fashion world with the launch of his New Look collection. The New Look marked a crucial turning point in the development of post-war fashion and signified some of the major new trends of the 1950s. Subsequently the phrase 'the New Look' was co-opted by journalists to describe other aspects of modern design that were undergoing a similarly dramatic change of appearance at this time: a style which later became known as Contemporary, because of its self-conscious modernity.

Similarly, in the early 1960s, it was a phrase originally coined by a fashion designer, Mary Quant, to describe her revolutionary new ready-to-wear youth fashions which perhaps best captures the spirit of the period. She referred to her clothes – and, significantly, the people who wore them – as having 'the look'. Speaking of one of her favourite models she said: 'She looked so beautiful wearing "the look" that other people were encouraged to try.' 'The look' was just one of the snappy phrases used by Quant in her breathless autobiography, *Quant by Quant*, published as early as 1965, which detailed the remarkable story of her rise from obscure boutique owner to international fashion icon, all in the space of less than ten years.

Another memorable phrase was Quant's reference to the 'youthquake' of the early 1960s, in which she herself was a prime mover, acting as a catalyst for the release of energy in others. She remarked in her book: 'Never before have the young set the pace as they do now. Never before have so many of the leaders, the trend-setters in all fields of design, been so young.'

Unlike Dior's New Look – the essence of luxury in the aftermath of austerity – 'the look' was something that money alone could not buy; it was as much about attitude as about clothes. As with the earlier Contemporary style, 'the look' affected furniture and fabrics as well as fashion. The Quant 'look', like the Habitat 'look' in interiors which was launched shortly afterwards, represented youthful energy and fun; it was a dynamic, cheap-and-cheerful, no-fuss style, and it prompted a consumer revolution. Unlike the New Look, 'the look' did not need a glitzy parade in a Paris fashion house to launch it. In fact, there was no launch as such; like the Beatles, it grew by popular demand, then all of a sudden exploded in the media, triggering off an international 'youthquake'. It was a revolution waiting to happen, the first of two revolutions that would shake the world of 1960s design.

The widespread popularity of Contemporary design, coinciding with the consumer boom of the latter half of the fifties, had meant that a much larger percentage of the public were aware of and affected by modern design. By the end of the decade, however, this style – originally so fresh and dynamic – was looking a little tired and was already starting to be rejected by the next generation of consumers. Amongst these were young people who had been born during or after the Second World War, with no direct recollection of the hardships that it caused or of the ensuing austerity against which the Contemporary style itself was partly a reaction. By the early 1960s the wheel had turned full circle and the newly-weds who had embraced Contemporary design when they had set up home during the early post-war period began to find that their once radical taste was now being dismissed as 'old hat'. In the early 1960s looking young and acting precociously, like Mary Quant and fellow English designer and entrepreneur Terence Conran (the founder of Habitat) – or at least being young in spirit and perennially precocious by nature, like the Italian polymath Ettore Sottsass – were essential attributes for attracting media attention and achieving commercial success. Contemporary design of the 1950s represented the belated popularization of the Modernist

opposite
Christian Dior's New Look collection, 1947. The nipped-in waist and long flared skirt of this suit emphasize the curves of the female form.

7

avant-garde aesthetic developed during the inter-war years. It was a self-consciously modern design style which affected architecture as much as, if not more than, home furnishings, and which responded to the need to create a more relaxed, informal and visually stimulating domestic environment. 'The look' of the 1960s went further still: in it, art, design and popular culture were all intertwined. Mary Quant was part of it, as were the Beatles, Bridget Riley, David Hockney, David Bailey and Twiggy, demonstrating that Britain was at the centre of things once again, having been on the margins for the previous twenty years. In 1966 the media suddenly latched on to the idea of Swinging London, and although this image would rapidly become a cliché, everyone who was involved in creating the Scene during the first half of the decade agrees that it existed, and that this was a particularly exciting and creative time.

During the late 1940s and early 1950s the Scandinavians and the Americans, having been less directly affected by the war, had taken advantage of the vacuum in Western Europe to market their new image and products abroad. Out of this grew the vogue for Scandinavian Modern and American Modern design, both of which continued, deservedly, to steal the limelight for the remainder of the 1950s. Having been so successful in establishing a distinctive identity for themselves during the early post-war period, it is not surprising that the Scandinavians and the Americans should continue to pursue this winning formula during the early 1960s. This element of continuity was important because it meant that public and commercial commitment to modern design was consolidated, but equally important was the introduction of an element of change and renewal. The major change that took place during the early 1960s was the emergence of two new design superpowers of international stature. For the remainder of the decade it was Britain and Italy that were the focus of world

Pierre Cardin in France (right) and Mary Quant in Britain (far right) were jointly responsible for creating 'the look' of the early 1960s. Arguably, Quant's impact was greater because she designed for the ready-to-wear market, whereas Cardin worked within the confines of the couture industry. The outfits shown here date from 1966–7.

attention: Britain in the fields of fashion, pattern design and popular culture; Italy in the fields of furniture, lighting and plastics. Both, in their own different ways, had an electrifying effect.

The decision to call this book *The Sixties – Decade of Design Revolution* was taken for a number of reasons. I have already suggested that what took place was not just one design revolution but two. 'Revolution' is a key word for the 1960s and I have used it in a number of different senses. Its most obvious and straightforward meaning is 'radical change' or 'dramatic upheaval'. The upheavals that design underwent during the 1960s were paralleled by major social upheavals. The first of these was positive and benign (the 'youthquake', which began to erupt around 1962); the second grew out of angry reactions to negative events and resulted in physical violence (the invasion of Czechoslovakia, and the student uprisings and Vietnam protests of 1968). This was revolution in the sense that John Lennon used the word, meaning 'wanting to change the world', although in both cases the motivation behind the desire for change arose from dissatisfaction with the Establishment. Revolution also has another meaning, however, which is equally pertinent to design in the sixties: this is revolution in the more literal sense of 'rotation'. This suggests the idea of the wheel of design history turning full circle, and of visual ideas and styles that had been out of favour coming back round into fashion again. The history of design is an endless cycle of action and reaction, and although there was much that was completely new and Space Age in the 1960s, historical revivalism – sometimes conscious, sometimes unconscious – is a thread that cannot be ignored during the second half of the decade. This in itself was 'revolutionary' (in the literal and conventional sense) after three decades of uncompromisingly modern and forward-looking design.

Whereas the story of design in the 1950s is one of coherence and convergence, the 1960s were characterized by abrupt changes of direction: a lot happened very quickly. This made it an exciting and inspiring time, but the resulting frenzy of creativity proved impossible to sustain. During the 1960s the concept of built-in obsolescence applied not only to the physical lifespan of domestic objects, but to the frenetic turnover of visual ideas. The attitude of 'here today, gone tomorrow' prevailed just as much in the world of design as in the world of fashion. New ideas arrived thick and fast, with old ideas – in the form of the rediscovery and reinterpretation of historical revival styles – following hot on their heels. In view of this, it is not surprising that many people ended the decade feeling confused rather than elated. Although superficially more accessible, therefore, the story of design in the 1960s is undoubtedly more complex than that of the 1950s. Nevertheless, in many ways these contradictions and ambiguities only serve to make the decade more interesting. An acknowledgement that they exist, and an acceptance of the idea of continuous revolution, lie at the heart of an understanding of the 1960s.

above
Tulip chair designed by Eero
Saarinen for Knoll, 1956,
shown here in an advert
from 1967. Ahead of its
time when it first appeared,
Saarinen's Tulip chair still
looked ultra-modern over a
decade later, and perfectly
complemented the Space
Age 'look' of 1960s fashion
and interiors.

one

consolidation of contemporary design

opposite
Dome House, Beachwood Canyon, Los Angeles, designed by Bernard Judge, 1960. Space frame structures, inspired by Buckminster Fuller's geodesic domes, were a distinctive feature of 'the look' of the 1960s. However, the Contemporary plastic dining chairs in this interior date back to the early 1950s and were designed by Charles Eames for Herman Miller.
right
Flamingo furnishing fabric designed by Tibor Reich for Tibor, 1957. Part of the Fotexur range, this textural abstract design was inspired by photographic enlargements of straw.

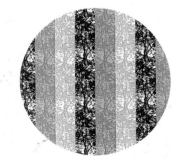

The story of design in the 1960s cannot be told without revisiting the 1950s. The fifteen years following the Second World War were crucial in establishing the distinctive social and economic conditions and the special creative climate in which domestic design would flourish during the 1960s. Just how special this climate was can only be fully appreciated by contrasting the upbeat mood that prevailed during the early 1960s with the pervasive mood of pessimism and anxiety that we have come to take for granted since the tide turned in the 1970s.

On 20 July 1957, the British Prime Minister, Harold Macmillan, made an apparently throwaway remark that some of the British population – or 'our people' as he rather patronizingly referred to them – had 'never had it so good'. The UK was not alone in experiencing a return to economic prosperity at this time. Conditions were the same, if not better, in Scandinavia, Italy and indeed most of Western Europe, while commercial confidence in the USA was at an all-time high and American standards of living were the envy of the rest of the world. This overt prosperity had a direct impact on the American public, whose optimism about the future reached a peak during the first two decades after the Second World War. After the frustrating and demoralizing experience of the war, people looked forward with genuine hope to a better and brighter future. By the early 1960s rising individual prosperity, along with more general positive economic indicators such as full employment, provided a sure sign that these improvements were on the horizon. Such confidence seems hard to countenance now because, since the 1970s, there has been

If the history of design in the 1960s starts with post-war Contemporary design, the history of Contemporary design has its roots in the inter-war Modern Movement, which in turn was a delayed response to the design reform movements of the nineteenth century. William Morris linked both the decline in standards of design and the moral decline of society to the rise of the machine. He actively explored and embraced the production techniques used by craftsmen in the Middle Ages, seeing them as a potential means of salvation on both fronts. However, it soon became apparent that the re-adoption of outmoded methods of hand-production meant that the goods that Morris produced could only be afforded by the very rich. This problem was to undermine and ultimately to destroy the Arts and Crafts Movement during the early twentieth century, as it came to be realized that the fundamental ideals behind it were economically unsustainable. Although studio potters such as Bernard Leach kept the craft ideology alive over the next fifty years, the crafts movement did not really revive again until the late 1960s and early 1970s, this time partly as a response to the impersonality of Space Age materials and technology, and partly as a delayed reaction against the aesthetics of the Modern Movement. During the 1960s the crafts movement remained very much a fringe activity, however, just one of several 'alternative' forms of expression being explored by artists and designers of the day, and one of a number of diverse options open to individuals for challenging Establishment values.

After the First World War the romantic notions about handicraft that had inspired the Arts and Crafts Movement seemed out of place, and the next design reform movement – Modernism – sought to re-establish a more positive relationship between the industrial designer and the machine. This time historical revivalism was rejected as a way forward and there was a radical reduction in the emphasis on decoration. What was deemed important now was that the form of an object should be a direct expression of its function, and that there should be no attempt to disguise the mechanical methods of production used in its manufacture. This led to a glorification of the machine aesthetic, and an expression of righteous indignation against 'senseless' decoration for its own sake, particularly surface decoration. However, just as the leaders of the Arts and Crafts Movement had transgressed the boundaries of common sense in pursuing their ideal to its 'logical' conclusion; so the Modernists went to extremes to make their point and, in so doing, not only alienated the wider public (the potential market for their newly reformed design), but also exposed their own inconsistencies. Many of the objects created at the Bauhaus and purporting to be expressions of a machine aesthetic were, in fact, largely hand-crafted. Thus the Modern Movement, although it presented itself as a style-less machine-based form of expression, exposed itself as being as idealistic and aspirational as the Arts and Crafts Movement had been fifty years earlier.

Ironically, it seems that it was partly the experience of the Second World War that finally brought the design world to its senses and made designers realize that extremism of any kind – whether pro- or anti- the machine, and whether pro- or anti-decoration – was not the answer. Truly modern or Contemporary design might be expressed through mass production, but equally, as the Scandinavians and the Italians demonstrated so well, it could find expression in hand-made

so much back-tracking. In order to appreciate the achievements of the post-war period, however, it is essential to understand the mindset of the architects and designers active at this time, and of the clients and consumers for whom they were working. This positive outlook was also the reason for the incredible success of entrepreneurial designer-retailers during the early 1960s: it gave them the confidence to break the mould and create new markets; and it gave the public the confidence to embrace the new products they were being offered and to come back clamouring for more.

Unlike the artificial economic boom of the mid-1980s, which was based on over-inflated property values and share prices rather than on increased prosperity from manufacturing, the optimism that prevailed during the early 1960s had a more solid and tangible basis. Furthermore, although desire for personal material gain was an incentive for many, at this time there was still a widely felt concern that standards of living should be raised, not just for the individual, but for society as a whole. As others have remarked, the 1960s was the age not of the 'Me' generation, but of the 'We' generation, a time when it was recognized that the well-being of the individual depended on the well-being of society. This sense of interrelationship – a feeling of mutual responsibility – between the individual and society provided a strong cohesive force bonding the two together. This bond, which had been so central to the ethos of the 1950s and early 60s, was finally shattered by the traumatic events of 1968, the repercussions of which were felt throughout Europe and the USA. After this visible crushing of revolt, many people, particularly the young, felt so betrayed by the Establishment that they sought to cut themselves off from society altogether. Some set up their own alternative communities, which often turned sour; while others sought artificial escape from their disenchantment through drugs, which in turn had a habit of destroying them. By the 1970s the age of innocence and optimism was well and truly over.

objects. Another radical feature of Contemporary design was that it openly recognized the basic human need for visual and tactile stimulation, an instinct that the Modern Movement had sought to suppress and deny. Inextricably linked to this, it acknowledged the strength of the impulse for creativity in the applied arts to be expressed in a purely aesthetic way through experiments with colour, pattern, texture and line. The frustrating and debilitating experience of the war made it more essential than ever that these creative impulses should once again find a means of expression. This, and the reaction against the earlier period of repression and denial, go some way towards explaining why the late 1940s and the 1950s were years of such dynamic creativity, because of the sheer intensity of the sense of release.

Aesthetically, Contemporary was one of the most coherent styles in the history of design. During the fifteen-year period between 1947 and 1962, architects and designers from all over the world seemed to be moving on a convergent path. Whether they were working in Brazil, Finland or California, it was remarkable how consistent and how complementary their visual ideas were. Similarly, there appeared to be a natural affinity between the fine and applied arts: not only did they stimulate each other, but they shared many common sources of outside inspiration, such as scientific imagery and organic forms in the natural world. Modern paintings and sculpture, along with Contemporary buildings, furniture, furnishings and domestic accessories, were more visually coherent than at any time since the second half of the eighteenth century, a period when architecture and the visual arts had been completely dominated in style and subject matter by the language of Neo-classicism. Contemporary design was equally comprehensive in its range and application, a complete New Look which brought unity and harmony to international design after a period of political disunity and conflict on a global scale. It brought people together in their tastes, and forged artistic links that had never existed before between different countries. Sometimes these countries were neighbours, as in the case of the Scandinavians, but more often they were geographically quite separate. In fine art, for example, there was the CoBrA alliance between artists in Copenhagen, Brussels and Amsterdam; in architecture new links were forged between France, India, Brazil and Japan, with Le Corbusier as the uniting thread; and in design, Finland, Denmark and Sweden, which had hitherto been considered on the margins of mainstream developments in the applied arts, were now accepted as being not only at the heart of Europe, but at the epicentre of the international design scene. The work of the Danish furniture designer Finn Juhl was celebrated in the USA, for example; the Finnish glass designer Tapio Wirkkala was feted in Milan and showered with Gold Medals at the Triennales; and the Swedish textile designer Astrid Sampe was welcomed as part of the design Establishment in Britain.

The situation at the start of the 1960s, therefore, was a remarkably healthy one. Creativity was rife. New buildings of all types – including housing, offices, factories, churches and schools – were in great demand, and were mostly designed in an unashamedly modern style. The new style of domestic design pioneered in Finland, Denmark and Sweden became internationally influential and triggered off initiatives in other countries such as Britain and the USA. Indeed, soon

after the war the USA itself emerged as a major new design superpower. During the 1950s the Italians were also growing in confidence. The particular strengths of the Americans were in architecture and furniture, while the Italians excelled in glass, ceramics, furniture and lighting. By the mid-1950s other countries such as Britain were also getting back on their feet, and after the lengthy period of disruption caused by the war, traditional industries such as textiles and wallpapers began to be infected by the excitement of the Contemporary style. Thus, by the end of the decade, the international pool of creative ideas was larger and more free-ranging than it had been since the turn of the century. In addition, international trade was flourishing; most Western economies were enjoying the benefits of a consumer boom, and this, in turn, fostered increased demand for new products. The 1950s was also an exciting time in the fine arts. Many of the great painters and sculptors of the 1930s – such as Joan Miró, Jean Arp, Henry Moore, Barbara Hepworth and Pablo Picasso – were still in their prime and extremely active. At the same time the art world was enlivened by the arrival of Abstract Expressionism in the USA, by the flourishing of various different forms of painterly abstraction in Europe, and by the birth of Pop Art in Britain. The combined effect of these diverse artistic and economic forces was unusually potent. It spawned a creative dynamo which turned art, design and architecture upside down during the first decade and a half after the war, and which presaged and paved the way for the subsequent design revolutions of the 1960s.

One of the factors that distinguishes the creative climate of the early 1960s so markedly from subsequent decades is the positive public attitude towards modern design. This too was a direct legacy of the 1950s, the decade that had witnessed the widespread acceptance of modern or Contemporary design after a worrying period during the 1930s when it had seemed that Modernism might forever remain stranded on the margins of public taste, the secret

above
Entenza House, Pacific Palisades, Los Angeles, designed by Charles Eames and Eero Saarinen, 1945–9. This house was among the early Case Study Houses commissioned by the progressive West Coast magazine, *Arts and Architecture*. With its flat roof, its floor-to-ceiling windows and its austere but elegant open-plan interior, the Entenza House was a classic of the Contemporary style.

right and far right
Two highlights of the Festival of Britain exhibition on London's South Bank in 1951 were the Dome of Discovery by Ralph Tubbs (right) and Skylon by Powell and Moya (far right). Spindly attenuated forms characterized both structures. In 1967 the Montreal Expo would have a similarly enlivening effect on public awareness of modern architecture, but this time on an international scale.

pleasure (some might say vice) of a tiny beleaguered European élite. The Second World War changed all that. In its aftermath it was essential that large-scale rebuilding programmes were rapidly undertaken using the most efficient and up-to-date techniques. With the new methods of construction came an opening for the new style of architecture pioneered by the Modernists, although by this date it had been subtly modified and tempered so that it was less clinical and drew upon a wider range of materials. With the New Look in architecture came Contemporary design, a self-consciously modern style showcased in the UK at the Festival of Britain; in Europe at the Milan Triennales; and in the USA at the 'Good Design' exhibitions held at the Museum of Modern Art in New York, and on the West Coast in the Case Study Houses promoted by the progressive magazine *Arts and Architecture*.

During the first two decades after the war, designers actively rejected revivalism and strove to break new ground. In the 1950s an overt commitment to Contemporary design, whether on the part of a designer or a consumer, really meant something: it was not just an expression of aesthetic judgement, it was a statement of moral values, a way of demonstrating an allegiance to a forward-looking vision. When it first came on the market, Contemporary design had real visual impact because it was so completely fresh and original. At the Festival of Britain in 1951, for example, the Dome of Discovery was literally a revelation: most visitors had never seen such a radical and futuristic building before. The same was true of the Atomium at the Brussels World Fair in 1958. During the 1950s applied art manufacturers that were committed to modern design enjoyed strength in numbers, and individual manufacturers benefited enormously from the creative cross-fertilization that took place both nationally and internationally, as well as across different disciplines. Because Contemporary design was adopted internationally, individual countries were less isolated; and because it was overtly accessible and geared towards mass production, this made it fundamentally democratic. Although not to everyone's taste, Contemporary design was certainly not limited in its appeal to the middle classes, but was adopted by a substantial cross section of society, in retailing terms from Harrods to Heal's to Woolworths. Its spontaneous rise in popularity during the course of the 1950s meant that by the turn of the decade it had won a large share of the market, and even in Britain where manufacturers and retailers were notoriously conservative, Contemporary formed at least part of the output of most firms.

As well as being visually distinctive, Contemporary design was also multifaceted: it influenced the form of both buildings and objects; it combined the decorative and the functional; it was embodied in both craft and industrial production; and it was internationally coherent at the same time as being culturally diverse. Contemporary was no mere passing fad: it continued to develop and mature throughout the course of the 1950s, and elements of it would continue to exert a strong influence on aspects of design throughout the ensuing decade. During the 1960s several different forces were in operation concurrently, with Contemporary (the face of the design Establishment) acting as a force for continuity and stability; and the 'youthquakes' of 1962 and 1968 (the first a revolution, the second a counter-revolution) representing forces for change. Only selected elements of the original Contemporary style survived beyond the end of the 1950s,

and the Contemporary style itself developed a more mature form of expression during its middle years. The 1960s began with a backlash against some of the more extreme and idiosyncratic visual characteristics of early Contemporary design, including over-exaggerated curvilinear forms, quirky linear abstract patterns, and mix-and-match colour schemes; in short, what were now perceived as the more frivolous, lightweight and playful aspects of the Contemporary style. By the end of the 1950s some designers had already begun to feel a little embarrassed about the naivety and gaucheness of their early post-war designs, and these elements were now rejected in favour of a more serious and sophisticated mode of expression.

Sophisticated Contemporary design was controlled and understated: it was the minimalist steel-framed furniture of Poul Kjaerholm rather than the exuberant sculptural wooden furniture of Finn Juhl. It was also literally more refined in the sense of being pared down to essentials: the functionalist lighting of the Finnish designer Lisa Johansson Pape for Stockmann, for example, rather than the fantastic and colourful lighting sculptures of Gino Sarfatti for Arteluce. Serious Contemporary design was an expression of both mood and moral values: it was embodied by textiles based on dense painterly abstractions rather than Miróesque doodles; controlled use of strong colour, rather than harlequin or rainbow schemes; and furniture designed for the needs of offices and corporate headquarters as well as for restaurants and the home. This growing divergence between what one might characterize as the juvenile and the mature expressions of Contemporary design, and the continued partiality of the Italians for the earlier, more playful version, perhaps accounts for the individual and overtly creative way in which Italian design was to develop subsequently. It is also at the root of some of the wider trends influencing design during the first twenty-five years after the Second World War. While the Americans and the Scandinavians, proud of their achievements during the first decade and a half after the war, and content with how things had evolved by the end of 1950s, were ready to settle down comfortably into middle age; the Italians continued to value and nurture the artistic expression associated with youth, even as some of their leading designers approached their middle years. It is significant that as British designers felt the first creative rumblings of the 'youthquake', a growing empathy would develop spontaneously between non-conformist British and mainstream Italian design.

The reason why the Americans and the Scandinavians championed the mature Contemporary aesthetic was because it enabled them to demonstrate the mastery that they had achieved over modern architecture and design. In the USA this mastery was typified by products such as the furniture designed by Charles Eames for Herman Miller. In Scandinavia the mature Contemporary style was embodied in ultra-refined domestic objects such as the stainless steel cutlery by the Swedish manufacturer Gense; Arne Jacobsen's designs for lighting by the Danish firm of Louis Poulsen; and the art glass and table glass designs of Timo Sarpaneva and Tapio Wirkkala for the Finnish factory littala. The American design Establishment had given its official sanction to the mature Contemporary aesthetic during the mid- to late 1950s by selecting such objects for inclusion in the 'Good Design'

top
Arts and Architecture from 1958. The magazine pioneered the programme of Case Study Houses from the late 1940s to the mid-1960s.
above
LCW moulded plywood lounge chair designed by Charles Eames for Herman Miller, 1946.

right
Melmex tableware designed by A H Woodfull for British Industrial Plastics (Gaydon). Plastic crockery, still something of a novelty in the 1950s, was widely used during the 1960s. This range, with its ovoid profiles, reflects the organic styling of the Contemporary era, and was displaced in 1966 by Woodfull's straight-sided Encore range.

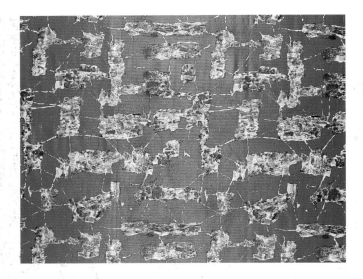

far left and left
There were two distinct phases in the development of Contemporary textile design. Early patterns, such as Lucienne Day's Herb Antony for Heal's, 1955 (see page 20), were linear and playful, influenced by the paintings of Miró and Klee. Later patterns were freer and more painterly, reflecting the influence of abstract expressionism. Oak, designed by Dorothy Carr for Heal's, 1958 (left), embodies this aesthetic, as does Fuma di Londra (far left), designed by Daphne Barder for the Italian firm J S A Busto Arsizio. The latter won an award at the Milan Triennale in 1957, and was subsequently marketed in Britain by Sanderson.

left
Aluminium-framed, moulded plywood restaurant chair designed for use on the QE2 by Robert Heritage for Race Furniture, 1969. Heritage symbolized the type of professional multi-disciplinary industrial designer approved by the Council of Industrial Design. Along with Robin Day and Robert Welch, he won numerous Design Centre Awards during the 1960s.

below
PK24 chaise longue designed by Poul Kjaerholm for E Kold Christensen, 1965. Made of wicker with a stainless steel frame, PK24 is a variant on an earlier chair dating from 1956. Kjaerholm's cool, minimalist style typifies the aesthetic of the mature Contemporary idiom.

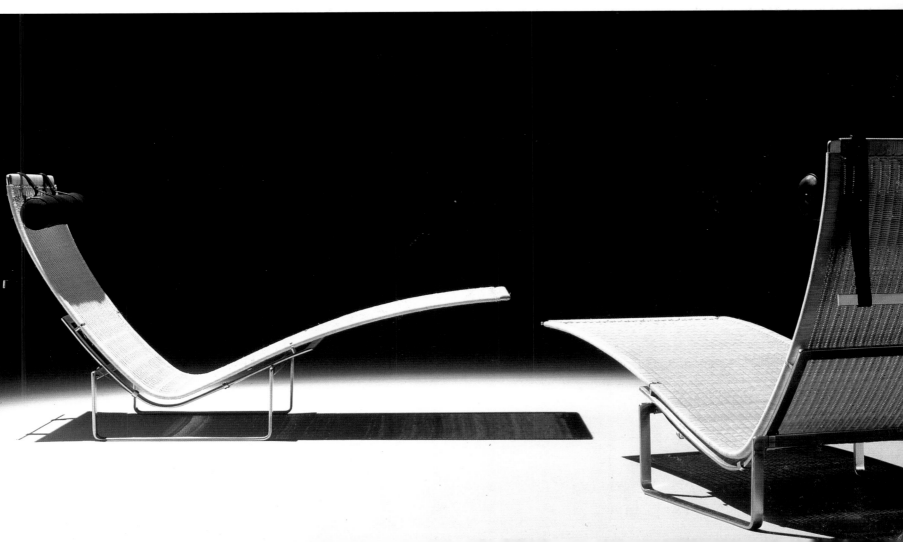

left
Age of Kings furnishing fabric commissioned for the Shakespeare Centre in Stratford-upon-Avon, built to celebrate the 400th anniversary of Shakespeare's birth in 1964. The fabric was produced by the local firm Tibor.

below
Herb Antony fabric designed by Lucienne Day for Heal's, 1955.

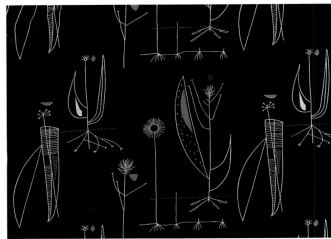

Danish Furniture

Examples from our extensive range of furniture imported exclusively and distributed in Great Britain by—Frederick Restall Limited.

STOCKISTS THROUGHOUT THE COUNTRY

Enquiries invited for the name and address of your nearest stockist.

FREDERICK RESTALL LIMITED.
Great Hampton Street, Birmingham 18.

Telephone: NORthern 2252 & 7501.

left and above
Advert for Danish furniture imported by Frederick Restall, 1961 (left). The sideboard in the centre is similar in shape to the Hamilton sideboard designed by Robert Heritage for Archie Shine (above), winner of a Design Centre Award in 1958. Danish furniture was exported in quantity during the late 1950s and early 1960s, and exerted a major influence on British and American design.

exhibitions held at the Museum of Modern Art in New York, while in Britain they were showered with Design Centre Awards. A relatively small number of design-led firms such as Herman Miller and Hille exerted a significant influence on the market, while increasing public exposure to the Scandinavian Modern style, which arose as a direct result of an export drive by Finland, Denmark and Sweden. This attracted widespread media attention and had a strong influence on the market.

Scandinavian furniture had a major impact in Britain during the late 1950s and early 1960s. Not only was it being imported on a large scale but the style of Danish furniture, in particular, had a significant influence on the output of British manufacturers. Typical of the furniture to which British consumers were being exposed were the ranges imported by the London-based wholesaler Finmar, and Frederick Restall of Birmingham. These included teak-framed armchairs and nesting coffee tables by firms such as France & Son and Poul Jeppesen, plywood dining chairs by Fritz Hansen and long, low coffin-shaped sideboards, some of which appear in an advert for Restall in *House and Garden* in March 1961. The influence of the Danish aesthetic can be seen in the Hamilton sideboard designed by Robert Heritage for Archie Shine, winner of a Design Centre Award in 1958, along with the innumerable other variants of this model which appeared on the market in Britain during the late 1950s and early 1960s, all aping the elegant low-slung form and teak finish of contemporary Danish furniture. Another indication of the British design Establishment's desire to associate itself with the mature Contemporary aesthetic was the introduction by the Council of Industrial Design of a new annual prize known as the Duke of Edinburgh's Award for Elegant Design. The first award was presented in 1960 to Neal French and David White for their Apollo tableware for Copeland, a range clearly influenced by Scandinavian ceramics such as those of Stig Lindberg for the Swedish firm Gustavsberg.

In some respects what was happening was a shifting of allegiances back towards the more rigorous and purist Modernist aesthetic. 'Decorative' was once again in danger of becoming a dirty word and, instead, functionalism was being trumpeted as the be-all and end-all of design. In Britain the 'design police', as Gillian Naylor has described them, were visibly out on patrol. The Criminal Investigation Department (CID) or Federal Bureau of Investigation (FBI) of the British design Establishment was the Council of Industrial Design (COID, later renamed the Design Council), while the Central Office of Information (COI, the official propaganda department of the British Government) was *Design* magazine in Britain and *Industrial Design* in the USA. This explains why, if judged purely by the contents of *Design*, British design during the 1960s appears rather limited and dull, because of the level of unofficial censorship being imposed. In fact the opposite was true: this was a time of unparalleled creativity and confidence, a fact inadequately acknowledged by the choices of the judges in the annual Design Centre Awards instituted by the COID from 1957 onwards. Although these awards do recognize some of the achievements of leading British designers and manufacturers of the day, the range of products that received the Council's endorsement was extremely restricted and does not represent the breadth of creativity which was starting to manifest itself in Britain at this time. The strength and diversity of pattern design in particular was undervalued

by the COID, with firms such as Sekers and Donald Brothers, manufacturers of plain dyed silks and traditional tweeds respectively, being singled out for praise, while the bold flamboyant printed fabrics of Barbara Brown for Heal's during the first half of the 1960s were overlooked, a choice that reeks of Bauhaus-influenced prejudices against printed patterns. Heal Fabrics and Hull Traders, Britain's two most creative furnishing fabric manufacturers during the 1960s, did both win Design Centre Awards, but somehow the extent of their creative dominance appears to have been underplayed by the COID because it did not entirely fit in with their vision of the new advanced Modernist Britain.

This undervaluing by the COID of the exuberance and sheer visual dynamism of British design in the 1960s, particularly in the fields of textiles, wallpaper and fashion, was in sharp contrast to the way in which other countries responded to Britain's achievements. By the middle of the decade not only British popular culture but British fashion, graphics and design were receiving considerable attention from foreign journalists who were keen to highlight the vibrancy of the British design scene. In addition to the famous article on 'London – The Swinging City' that appeared in *Time* magazine on 13 April 1966, there were important features in several other American magazines, such as *Life* and *Esquire*. The international design press also suddenly began to pay attention. An article entitled 'Good Day London' appeared in the Swedish magazine *Form* (no 9) in 1966, for example. This was followed by an 'English Tour' in the American magazine *Interiors* in December 1966, subtitled 'An informal report on the Anglican iconoclasts'; while the following year their sister magazine *Industrial Design* printed a feature in October 1967 called 'Action in England' by Michael Webb, describing how 'Young designers with young ideas have transformed "merrie olde" England into a designer's avant-garde workshop.' The Italian design Bible *Domus* published two photo-essays about the London 'scene' by Ettore Sottsass, the first in January 1967, the second in November 1969; and the Danish furniture periodical *Mobilia* produced a special issue devoted exclusively to British design in March 1968. Thus, within the space of two years, Britain was recognized by the leading design nations of the world as one of the new creative superpowers of the 1960s.

While foreign commentators, both lightweight and serious, were singing the praises not only of the Beatles but of British design in its more populist manifestations, the COID apparently failed to appreciate the significance of what was happening on their own doorstep. With a few exceptions, writers in *Design* magazine tended to speak in somewhat disparaging and disapproving terms of the dangers of Pop design and the evils of Carnaby Street, the latter being synonymous with all that was aesthetically and commercially unacceptable to the design police. Although this narrow-minded and judgmental attitude was gradually relaxed during the course of the decade, in general the type of products endorsed by the COID and illustrated in *Design* magazine continued to fall into the category of Modernist-style reformed Contemporary design. Typical of the firms which advertised in and were openly endorsed by *Design* was the lighting company Allom Heffer, which worked mainly for the contract market. Its designs were so low key and pared down in aesthetic terms as to be almost devoid of any identifiable element of visual expression. This was Functionalism, and the idea of form following function, taken to its logical conclusion. The problem was that, whereas such an anonymous approach might well be suited to offices, it did not provide much stimulation in the domestic environment.

It was in the domestic furniture and lighting market that the Italians triumphed during the 1960s, just as the Danes had done during the previous decade. After the Second World War the Italians had concentrated on renewing their design strengths and building up their industries. By the early 1960s small workshops serviced by freelance architects were developing into factories, and the number of architects offering their services as designers was proliferating. Whereas during the 1950s the Italians had been content to act as hosts at the international exhibitions to the Scandinavians and the Americans, and had welcomed and celebrated the creativity of these foreign design superpowers, during the 1960s the Italians themselves grew in confidence and gradually came to dominate the exhibitions and trade fairs. Increasingly the exhibitions of design that they mounted focused on their own creative output and became a celebration of the renaissance of Italian design. By the second half of the 1960s, in addition to the Milan Triennales, which focused on decorative art and design in general, an annual Furniture Fair was now held in Milan which began to rival the more established international trade fair at Cologne. Meanwhile Italian glass continued to be celebrated at the Venice Biennales alongside the major international art exhibition, and in 1966 *Domus* magazine launched another new exhibition initiative called *Eurodomus*, which alternated between the twin design capitals of Milan and Turin. Having ousted virtually all foreign competition from Italy itself, not by imposing trade embargoes but simply by the sheer volume and quality of work being produced at home, the Italians set about invading the rest of Europe, including hitherto self-sufficient Scandinavia. Towards the end of the decade they began to set their sights further afield across the Atlantic, a plan of campaign culminating in the triumphant and provocative exhibition *Italy – The New Domestic Landscape* at the Museum of Modern Art in New York in 1972.

While the Italians represented the force of change within the international design community and aspired to achieve something more than the pursuit of good taste in the accepted mature Contemporary idiom, the Scandinavians retained a strong core allegiance to the ideals and the aesthetics of Contemporary design right through until the end of the decade. This attitude is reflected in an article called 'Function, Sensuality and Morality' written in 1962 by Arthur Hald in issue no. 3 of *Form*, the mouthpiece of the Svenska Slöjdföreningen (the Swedish Society for Industrial Design), where he reasserted his faith in the post-war ideal of Modernism with a human face: 'We need a utility product which is sensual, a product combining the considerable functional and aesthetic import that a heightened standard of living has made feasible.' Similar views were expressed by the Swedish furniture designer Carl-Axel Acking, writing in *Form* (no. 4) the following year in a review of the annual Swedish Furniture Fair: 'If one was expecting novelties in design and construction, this year's fair wasn't remarkable. However, an even, high technical quality was shown, an exemplary display of orthodoxy and unity with strong ties to a democratic way of life.' Although this continued commitment to the Contemporary style did not preclude new departures – the work of the Danish designer Verner Panton in the field of furniture; Lars Hellsten and Ann and Göran Wärff in the field of Swedish glass; and Marjatta Metsovaara and Marimekko in the field of Finnish textiles, all provide good examples of the injection of 'new blood' into mainstream Scandinavian design – the dominant aesthetic of the majority of applied art manufacturers in Scandinavia during the 1960s remained the Contemporary style of the previous decade.

This was hardly surprising given the achievements of the 1950s. The Finns, Danes and Swedes had initiated a dramatic renaissance in the applied arts after the war and had established standards of design and production hitherto unparalleled in Scandinavia. They had also earned enormous critical prestige on the international stage, and through their active export drive they had achieved considerable commercial success. Scandinavian design literally put Scandinavia itself on the cultural map during the 1950s, so it was understandable that they should be cautious about risking the loss of their new-found success after having established a winning creative and commercial formula. This attitude comes through clearly in a comment made by Erik Berglund in *Form* (no 9) in 1961. Remarking on an exhibition called 'Dream Homes' mounted by a group of Stockholm furniture dealers, Berglund noted that: 'Several types can be differentiated among the dream homes of 1961. First there is the Nordic blonde interior which is still wearing well. Another type could be called the romantic and a third is akin to the modernistically angular.' What Berglund describes as 'Nordic blonde' was what others would characterize as the Scandinavian Modern style. Its continuing commercial success explains why there was no abrupt change of direction in Scandinavian design at the start of the 1960s, and no sudden rejection of the achievements of the pioneers of the early post-war period. Equally, however, although there were no immediate radical departures, there were no signs of stagnation either and Scandinavian design would continue to look fresh for several years to come.

The designers who had been responsible for creating the Scandinavian Modern style continued to practice actively, and to develop and hone their expression during the 1960s. Originally, during the late 1940s, Scandinavian designers had been working in a vacuum, which was part of the reason why they made such a big impact; by the early 1960s their designs were being launched in an entirely different context, both in terms of audience familiarity and market buoyancy. High standards were now expected as a matter of course, and it was taken for granted that the levels of creativity and quality that Scandinavian designers and manufacturers had achieved during the 1950s would be sustained. To demonstrate how Contemporary design was consolidated and developed in Scandinavia during the 1960s it is worth examining the later careers of some of the leading protagonists: the furniture designers Arne Jacobsen and Hans Wegner in Denmark; the ceramic designer Stig Lindberg and the glass designer Ingeborg Lundin in Sweden; and Finland's two leading glass artists, Tapio Wirkkala and Timo Sarpaneva, both of whom also worked in different media, including ceramics, wood, metal and textiles.

In the case of the architect Arne Jacobsen, his work illustrates the seamless transition from one decade to another.

above and right
St Catherine's College,
Oxford, completed in 1963
by the Danish architect,
Arne Jacobsen, contrasts
severely rectilinear architecture with organic furniture.

below, bottom left, bottom centre
The career of the Danish architect, Arne Jacobsen, demonstrates the evolution of the mature Contemporary style into 'the look'. His ply-wood Ant chair of 1952 (bottom left), and his leather-covered Egg chair of 1958 (bottom centre), both for Fritz Hansen, reflect the fluid, plastic forms popular during the 1950s. His Cylinda-Line stainless steel tableware (below), for A S Stelton, developed between 1964–7, is the per-fect embodiment of the geo-metric 'look' of the 1960s.

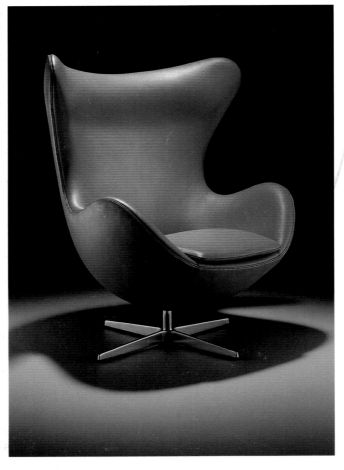

above
Wishbone chair designed by Hans Wegner for Carl Hansen, 1950. Whereas the stylistic development of most designers can be easily traced chronologically, Wegner followed a less obvious course and returned to particular themes – in this case the Chinese Chair form – at intervals throughout his career.

His great masterpiece of the early 1960s, St Catherine's College in Oxford, had in fact been designed during the late 1950s, although it was not finally completed until 1963. Perhaps because of the lengthy period from genesis to fruition, it embodies both the culmination and the summation of his design ideas of the 1950s. In architectural terms it represents a further refinement on his earlier buildings. Jacobsen himself considered it his best work: for him it represented an epiphany because of the satisfyingly complete way in which he was able to combine and unify all the hitherto disparate areas of his design activities. What Jacobsen created in this building was the ideal controlled environment in which to house his earlier furniture, lighting and metalwork designs. In addition, though, as with previous projects such as the Royal Hotel in Copenhagen (1959–61), he created some completely new designs specially for this building, notably the Oxford chair series and the St Catherine range of lighting. The original high-backed Oxford chairs with their elegant curvilinear profile were prompted by the specific nature of the brief, to design a set of chairs suitable for the high table in the college dining room. It was important that this furniture should subtly differentiate the fellows of the college from the students, although at the same time it had to blend in aesthetically and not appear grand or pretentious. The original Oxford chair spawned other variants, including an upholstered armchair made of laminated and bent wood, which was used in the students' study bedrooms. The St Catherine range of lighting came in three versions, wall-lamps, pendant lamps and table lamps, and was designed for use in the college common rooms, library and dining room. The common feature was an elliptical opal glass shade with varied mounts and casings. What characterizes both these designs, and Jacobsen's other designs of the 1960s, which include his Cylinda-Line stainless steel tableware range for A S Stelton in 1967, and the Vola range of sanitary fittings (including taps and shower fittings) for the firm of I P Lund in 1969, was their restraint. The designs themselves are expressive, but the expressive element has been pared down to a minimum, thus heightening its intensity. A comparison with some of Jacobsen's earlier designs from the 1950s illustrates how he developed and refined his version of the Contemporary style over a period of seventeen years between 1952, when the Ant chair appeared, and 1969, when the Vola range was launched. Both the Ant chair and Series 7 group – all made of moulded plywood with thin insect-like tubular steel legs – although extremely practical, were visually playful and quirky. This description also applies to the organic forms of the later Swan and Egg chairs of 1958. A turning point came in 1959, however, with the design of the much more angular and severe AJ lamp, originally created for the Royal Hotel in Copenhagen, and from this date onwards Jacobsen's designs were much more simple and austere: organic elements were reduced and geometric forms became the dominant aesthetic, but in a highly controlled and self-contained way.

Although Jacobsen's designs have become classics, and have thus transcended the time in which they were originally created, it is possible to hazard a guess at the approximate date they first appeared as each has distinct visual characteristics recalling a particular period. The same cannot be said for Hans Wegner whose designs, produced over a forty-year period from the late 1940s onwards, are genuinely timeless. There is very little that differentiates the designs from his early career from those created more recently, or which pinpoints them to a specific moment in time such as the 1960s. Wegner has always had a series of recurrent themes in his work, and what has prompted him at a certain moment in time to return to a particular idea in order to explore it further has had little to do with the outside forces of fashion. So although Wegner's work has clearly progressed over time, it has not followed an obvious linear or chronological course. In 1944 Wegner designed his first oriental-inspired chair, the Chinese chair, made of solid cherry or mahogany. This was followed a year later by a second Chinese chair for P P Møbler, with a distinctive steam-bent, all-in-one back and arm rail made of solid ash. These were succeeded by a classic design known simply as The Chair dating from 1949; the Wishbone chair of 1950 and the Cowhorn chair of 1952. Although there are some similarities between these designs, each has its own distinct character. Elements of all five of these earlier designs can be seen in the PP201 armchair designed by Wegner in 1969 for P P Møbler. Made of solid ash, oak or mahogany, this chair has the same all-in-one curved back and arm rail, a woven cord seat and, like the Cowhorn chair, the back rail is inlaid with a darker coloured wood, in this case wengé, to highlight the joints between the different sections of laminated wood. The Cowhorn chair had an even more direct successor nine years after it was created in the Bull chair, also manufactured by Johannes Hansen. The Ox chair of 1960, produced by Erik Jørgensen Møbelfabrik, although it has a similar-sounding name, was quite different to the Bull and the Cowhorn chairs, being a large-scale foam-padded, leather-upholstered armchair with legs made of chromium-plated tubular steel. During the 1950s, Wegner's name became synonymous with Danish furniture, and Danish furniture became synonymous with the Scandinavian Modern version of the Contemporary style. This relationship and these associations continued throughout the 1960s, and were one of the ways in which design continuity was maintained at a time of rapid change.

Before new blood was injected into the Swedish glass industry with the arrival of a squad of iconoclastic young designers and proto-studio glassmakers in the mid-1960s, new developments were dependent on the initiatives of designers whose careers dated back to the thirties, forties and fifties. Ingeborg Lundin was one of the younger designers and it was she, along with Nils Landberg, Edvin Öhrström and Sven Palmqvist, who had pioneered the Contemporary aesthetic at Orrefors during the 1950s. Of the four, it was Lundin who went on to produce some of the most interesting and innovative designs during the ensuing decade, helped from 1959 onwards by a new recruit, Gunnar Cyrén. There were particular techniques at Orrefors such as Ariel and Graal which, because they had been pioneered at the factory by earlier designers such as Edward Hald and Edvin Öhrström, had become indelibly associated with the output of the firm. In this area it would have been easy for the company to fall back on tried and tested designs, but what Lundin did during the 1960s was to update the application of these techniques by formulating a new aesthetic. For the Ariel range, in which air bubbles were captured within the walls of the vessel, she created a simple straight-sided vase decorated with a strong geometric pattern of squares and triangles. The Graal

above
Advert for the New York showroom of Frederik Lunning in 1961, illustrating the wide range of Hans Wegner chairs he was importing from Denmark at this date.

technique, in which veils of transparent coloured glass were suspended in the walls of the vessel, was redeployed in an entirely new way to create patterns with criss-crossing optical effects on vessels with angular shapes. Prior to this, both the Ariel and Graal techniques had been primarily associated with fluid organic patterns and shapes, but Lundin broke new ground by introducing this element of geometry. Geometric precision was also a feature of Lundin's cut patterns of the 1960s, whereas, by contrast, in her engraved designs she developed an entirely different form of expression which was much more free and painterly. During the 1950s, Lundin had created some exquisite and highly distinctive linear engraved patterns, often semi-representational with surrealistic subject matter. During the 1960s, however, she abandoned linear engraving in favour of much flatter and broader markings resembling daubed brushstrokes, which were deliberately left raw and unpolished. These designs, which were first shown in 1963 in a joint exhibition with Gunnar Cyrén at Svensk Form, had a magical airy quality which was completely new in glass at this date. Lundin showed herself to be open to new ideas throughout the decade, and by 1968 her work was starting to reveal the influence of the burgeoning studio glass movement, with a further shift away from geometric precision towards self-consciously lumpy and inelegant forms decorated with random specks of colour.

For designers such as Lundin, who had scaled such creative heights during the 1950s, it was a challenge to sustain these levels of achievement and to go on to produce something new during the 1960s. For Stig Lindberg, who had begun his career fifteen years earlier and who had an even longer personal track record and even higher public expectations to contend with, the challenge was proportionately greater. Having worked for Gustavsberg since 1937, Lindberg decided to step down as artistic director of the factory in 1957, although he continued to play an active role in fostering the work of artists from the next generation, such as Britt-Louise Sundell and Lisa Larson. He also taught at the Konstfackskolan, the Swedish State School of Arts and Crafts, from 1957 onwards, and in his capacity as a lecturer he exerted a strong influence on the development of design in Sweden in general. As one might expect, Lindberg was an inspirational teacher, but in ensuring that the work of others was nurtured and promoted, however, attention was inevitably distracted from Lindberg's own work, although in fact he continued to be productive throughout the decade. Adverts for Gustavsberg appeared regularly in *Form* magazine during this period, and although only a few of these illustrate works by Lindberg himself, his presiding spirit can still be felt very strongly. As during the 1950s, Lindberg's involvement in the output at Gustavsberg was on many different levels: both shapes and patterns for industrially produced tableware and cookware (such as the LO bone china service of 1961, and the pretty Prunus pattern of 1962); as well as one-off pieces, both vessels and ceramic sculptures, created in the Gustavsberg Studio. It was through his parallel input into these areas that such a high level of creative achievement was sustained.

Lindberg's main problem as a designer during the 1960s was that his work was deeply rooted in the mood and the aesthetic of the late 1940s and early 1950s, the playful early period of Contemporary design. Because this type of

top and above
After he stepped down in 1957 as artistic director at Gustavsberg, Stig Lindberg continued to generate designs for ceramics. His Domino range of 1955 (top), with its geometric shapes and pattern, prefigures 'the look' and remained in production until 1970. By contrast, his Prunus tableware of 1962 (above), recalls Contemporary style.

above right
Ingeborg Lundin, the creator of the Apple vase, a classic of Contemporary design, continued to produce stunning work throughout the 1960s. Illustrated here is a large straight-sided vase which reflects Lundin's interest in abstract pattern-making. Decorated with 'raw' unpolished engraving, it was made for an exhibition at Svensk Form in 1963.

levity suited his nature, he never fully engaged with the later mature version of Contemporary design, which is why some of his work of the 1960s, particularly his figurative ceramic sculptures, seems somewhat anachronistic. However, this whimsical element was by no means completely alien to the 1960s, as the popularity of Bjorn Wiinblad's designs underlines. An important new area in which Lindberg became increasingly involved from the late 1950s onwards was the creation of large-scale ceramic relief wall sculptures, which were in great demand because of the building boom at this time. A series of monumental murals were produced from 1958 onwards for colleges, libraries, hospitals, department stores, corporate headquarters and banks throughout Sweden. Each of these works was a major undertaking and some were produced using the sand-casting technique devised by Anders Liljefors, his colleague at Gustavsberg. Some panels had figurative elements and were painted in enamels, others were more abstract and relied on purely textural patterns for their effect. A new area of industrial design in which Lindberg became involved during the 1960s was plastics, a field into which Gustavsberg expanded in order to make a pre-emptive strike on a potential area of competition.

During the late 1940s and early 1950s two giants emerged in the field of Finnish glass design, Tapio Wirkkala and Timo Sarpaneva, both of whom worked for the firm of littala. Together they dominated Finnish design for the next twenty years. At the start of the 1960s they were both at the height of their powers, and their work was stunningly showcased, along with that of Finland's other major designers, in the *Finlandia* exhibition designed by Sarpaneva, which toured to several different countries in 1961. Wirkkala got off to an incredibly strong start with the launch of his Paader's Ice range of vases in 1960, craggy and striated forms of varying heights, intended to be grouped together for maximum effect. These strongly sculptural and richly textured cast vessels, which won a Gold Medal at the Milan Triennale in 1960, marked a new departure for Wirkkala. Both their shapes and surface textures alike were formed as a result of contact with the surface of a mould, rather than, as previously, being free-blown and engraved (as in the case of the Kantarelli vases of 1946–7), or shaped by cutting (as in the Iceberg vase of 1952), or manipulated and acid-etched (as in the Lichen range of 1950). The new methods that would dominate the 1960s were casting (sometimes using centrifugal force, as in the case of Wirkkala's Hole in the Ice dish of 1970) or blowing the molten glass into a textured mould. Such methods opened up new possibilities for creating rugged and irregular sculptural forms and for exploring rich and unusual textures. The benefit of these processes was that they could be applied both to limited-run art objects and to production tableware, as in the case of Wirkkala's hugely successful and influential Ultima Thule range of 1968, which captures the effect of melting and dripping ice. Although his designs were highly sophisticated and carefully controlled, throughout the 1960s Wirkkala promoted the idea of himself as a rough-and-ready, down-to-earth, peasant-artisan, living close to nature and in tune with the natural world. Although not a studio glassmaker himself, indirectly his work fostered the growth of the craft movement and the craft aesthetic. This was because, although highly controlled, Wirkkala's work suggested that elements of spontaneity and chance were involved in the

designing and making process. A comparison between Wirkkala's exquisite designs and the inept lumpen creations of the first generation of studio glassmakers, however, is enough to counter that suggestion.

With the work of Timo Sarpaneva, however, there is perhaps an element of truth in this idea because, in his Finlandia series, produced from 1964 onwards, chance did play a part in shaping the final forms. This was because, rather than using metal moulds, Sarpaneva's glass was blown into carved alderwood moulds and, as a result of the contact between the hot glass and the wood, the inside of the mould was set alight, and the glass took on the texture of the charred wood. Thus the precise patterning varied from piece to piece, moulds had to be regularly replaced, and each object produced by these means was essentially unique. Whereas Wirkkala had explored the theme of texture in many different ways in his work of the 1950s – so that Paader's Ice, although revolutionary, can be seen as the natural development of earlier ideas – Sarpaneva's designs of the 1950s, right up to his Sleeping Birds of 1960, had had perfectly smooth surfaces, a refinement often achieved through extensive cutting and polishing, as in the case of his Brancusi-esque *Kayak* sculpture of 1954. The sudden adoption of exaggeratedly crude, misshapen forms and of charred surfaces came as a genuine shock, therefore, and indicated the extent to which Sarpaneva was determined to break the mould of Finnish glass. The use of wooden moulds was not viable for mass-production wares, however, because the mould was destroyed so rapidly during the making process. Tablewares, in any case, needed to be of a consistent size and shape in order to be commercially saleable. What Sarpaneva did, therefore, as with Wirkkala in his Ultima Thule range, was to devise a more durable metal mould into which tableware could be cast (in the case of stemware) or blown (in the case of hollow vessels). This led to the development of a textured range originally known as Juhlalasi, later renamed Festivo, launched in 1968, which continued in production for several decades. This range proved influential in two respects, primarily because of its rough surface texture, but also because of its flanged forms. The flanging was particularly pronounced on the candlesticks, produced in eight different sizes. The extent to which the Festivo range and the earlier Finlandia pieces were used as a source of inspiration by other glass manufacturers is indicated by how widely moulded textured surfaces were adopted for glass tableware during the late 1960s and early 1970s. In Britain its influence can be seen in the Glacier and Everest tableware ranges produced by Whitefriars Glass during this period, although Whitefriars' chief designer, Geoffrey Baxter, had in fact hit upon the idea of mould-blown Bark textured vases independently in 1966. A further measure of Sarpaneva's international influence, and the enduring popularity of the Festivo range in particular, is provided by the machine-produced Siesta range made by another British firm, Ravenhead Glass, from the early 1970s.

Interesting by-products of Sarpaneva's Finlandia range were the cast-off wooden moulds that were displayed in their own right as works of sculpture. Five hundred sections were displayed together in a huge installation called *Drift Ice* at the Montreal Expo in 1967. Also on display at the Expo, and one of the highlights of the Scandinavian Pavilion, was a major

above
Orrefors, the leading Swedish glass factory of the 1950s, retained its pre-eminence during the following decade. This Ravenna vase designed by Sven Palmqvist, reflects the geometry of the early 'look'. It was made for an exhibition at the Nordiska Kompaniet department store in Stockholm in 1963.

new sculpture by Tapio Wirkkala called *Ultima Thule*. Made of carved laminated birchwood, it was inspired by an aerial view of a river valley in Lapland. Wirkkala's career took on a significant international dimension during the 1960s through his participation in events such as this and through his work for foreign manufacturers. In his designs for the Italian glass manufacturer Venini, Wirkkala took the opportunity to explore techniques and colours which were traditional to Italy rather than to his native Finland, and thus he created some vessels which used the filigree technique, and others which combined rich colours and metallic inclusions such as gold foil. Working in Italy was like being in a parallel universe: here Wirkkala could indulge in the type of fantasies which simply would not have been appropriate on his home territory. Another foreign manufacturer with which he collaborated on a regular basis throughout the 1960s was the German ceramics firm Rosenthal. As well as designing tableware in the Modernist idiom, Wirkkala created some unusual vases in matt white porcelain in 1964, the outlines of which were composed of a series of deep striations. Thus Wirkkala introduced into another medium visual ideas which he had already begun to explore in glass, although the material and the processes of production ensured that the two were visually quite distinct.

In Britain two designers who had begun their careers during the 1950s, and who continued to uphold both the ideals and the aesthetics of Contemporary design throughout the ensuing decade, were Robert Welch and Robin Day. Welch is best known as a metalwork designer, although in fact his designs from the 1960s encompassed a wide range of other products, including ceramics, glass, clocks, tools,

kitchenware and lighting. During the 1960s he continued to act as consultant designer for the West Midlands stainless steel manufacturer J & J Wiggin, which marketed its domestic products under the name of Old Hall Tableware. This alliance had begun in 1956 when Welch had designed a successful tableware range called Campden along organic Scandinavian lines; the cutlery was a result of a collaboration with fellow Royal College of Art graduate, David Mellor. By the early 1960s Welch's work for Old Hall had become both more confident and more distinctively English, the well-proportioned and subtly detailed Alveston range of 1962 being one of his best designs. The tableware in this range was angular without being severe, while the outlines of the accompanying cutlery were fluid and attenuated, making an interesting and stimulating juxtaposition. Two years later, with his robust and highly practical Bistro range of 1964 with its square-shaped, rosewood handles, Welch became one of the first post-war metalwork designers to abandon all-metal cutlery in favour of a combination of wood and metal. Stainless steel was by no means the only metal with which he worked. He produced one-off commissions in precious metals as well as production designs, such as an attractive range of domestic silver designed for Heal's in 1964. He also experimented with base metals, in particular cast iron, an unfashionable material which he completely revitalized. Foremost among his other product designs of the 1960s were ceramics (including a range of Government-issue crockery as well as work for a commercial manufacturer); lighting (a range of floor, table, wall and pendant lamps for Lumitron with dome-shaped smoked perspex hoods over opalescent shades); and clocks (including both

above left and above
The Finnish glass factory, littala, which had won so many accolades during the 1950s, continued to set the trend in the 1960s. Timo Sarpaneva's Finlandia range, 1964 (above left) was blown in charred wooden moulds. Later, the textured 'look' was applied to production tablewares, including Tapio Wirkkala's Ultima Thule drinking glasses (above), 1968.

alarm clocks and wall clocks for the Scottish firm of Westclox). While Welch's work was clearly driven by the Modernist urge to create objects that were undeniably functional and served a real and useful purpose in the home, the Scandinavian urge to create something beautiful (in a quiet unassuming way) as well as useful, was equally strong. Welch himself had visited Sweden and Norway during 1953–4 and maintained strong links with the Scandinavian design community throughout the 1960s. He was a great admirer of the Danish furniture magazine *Mobilia*, which returned the compliment by publishing a special feature on his work in August 1967. In his designs of the 1960s Welch effortlessly combined the mature Contemporary aesthetic with visual forms that were an expression of their time.

Like Robert Welch, Robin Day's early work was deeply imbued with the positive spirit of Contemporary design, while at the same time aspiring to seriousness through its exploitation of new materials and its functional intent. Day had a head start of almost ten years on Welch. In 1948 he had witnessed the conception of Contemporary design in the USA at the Low-Cost Furniture Competition organized by the Museum of Modern Art in New York; and three years later he was present at the birth of the Contemporary phenomenon in the UK at the Festival of Britain in 1951. Responding enthusiastically to the flood of new ideas emerging from both North America and Scandinavia after the war, but particularly the former, Day succeeded in creating a style of furniture for Hille that combined elements of both, but which was at the same time highly original and uniquely suited to the English market. By the end of the decade Day was well established in the public eye as Britain's leading designer of modern furniture, and was being lionized by popular interiors magazines such as *Ideal Home*, which commissioned him to design a living room that

was featured in their February 1960 issue. This commission marked the launch in Britain of an important new furnishing concept: modular furniture. Day's Modulus range, later renamed the Form Group when it was manufactured by Hille, was composed of interchangeable seating and table units supported by a basic square-section steel-bar frame, an idea which was praised by *Ideal Home* for achieving 'unity allied to flexibility' and for combining 'simplicity with variety'. It was followed around 1965 by the Plus Group which adopted similar basic principles but utilized a more solid wooden structural framework.

The respect with which Day's work was regarded by the design profession in Britain is indicated by the fact that already, by the end of the 1950s, he had been honoured as a Royal Designer for Industry. Throughout the 1960s, along with Robert Welch, he was also one of the most regular recipients of the Council of Industrial Design's Design Centre Awards. In 1962, for example, he received the award for an ultra-functional bench that he had designed for British Rail; in 1963 the Form Group was selected; and in 1965 there was a certain inevitability to his receiving the award again, this time for his famous Polyprop stacking chair, the first chair to be manufactured from Shell's new wonder plastic, polypropylene. Although many of Day's furniture designs of the 1960s adopted the new angular look – which obviously fitted in well from a practical point of view when it came to the design of modular furniture, the square being the basic building block for such ranges – some designs retained the curved forms that had characterized most of his earlier Contemporary designs. The Scimitar chair of 1963 provides a good example of this, its evocative title referring to the shape of the all-in-one, free-standing, pre-formed back and arm unit. An organic shape was also the most appropriate and practical form for the moulded shell of the Polyprop chair.

One thought: many forms

Robin Day's Form Group matches good design with adaptability and won a Council of Industrial Design Award for doing it so well. The idea of changeable groupings begins with three black steel frames 4′8″, 7′ and 9′4″ long, and the combinations of chair units, seat units, table tops and cabinets they support. The chair unit, with or without arm, has a solid makore or teak frame, rubber webbed, supporting foam back and seat cushions. The seat unit has a similar frame and single foam cushion. All cushions are fitted with removable covers of any Hille fabric you select: Table tops are either black or white melamine, mahogany or teak veneer, always makore or teak edged. The cabinet is mahogany or teak veneer with lift up lids. Square section steel legs have floor-protecting plastic feet. The scope for different arrangements is prodigious.

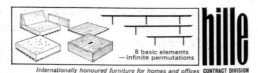

hille

8 basic elements — infinite permutations

Internationally honoured furniture for homes and offices **CONTRACT DIVISION**

LONDON: 41 Albemarle Street, W.1. Hyde Park 9576 □ BIRMINGHAM: 24 Albert Street, Birmingham 4. Midland 7378 □ MANCHESTER: Sackville Street, Manchester 1. Central 6929 □ WATFORD: Hille House, St. Albans Road.

left, below left and below right

Three publicity images from the 1960s illustrating designs by Robin Day for Hille. Form Group modular seating (left), winner of a Design Centre Award in 1961. Polyprop chair, 1963, (below right), designed with two basic components, a plastic shell and tubular steel legs, which could be dismantled to reduce space during transportation. Scimitar chair (below left), shown in a stylish advert dating from 1963.

Along with stackability and modularity, another important practical factor that first came to the fore during the 1950s, but which only became a major design issue during the 1960s, was flat-packing. As transport costs rose, the question of how much space a piece of furniture occupied while in transit was closely scrutinized, especially because of the need to compete both nationally and internationally. In response to this, Robin Day created his aluminium-framed, plywood-seated Axis chair of 1966, its name suggesting a possible debt to Peter Hvidt and Orla Mølgaard Nielsen's classic knock-down Ax chair of 1950. The latter was an attractive all-wood chair, made by the Danish manufacturer Fritz Hansen, which had a laminated beech X-shaped frame and a plywood seat and back. Imported into Britain by Finmar, it represented one of the earliest post-war attempts to design a flat-packed chair for export. In an advert that appeared in the *Architectural Review* in March 1967 Day's Axis chair was illustrated in a not dissimilar way, both in pieces and fully assembled, and was championed using a clever play on words: 'Knock-down assembly. Knock-out chair.' It was followed later the same year by the demountable Disque table, designed to cater to the Habitat-conscious youth market which wanted cheap, simple, flat-packed self-assembly furniture that could literally be carried away from the shop.

Throughout the 1960s it was the Polyprop chair that was the great design success of the decade for Robin Day and Hille. After the launch of the original model in 1963 following a lengthy period of experimentation, the Polyprop, like its precursor, the Eames fibreglass shell chair, was produced in innumerable variants, and was re-launched in 1967 in an armchair version. A witty advert that appeared in the *Architectural Review* in September 1966 asked: 'What has forty-four legs but is very light on its feet, a weatherproof shell yet wears many different covers, sometimes has arms – sometimes hasn't, works alone, or in large groups, can be seen all over the world, but is only three years old?' The answer, of course (illustrated upside down at the bottom of the page) was the Polyprop, which by this date had already proved to be so successful that it was being exported and produced under licence all over the world, including in the USA via the agency of John Stuart. In view of this, it is perhaps somewhat surprising that it was the Italians who were the most active in following up Day's enterprising early lead in the exploitation of new forms of plastic by the furniture industry. Italy, more than any other country, recognized that plastics were the key material of the 1960s in functional, aesthetic and symbolic terms, and exploited their potential applications to the full.

What this demonstrates is that it was not the availability of new materials alone that prompted a change of direction in the 1960s. In purely material terms, the same design options were available to Robin Day as to Vico Magistretti and Joe Colombo, but whereas Day made a conscious decision in the early 1960s to follow in the footsteps of the revered Charles Eames and to refine the Contemporary aesthetic rather than to abandon it, Magistretti and Colombo, although influenced and to a certain degree shaped by Contemporary design, clearly felt that the time was right to move on and to start exploring other avenues. This was the difficult choice with which all designers were faced at the turn of the 1950s: should they continue on the same path, or should they strike out in a new direction? Some, such as Day

and Welch, who were basically satisfied with the way in which design had developed in recent years, were content with the idea of consolidating the mature Contemporary idiom. Others, such as Verner Panton, described in *Form* magazine (no. 6) in 1963 as 'the *enfant terrible* of the Danish furniture world', were already restless by the end of the 1950s and were actively seeking an alternative to the comfortable Scandinavian Modern style. Designers such as Panton and Colombo resisted the pressure to conform and adopted a standpoint that called into question some of the basic tenets of Contemporary design. They were not interested in consolidating what had gone before; they wanted to create something completely new. Ettore Sottsass was another designer who was presented with a stark choice at the start of the 1960s, after having been engaged as a consultant designer by Olivetti. The choice he faced was whether to submit to the pressure of multi-national conformity, or whether to take up the challenge of making the company itself rethink its basic approach to design. Over the course of the next decade this is exactly what he did. Also, by remaining independent of Olivetti and pursuing many other different art, craft and design experiments, and by travelling extensively and actively exposing himself to a multiplicity of foreign cultural influences, Sottsass was continually reinventing himself during the course of the 1960s, and in so doing, reinventing Italian design. It was he who embraced most completely the idea of the need for continuous revolution, and in so doing he opened up many new creative avenues for others to follow.

opposite
Polyprop range of polypropylene chairs designed by Robin Day for Hille. The original stacking chair, bottom left, dates from 1963, while the armchair version, centre, was introduced in 1967. Like the classic Eames fibreglass chair produced by Herman Miller from 1950 onwards, the Polyprop shell was designed to fit on a wide variety of bases, thus maximizing its potential applications.

the consumer revolution

two

The Contemporary style remained the dominant aesthetic until the early years of the 1960s. Contemporary did not just evaporate at the turn of the decade: it remained a significant thread running through design for at least another ten years. Nevertheless, in spite of its continuing influence, the 1960s was a decade of radical change. The first revolution took place around 1962 when 'the look' of the sixties – to co-opt a phrase from Mary Quant – began to displace the 'New Look' of the post-war period. From this date onwards there was a clear shift in emphasis: youth and 'the look' associated with youth culture were in the ascendant; the Establishment and the Contemporary aesthetic were marginalized, and during the late 1960s came under direct attack.

During the 1960s there were some astonishing commercial success stories, many related to retailing of one sort or another, with fashion and home furnishings being at the forefront of the consumer revolution. Because this was a time of virtually full employment and economic prosperity, consumers had more money to spend than ever before. Initially, though, supply lagged behind demand, at least in terms of the range of goods on offer. Many shops were old-fashioned, both in their decor and their archaic sales practices. Even in a large store like Heal's, which was closely associated with progressive trends in design, the salesmen in the furniture department were forbidden to approach customers directly at the start of the 1960s; they had to go through the formality of being introduced by a third party. This acted as an unnecessary obstacle to both buying and selling.

The 1960s was the age of the entrepreneur, and for those with design skills, commercial intuition and personal drive, there were large and lucrative markets to be exploited and considerable fortunes to be made. The young, in particular, as well as being more independent-minded and culturally aware, were better off and had more money to spend. The most successful entrepreneurs were the ones who targeted this market, both through the goods they designed and manufactured, and the new shopping environments they created. That is why the name Habitat was so evocative, because it suggested that the shop itself provided a sympathetic environment for consumers. Habitat was bright, colourful and welcoming, and like Mary Quant's Bazaar, it highlighted the fact that shopping could be an exciting and stimulating experience, purely pleasurable in its own right. Design alone could not

above
Vaulted interior of Just
Looking boutique, King's
Road, London, 1968,
designed by Garnett,
Cloughey, Blakemore and
Associates, lined with polished aluminium. Shopping
became a primary leisure
activity for the young during
the 1960s, and interiors
such as this made the
experience as exciting as
going to a discothèque.
above right
Shop front painted with a
giant toadstool to attract
customers through a side
alley off Carnaby Street.

have brought about the revolution in taste and lifestyle that happened during the 1960s; the key figures of the decade were the popularizers, those who actively and directly promoted 'the look' and made it available to a mass audience.

This desire to popularize – what Jennifer Harris has referred to as the democratization of the avant garde – was a process that had got underway in the 1950s, but that gained considerable momentum during the early 1960s. By 1964, the year when both Habitat and Biba opened, it had gained such a head of steam that the consumer revolution presaged by Bazaar in 1955 finally took place. When the world discovered 'Swinging' London in 1966, what people were most interested in was shopping. This was the start of the era of conspicuous consumption. With the opening of Habitat and Biba, shopping became an end in itself, rather than simply a means to an end. Shops became places to meet people, and places to visit simply to experience an ambiance. Shopping became a primary leisure activity for young people, along with watching television and listening to pop music. Shopping was also an avenue for the expression of popular culture, both in terms of what was now being sold, and through the way shops were designed.

What happened during the 1960s was that areas of activity that had previously been the preserve of a cultural or economic élite were opened up to a mass audience. The restrictive conventions and judgmental attitudes of earlier decades were challenged. One by one the taboos of how people dressed, what music they listened to, what they ate, how they behaved, and how they furnished their homes, were all swept away. Included in this list of transformations was how people shopped, whether this was food shopping in the new supermarkets, fashion shopping in the new boutiques, or shopping for furniture and furnishings through the new Habitat chain. Shopping had a major impact on people's lifestyles: by

making available goods that people had never seen before, and by creating a sympathetic environment in which to appreciate them, people's perceptions were altered, their expectations raised, and their horizons broadened. Instead of knowing what to expect when they went out shopping, there was now a new and refreshing element of surprise which made the whole experience more exciting and, significantly, more addictive. This sense of novelty was prompted not just by the broader range of goods on offer but, in the case of fashion and home furnishings, as a result of a heightened awareness of the rapid turnover of styles. As Terence Conran remarked in an interview in *The Ambassador* in August 1965: 'Taste is constantly on the move … People have become enormously aware of colour and design, and they are prepared to have more exciting things provided they are less expensive and more expendable …. "Expendability" is no longer a dirty word.'

Conran preferred the word 'expendability' to 'obsolescence': expendability suggested pragmatism on the part of the manufacturer, while obsolescence suggested cynical exploitation. Conran did not approve of objects that were designed with a deliberately short life so that they would have to be replaced after a limited time (built-in obsolescence), but he did recognize that, in the case of home furnishings, people might want to make changes every few years for purely aesthetic reasons, in which case there was no need to go to the expense of supplying them with things that would last forever.

The link between the widening acceptance of the concept of expendability and the growth of shopping as a leisure activity – a new fashion which was at the heart of the consumer revolution – was made in an interesting article in *Nova* in May 1967 called 'Where are all the three-piece suites?' Alongside a photograph of a morass of drinks cans and plastic bottles, the article illustrated pictures of paper dresses and cardboard furniture, the latest expendable designer accessories at this date. The accompanying text described how, in the past, people had been conditioned to believe that, when they set up home, they needed to buy furniture that would last a lifetime. Now attitudes had changed, however; expendability was accepted as the norm, so people were less concerned about wear and tear:

Let the kids beat up the furniture, scratch the table or even paint all over the chairs – for you can buy very cheap, well-designed expendable furniture. When it gets broken, marked or stained, you can throw it away. Cheap materials and mass-produced methods are providing the consumer market with a whole range of goods which are efficient – and so cheap that you can discard them when you like without feeling guilty. Everything is changing at such a rate today that it is a drawback not to be able to change your belongings too, at frequent intervals.

It was highly appropriate that such an article should appear in *Nova*, as this magazine, launched in 1964, the same year as Habitat, was at once an opinion-former and a reflection of the times in terms of lifestyle trends.

Although the consumer revolution of the 1960s was an international phenomenon, and creativity in design fuelled consumerism in many countries, the fashion for shopping – or rather, shopping as a fashion – was particularly prominent in Britain. More than in any other country, shops in Britain were used as a direct and vivid expression of the latest trends in design during the 1960s, particularly those associated with youth fashion. Originally this happened spontaneously as part of the anti-Establishment movement associated with the 'youthquake', but by the second half of the 1960s, once 'the look' itself had become part of the Establishment, interior design was used in a more calculated and commercial way to attract a specific target sector of the market. In the Mary

Quant shop on New Bond Street, designed by Jon Bannenberg in 1967, two design features were used as key signifiers of modernity (the cylindrical capsule-shaped changing cubicles, and Eero Aarnio's 'Globe' chairs), and another as a brand image (the Mary Quant daisy logo incorporated into the pattern of the carpet). Even Harrods, the ultimate symbol of the British retailing establishment, jumped onto the 'youthquake' bandwagon towards the end of the decade with their self-consciously trendy and youth-orientated Way In boutique of 1967, and their Dress Circle restaurant of 1968, both designed by Maurice Broughton and Associates. The interiors of shops and restaurants were used to embody the ethos of the goods or food sold in them, and attracted customers who were as interested in experiencing the atmosphere of the boutique or restaurant as in buying the merchandise or eating the food. Patrick Gwynne's Space Age restaurants in Hyde Park, London, and the Theatre Royal, York, provide good examples of attempts by restaurateurs to attract a more youthful clientele through association with the latest trends in modern architecture. In shops, image was all-important. This was as true for the clean lines and bright lights of Habitat as for the exotic, dark, cluttered interior of Biba, and the psychedelic frontages of the boutiques on the King's Road.

That the fashion for shopping was perceived as being central to the revitalization of design in Britain during the 1960s and to the phenomenon known as Swinging London, is indicated by the media obsession with particular shops such as Bazaar and Biba, and specific shopping locales, such as Carnaby Street and the King's Road. From the middle of the decade onwards, 'Carnaby Street' was widely used as a generic term for a particular type of design: brash, brightly coloured, with highly decorated surfaces, including the ubiquitous Union Jack. After the initial catalyst article called 'London – The Swinging City' which appeared in *Time* magazine on

below
Nova, launched in 1964, was a major commentator on contemporary culture.
right
Way In boutique at Harrods, 1967, designed by Maurice Broughton and Associates. Even upmarket department stores made an effort to cater for the youth market.

above
I Was Lord Kitchener's Valet, a shop on Portobello Road which sold second-hand military uniforms and reflected the eclecticism of men's fashion during the late 1960s.
above right
'Mummy takes a Trip', a cartoon by Mark Boxer which appeared in *The Listener*, 1967. The title refers to the boutique on the King's Road called Granny Takes a Trip.

15 April 1966, hoards of foreign journalists descended on London to find out what was going on. Among those from the international design media, while some paid lip service to the work of the design Establishment in the form of the Council of Industrial Design, what they were really interested in was the streetlife in Kensington and Chelsea, and the buzz surrounding shops like Habitat and Biba. The way in which their articles focused so heavily on retailing highlights the importance of the consumer boom in 1960s Britain. An article on Finnish design or Dutch design during the same period, for example, would concentrate on specific products and would be unlikely to investigate the domestic market or the mechanisms of retailing practised in those countries. Any article on British design, however, would be as much about shopping as about design *per se*. Observing the crowds milling along the King's Road on a sunny afternoon, the Danish designer Rolf Middelboe made an evocative record of his impressions in *Mobilia* in March 1968:
A flowing stream of people, old people in uniforms, and young people in uniforms. Theatre and reality, personal inventions coupled with the latest fashions, kaleidoscopic copiousness, grandma's shawl, Indian fabrics remade into men's jackets, mini and maxi skirts alongside old veterans from the Great war in uniforms with their service medals jingling together with the bells worn on the fancy cowboy dresses of young girls and men, striped shirts and embroidered leather waistcoats.
What made Britain different was that it had its own 'scene', which meant that it was much more self-sufficient in cultural terms. In some ways the situation in Britain was similar to that in Italy, which was also very buoyant, although in Italy this buoyancy was less closely bound up with consumerism and popular culture, and more closely allied to science, technology and the visual arts. In both cases, however, it was the fact that creativity and commerce were thriving which gave these countries such a confident air.

Media commentary, both at the time and retrospectively, has focused on the middle of the sixties – 1966 in particular – as being the pivotal years of the decade. But as is often the case when a new trend emerges, the media arrived several years late, and what they recorded was the tail end of a phenomenon rather than something that had just begun to happen. Also, by adopting the phrase 'Carnaby Street' as a generic name for 'the look', and by focusing on the highly commercialized 'Carnaby Street' phenomenon to the exclusion of virtually everything else, they belittled the breadth, strength and aesthetic significance of what had been happening, not just city wide but nationwide, which was itself part of a

mounting international 'youthquake'. According to Ken and Kate Baynes writing in *Design* magazine in August 1966, '"Carnaby Street" has turned into one of those phrases that sets the adrenalin pumping into your bloodstream. It tends to make you feel either young, stylish and hyper-aware – or else old, old and old.' The 'scene' and 'the look' with which it was associated, had actually begun to take off as early as 1962. This fact has been appreciated in relation to the Beatles – 1962 was the date of their first British chart success – but it has been less well understood in relation to visual culture.

The convergence between these new developments in popular culture – 'the scene' – and the emergence of new directions in contemporary design – 'the look' – was no coincidence. One of the main reasons for the explosive impact of the 'youthquake' of the early 1960s was because of the integral relationship which existed at this moment in time between pop music, Pop Art, (two terms which were already widely accepted at this time) and what have been described as pop fashion and pop design. Analogies between these different branches of the arts were constantly being made, not only by outside commentators but by the protagonists themselves. Thus Mary Quant was described as the Beatles of the fashion industry; and when Terence Conran opened his revolutionary shop Habitat in 1964 his aspirations in the field of home-furnishings were, in turn, compared to those of Mary Quant, and both she and the Beatles were among his most enthusiastic early customers. To illustrate this nexus between art, design and shopping, in April 1964 (a month before the opening of Habitat) *The Ambassador*, the upbeat trade magazine of the British textile industry, presented a lively article called 'Fab Fash Pop' in which they photographed some of the latest fashions by Mary Quant, Foale and Tuffin, Jean Muir and the young French designer Emmanuelle Khanh being modelled in the surroundings of an American Pop Art exhibition in a leading contemporary art gallery. The photographs were accompanied by the following commentary:
The awareness and exhilaration of modern city life in the Rauschenberg exhibition makes London's Whitechapel Art Gallery the most relevant setting for our fashion on the same wavelength. It is this awareness which produces the group identity of young British fashion designers, and gives our ready-to-wear additional impetus all over the world. The acceptance of social and other shifts is interpreted with wit and enthusiasm.
What this feature demonstrates is that image, attitude and associations – in other words, 'the look' – were as important

left
The Beatles in 1963
wearing the round-necked,
collarless, grey suits
specially designed for
them by Pierre Cardin.
below left
The Finnish version of 'the
look': a girl on a moped
wearing a Marimekko dress.
Lens fabric designed by
Kaarina Kellomäki, dress
designed by Annika Rimala,
1966. The name Marimekko
means 'a dress for Mary',
and the key to the firm's
success was the fact that
they used the same type
of bold abstract prints on
their dress fabrics as in
their furnishing textiles.
below right
Cover of *Time* magazine,
dated 15 April 1966, with
its influential feature on
'London – The Swinging
City'.

as the actual content of the product itself, whether this be a painting, a record, a dress or a chair. 'The look' was a total package, and it was the decision to embrace it in its entirety which was to have such a dramatic effect on the early career of the Beatles. It was not until the group abandoned the type of music and styling associated with the 1950s (leather jackets, greaser haircuts and rock n' roll) in favour of 'the look' of the 1960s (clean-cut collarless suits – courtesy of Pierre Cardin – mop tops, and a new brand of infectiously melodic home-grown English pop music) that they hit the big time and became internationally successful. Adopting 'the look', and thereby matching their appearance to their music, was a crucial part of the Beatles' winning formula, as their manager Brian Epstein and Astrid Kirchherr, the German photographer who helped to shape their new image, were both astute enough to realize.

The Beatles continued to shape and be shaped by 'the look' until the middle of the decade, adding first television, then film, and finally publishing, to the list of media through which they communicated 'the look', and finding in director Richard Lester a perfect amanuensis for translating 'the look' on to the big screen in their two feature films, *A Hard Day's Night* (1964) and *Help!* (1965). By 1966, however, they were clearly flagging and, having exhausted themselves through touring, they began to withdraw from the public arena. As their

quest to discover other avenues of individual and collective fulfilment and self-expression began to take shape, so they began to disassociate themselves from 'the look'. This makes it all the more ironic that it should be in 1966 that the international media suddenly discovered the London 'scene' and decided that Britain had got 'the look' which the rest of the world wanted. By the time Carnaby Street began to attract the attention of the world, 'the look' was already on the wane, and another 'scene' had begun to develop, which would soon overtake and eclipse this earlier style. While 1966 was indeed a pivotal year, it was more because it marked the culmination of the first phase of the cultural revolution of the 1960s, and presaged the birth of the subsequent counter-revolution, than because 1966 itself was intrinsically significant. In any case, for many of the key players in the British design revolution of the early 1960s – Mary Quant, Terence Conran, David Queensberry, Barbara Brown, to name but four – the seeds of change had actually been sewn back in the 1950s, and it was only because of the pioneering groundwork carried out then that the design explosion finally happened when it did.

The delayed shell-shocked response of the media to the impact of 'the look' was not confined to the international press. Apart from Reyner Banham, most design commentators in Britain had also failed to appreciate its significance. It was not until 1966, for example, that *Design* magazine, having finally noticed 'the collision that is now taking place between design and fashion, between durability and obsolescence', took the plunge and commissioned a series of articles by Ken and Kate Baynes examining the phenomenon of popular culture and its interaction with design. The first article, published in February 1966, was called 'Eating Out Can Be Fun' and looked at the growth in the market for cheap restaurants. These included not only the American-inspired Wimpy chain, but light-hearted English variants such as The Sizzling Sausage and the wittily titled Chips with Everything, the interior and graphics for which were designed by Main, Wolff, Olins and Partners and were themselves the subject of a feature in the *Architectural Review* in September 1966. The authors' conclusion about Chips with Everything was that: 'The balance it strikes between the smelly, tawdry, gorgeous world of genuine pierhead pop and the growing sophistication of the mass audience is a very interesting and probably valid interpretation of contemporary fashion.' Such outlets clearly plugged a gap in the market, and in their use of bright colours and inventive pop graphics to evoke 'the look', were clearly aimed at a youthful clientele. The biggest catering success story of the decade at the popular end of the market was The Golden Egg, a chain of speciality restaurants established by the Kaye brothers, in which great attention was paid to design detailing, and the graphics and the decor were all on a related theme. Geoffrey Cockcroft, one of their designers, installed a panel of brightly coloured stained glass made by the firm of Whitefriars Glass in the window of their Leicester Square branch, which cast luminous shades of red and yellow throughout the interior. Special sculptures were also commissioned, such as the flock of ceramic geese made by William Newland for the Victoria Street branch. Graphics, in particular, were recognized as being of primary importance, a distinctive feature of The Golden Egg being their giant egg-shaped menus. The authors concluded that the vividness and visual wit of these restaurants was an

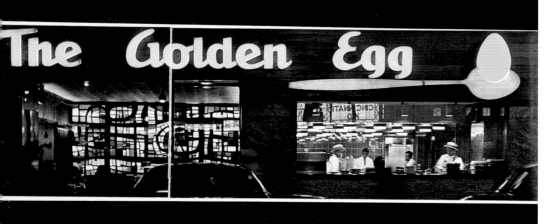

essential part of their 'look', and it was the vibrancy and completeness of 'the look' which made them so attractive to the public. On these grounds, therefore, they could not be faulted:

If they reflect a growing public awareness of colour, visual excitement and richness, it is a bit absurd to complain that they are vulgar. They are a tremendous, even a fantastic, advance on the vacuum that existed a few years ago. And it is only fair to say that we often enjoyed the spoof for its own Rococo sake.

This article was followed in August 1966 by a feature called 'Behind the Scene' which investigated the dynamic world of contemporary British youth fashion, and the personalities behind it. Once again the authors noted the relationship between design and popular culture:

The origins of the movement are deep in the larger revolution which has grown out of teenage affluence and the wider rejection of conventional values... This new world is an entertainment world, inevitably linked with pop, and it reflects the same curious mixture of grass roots exuberance and big business success.

The individuals identified as being responsible for creating 'the scene' were Mary Quant, John Stephen, John Michael, Barbara Hulanicki, and Marion Foale and Sally Tuffin. Of these, the single most important figure of the decade, both as an image-maker and as a retailing entrepreneur, was Mary Quant.

In 1955, motivated by the fact that the designer herself was dissatisfied with the range of clothes on the market for young women and felt she could provide something better, Quant and her partner Alexander Plunket Greene opened their fashion boutique, Bazaar, in the King's Road. The original idea for Bazaar, as outlined by the designer in her autobiography, was that it should be 'a *bouillabaise* of clothes and accessories', and that Quant herself, who was well-known in her own circle for her idiosyncratic style of dressing, should be the buyer. The problem was that, apart from jewellery and a few accessories, Quant could not find the type of stock she wanted to sell, particularly clothes. It was as a result of this, and the fear of a newly opened but empty shop, that she started to design clothes herself, making use of the services of a dressmaker for a few hours each day to help produce the garments

which would go on sale the following morning. Catering to the middle market in terms of price, the shop was an instant success, demand constantly outstripped supply, and the designer rapidly became aware that most young women felt the same way that she did and would snap up anything she could produce. Within the space of two years a second shop had been opened, this time in Knightsbridge, which was even more successful than the first. From these humble beginnings the Quant empire was to grow. Within the space of less than ten years her manufacturing base would expand from Britain to North America, and by 1966 she was working with eighteen different manufacturers concurrently, and the Quant name itself had become a brand.

Quant attributed her phenomenal success in part simply to the fact of being in the right place at the time: *I just happened to start when that 'something in the air' was coming to the boil. The clothes I made happened to fit in exactly with the teenage trend, with pop records and espresso bars and jazz clubs. The rejuvenated* Queen *magazine,* Beyond the Fringe, Private Eye, *the discothèques and* That was the Week That Was *were all born on the same wavelength.* However, while it was undoubtedly true that Quant opened Bazaar at an opportune moment, she was certainly not passively swept along by the *Zeitgeist*. When she started out she was very much ahead of her time. Although Quant began by literally making clothes by hand, this was out of necessity rather than choice, and once her business took off she was more than happy for her garments to be mass-produced in factories. What excited and motivated her was the idea of making her clothes available to the largest number of people at the cheapest possible prices. In her autobiography she asserts: 'the whole point of fashion is to make fashionable clothes available to everyone. Fashion is an inherent thing and should not be something which depends solely on beautiful and expensive cloth and hand work. It should be mass produced.' Having cracked the American market, Quant was able to put her ideas into practice on an international scale. What was always difficult to master, though, was how to adapt a design for mass production without losing 'the look'. Because 'the look' was strongly associated with a particular type of physique – thin, boyish and flat-chested – Quant worried that

Catering to the hitherto neglected youth market, Mary Quant created a 'look' which sent shock waves through the fashion industry during the early 1960s, and shifted attention from the élitist world of couture to the ready-to-wear market.

right
'The look' was created not just by the clothes alone, but through hairstyles, make-up and fashion accessories. Fashion photography, such as this publicity image from c1965, reinforced the impression that Quant's clothes were dynamic, wacky and fun.

above right
Sketches of three of Mary Quant's most popular early designs. From left to right: Pinafore Pleats, a grey flannel sack dress with box pleats, 1958; Peachy, a woollen A-line dress with a kick pleat, intended to be worn with a polo-neck sweater and thick tights, 1960; and Rex Harrison, a V-neck button-up shirt dress with two pockets just above the hem, 1960.

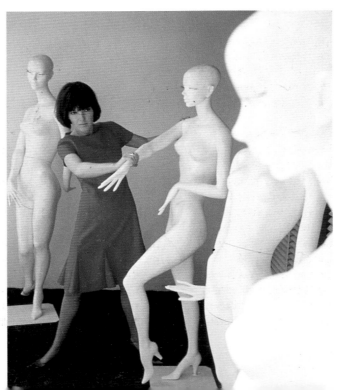

above
Mary Quant and her husband, Alexander Plunket Greene, who together created the Quant empire.

left
Quant took a hands-on approach to design. Her early creations were variants of the clothes she made for herself.

far left
Mary Quant's original Bazaar boutique on the King's Road in Chelsea opened in 1955.

her style would become watered down or incoherent when the garments were made up in different sizes. Part of the skill of the designer was in compensating for these compromises, but in spite of the risks, her commitment to mass production remained undiminished.

The fact that Mary Quant was actively responsible for creating 'the look' was acknowledged by an American commentator writing in *Women's Wear Daily* during the designer's first promotional visit to New York: 'These Britishers have a massive onslaught of talent, charm and mint-new ideas. English chic is fiercely NOW ... by the young for the young.' Quant recognized that she was part of a wider 'youthquake' and that her primary market was forward-looking young people like herself. Reflecting on the start of her career, in 1965 she wrote: 'It is the Mods ... who gave the dress trade the impetus to break through the fast-moving, breathtaking, uprooting revolution in which we have been a part since the opening of Bazaar.' Perhaps Mary Quant's most significant achievement was the promotion of the cult of youth over the cult of middle age. In 1965 she was able to reflect with some satisfaction: *There was a time when every girl under twenty yearned to look like an experienced, sophisticated thirty ... All this is in reverse with a vengeance now. Suddenly, every girl with a hope of getting away with it is aiming to look not only under voting age but under the age of consent ... Their aim is to look childishly young, naively unsophisticated. And it takes more sophistication to work out 'the look' than those earlier would-be sophisticates ever dreamed of.*

Although Quant recognized that 'the look' which she created was part of a wider movement encompassing photography, graphics and pop music along with domestic design, she was keenly aware of the significance of fashion in particular in pioneering change, and in leading and defining a shift in social attitudes. As social conventions became more relaxed, people wanted their clothes to reflect this increased informality. Women wanted clothes in which they could feel comfortable the whole day through, whether at work or socializing in the evening. Quant believed that clothes should be flexible and adaptable. Increasingly, fashion was becoming a signifier not of social position but of social attitudes. Quant clearly delighted in the fact that her clothes challenged Establishment values and appealed to all sectors of society. In her autobiography she wrote approvingly of the democratization of fashion that had taken place during the first half of the 1960s: 'There was a time when clothes were a sure sign of a woman's social position and income group. Not now. Snobbery has gone out of fashion, and in our shops you will find duchesses jostling with typists to buy the same dresses.'

Like Quant in the field of women's fashion, self-taught menswear designer John Stephen realized that young men like himself wished to express themselves through their clothes, but that this was difficult because there was a gaping hole in the market for stylish menswear. Stephen's unconventional outfits broke the mould and helped pop groups such as the Beatles to establish their musical identity through 'the look'. He opened his first boutique on Carnaby Street in 1959, thus triggering off interest in a narrow street in a previously obscure part of London which, within the space of seven years, would become internationally renowned. By 1966 Stephen was so successful that he owned ten shops on Carnaby Street, and he was working with four different factories in order to satisfy the growing international demand for his clothes, particularly in the USA and Canada where he ran a chain of boutiques within department stores.

Following the lead set by Mary Quant, another leading menswear designer John Michael chose the hitherto unfashionable King's Road as the location for his first shop in 1957. He met with such phenomenal success that by 1966 he was in charge of a large public company exporting to Europe and the USA, and the original boutique had been transformed into a chain with seventeen branches. John Michael's background was in women's fashion, and like Stephen he believed that it was because of his lack of training that he was able to come up with unconventional solutions. Catering mainly to style-conscious young professionals, the John Michael 'look' was considerably more expensive than that of Stephen, and the image he projected through his shop interiors and graphics as well as his clothes was one of urbane sophistication. Pitching their work at a similar market, but in the field of women's fashion, and selling their clothes in a similar price bracket, were Marion Foale and Sally Tuffin. Foale and Tuffin, as they were known, arrived on the scene slightly later than Quant, Stephen and Michael, and unlike them had been professionally trained at the Royal College of Art. After leaving the RCA in 1961 they secured orders from the newly established 21 Shop, a boutique-style fashion outlet which operated from within the trend-setting department store Woollands. A feature in *Vogue* brought them additional exposure, after which they moved into the contract market. By 1966, as well as running their own ultra-stylish boutique, their designs were being produced under licence by an American manufacturer.

The question of the optimum scale of a creative business is very much an issue when considering developments in retailing during the 1960s. A leading company that eventually became a victim of its own success was Biba. Founded in 1963 by fashion illustrator Barbara Hulanicki and her advertising executive husband, Stephen Fitz-Simon, the company originally began life as a mail order business, Biba's Postal Boutique, with initial sales being generated on a one garment at a time basis as a result of newspaper coverage. After a slow start the company suddenly took off in May 1964 when a pink gingham dress was featured in the *Daily Mirror*. Soon the distinctive Biba style began to attract the attention of pop stars such as Cilla Black, and youth style gurus such as Cathy McGowan, the modish young presenter of the pop programme 'Ready, Steady, Go'. The favourable publicity arising out of this high-profile television and media exposure gave Biba direct access to the mass youth audience which Mary Quant had successfully begun to tap into. This led, in 1964, to the opening of the first Biba shop in Abingdon Road, Kensington, initially conceived as a sideline to the main mail order business, and as a way of offloading surplus stock. The boutique was an immediate success in its own right, however, partly because of 'the look' of the clothes on offer, which included vibrant Op Art mini dresses, but also because of the unique ambiance which Hulanicki and Fitz-Simon created in the shop. The walls were painted navy blue with plum and navy curtains, an early example of historical revivalism being demonstrated in the choice of a William Morris print for the curtain fabric. This was a highly unusual and original decorative scheme for 1964, and the colours would later reflect the tones of the fashion accessories on offer, dyed in rich deep mulberry, blueberry, rust and plum.

The combination of unusual fashions and an unconventional interior proved a magnet for young people. In Hulanicki's autobiography, *From A to Biba*, she describes the impact that the shop began to exert on people's lives, her own and her husband's included:

It became a meeting place. Years later I had letters from people who met at Biba, spent their courtship in Biba on saturdays, married, had babies and wrapped them in Biba purple nappies … All classes mingled under the creaking roof of O'Grady's wobbly house. There was no social distinction. Their common denominator was youth and rebellion against the establishment.

Because of its phenomenal success, Biba quickly grew out of its original premises, and in 1966 this led to the opening of a larger shop in Kensington Church Street. By this date Biba was attracting attention not only from television celebrities but from film stars, such as Julie Christie. Famous visitors became increasingly common following the frenzy of media attention in 1966, including Mia Farrow, Barbra Streisand, Marianne Faithfull and Brigitte Bardot.

Apart from providing a case study of the 1960s consumer boom, the Biba story is interesting from a purely stylistic point of view as it documents the dramatic change of image that took place during the second half of the decade. Between 1963 and 1966 'the look' that young women aspired to was what Hulanicki refers to as the 'Biba dolly':

She was pretty and young. She had an upturned nose, rose cheeks, and a skinny body with long asparagus legs and tiny feet. She was square-shouldered and quite flat-chested. Her head was perched on a long, swanlike neck. Her face was a perfect oval, her lids were heavy with long spiky lashes. She looked sweet but she was as hard as nails.

During the second half of the 1960s, however, Hulanicki's conception of the ideal woman changed quite radically:

As time went by my Biba girl became more dreamy and untouchable. Her long straight hair turned into a halo of golden ringlets, her cheeks were hollowed by brown powder, and her lips stained with sepia lipstick. The thin line of her brows framed her sparkly blue eyes … Once she was inside Biba, the music thundered, the lighting was soft, and she became more mysterious. It was extraordinary to see how people applied, often successfully, my dream image to themselves.

This dramatic change of image from a clean-cut boyish dolly bird to a gaunt, dreamy, strongly feminine woman reflects the wider cultural changes taking place in society at this time, in particular the shift from the playful innocence of the Pop era to the quasi-mysticism and drug-induced dreaminess of the hippy era. A decision to revive the mail order side of the business, but this time by means of illustrated catalogues, enabled Hulanicki to exert an even more direct influence over the shaping of the image of the Biba girl, as she was now able to pick the models (including Twiggy) and dictate the styling of the photographs used to promote her clothes. Launched in the summer of 1968, the first Biba catalogue confirmed the company's status as one of the most influential forces in British fashion.

During the late 1960s Biba rode on an incredible tide of success, culminating in 1970 with its expansion into the American market, initially via the agency of the prestigious Bergdorf Goodman store in New York, subsequently by entering into a partnership with Marcia Israel, the most powerful figure in the West Coast clothing industry. At the end of the decade, spurred on once again by the pressure of success, Biba moved for a third time, this time to larger premises in Kensington High Street. When it opened in September 1969 the new shop was an instant success. Hailed by *The Sunday Times* as 'the most beautiful store in the world', it attracted as many as thirty thousand customers in a single day. In order to finance this expansion, however, Hulanicki and Fitz-Simon had been obliged to bring in new business partners in the form of Dennis Day, a large garment manufacturer, and Dorothy Perkins, a major fashion retailer. Initially this merger was successful as it provided the capital required in order to expand. In the longer term, however, it led to the downfall of the company following the 1972 take-over of Dorothy Perkins by a property developer called British Land, which knew nothing about the fashion industry and was motivated purely by commercial gain.

What prompted the final collapse, although it was not in itself the cause, was the creation of Big Biba, when the shop moved in 1973 into the magnificent Art Deco surroundings of the former Derry and Toms department store in Kensington. Things might have been very different if Hulanicki and Fitz-Simon had been able to retain artistic and commercial control over this venture, but because events had conspired to ensure that this was no longer the case, what should have been the apotheosis of the Biba dream eventually turned into a nightmare. Big Biba was so huge and so complex to run in comparison to the three earlier stores that, without the vision of its creators to drive it forward, it soon fell apart. After Hulanicki and Fitz-Simon withdrew from direct involvement, the quality of the merchandise and its presentation rapidly declined, and within the space of two years Big Biba was closed and the entire contents auctioned off. Pressure of success had forced the expansion, but in the end the company became a victim of its own success when others saw an opportunity of exploiting it and moved in to make a killing. Although, in the case of Biba, the bubble did not finally burst until the 1970s, the seeds of commercial disintegration had been sewn during the late 1960s, and it was at the end of the decade that the process of fragmentation began.

These processes of disintegration and fragmentation are what characterize the late 1960s. Commercial disintegration, prompted by artificial hot house growth, was just one of several mechanisms by which this took place. Stylistic disintegration, prompted among other things by the new interest in historical revivalism, was another. It should be remembered, however, that the spirit of design typified by the later fashions of Biba and the early work of Laura Ashley was born during a period when historical revivalism was still being enjoyed as a genuine novelty. Initially there was an innocence about it; it was only later, during the 1970s, when manufacturers began to rely on revivalism as a formula, that it got out of hand and turned from something novel and charming into something cynical and sinister. What was remarkable about Terence Conran's retailing enterprise was that he managed to harness the modern and traditional in tandem, and it was this unique blend that made Habitat such a success, commercially and aesthetically. The important thing about Conran's appreciation of the traditional and the vernacular – his enjoyment of the 'below stairs' furniture of the Victorian period, and traditional French ironmongery, for example – was that it arose out of a genuine commitment to the simple and the unpretentious in design.

below
Barbara Hulanicki's Biba
originally started out in a
similar mould to Mary
Quant's Bazaar, but by the
mid-1960s it had developed
into something quite different, with a new emphasis
on femininity and glamour.
bottom left
Cosmetics counter in
the Kensington High
Street shop, which opened
in 1969.
right
Art Deco-inspired Exotics
counter in the opulent Big
Biba store, 1973.
.

below centre
Image from a Biba cata-
logue, 1969. During the late
1960s and early 1970s the
Biba style changed dramatically and became a celebration of Art Deco revivalism.
below far right
Model wearing an Op Art
trouser suit, posing outside
the original Abingdon Road
branch of Biba, which
opened in 1964.

Ultimately it was not a question of whether something was new or old, simply of whether the underlying approach to design was genuine or not.

Conran's philosophy of design had been formulated during the early post-war era, at a time when modern design was being promoted with a missionary zeal, as if it heralded the path to aesthetic salvation. Although the Contemporary style provided a much-needed shot in the arm to the applied arts in Britain during the early 1950s, ultimately in many ways it encouraged customers to be as indiscriminate in their purchases of modern design as they had been of traditional furniture and furnishings. Consumers became caught up in the new fashion for its own sake: it did not matter whether a design was good or bad, as long as it was Contemporary. Although Conran himself produced designs for textiles, furniture, ceramics and accessories which were classics of the Contemporary style, by the early 1960s he was no longer concerned with the superficial trappings of fashionable forms, patterns and materials; what interested him instead were designs which expressed their presence in a stronger and more direct way, and that were less overtly idiosyncratic.

The reason why Habitat came about was not because Conran had a burning desire to enter the world of retailing, but because, having recently initiated a major expansion on the furniture-making side of his business, he was concerned to ensure that the products being made in his new factory had guaranteed outlets. Conran's network of business interests had been gradually growing since the early 1950s when, after working independently as a freelance designer for a number of years, he had set up the Conran Design Group in 1956. An important part of the Conran Design Group was Conran Contracts, who were responsible for fitting out the interiors which the Design Group created. It was during the first half of the 1950s, too, that Conran had established his two manufacturing concerns, first Conran Furniture, then Conran Fabrics. During the mid 1960s a series of adverts appeared in the *Architectural Review* drawing attention to the sampling service offered by Conran Fabrics to architects and designers, indicating how important the contract market was still considered to be at this date. Conran himself designed for both firms, and the Conran Design Group, in turn, would specify products by these two companies in the interior design work it carried out. It was all very incestuous but it made excellent commercial sense, as the securing of work for one side of the business had the knock-on effect of generating further work for another part of the company. It also ensured a vital element of control for the designer himself, particularly in the areas of quality and consistency, something that would be increasingly important as the Conran empire expanded.

By the early 1960s the Conran Design Group was becoming increasingly multi-disciplinary, carrying out work in fields as diverse as furniture, textiles, exhibitions, graphics and interior design. Meanwhile, both Conran Furniture and Conran Fabrics had expanded into the field of imports as well as manufacturing. Conran was keenly aware of the importance of the work being carried out in design-led countries such as Italy and Finland, and part of his mission to reform domestic design in Britain was simply to make high quality goods from abroad available in the UK. This was central to the ethos of Habitat, although even before the store opened Conran had already begun to import the stunning printed fabrics produced by

Marimekko in Finland, and since the mid 1950s he had been importing a variety of furniture from Italy, including Gio Ponti's Superleggera chair by Cassina, and the traditional Chiavari chairs made by the firm of Sanguinetti. A feature in *Ideal Home* in April 1961 illustrated a range of Danish oiled teak chairs and sofas available from Conran Furniture, and an advert in *Design* in September 1964 drew attention to a new range of office chairs imported from Finland. During the early 1960s an important and influential addition to the Italian furniture range was the Carimate dining chair designed by Vico Magistretti. Originally designed for the restaurant of the Carimate Golf Club in Italy in 1959, the Carimate chair was put into production the following year by Cassina. Produced under licence by Conran Furniture for many years, the chair was described as 'people proof' in an advert in *Design* in November 1964, and was distinguished by its curved arms, its bright red lacquered frame, and its woven straw seat, thus combining traditional and Pop elements.

In addition to Italian and Scandinavian furniture, Conran also greatly admired the two major design-led American furniture firms, Knoll and Herman Miller, and in terms of his own manufacturing base, it was to this level of production that Conran aspired, rather than the workshop-based methods of the Italians. Most of the office furniture produced by Conran Furniture during the early 1960s was strongly influenced by the ideas and aesthetics of American designers such as Charles Eames and Eero Saarinen, and in Britain by the work of Robin Day for Hille. A series of striking full-page adverts in *Design* magazine during 1963–4 urged potential customers: 'Don't just sit there … sit there ergonomically', and informed them that 'Conran have a range of office chairs specifically designed to solve every office seating problem comfortably, from the switchboard to the conference room.' Although Conran respected craftsmanship, he was fully committed to mass production as a way of reducing costs. He revered simplicity of design and he hoped that by pursuing these ideas to their logical conclusion, taking on board ideas such as knock-down construction methods *en route*, he could come up with products that were both cheap and well-designed. In 1964 he launched a handsome new series which prefigured the Habitat style. This was the Pythagoras range of office furniture, which included desks, tables, chairs and storage units. Solid in appearance and strongly rectilinear in form and construction, the furniture had solid oak frames, with oak-veneered or lino-covered surfaces.

In pursuit of his aim to mass produce good quality simple furniture at an affordable price, Conran expanded his furniture-manufacturing capacity by moving out of London to a larger factory at Thetford in Norfolk. The steel-framed building clad with timber and brick and the machinery it contained were both ultra-modern. Prior to its relocation, Conran Furniture had launched a new range of domestic furniture called Summa, in a bid to move beyond the confines of the contract market. In addition to seat furniture, the Summa range was later expanded to include bedroom furniture, tables and an extensive selection of storage units made of solid Swedish pine, including kitchen cupboards and shelving, and even tongue and groove cladding to line walls. According to the promotional copy in an early brochure, the Summa range was 'designed to match the mood of present day living. What people want now for their homes is lively practical furniture in good basic shapes and

left
Range of products sold at Habitat, 1967. The use of lower case lettering for their graphics was an essential part of the Habitat 'look'.
below left
Much of the furniture sold by Habitat during the 1960s was made by Conran Furniture. The Summa range, dating from 1962, was the first domestic range manufactured by the company.

bottom right
During the 1950s Conran also worked as a freelance designer, supplying patterns for firms such as the textile company, David Whitehead, and the ceramics manufacturer Midwinter. Illustrated here is a printed pattern for Midwinter called Nature Study, 1955.
far right
Contemporary style chairs designed by Terence Conran for the Leather Institute, 1958.

the whole boiling
(including the kitchen sink)

Now Conran's Summa Wall Storage kit has a sink, as well as fabulous (solid Swedish pine) storage for everything you could ever want in your kitchen. Even the walls are part of the package—fix them first and from them hang your own arrangement of storage and working tops (or fix the units directly to your own walls).

New too is the £22 kitchen table—solid pine all the way—with a boarded top to absorb any amount of chopping, beating and bashing. People proof chairs by Magistretti are made by Conran and retail from £12 each.

See Summa kitchens at our local stockists or at our showrooms 5 Hanway Place, London W1 3 Smithy Lane King Street West, Manchester 3 and Thetford Norfolk, or clip the coupon and send it to us for full catalogue and stockist details.

Please send details of Summa Wall Storage   d1

Name _____

Address _____

Conran [c]
5 Hanway Place London W1

left
Advert from 1964 showing Summa kitchen units and table made from Swedish pine, complemented by 'sizzling red' Carimate chairs designed by Vico Magistretti for Cassina, produced under licence by Conran in the UK. Summa wall storage shelving, which could be purchased as a kit with accompanying tongue-and-groove cladding, was described in promotional literature as 'bang on the trend for cosy countrified living'.

top left
Exterior of the first Habitat store at Brompton Cross, London, opened in 1964.
above
Habitat carrier bags, 1975. From its outset in the mid-1950s the corporate identity of the Conran Design Group was carefully controlled. When Habitat was set up in 1964 the same attention was paid to detail.
right
Display of Habitat products at the Design Centre, London, 1969. During the course of the decade the number of Habitat shops grew, and the Habitat 'look' became increasingly influential. Like Mary Quant's fashions, it particularly appealed to young people.

warm unspoilt materials – natural timbers, leather, canvas – set off by bright fabrics.' In terms of its domestic sales, however, in spite of its attractive publicity brochures, the Summa range was only moderately successful when it was first launched in 1962, the main constraint being the lack of sympathetic retail outlets through which it could be sold. Conran vented his bitterness about this situation in an interview in *The Ambassador* magazine in August 1965:

The sales people and the buyers of this country are just sitting in a solid black block cutting off a much livelier public on one side from groups of manufacturers – more lively than they are given credit for – on the other. Sometimes the whole complex of selling is so turgid that the prospect of getting the design right the way through is remote. New design needs a new marketing and sales approach ... The most important job the Council of Industrial Design has to do is to persuade buyers and retailers of the need to buy and sell good design. The whole attitude of these people towards design needs to be revitalised.

It was largely as a result of his frustration with this situation that Conran finally decided to take the plunge and set himself up as a retailer. He realized eventually that he could no longer confine himself to designing and making. Only then could he increase public access to his work, and popularize his style. Furthermore, in order to exert greater control over the selling of his furniture to the public, Conran realized that he would have to challenge traditional patterns of furniture selling. This meant deliberately livening things up by setting out to target the new youth market. A high profile early commission for the Conran Design Group had been Mary Quant's new Knightsbridge Green shop in 1957. Conran was a great admirer of the way that young fashion designers like Quant, and later Foale and Tuffin, had challenged the status quo, not only through their design work, but by setting up their trend-setting boutiques. In many ways it was these shops that were the inspiration for Habitat because they had drawn attention to, and opened up, a whole new market. In terms of the range of goods on sale, another influence on Habitat was the enlightened Danish department store Illums Bolighus, which Conran had visited in Copenhagen, that sold good quality modern furniture and furnishings at an affordable price. In his interview with *The Ambassador* magazine in August 1965 Conran suggested that:

Furniture designers haven't yet moved into the commercial groove in the same way as fashion designers ... The ideal situation is one wherein manufacturer, designer, retailer and consumer are involved in a balanced and integrated relationship.

The choice of a name for Conran's new venture came about through looking up associations for the word 'house' in *Roget's Thesaurus*. The site chosen for the first Habitat shop was Brompton Cross on the Fulham Road, at this date largely a residential area, but one which Conran felt intuitively had great potential for retailing. The interior was designed by Conran himself and Oliver Gregory from the Conran Design Group, and the stock, which was drawn from Scandinavia, France and Italy, as well as from his own factories, and included a wide range of domestic accessories, as well as furniture and furnishings, was all personally selected by Conran. In terms of its interior design, the first Habitat provided a template and set a standard against which all the other later branches would be judged. With its quarry tiled floor, its whitewashed

brick walls, its suspended wooden ceiling, and its use of spotlights, the interior had a refreshing simplicity, clarity and openness. Although distinctive, the interior was designed so that it did not compete for attention with the goods on show. One of the most striking things about Habitat was the way in which the merchandise was displayed in bulk on deep open shelves. This was the truly revolutionary nature of its appeal and the key to its success, rather than the quality or rarity of the products themselves. Individually they were often unremarkable, but *en masse* they had a completely different aura, and it was their association with the shop itself which gave them their particular *cachet*.

Opened on 11 May 1964, Habitat was an immediate and spectacular success. It rapidly became the talk of the town, and the media, including the influential new colour supplements and trend-setting magazines, such as *Queen, About Town* and *Nova,* lapped it up. Much in the same way as Bazaar and Biba, Habitat attracted both the stars and a mass market audience, and was used by consumers in much the same way, as a place to meet like-minded people. According to Conran's biographer, Nicholas Ind:

Habitat was not so much a design triumph as a marketing one ... The shop was successful for a variety of reasons: Terence's vision and drive and eye for products, the quality of the staff, the cohesiveness of the stock and the marketing of the concept.

Within the space of two and a half years, a second store had been opened, this time close to its rival, Heal's, on Tottenham Court Road. The juxtaposition of the design Establishment in the form of Heal's, with the new face of design in the form of Habitat, was particularly fascinating, and Conran's choice of site was deliberately provocative. As in the case of Biba when it moved to a new site on Kensington Church Street in 1966, the opening of the second Habitat shop coincided with the intense international media focus on Swinging London. In both cases, however, rather than jumping on a bandwagon, the designers had prefigured and helped to establish a trend which the international media only discovered somewhat after the event. By the time they arrived, both Hulanicki and Conran had already moved on to the second phase of their expansion.

Physical growth, initially a symbol of success for both Biba and Habitat, was also at the root of their future difficulties, however. Neither were able to sustain the exactingly high standards and the unique identity of their shops, key factors in their original success. This was particularly so in the case of Habitat because, instead of moving from one site to another, the number of stores increased incrementally year by year, with two new shops opening in Manchester and Kingston-upon-Thames in 1967, and a total of nine shops in operation around the country by the end of 1969. Habitat retained its reputation for cheap chic right through until the end of the decade, although once it began to expand outside London, the Habitat 'look' inevitably lost something of its mystique.

In its impact on people's taste in home decor and in its influence on shopping habits in the field of furniture and furnishings, Habitat was probably the single most important domestic design phenomenon in Britain during the 1960s. Although this was partly because the British had been so unadventurous hitherto in their approach to furniture design and retailing, the Habitat approach was recognized as being significant in an international context and was praised for its

above
Interior of the Danish department store, Illums Bolighus, during the early 1960s. Conran cited this shop as an influence on Habitat.

freshness and its directness by foreign commentators, particularly the Americans and the Scandinavians. In a feature in *Mobilia* in September 1969, Conran was singled out for praise. He was only 38, yet he was at the height of his creative and commercial success. According to the Danes:

Terence Conran is the natural consequence of the line that goes from William Morris to Gordon Russell. Everything Conran designs is created for modern people, easy to live with, light and colourful, and the best thing in connection with their simplicity is that they are reasonably priced.

Herein lay his greatest achievement, making modern design available to a wider audience by solving the age-old problem of bringing down the price, and it was in this that Conran succeeded where William Morris had failed.

Apart from the Habitat retailing phenomenon, the aspect of British design that most fascinated foreign observers was Pop design, particularly graphics. John Heyes, writing in *Design* in June 1968, acknowledged that 'a new image of Britain created by more ephemeral designs has an important contribution to make as a selling point'. In this article, called 'Design for Export', he noted that in North America, not only were British fashions and hairstyles all the rage, but also British cars and even British bicycles. Graphics were one of the most distinctive areas of British commercial design during the 1960s, especially the patterns applied to household and ornamental goods. Leading firms in this field included Dodo Designs, Goods and Chattels and Xlon, whose printed tinwares designed by Pauline Butler were sold through leading department stores around the country. For Goods and Chattels in 1969 Nigel Quiney created a series of exuberant psychedelic designs for wrapping papers and paper bags which, although as ephemeral as design could possibly get, reflected some of the most creative and exciting visual ideas of the period. Other designers working with Goods and Chattels included Derek Hodgkinson and Astrop Hill Associates; while the designer and illustrator Jan Pienkowski established a company called Gallery Five making wrapping paper, greetings cards and jigsaw puzzles; Cliff Richards designed zany printed gift boxes manufactured by Michael Stanfield Products, which were sold through Habitat; and Ian Logan was the chief designer at JRM Designs, makers of brightly coloured ceramics and printed patterned metal accessories such as trays, caddies and wastepaper bins.

It was firms such as these, along with the leading fashion boutiques, who were responsible for creating the design phenomenon known as 'Carnaby Street', and it was the 'Carnaby Street' phenomenon that was largely responsible for the growing interest in British design abroad during the second half of the decade. According to John Heyes:

The success of the young fashion world – particularly Mary Quant, Barbara Hulanicki and John Stephen – and of the idiom corporately familiar as 'Carnaby Street', have similarly contributed to this clearing of dead wood. Together these innovators have created a coherent though kaleidoscopic pattern, best caught within the vivid, amusing and attractive British pavilion at Expo 67.

In spite of acknowledging Pop design as an important factor in the marketing of British design abroad, however, the main thrust of Heyes's article was that it provided manufacturers of 'serious' goods with openings to secure increased exports. In the eyes of the British design Establishment there was a sense of embarrassment that Britain was having to go 'downmarket' to win orders for the quality goods that might otherwise be overlooked in foreign markets. What the design Establishment found difficult to accept, except in the case of fashion, was that their perception of 'downmarket' was now outmoded. Being commercially successful did not necessarily mean making compromises or reducing standards; it simply meant targeting a wider audience, and making goods available at prices more people could afford. This was exactly what Mary Quant did by choosing to design, not for the couture industry, but for the ready-to-wear market; and this was what Terence Conran did by expanding Conran Furniture and opening Habitat. The 1960s was a genuinely democratic age, and it was no longer the aspiration of young designers to create products for an élite. They wanted to reach as many people as possible, and to improve people's quality of life by improving the quality of everyday design. In their article 'Behind the Scene' in *Design* in August 1966, Ken and Kate Baynes concluded that 'Fun' could be 'a weapon of revolution', and that:

One day, 'Carnaby Street' could rank with 'Bauhaus' as a descriptive phrase for a design style and a design legend. Just as the Bauhaus has come to stand for a moment in the history of design when nineteenth-century assumptions were shaken by a new attitude which was part aesthetic, part social, so today the revolution in attitude to things like obsolescence and decoration goes with economic and social changes.

This is a fascinating statement because it forges a link between the Carnaby Street phenomenon and the rejection of Modernism. The underlying tenets of the Bauhaus revolution of earlier in the century embodied in the Miesian statement 'Less is More', and Adolf Loos's dictate, 'Ornament is Crime', became inverted and subverted during the 1960s so that the guiding philosophies of Carnaby Street were 'More is More' and 'Ornament is Sublime'.

It was this aspect of British design to which the Italians responded most positively. When Ettore Sottsass visited London at the end of October 1966, for example, he made no mention of Habitat, but he was clearly overwhelmed by the colourfulness of the street life in the capital, in particular the eclectic shop frontages of the many small boutiques that had sprung up in recent years, with their dark cramped interiors and their lively *ad hoc* signage. This experience made a deep impression on him and inspired a photographic essay published in *Domus* in January 1967. Sottsass's return to London on a flying visit in 1969 prompted a second creative outpouring in *Domus*, 'London Shop Fronts', published in November 1969. This took the form of a series of photographs of some of the striking painted shop windows and facades he had witnessed on a taxi trip around the capital, conducted at breakneck speed, with accompanying text by the writer Richard Carr. In Sottsass's introduction, he lamented the disappearance of the famous mural on the exterior of the headquarters of the Beatles' company Apple by a group of artists called the Fool, which had been painted over following the threat of legal action by the owners of adjacent properties. However, he remarked with some satisfaction: 'here and there are still humbler-scale trips on offer, suggesting that perhaps there is still room for creativity and invention.'

One of the most famous 'trips on offer' in London during the second half of the 1960s was the legendary Granny Takes A Trip boutique on the King's Road, which underwent

right
Beakers and storage jars
by Hornsea Pottery, 1967.
This colourful range reflects
the graphic exuberance of
British design during the
1960s. Hornsea's Heirloom
tableware range, which
was similar in style, proved
enormously popular during
the late 1960s.

left
Optik Art perspex jewellery,
1965, designed and made
by Wendy Ramshaw, sold
through outlets such as
Mary Quant's Bazaar; and
Something Special paper
jewellery, 1967, designed
and manufactured by
Wendy Ramshaw, sold flat-
packed through outlets
such as the Way In bou-
tique at Harrods. The patterns on this jewellery and
the materials from which it
was made were considered
revolutionary at the time,
and typify the graphic inventiveness and technical ingenuity of British design during
this period.

above
Ceramic accessories
designed by Helena Uglow
for JRM Designs, 1969,
reflecting the square, cylindrical and spherical forms of
'the look'. White and orange
were also popular colours
for plastics at this time.

various transmutations over time, but which was at this date adorned with a car emerging out of the front of the building. Another was Gandalf's Garden, a shop specializing in hippy clothes, handicrafts and wholefoods, named after the white wizard in J R R Tolkien's cult novel, *The Lord of the Rings*, and decorated with pseudo-mystical imagery. In both cases the shops had no window displays, the attraction being the way in which the window itself was used as a mural. Whereas Habitat was designed to be light and open, and to draw people in off the street by making what was inside as visible as possible, these boutiques operated on the opposite premise. By completely obscuring the interior and the merchandise, they attracted people to enter out of curiosity, having first grabbed their attention by the unconventional decoration on the exterior. Thus what might be interpreted as an anti-consumerist statement was, in fact, used to lure people inside to spend money. What distinguished Habitat from the ephemeral boutique culture of the day was that, although it appealed to the youth market and sold products which were expendable, the Habitat shops themselves had a more timeless quality. A symbol of its enduring qualities is the fact that the lower case typography adopted for its original graphics is still in use over three decades later, and some of its stores are still in their original carefully chosen locations. In spite of Terence Conran's views on expendability, Habitat itself was not a here-today, gone-tomorrow boutique, but something much more substantial. By contrast, many of the boutiques on Carnaby Street and the King's Road that had attracted the interest of the international media in 1966 and which subsequently became the destination of all tourists doing the Grand Tour of London, were looking decidedly dated and shabby by the end of the decade. As soon as other people realized there was money to be made out of them, they were threatened by cynical commercial exploitation. Richard Carr concluded his commentary on Sottsass's photographs with the lament: 'So farewell Carnaby Street and King's Road. Long may you live even though the vultures are upon you. For because of you both clothes and shopping will never be the same again.'

right
Psychedelic mural above Lord John boutique on Carnaby Street, 1967.
below
Mary Quant having her hair cut by Vidal Sassoon, 1964. By contrast with the organic Contemporary style, 'the look' of the 1960s was geometric and angular. The neatly cropped boyish hairstyles developed by Sassoon perfectly complemented Quant's simple pinafores and mini-dresses.

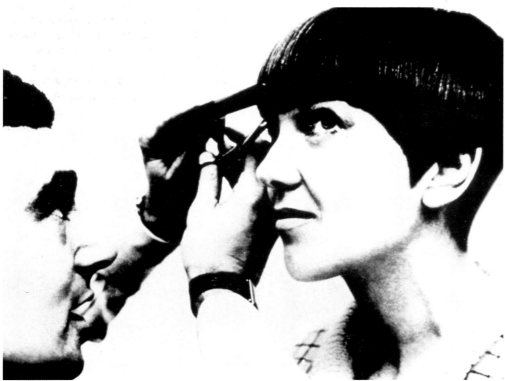

left and above
Murals and novelty window features formed an essential part of London streetlife in areas such as Carnaby Street and the King's Road during the second half of the 1960s. Granny Takes a Trip (left), and Gandalf's Garden (above), were two of the shop fronts on the King's Road singled out for attention by Ettore Sottsass in *Domus* in November 1969. The car emerging from the facade of Granny Takes a Trip was created by Nigel

Waymouth of Hapshash and the Coloured Coat. The shopfront of Gandalf's Garden was painted by Ian Culow and Muz Murray. This shop, named after the white wizard in J R R Tolkien's novel *The Lord of the Rings*, was described in *Domus* as 'a meeting place for soul gardeners, occultists, yogis and others in search of gentle peace'. It sold hand-made pottery, candles, clothes and leathergoods, as well as alternative literature and wholefoods.

'the look'

three

opposite
opposite
Piazza furnishing fabric designed by Barbara Brown for Heal's, 1964. The circular motifs which dominate domestic objects and buildings of the early 1960s also crop up repeatedly in textile designs. Barbara Brown's large-scale geometric patterns were as important in defining 'the look' as the playful linear patterns of Lucienne Day had been in establishing the earlier Contemporary style.

above left
Detail of circular patterned facade of the Parke-Davis Building, Los Angeles, designed by Charles Luckman, 1960.

above right
Wire stool by Plus-Linje and carpet by Unika Vaev, both designed by Verner Panton, c1960. The *enfant terrible* of Danish design, Panton played a key role in evolving the aesthetics of 'the look'.

The Carnaby Street approach which started with clothes is now spilling over into other areas, and what has happened is of great significance for design as a whole. It seems likely that fun and entertainment – which people have always wanted from the things they use everyday – may even come to be accepted by designers as an important requirement.
Ken and Kate Baynes, 'Behind the Scene', *Design*, August 1966

As in the world of fashion, 'the look' in domestic furniture, furnishings and accessories arrived as early as 1962. Perhaps the best way to define 'the look' is to make direct comparisons with the Contemporary style, to contrast the *old* new with the *new* new. This in itself is a highly significant point: the 'look' was not a retrogressive backlash style; it represented a positive step forward from an already advanced position. The key to an understanding of what happened during the early 1960s is to recognize that one form of modernity displaced another. In design terms, by way of analogy to *film noir*, it was a case of double indemnity. By contrast, what began to happen during the second half of the decade – the counter-revolution – was the start of a reaction against the concept of modernity itself. Unlike 'the look', the counter-revolution, although positive and creative in many respects, contained strong elements of negative backlash, manifested most obviously through a renewed interest in self-conscious historical revivalism. The use of artificial stimulation in the form of hallucinogenic drugs was another new phenomenon which would influence the character of design during the second half of the decade, most obviously in the field of graphics, but also in other forms of pattern design. The general trend during the late 1960s was to seek alternative design solutions outside the Establishment framework, thereby confounding expectations and disrupting projected patterns of development. There was also a greater reliance on, and acceptance of, the concept of derivation rather than innovation, demonstrated by the impulse to explore alternative ideas gleaned from traditional ethnic sources. Whereas the early 1960s can be seen as a period of convergence, a time when existing trends were strengthened and intensified, the later 1960s, by contrast, were distinguished by divergence and fragmentation. By way of analogy to fashion, if Mary Quant typifies the first phase, then Biba characterizes the latter. Thus the two design revolutions which occurred during the course of the decade had a markedly different flavour, and carried design in opposite directions.

Returning to the 1950s, however, and to a comparison between the *old* new style – Contemporary – and the *new* new style – 'the look'; in visual terms 'the look' defined itself by the extent to which it departed from the conventions of the New Look. Contemporary design had been strongly influenced by the abstract organic sculptures of artists such as Jean Arp, Henry Moore and Barbara Hepworth. As a result, the Contemporary forms were soft and plastic, and shapes were fluid and free-form in outline. Frequently objects were asymmetrical or irregular in some way, such as chairs and tables with three legs instead of the more usual four. Another distinctive characteristic of the Contemporary style was excessive exaggeration and distortion of form – the 'Tulip Phenomenon' – whereby the width or diameter of individual objects varied from one extreme to another. In Italy the Contemporary style had been dubbed Neo-Liberty, because it was so exaggeratedly curvilinear that some designs recalled the whiplash lines of Art Nouveau. During the early 1960s, as people tired of the excesses of Contemporary, there was a reaction against many of these organic trends, and in linear terms what might be described as a backlash against the whiplash. The evolution of 'the look' was marked by a return to geometrical correctness, characterized not only by the widespread adoption of pure geometric forms, but also more generally by characteristics such as formalism, precision, balance, repetition and symmetry.

The adoption of geometric forms in architecture and design during the early 1960s was but the start of a more general shift in design away from free forms to controlled forms. This sudden and decided change of direction was at the heart of 'the look'. Although by the end of the decade in some media such as glass, ceramics and textiles this revolution would itself already have been put into reverse as part of a counter-revolution, at the start of the 1960s the general trend was to replace the overtly loose, informal, soft forms and expressive patterns of the 1950s with highly controlled shapes and patterns. Geometric precision was what designers of 'the look' aspired to, whether this be in the pattern on a textile or a dress, or the shape of a lamp or a cruet set. If a shape was round, it had to be a perfect circle or half circle. If a shape was rectilinear, it had to be either a cube or a square, or be based on a modular system. The fluid, asymmetrical shapes of Contemporary design were now dismissed as lax, as was the arbitrariness of Abstract Expressionism in the field of pattern design; both were abandoned in favour of rigid symmetry and undisguised repetition. Although the mood of the age was increasingly informal, therefore, 'the look' of the early 1960s was highly regulated, precise and even somewhat severe.

Control, and the desire to exert control, were essential characteristics of both 'the look' and the *Zeitgeist* of the early 1960s, particularly during the period before the escalation of the Vietnam War. Designers and manufacturers openly aspired to the imposition of control aesthetically (in relation to shapes and patterns), practically (in terms of function and the processes of manufacture), and commercially (in terms of manipulating the market). Actively interventionist systems of control were in fashion at this date, particularly in large commercial organizations run on corporate American lines, and such systems were openly encouraged by professional organizations such as the Council of Industrial Design in Britain and the Svenska Slödjföreningen (the Swedish Society for Industrial Design) in Scandinavia. Even in the world of fashion, the

motivating force behind the Quant 'look' was to give young women a greater degree of control over their own lives. The way this was done was by creating an image which was itself a manifestation of control, although in practical terms what it actually gave them was freedom. Thus they achieved informality through self-imposed formalism. The essential point was that this was a discipline imposed by the young on themselves, rather than a control system imposed from outside by the older generation.

One can only speculate on the reasons behind this obsession with control during the early 1960s. Perhaps it was partly a delayed reaction against the Second World War, when the world quite clearly went out of control; perhaps it was a more immediate reaction against the nature of art and design in the 1950s which, in encouraging self-expression, had become somewhat self-indulgent. (All those exaggerated and impractical shapes. All those clashing primary colours. All those drips and daubs.) More likely, however, this desire to exert control arose from a growing confidence in the value of science and technology, and of the perceived benefits that a controlled 'scientific' approach to design could bring to the designer, the manufacturer and the consumer. Since the war there had been unprecedented advances in almost all branches of science and technology, and the fruits of this progress were apparent in many areas of manufacturing, as well as in everyday life. People were very conscious of how scientific progress was affecting their lives and, on the whole – except in relation to nuclear weapons – the consensus view was that scientific progress was a good thing. As with fashion, what people wanted was to be able to exert greater control over their own lives, and they believed that it was through technological advances, whether in the field of health, housing or hi-fis, that this would come about. Architects and designers, like scientists, were riding on a wave of public confidence during the early 1960s: confidence in the achievements of the recent past, and confidence that they were moving forward in the right direction. Harold Wilson's rousing speech at the Labour Party Conference in 1963 about his vision of a country driven forward by 'the white heat of technological change' only served to endorse this view. It came as no surprise the following year, therefore, when Wilson was elected to power. Clearly he had pressed the right button.

Looked at in this way, one can understand why, in the context of design, control came to be associated with particular forms and patterns during the early 1960s. By contrast, it is easy to see why free-form shapes could be perceived as unsettling and disturbing. This was one of the reasons why they had appealed to the Surrealists during the 1930s, because they appeared to provide a link with the irrational and the subconscious. Geometric shapes, by contrast, were reassuring simply because they were predictable. Even when only part of a profile or outline was in view, the eye was confident of the remaining shape or pattern at a glance: there was nothing to throw it off course. Geometric shapes, therefore, were the embodiment of moral and aesthetic certainty. The same was true of abstract geometric patterns, but to an even greater degree, as these combined the outline of geometric shapes with the additional element of repetition. That some designers were conscious of at least some of these phenomena and were aware of how they were operating at a psychological level is indicated by the titles of a series of furnishing fabrics

top and above
Children's toys designed by Hans von Klier for Il Sestante in Milan, 1962, illustrating the 'family of forms' which define 'the look' of the 1960s.
opposite
With their bold, self-consciously repetitive, geometric patterns, British furnishing fabrics of the early 1960s were ideally suited to complement 'the look' of modern architecture. These textiles are both by Heal's, the most progressive manufacturer of the decade. Colonnade designed by Barbara Brown, 1964 (opposite top). Alternation designed by Doreen Dyall, 1962 (opposite below).

produced by one of the most dynamic and forward-looking British textile companies of the period, Heal's. Between 1962 and 1964 Barbara Brown produced a series of strongly geometric and highly controlled patterns with names such as Symmetry, Recurrence and Reciprocation. Another Heal's designer, Doreen Dyall, produced two patterns in 1962 called Alternation and Repetition. Even without seeing these fabrics, the titles are highly evocative of the tightly controlled nature of the designs.

In December 1962 *Domus* published a feature on some children's toys by the designer Hans von Klier for the Milanese firm of Il Sestante. Klier had designed a range of painted wooden blocks in different geometric shapes which enabled children to build their own totemic structures. These wooden components provide a representation in miniature of the new repertoire of shapes which designers were to draw upon during the early 1960s. They also suggest how such shapes could be juxtaposed to contrast with or complement each other, or alternatively how they could be grouped into families of related forms. The new orthodoxy of approved geometric shapes was composed of three distinct families. Firstly, the circle family, which in addition to circles themselves included cylinders, tubes, spheres, domes and discs. Secondly, the square family, which included diamonds, rectangles, cubes and other three-dimensional rectilinear forms. Thirdly, the triangle family, which in addition to triangles included cones and pyramids, and which was closely related to hexagons and geodesic domes. The use of geometric forms and patterns was a central feature of 'the look' of the sixties, and this vocabulary, although in some areas it may have started out as an expression of the avant-garde, was immediately picked up by a wider audience and rapidly became mainstream. Although it may seem simplistic to suggest that 'the look' of the early 1960s arose primarily because designers exploited this basic repertoire of geometric forms, closer analysis of the actual objects and patterns produced between 1962 and 1967 suggests that this was indeed the case: the use of these forms was not limited to a few isolated and unrepresentative examples but was extremely widespread.

Cylinders
Of all the geometric forms that were utilized during the 1960s, it was those based on the circle which had the greatest resonance. Yet the most widespread change was perhaps the least dramatic, and one that could easily be overlooked and taken for granted. This was the adoption of the cylinder as the new standard form for the vessel, marking a move away from tapering forms and the organic and curvilinear shapes of the 1950s, such as the hour-glass, the pear shape and the rounded rectangle. This trend applied equally to tableware and light fittings, and was as marked in new materials such as stainless steel and plastics, as it was in traditional media such as ceramics and glass. A classic example in the field of metalwork was Arne Jacobsen's stainless-steel Cylinda-Line range (see page 24) for the Danish firm of A S Stelton, introduced over a period of several years between 1964 and 1967, where even the title draws attention to the newly evolved cylindrical shapes (see page 24). As with all his work, Jacobsen paid great attention to detail, both aesthetic and functional. The lids of vessels such as the coffee pot, for example, lie flush with the rim, so as not to interfere with the creation of a

perfect cylinder. Circular motifs were incorporated throughout the range to complement the cylindrical forms, and can be seen in the pierced decoration on the tongs accompanying the ice bucket, and in the exposed rivets on the ice bucket itself. A combination of circles and right angles were used for the design of the black plastic handles, a detail that clearly demonstrates the rigour and discipline of Jacobsen's design. Although Jacobsen's buildings of the 1950s and 1960s had been rectilinear rather than curvilinear – with the exception of his Round House of 1957– until 1964 most of his designs for furniture and metalwork had followed the prevailing organic trend. For Jacobsen, therefore, the Cylinda-Line range marked a conscious departure from the aesthetics of the 1950s and, without rejecting the validity of his earlier work, signified an acceptance of 'the look' of the sixties.

Similar trends, and a similar rigour, are apparent in the work of Robert Welch during the early 1960s. Just as the Cylinda-Line range was a pivotal design for Jacobsen, so the Alveston tableware range of 1962 marked a significant turning point for Welch. Hitherto inspired by Scandinavian design, Welch had previously designed shapes that were overtly organic or that relied on tapering or attenuated forms. Henceforth his shapes would be much more compact and robust, often based on circles, discs, cylinders, domes and cones. The basic vessel shapes and the detailing of the Alveston range arise from an imaginative juxtaposition of cylindrical, conical and triangular elements, the latter being expressed in the open handles, while conical forms determined the shape of the knob handles on the lids, and the flared bases and drip pans of the candlesticks. The vessels themselves were basically cylindrical, although the upper and lower sections tapered at an angle to form truncated cones. Slightly rounded angles, where these different formal elements meet, make the design seem less severe. Details such as these, along with a more profound understanding of Functionalism, are what differentiate the geometrical correctness of the 1960s from that of the 1930s, a period when geometric forms had also been adopted by designers working in both the Modernist and Moderne camp.

A second range of domestic objects designed by Welch in which circular forms played a major role – in this case the circle itself, along with the disc and the cylinder – were his cast-iron kitchen accessories designed between 1962 and 1966. The choice of the then unfashionable material of cast iron for this range, treated with a matt black enamel finish, was itself radical at the time, and demonstrated the extent of Welch's originality. It reflected his commitment to robust forms, the material itself dictating a strong approach to design. The range included a chunky cylindrical pepper grinder and nutcracker, and a circular fruit bowl decorated with sharply defined radiating lines. The most memorable item in the range, however, was the flanged candlestick dating from 1962, also known as the Disc candlestick because the flanges were in the form of circular discs stacked at intervals along the length of its stem. Made in three different heights, and cast in the shape of a solid notched tube, an idea Welch had previously explored through the medium of silver, the Disc candlestick was ideally suited to cast iron. The influence of its flanged form can be detected in the clear colourless textured candlesticks in Timo Sarpaneva's Festivo range for littala dating from 1968; and even more directly in Ronald Stennett-Willson's

below
Flanged cylindrical forms were common during the 1960s. Robert Welch set the trend with his cast-iron Disc candlesticks of 1962.
bottom
Similar ideas were later adopted by Ronald Stennett-Willson in his Sheringham range of glass candlesticks, 1967, originally produced by King's Lynn Glass, and subsequently by Wedgwood.

above left
Palio printed textile designed by Alexander Girard for Herman Miller in 1964, was similar in aesthetic to the simplified, flat, two-colour pop patterns created by Susie Cooper for Wedgwood between 1967 and 1969.
left
The evolution of the cylindrical vessel form associated with 'the look' can be traced in the Can, Variation and Fine tableware ranges. Can coffee cups designed by Susie Cooper, 1958, decorated with a pattern called Carnaby Daisy which was introduced in 1968. The title refers to Carnaby Street and the motif recalls Mary Quant's stylized daisy logo.
top
Variation tableware designed by Tapio Wirkkala for Rosenthal, 1962.
above
Fine tableware designed by David Queensberry and Roy Midwinter for Midwinter, 1962, decorated with a pattern called Queensberry Stripe.

'the look'

Sheringham range dating from 1967. Initially produced by Stennett-Willson's firm, King's Lynn Glass, subsequently taken over by Wedgwood in 1969, the Sheringham candlestick was made in various heights with up to six flanges, and was produced in dark colours, as well as clear glass.

In the field of industrial ceramics there were numerous instances of the shift from organic body forms to regular straight-sided cylindrical vessels during the early 1960s, although the trend had, in fact, begun during the late 1950s. As early as 1958 Susie Cooper – perhaps the single most consistently original British ceramic designer of this century – introduced her new Can shape, produced in bone china, the form of which was inspired by late eighteenth- and early nineteenth-century porcelain coffee wares. The coffee pot and jug forms were tall oval cylinders, but the cups were circular, making this the earliest documented re-appearance of the cylindrical vessel form that was to dominate ceramics in the 1960s. An appreciation of the significance of Cooper's Can shape has been hindered partly because the shape remained in production so long that its originality has been overlooked, and partly because, when it was first launched, the organic and classical printed patterns with which it was decorated lagged behind in terms of modernity. It was not until the second half of the 1960s that Susie Cooper devised a range of patterns bold enough to match the aesthetic potential of the shape. These included Heraldry (1967), Pennant (1969), Diablo (1969), Keystone (1968) and Carnaby Daisy (1968), the latter inspired by Mary Quant's daisy logo. These highly stylized and strikingly simple one- or two-colour quasi-abstract printed designs encapsulated 'the look' of 1960s patterns, and perfectly matched 'the look' of Cooper's cylindrical vessel form. Apart from Carnaby Daisy, the basic ideas for most of these patterns were, in fact, derived from historical sources. In this, and in the bold simplicity of their design, they resembled the Palio range of printed textiles designed by Alexander Girard for Herman Miller in 1964, which were inspired by the patterns on the medieval banners used at the Palio, a ceremonial horse race held in Siena twice each year.

David Queensberry has also pointed to the introduction of the Berlin shape, designed by Hans Theo Baumann for Rosenthal in 1959, as a turning point in ceramic design: it was this shape that prompted Queensberry to abandon organic forms. Vessels in the Berlin range were straight-sided but flared outwards at the rim, and their lids and knobs retained the organic tapering contours of the Contemporary style. Although its new cylindrical outline must have seemed quite radical when it first appeared, the Berlin shape did not, in fact, embody all the fully developed features of 'the look', and in historical terms it should be considered as transitional. After Susie Cooper's Can shape, therefore, it is David Queensberry's Fine range for Midwinter, and the Variation service designed by the Finnish designer Tapio Wirkkala for Rosenthal, both launched in 1962, that ought to be recognized as two of the most important breakthrough ceramic designs in Europe during the early 1960s. Both had a major impact on the designs produced by direct competitors within their own countries: Thomas China in the case of Rosenthal, and J & G Meakin in the case of Midwinter. With these shapes Wirkkala and Queensberry made a complete break with earlier organic trends: vessels were straight-sided instead of curvilinear; plates were circular instead of oval or quartic; and knobs

and handles were consistent with the design of the main vessel, instead of being used as a vehicle for a flamboyant design statement. In fact, when Queensberry came to remodel the Fine range in 1966, like Jacobsen with his Cylinda-Line range, he removed the knobs on the lids altogether.

Like Rosenthal in Germany, under what Queensberry has described as the 'inspired leadership' of Philip Rosenthal, Midwinter, headed by the dynamic Roy Midwinter, was recognized as the most forward-looking ceramics manufacturer in Britain after the Second World War. At the start of the 1960s Roy Midwinter was determined that his firm should continue to lead the British market in a dynamic and proactive way, as it had done throughout the 1950s. Midwinter's two previous shapes, Stylecraft (designed in 1952), and Fashion (dating from 1955), had both been overtly organic, so the adoption of a new cylindrical vessel form marked a conscious and strategic move in a new direction. In addition to the influence of eighteenth-century Neo-classical creamware, a source which David Queensberry has acknowledged in the design of Fine, Roy Midwinter, who collaborated on the design, indicated that the form of the coffee pot was also inspired by the shape of traditional English milk churns. Midwinter drew creatively and constructively on the Staffordshire ceramic industry's heritage, but did not allow itself to become trammelled by historical revivalism. The desire to produce a design which, although modern and of its time, was distinctly English, rather than just to mimic the latest continental leads, was a strong motivating factor, not only for Midwinter and Susie Cooper, but for Britain's leading domestic glass factory, Whitefriars Glass, during the 1960s. This helps to explain why British design developed so strongly at this date, because of a conscious striving for originality through a redefinition of national identity.

One of the main differences between Queensberry's Fine and Wirkkala's Variation was that the latter was produced in porcelain in a sophisticated but stark combination of plain black and white, whereas Fine was produced in earthenware, albeit of a specially refined nature, which emphasized its 'china whiteness'. With the Wirkkala design the decoration – a pattern of irregular fine ribbing on the vessel sides – was integrated with the shape; while with the Queensberry shape, overglaze enamel printed patterns were applied to the sides of the straight-sided vessels and the rims of plates and bowls. The suitability of the Fine shape for the application of printed surface patterns was one of the reasons why Queensberry favoured the cylindrical vessel form over the earlier organic forms of the 1950s with their awkward compound curves. Queensberry himself designed one of the most successful patterns used on the range, a textural vertical abstract design in muted mustard-brown, grey and black known as Queensberry Stripe, dating from 1962.

Apart from Midwinter, the most adventurous British ceramics manufacturer of the 1960s, and the company that pushed the cylindrical vessel form to its furthest limits, was the new firm of Portmeirion Pottery. Portmeirion grew out of the established Staffordshire decorating company of A E Gray, or Gray's Pottery, which had been well known and highly regarded during the 1930s. The firm was completely reinvented, however, after it was taken over by the designer Susan Williams-Ellis and her husband Euan Cooper-Willis in 1959. Susan Williams-Ellis was the daughter of Clough Williams-Ellis,

opposite above left
Portmeirion Pottery, run by the designer Susan Williams-Ellis, achieved remarkable success with its Cylinder shape, launched in 1962. Originally decorated with flat printed patterns, from 1963 it was produced with a raised moulded design called Totem, the geometric motifs of which complemented the vessel's form.

opposite above right
Cylindrical vessel forms were widely adopted by British ceramics manufacturers during the first half of the 1960s. J & G Meakin's Studio shape was designed by Tom Arnold in about 1964. Decorated here with a printed sunburst pattern called Aztec dating from 1965, the vessel is a cross between Midwinter's Fine tableware and Portmeirion's Cylinder.

opposite below
Denby's Chevron range designed by Gill Pemberton, 1963, is decorated with an impressed geometric pattern which complements the form. This service also included a double-height coffee pot.

the architect of the famous fantasy village of Portmeirion in Wales, hence the title chosen for the new factory when Gray's Pottery was renamed in 1962. She herself had trained not as a ceramic designer but as an artist, including a period of study at Chelsea School of Art under Henry Moore and Graham Sutherland. This presumably accounts for the unconventional and, by Staffordshire standards, iconoclastic approach to ceramic design that she adopted when she assumed the role of chief designer at Portmeirion during the early 1960s.

The first fruits of her labours appeared on the market in 1962 with the launch of the new Cylinder vessel form, originally decorated with a silk-screen printed enamel pattern called Talisman. The vessels in the resulting coffee service were so exaggeratedly tall and narrow that they looked more like tubes than cylinders. By comparison with earlier tableware, these vessels were up to double the height of their predecessors. The spouts were incredibly long, rising from near the foot almost to the rim of the coffee pot, while cups and coffee pots had long strap handles which also extended for virtually the full height of the vessel. Cone-shaped lids further increased the height, and were crowned with a spherical knop. Talisman was followed in 1963 by the Totem range, which used the same cylindrical shape, but this time decorated with a raised relief-moulded pattern. Through this design the astute Williams-Ellis created a service that was the embodiment of 'the look'. She took the fashionable cylindrical theme but developed it in an even more pronounced fashion than either Queensberry or Wirkkala. In addition to its dramatic shape, an essential element of the visual impact of Totem was the relief-patterned surface decoration, the raised pattern being produced from the reverse impressions of a mould during the slip-casting process. Here the pattern was composed of columns of circular motifs made up of lines and dots, a simple but highly effective visual device. Some motifs resembled snowflakes, others looked like molecular structures; the overall effect was suggestive of ancient totems in the guise of modern-day abstract art. Decorated with glossy translucent monochome 'flow' glazes in rich dark blue, amber and green, the raised patterns remained prominent while the glaze pooled more darkly on the flat surface below. Some later pieces, such as a range of storage jars with enlarged motifs, were decorated in matt white glaze, thus producing a rather different visual effect. Totem had a major impact on the British ceramics industry and proved to be the making of Portmeirion Pottery.

A second shape, Serif, introduced by Portmeirion later in 1963, was used as the basis for two further relief patterns: Cypher, which resembled hieroglyphics, and Jupiter, decorated with large indented circles, which echoed the form of the cylindrical vessel. The Serif shape retained the tubular vessel form, but added a flared lip and introduced a new pointed handle – a reference to the Serif of the title – and a flattened knob on the lid. Both the original Cylinder shape and the later Serif shape were produced with a variety of overglaze enamel printed patterns, the decoration, whether printed or in relief, being an essential ingredient of 'the look'. Two screen-printed patterns from 1964 were Variations and Tivoli, the latter inspired by a trip to the Tivoli Gardens in Copenhagen. Montesol dating from 1965 reflected a Moorish influence, while Magic City was more eclectic still, suggesting

above right
Cylindric cigarette lighter designed by Dieter Rams for Braun, 1968. Cylindrical forms influenced 'the look' of a wide range of products during the 1960s.
above
Vessel by Ettore Sottsass from the Ceramics of Darkness range, 1959. The circular form and patterns of this range were emblematic of his designs until the mid-1960s.
right
Nova stacking tableware designed by David Harman Powell for Ekco Plastics, winner of the Duke of Edinburgh's Award for Elegant Design in 1968.

an imaginary architecture as fantastical as that of Clough Williams-Ellis himself. While Magic City was extremely successful, having once again captured the mood of the time, Magic Garden, launched in 1970, did not take off, arriving too late after the peak of the the flower-power craze.

Another British ceramics manufacturer that combined cylindrical vessel forms with textured surface patterns was Denby Pottery in its Chevron range of 1963 designed by Gill Pemberton. Chevron was extremely successful and remained in production for many years. Made of stoneware, the vessels were hand-thrown then decorated with bands of impressed chevron patterning using a tool called a roulette, which produced indentations in the soft clay. It is significant that, as with Portmeirion's Totem and Jupiter, the relief pattern chosen to decorate Chevron was strongly geometric. As with the Portmeirion ranges, Chevron was decorated with a monochrome glaze which pooled around the relief pattern, although in this case the glaze was an opaque greyish-green colour, and was much thicker with an eggshell finish. Although cylindrical forms were adopted for this range, they were not as severe as those of Portmeirion, and only the coffee pot and the oil and vinegar bottles were exaggeratedly tall; all the other vessels in the range were of more conventional proportions. A later Denby range, Arabesque, dating from 1964, also by Gill Pemberton, used exaggeratedly tall but modified cylindrical forms which were high-waisted and angular. Loosely inspired by Hispano-Moresque patterns, the pattern, hand-painted in coloured glazes, was composed of rings or bands of large and small circles, the larger circles containing simplified star-shaped motifs. The appeal of Moorish design lay in the fact that it was entirely based on geometric forms, and thus was an appropriate source of historical inspiration for 'the look' of the 1960s.

Wedgwood also created a modified cylindrical shape in their traditional Black Basalt body around this date. Designed by Robert Minkin in 1964, this range was tall and thin but the sides were slightly convex rather than straight. Vessel heights peaked in the mid-1960s, but from this date onwards they started to decline as it came to be appreciated that tall coffee pots, although elegant, were not very practical. A more modestly proportioned shape, the Studio range, was produced by J & G Meakin from around 1964 designed by Tom Arnold. This had a distinctive tall cylindrical coffee pot with a deep square handle on the side and a wide round flattened handle on the lid. The accompanying cups, however, were flared and did not follow the cylindrical contours established by the coffee pot. Like Midwinter's Fine, Meakin's Studio shape remained in production for the remainder of the decade, and was decorated with a variety of printed overglaze enamel patterns over the years, each reflecting the visual trends of the time.

Apart from Britain, the country that witnessed the most decided shift away from the organic towards the geometric during the early 1960s was Italy. This happened concurrently with developments in the UK, and can be seen in a wide range of products in various materials. These included the bold geometric abstract patterns used by Ettore Sottsass to decorate a range of enamel bowls for Il Sestante of Milan, illustrated in *Domus* in September 1961, and a series of aluminium-cased glass flower vases designed by Enzo Mari for the adventurous new firm of Danese, also based in Milan,

right
Stroma water set designed by Domhnall O'Broin for Caithness Glass, 1964, a subtle variant on the standard cylindrical form. Like Portmeirion's Cylinder coffee pot, this decanter is exaggeratedly tall and narrow.
below
Angular range designed by Geoffrey Baxter for Whitefriars Glass, 1962. These vases were mouth-blown into a mould but the necks were finished by hand, hence the variations in form.

left
Conical tumblers designed by Alexander Hardie Williamson for United Glass, St Helens, Merseyside. The glasses were machine-made, with screen-printed enamel decoration. Initially made at the Sherdley factory from 1956, production was transferred to the Ravenhead plant in 1964. From left to right, the patterns reflect the influence of Op Art, Flower Power and the Contemporary style.

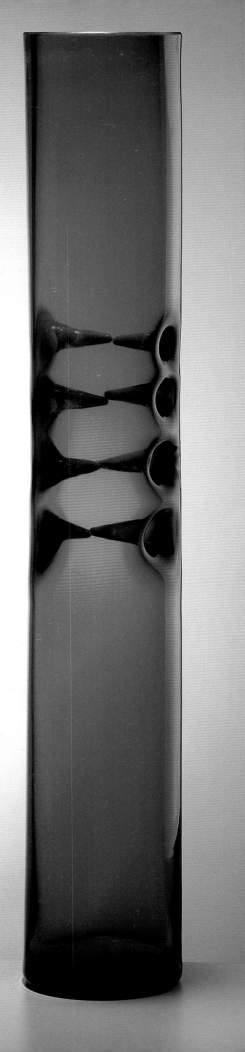

top
At the Finnish firm of
Nuutajärvi, Kaj Franck
adopted cylindrical elements
for both the wide stems and
the bowls of these richly
coloured goblets which date
from 1968.
above left
Harlequin range of cut
glass, designed by David
Queensberry for Webb
Corbett. Decorated with
matt and polished diamond
cutting, this range won the
Duke of Edinburgh's Award
for Elegant Design in 1964.

above
The Finnish designer, Nanny
Still, who worked for the
Riihimäki glassworks,
played an important role in
updating 'the look' of
Scandinavian design in the
1960s. Still's Ambra candlesticks of 1961 balance
discs on top of cylinders.
right
Cylindrical vase with sunken
decoration, designed by
Pavel Hlava for Ceský
Kristál, Czechoslovakia,
1964.

featured in *Domus* the following month. The idea for the latter was highly unusual and involved placing a thin anodized aluminium sheath around a cylindrical glass vase, the casing having first been cut with a simple abstract geometric pattern. Thus geometric forms and patterns were combined to create a chic Italian version of 'the look'. The fact that cylindrical forms re-appeared in a second range of objects designed by Mari in 1962, including an aluminium umbrella stand, indicated that this new departure was not just a one-off, but was set to become a wider trend. Later, the fashion for geometric forms in general and cylindrical forms in particular was to spread to most branches of the applied arts in Italy, including glass, ceramics, furniture and plastics. A good example of the latter was the Compact range of melamine tableware designed by Massimo Vignelli for ARPE, winner of a Compasso d'Oro award in 1964, and shown at the Milan Triennale later that year. This range, illustrated in *Domus* in November 1964, was composed entirely of square, rectangular and cylindrical items, with cylinders being the most common. The design-conscious American firm of Habitat Inc. (no relation to the British shop), which produced furniture, lighting and accessories, made a concerted attempt to assume 'the look' embodied by Italian design in the mid-1960s by adopting forms such as cylinders and spheres. In 1966, for example, Paul Mayen designed a combined litter bin and ashtray made of aluminium, which was cylindrical in form with a sand tray on the top and a circular opening for depositing rubbish below. This was complemented by an aluminium umbrella stand in the form of two adjoining open cylinders. Variants of these designs were widely adopted internationally from the mid-1960s onwards.

Cylinders and modified cylinders were a prominent feature of glass design during the first half of the 1960s, and can be seen in the work of existing design-led companies such as Iittala and Riihimäki in Finland, as well as in the products of new companies such as the Scottish firm Caithness Glass. Caithness Glass was established in the town of Wick in the far north of Scotland in 1960 as a special employment initiative. Inspired by the purity and simplicity of contemporary Scandinavian glass, the company's designer Domhnall O'Broin aspired to create high-quality hand-blown domestic designs which embodied 'the look' of the sixties. The result was a range of starkly simple, undecorated vessels, including the narrow cylindrical Lochshiel vases of 1965 produced in coloured underlay, and some stylish angular tablewares typified by the Stroma water set of 1964. Produced in dark brown, dark grey and clear glass, the tumblers in this range were slightly flared, and the decanter was an attenuated cylinder which tapered towards the rim. The following year saw the appearance of the Morven decanter, which was strictly geometrical, being composed of a tube-shaped neck surmounting a wider cylindrical body.

Establishing a new glass factory in a region with no previous history of glass-making was refreshing in one way because there were no preconceptions to overcome and no bad habits to undo, but restrictive in another way because the skills of the workforce were limited through lack of experience. This was another factor that may well have influenced the adoption of ultra-plain undecorated straight-sided vessel forms at Caithness Glass during the early 1960s. Because cylindrical vessels were so much easier for machines to produce, however, the trend away from the organic to the

geometric was also ideally suited to fully automated manufacturing plants such as Ravenhead Glass in St Helens, which formed part of the international container glass company United Glass. During the 1960s Ravenhead produced three basic types of tumbler, all designed by Alexander Hardie Williamson: the slightly flared Conical range, originally introduced in the 1950s, and renamed Coolers in the 1960s; the barrel-shaped Gaytime range; and the Slim Jims, tall, narrow tube-like tumblers which typified 'the look'. All three were decorated with a wide range of machine-applied silk-screen printed enamel patterns, designed by the prolific Hardie Williamson, which reflected the many different stylistic trends of the decade, from Op Art to flower power. Although catering to different sectors of the market, and although one company relied on visual restraint for its appeal while the other exploited visual panache, both Caithness Glass and Ravenhead were alike in adopting tall narrow tubular forms as a mechanism for associating themselves with 'the look'.

Ravenhead and Caithness were by no means isolated examples of the new geometric precision in British glass design during the early 1960s. Whitefriars Glass was also noticeably affected by the new trend, and 'the look' was reflected in the Angular range of thin-walled turn mould-blown soda glass vases launched at the Blackpool Gifts and Fancy Goods Fair in 1962. Although produced in Scandinavian-inspired deep smokey colours, such as amethyst, shadow green and midnight blue, the new range marked a departure from the thick-walled heavy Scandinavian Modern-style organic vessels that Whitefriars had produced during the second half of the 1950s. Designed by William Wilson and Geoffrey Baxter, these new vessels were lightweight and decidedly angular, giving them a different feel as well as a new aesthetic, a fact noted by the *Pottery Gazette and Glass Trade Review* which commented on the 'modern harmony' of the range in March 1962.

Another well-established English glass factory that made a conscious decision to modernize its image during the early 1960s was the Stourbridge firm of Webb Corbett. During the 1950s it had worked with the talented young designer Irene Stevens, who had pioneered the adoption of Contemporary design via the traditional avenue of cut glass. After Stevens left in 1957 to embark on a career in teaching at the Stourbridge School of Art, Webb Corbett retained its commitment to modern design, and during the early 1960s engaged the freelance designer David Queensberry. By this date Queensberry had already scored a notable success with his straight-sided Fine tableware range for Midwinter. Now he applied the same winning formula to the field of domestic glass by creating a new range of cut-glass bowls and vases which embodied 'the look' of the sixties in both their shapes and patterns. Launched in 1963, and the winner of the prestigious Duke of Edinburgh's Award for Elegant Design the following year, this range was one of the most significant British glass designs of the decade, and was described in *The Ambassador* in December 1963 as 'hand-cut in the traditional manner, yet completely in the modern idiom'. The vessels, produced in four shapes, were basically cylindrical, tapering at an angle at the foot. Of the four patterns that won the award, two were based on linear designs (Mitre, decorated with irregular vertical fluting, and Random, decorated with irregular vertical and horizontal mitre cutting); and two on all-over diamond

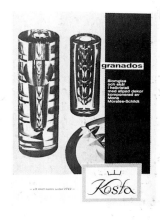

above
Mona Morales-Schildt used bold cutting to emphasize the optical qualities of glass in her thick-walled cylindrical Granados range for the Swedish firm, Kosta, shown here in an advert dating from 1963.

Gondolieri vases designed
by Tapio Wirkkala for Venini,
1966. The vivid colours of
the glass suggest luxury,
although the vessel forms
themselves are tempered by
restraint.
opposite
Scolpiti bowl and vases
designed by Toni Zuccheri
for Venini, 1968. Towards
the end of the decade
Italian design began to
revert from the geometric
to the neo-organic, a transition reflected in the plastic
qualities of these sculptural
vessels.

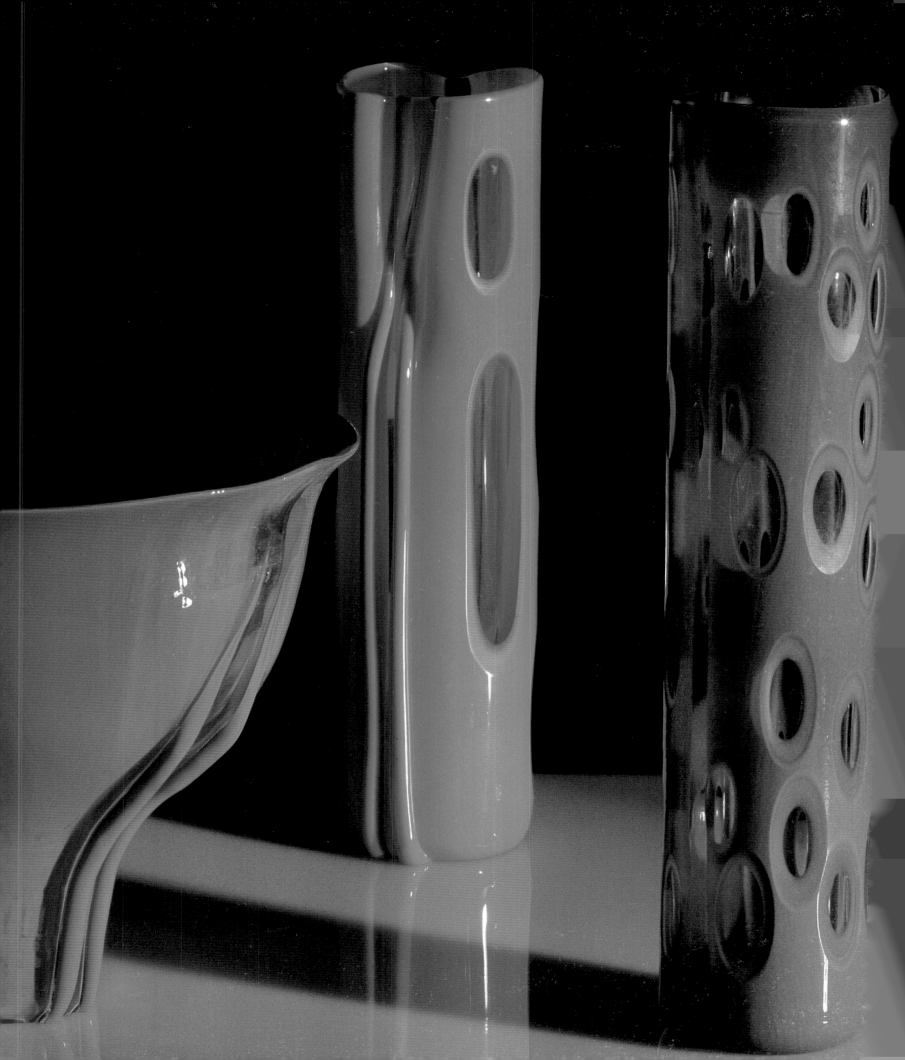

above
Beach house in Malibu,
California, designed by
Conrad Buff and Donald
Hensman, 1969. Buff and
Hensman had contributed
to the Case Study House
programme on the West
Coast during the 1950s, the
enduring legacy of which
can be seen in this house.
Features reflecting 'the look'
of the 1960s are the open-
tread spiral staircase and
the tiered, cylindrical,
pendant light fitting.

right
Tubular light fittings
dominated the early 1960s.
Advert for Tubelight series
designed by Paul
Boissevain for the British
firm, Merchant Adventurers,
1963.
far right
Suspended lighting fixture in
the private dining room at
Manchester Airport (formerly
Ringway Airport), designed
by James Cubitt and
Partners, 1962.

Tubelight series

Merchant Adventurers Limited

patterns (Diadem, which had polished cutting, and Harlequin, which contrasted matt and polished diamonds). Later, another design called Domino was added to the series, a mitre-cut square-grid pattern launched in 1966.

The highly controlled geometric forms and patterns seen in the Queensberry range contrasted markedly with the earlier overtly plastic and organic shapes that had dominated Contemporary glass design in the 1950s. Equally, however, they were also in sharp contrast to the new trends in glass design that would gather momentum later in the decade via the agency of the studio glass movement. The morality and the aesthetics of the studio glass movement were rooted in the idea of individual creativity, 'direct action', and freedom of expression, the results of which were embodied in irregular forms and random decoration. 'The look', by contrast, was about exerting total control over glass as a medium, whether in the shaping or colouring of the metal while in its molten state, or the marking of the surface once cold. Straight-sided cylindrical vessels were the embodiment of control because they symbolized the restraint of fluidity; while in terms of decoration, cutting was the ultimate control system because there were strict limitations on the types of cuts that could be made and the way in which these could be arranged.

Britain was by no means the only country to impose a controlled aesthetic in glass design during the early 1960s. Hans Theo Baumann, creator of the influential Berlin service, and another designer who, like Queensberry, worked across various different media in the tableware field, designed a range of mould-blown cylindrical tumblers with pedestal bases for Thomas Glas of Selb in Germany in 1965. In neighbouring Czechoslovakia, where art glass was the acknowledged speciality, Jirí Harcuba used tall narrow tubular vases as a vehicle for a series of linear geometric and stylized representational engraved patterns during the first half of the 1960s. The cylindrical 'look' was also widely adopted in Scandinavia, where it was treated to a variety of interpretations. One of its earliest incarnations was in Nanny Still's Ambra candlesticks, designed for the Finnish firm of Riihimäki in 1961, which used the simple device of a disc surmounting a solid, narrow, straight-sided foot. Interestingly, it was Still's Harlequin tableware range of 1958, composed almost entirely of spherical and cylindrical components, that had prefigured the fascination with geometric forms during the ensuing decade. In the mid-1960s Tamara Aladin designed a range of flanged cylindrical vases for the same firm. Cylindrical elements of different gauges, made of bands of richly coloured, partly lustred glass, were combined to create Kaj Franck's goblets, designed for another important Finnish firm, Nuutajärvi, in 1968. Prior to this, in 1966, Franck had designed a stunning circular plate decorated with concentric circles of vibrantly coloured glass, which had prefigured his new interest in geometric shapes and patterns. In Sweden one of the most dramatic embodiments of the new aesthetic was the Granados range of coloured underlay vases designed by Mona Morales-Schildt for Kosta from around 1962. Decorated with large optical mirror cuts, these vases were cylindrical in form, and were sometimes sliced diagonally across the rim to give them an even more severe clinical appearance, radically different to the organic designs of Vicke Lindstrand for Kosta during the 1950s.

right
Monumental chandeliers made of clusters of glass tubes dominate the concourse at Manchester Airport. Designed by Stefan Buzas for James Cubitt and Partners in 1962, they were made by the Italian firm Venini.
below
Space Age cylindrical telephone kiosks were also purpose-designed by the architects for the new airport. 'The look' was reflected in every detail of the interior.

Cylinders and modified cylinders were also adopted as part of the new aesthetic of Italian glass during the early 1960s. They were among the forms in the Thomas range of vases created by the American designer Thomas Stearns for Venini in 1961; and two years later cylinders and spheres formed the basic repertoire of shapes in a new range designed for Venini by Massimo Vignelli, which was unusual in combining silver with glass. In 1963 Fulvio Bianconi designed a range of cylindrical vases decorated with fine coloured spirals for Venini's rival, Vistosi, which was awarded a Compasso d'Oro prize that year and was subsequently shown at the Milan Triennale. In 1966 the Finnish designer Tapio Wirkkala, like Nanny Still before him, used the idea of balancing a disc on top of a cylinder in his Gondolieri vases for Venini. This range was produced using the 'incalmo' technique to create clearly defined rings of colour which further emphasized the circular theme. Stacked cylindrical elements, sometimes offset, sometimes aligned, were another recurrent motif of the 1960s, and can be seen in a range of vases designed by Gino Vistosi for Vistosi in 1964.

Tubular forms became a mainstay in the field of lighting design during the early 1960s, particularly in Britain. One of the earliest light fittings to evoke 'the look' was the elegant Chelsea range of pendant lamps designed by Richard Stevens and Peter Rodd for Atlas Lighting. In this design a narrow bulb was held in a tubular black metal fitting, and a glass shade of the same diameter formed a continuation of the tube below. This design won a Design Centre Award in 1960, and set the trend in Britain for the next few years. For example, in 1963 'cylindrical pendants in corrugated glass' were advertised by Troughton and Young; a range of 'break-resistant' opal, black and coloured pendant cylinders were advertised by Plus Lighting; and the name Tubelight was given to a range of pendant light fittings designed by the architect Paul Boissevain for Merchant Adventurers. Merchant Adventurers was a family firm run by three brothers, Walter Boissevain (managing director), Roland Boissevain (marketing manager) and Paul Boissevain (chief designer), which expanded rapidly during the early 1960s to service the growing market for modern lighting with the all-important 'look'. The Tubelight series was promoted in advertisements in the architectural press as 'elegant and dramatic vertical fluorescent units'. Made of extruded white opal plastic, they acted as casings for either 2-foot or 4-foot long fluorescent bulbs, which could be hung either singly or in multiple clusters.

Later in the decade tubular casings were also widely used for tungsten spotlights and for downlighters. Adverts for spotlights of this type produced by Plus Lighting appeared in the *Architectural Review* from 1965, while Merchant Adventurers advertised a wide range of such fittings in *Design* magazine in August 1966. Variants of the tubular 'look' in lighting remained popular in Britain until the end of the decade. Cylindrical opal glass lampshades, some long, narrow and tubular, some broader and shorter, were advertised by the firm of Lumitron in 1967, for example; while austere cylindrical and square downlighters in the pared-down Modernist Contemporary style were featured in an advert for Allom Heffer in 1968. Towards the end of the decade a British firm called Phosco, which until this date had specialized in street lighting, decided to diversify into the domestic market, and employed the Industrial Design Partnership to help them

develop a new range of products. In 1969 they launched their Solar range of table, wall, clamp and floor lamps which, to the great satisfaction of *Design* magazine (which carried an approving article about the firm in September 1969), made use of the metal spinning, casting and bending processes that the company already employed in the production of their street lighting. All the various components of the Solar range were made from either tubular or cylindrical elements: a cylindrical lampshade made of either opal perspex or spun aluminium; adjustable height chromium-plated tubular steel supports; and an open base made from a ring of steel. Thus the circular theme was reiterated thrice over.

At the other end of the lighting design spectrum, cylindrical forms could be used in a highly expressive way. A good example of this is provided by the four spectacular glass chandeliers made by Venini for the concourse of the newly opened Manchester Airport in 1962, the interior of which, including the chandeliers themselves, was designed by Stefan Buzas for James Cubitt and Partners. Each chandelier was composed of a cluster of hundreds of tubes up to several metres long, suspended by steel wire at different levels. Thus, although the individual elements were relatively restrained, the effect of the tubes *en masse* was rich and luxurious. Another example of tubular forms being used in an expressive way was the Falkland lampshade designed by Bruno Munari for Danese in 1964 (see page 157). Based on a modified cylinder, this lamp was made of a 1.5-metre length of elasticized tubular nylon hose, held open at intervals by metal rings of varying diameter. By the end of the 1960s the wheel of design had turned full circle and a strong neo-organic trend was discernible once again. Such ideas were prefigured in the Falkland lamp and were embodied in fully fledged form later in the decade in Livio Castiglioni and Gianfranco Frattini's Boalum lamp of 1969, produced by the adventurous Milan-based firm of Artemide (see page 193). The Modernist approach, epitomized by the British firm Allom Heffer, had been to treat the lighting source as though it were an end in itself. Allom Heffer offered minimum design intervention: their contribution was simply to supply the most discreet casing possible to house the bulb. The Italian approach was quite different. They recognized that lighting in general, and domestic lighting in particular, served a purpose far beyond pure function. For this reason they had no qualms about exploiting lighting as a direct avenue for creative expression.

Cylinders and tubes were perhaps a less obvious source of forms for the design of furniture, although in fact they crop up in a surprising number of different guises throughout the 1960s, especially in Italy during the first half of the decade, where drum-shaped forms were particularly important in both seating and storage. In 1956 Tobia Scarpa had adopted the half-cylinder as the outline for the frame of his Pigreco chair, produced for the forward-looking firm of Gavina from 1958. Several years later, in 1962, Gavina produced the remarkable Giro armchair designed by Achille and Pier Giacomo Castiglioni, which combined cylindrical and tubular elements in a particularly striking way. The basic chair was drum-shaped, with the upholstered seat cut out in the shape of a cube, the seat itself being supported by four straight cylindrical steel legs. Although this type of chair leg seemed a little idiosyncratic when it first appeared, within the space of a year a similar idea was being used by Vico

top
Cylindrical and semi-cylindrical components were used for the legs of two all-plastic chairs produced by the Italian firm Kartell. Children's chair (model K1340) designed by Marco Zanuso and Richard Sapper, for Kartell, 1964.
above
Universale chair (model 4860) designed by Joe Colombo, 1965, produced by Kartell from 1967.
opposite
Joe Colombo began to explore circular themes in his work in the early years of the decade. The Roll armchair he designed for Comfort in 1962, for example, had exaggerated tubular padding.

Magistretti in a wooden-legged leather-upholstered armchair for Cassina; while later in the decade, in 1968, cylindrical metal legs were used as supports for two tables designed by Joe Colombo for Zanotta, the Poker and the Mastro. Perhaps the best known example, however, is Marco Zanuso and Richard Sapper's plastic children's chair for Kartell (model K1340). Exhibited at the Milan Triennale in 1964, this chair represented a landmark in the history of plastic design, being the first piece of furniture to be produced entirely from injection-moulded low-density polythene. The cylindrical leg form was adopted because of its strength, and was designed so that the chairs themselves could be used by children as building blocks as well as seating. Joe Colombo's plastic Universale chair (model 4860), designed the following year, also for Kartell, but not produced commercially until 1967, appears to pay homage to the earlier Sapper/Zanuso chair via the shape of its legs, which are in the form of half-cylinders, split lengthways down the centre. Made of injection-moulded ABS plastic, this was the first one-piece plastic chair to be produced, apart from its feet which were made separately. These early plastic chairs were given wide rounded legs, partly to provide them with the necessary strength to act as supports, and partly because such forms made them much better suited to the injection-moulding process. In these two cases, therefore, the use of cylinders and half-cylinders was for pragmatic, not just aesthetic, reasons.

The prevalence of cylindrical forms in Joe Colombo's furniture throughout the decade, however, indicates that he did have a particular affinity for circular shapes. In 1962, for example, he used narrow tube-like forms for the upholstered cushions on his Roll armchair designed for the firm Comfort. The frame of this chair was made of flat chromium-plated steel bars, while the seat was composed of six large rolls of leather-upholstered foam. Although ribbed upholstery was to become widespread towards the end of the decade, this was an unusually early and striking example. A similar idea was

later used by Fabio Lenci in a chair designed for the Rome-based firm La Comfort-Line, which was shown at the Milan Furniture Fair in 1967. The seat of this chair was composed of eight upholstered rolls, supported by a transparent tempered glass frame. Both these chairs were, in turn, indebted to the Transat chair by the pioneer Modernist Eileen Gray, dating from the late 1920s. At the end of the decade Colombo returned to the cylinder as a direct source of inspiration for his radical Tube chair of 1969. Produced by Flexform, this chair was composed of four separate foam-covered and upholstered plastic cylinders, held together by special clamp-like joints made of rubber and metal. The cylinders were of different diameters so that they could be stored concentrically, one inside the other. Apart, they could be combined in any order to create a variety of chairs, sofas and stools.

As well as being the single most important furniture designer of the 1960s, and particularly outstanding in his adventurous choice of materials and the diversity of the forms he created, Joe Colombo was a designer whose work epitomized 'the look' of the sixties. Varied though his use of materials and his visual ideas were, at the root of the Colombo aesthetic was a fascination with geometric forms. These were used both as the basis for the overall form of pieces of furniture, and as a repertoire of shapes for the individual elements or components upon which the designer drew in order to create his designs. Colombo's most significant contribution to the cylindrical furniture phenomenon – and one of the most important designs of his fruitful but short-lived career – was his tall drum-shaped multi-purpose storage unit known as the Combi-Centre, designed in 1963 for the firm of Bernini. This was a flexible unit which could be used either as a bookcase, or more correctly a book tower, or alternatively for storing domestic objects or tools. Built up in disc-shaped layers of different depths which could be combined in various arrangements, there were several different units, including shelves, drawers, cupboards and even built-in lighting. Raised

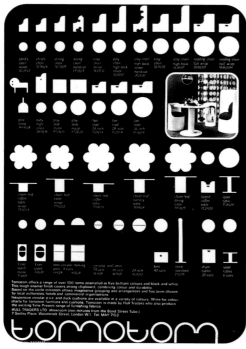

far left
Advert from 1969 for Tomotom furniture designed by Bernard Holdaway for Hull Traders. The circular theme underlying this range of cardboard tube furniture is obvious in these diagrams.

left
Advert for Kartell, 1967. The furniture includes the Universale chair by Joe Colombo; stacking children's chairs by Richard Sapper and Marco Zanuso; the 600 circular pedestal table designed by Achille and Pier Giacomo Castiglioni; and a stackable square storage unit (model 4970) designed by Anna Castelli Ferrieri.

on castors so that it could be wheeled into position, the
Combi-Centre was designed so that its various disc-shaped
components could be offset without becoming unbalanced.
As with many of Colombo's designs, the Combi-Centre was
many years ahead of its time when it first appeared in 1963. It
spawned a host of drum-shaped storage units by other
designers and manufacturers later in the 1960s, including the
Barboy drinks unit designed by Verner Panton for Bisterfeld
and Weiss in 1965, which had disc-shaped shelves that could
be pulled out from a central axis; the Jamaica B 106 drinks
cupboard, also on castors, designed by Eugenio Gerli for
Tecno in 1967; and the Round-Up range of cylindrical plastic
containers designed by Anna Castelli Ferrieri for Kartell in
1970. Panton also designed a second drum-shaped unit in
1965 for Bisterfeld and Weiss called the Party Set. Made of
moulded wood, this was a series of circular stools designed
in graduated sizes so that they could all be stored one inside
the other, the largest being a small table on which to serve
drinks. The concept behind this range was very much in the
Colombo spirit, and, in fact, of all his contemporaries it is
Panton whose work most closely equates with Colombo's in
terms of its adventurousness and creativity.

The 1960s was a decade for design mavericks
some of whom are remembered today for individual offbeat
one-off designs rather than for a whole body of work spanning the entire decade like Colombo. Bernard Holdaway's
decision to design a range of furniture made of cardboard
prompted an alliance outside traditional furniture-manufacturing circles. The makers, Hull Traders, were in fact a progressive furnishing textile firm for whom Holdaway had already
designed both textiles and graphics, and for whom his wife,
Shirley Craven, acted as the art director and chief designer.
The Tomotom range of 1966, however, marked a completely
new departure for the firm. It exploited the novel idea of using
large compressed cardboard tubes as the basic structure for
the frames of seat furniture, storage units and tables. Circles
of chipboard were used for the flat surfaces of seats, shelves
and tabletops, and the furniture was painted all over in tough
brightly coloured enamels. Stools and chairs were basically
tubular, with variously shaped cut-away sections in the side,
while the seats themselves were circular with optional loose
disc-shaped upholstered cushions. Tables had central tubular
supports with either circular tops or more complex Cloverleaf
tops composed of multiple circles, the form of which, coincidentally, was not dissimilar to the Mary Quant daisy logo. The
Tomotom range was promoted for use by both children and
adults, and it proved so successful that by 1969 there were
over a hundred different items in the range. An advert in
Design in April 1969 emphasized the flexibility of the range
and the importance of the circular forms: 'Based on the circle,
Tomotom allows imaginative grouping and arrangement and
has been chosen by local authorities, hotels and commercial
organisations.' By this date the range included dining chairs,
easy chairs, and reading chairs of differing diameters, as well
as a baby's high chair, a play horse and various other child-
sized chairs. There were also footstools, play desks, bins,
tiered stands, shelving units and a standard lamp. Among the
wide range of tables were full-size and nursery tables, some
drum-shaped, some spool-shaped, in addition to the distinctive six-sided Cloverleaf tables. Towards the end of the
decade two new light fittings were introduced, one of which

right
Reiner Residence, Silvertop,
Los Angeles, designed by
John Lautner, 1963. This
luxurious house, complete
with scalloped canopy,
curved feature fireplace,
crescent-shaped swimming
pool and panoramic hillside
view, reflects the affluent
lifestyle to which wealthy
Americans aspired during
the 1960s. By this date, the
self-imposed austerity of the
early post-war period had
been abandoned in favour
of comfort and conspicuous
consumption. 'I love this
house,' says Lautner, 'it was
a pleasure to build. Reiner
would not compromise on
materials or design. We
travelled abroad to find the
perfect finishes. Whatever I
wanted was done, and the
house shows the care that
went into it.'
above
Extension to Dumbarton
Oaks Museum, Washington,
DC, designed by Philip
Johnson, 1963. With its
cylindrical galleries, its round
marble columns and its
domed ceilings, this small
building celebrates the circle,
and captures Johnson at his
most inventive, relishing his
new-found creative freedom
after abandoning the restrictive tenets of Modernism.

opposite
Cylindrical buildings captured the imagination of architects on a global level during the 1960s. Birmingham city centre was transformed by the Bullring shopping centre and the Rotunda office tower, the latter designed by James A Roberts and completed in 1964.

above
The Japanese architect, Kiyonori Kikutake, dreamt up a memorable vision of the future called Ocean City in 1965, the cylindrical forms of which resembled the Post Office Tower in London, a potent new city landmark constructed in 1966 (see page 74).

centre right
In Milan, Angelo Mangiarotti and Bruno Morasutti designed a tripartite drum-shaped apartment block during the early 1960s.

right
Peter Womersley, one of Britain's most imaginative post-war architects, designed a doctors' surgery at Kelso in the Scottish Borders composed of a cluster of sliced cylinders. It was completed in 1966.

was described in the press release accompanying the launch as a 'Drum Table-come-lamp with a letter box slot near the top for the light'; and the other as 'a tall cylindrical table lamp with an oval porthole type aperture'. Thus the circular theme which had inspired the original Tomotom range in the mid-1960s, still formed the basis of 'the look' of the new pieces being introduced into the range at the end of the decade.

By no means all furniture designers of the late 1960s embraced the concept of obsolescence, however; there were still many who remained wedded to Modernist principles and aesthetics. One of these was the British designer William Plunkett, who set up his own furniture company, William Plunkett Ltd, in 1963 so that he would be able to exert control over both the design and the manufacturing sides of the business. Championed by the Council of Industrial Design, this small firm was one of the commercial success stories of the 1960s, and the designer's achievements were acknowledged in 1968 when he received two Design Centre Awards. One of these was for his elegant Reigate rocking chair, designed five years earlier, the steel runners of which resembled a section from a wheel. A later design of 1966 was for the steel and glass Coulsden coffee table, the basic form of which was an open cylinder. The circular theme explored in this design was emphasized in the description of the table in *Design* magazine in May 1968 at the time of the awards:

The frame is made from two identical steel sections with bright or satin chrome finish; each of these consists of a half-circle base welded to a vertical upright which in turn is welded to another half-circle top. The two sections are held together firmly with four cylindrical distance pieces, the glass top resting securely within the two upper half-circles exactly level with the surface of the metal frame.

The minimalist aesthetic of this design, and in particular the use of steel and glass, were reminiscent of the work of Eileen Gray. Between 1926 and 1929, for example, Gray had designed the small adjustable-height circular tubular steel and glass E1027 table for the interior of a house at Roquebrune in France. Significantly, this was one of the classic Modernist designs later put back into production by Aram Designs. This is not to suggest that Plunkett's design was retrogressive or that it was inspired by historical revivalism; it was simply that by the 1960s the wheel of design history had turned full circle, and geometric forms which had been in vogue during the inter-war period, and which had at that time been associated with cutting edge Modernist design, had come back into fashion again. While some designers were conscious of the fact that history was repeating itself, others appear to have been unaware of the similarities between their ideas and those of their predecessors, and were simply reacting against the previous generation who had rejected the geometric in favour of the organic. This time around, however, pure geometric forms were adopted not because of their associations with the Machine Age but because they were the embodiment of Space Age design. William Plunkett was clearly aware of his Modernist inheritance, but although conscious of the past, he was at the same time wedded to the future.

The fashion for cylindrical forms began to spread from objects to architecture during the early 1960s, and can be seen in a variety of drum-shaped and cylindrical buildings. High-profile large-scale examples in major cities, which have since become well-known landmarks, include the Hotel

Budapest on the outskirts of Budapest in Hungary; the American Embassy in Dublin designed by John Johansen, completed in 1964; the Post Office Tower in London, designed by the Ministry of Works and completed in 1966; and, most impressive of all, Marina City in Chicago designed by Bertrand Goldberg in 1964 and completed two years later. This development, located on the north bank of the Chicago River, is composed of two tall adjacent circular towers, and is original both for its shape and for the fact that it provides an early example of mixed-use development, containing both offices and apartments, serviced by a car park on the lower floors with an impressive helical ramp. A variety of other commercial and recreational facilities are also built into the towers, such as shops, restaurants, a theatre, a skating rink and a bowling alley. Each floor has sixteen semi-circular projecting balconies made of reinforced concrete which give the towers their distinctive lobed appearance and which prompted their nickname, 'the concrete corncobs'. In Britain perhaps the most famous cylindrical building is the Rotunda office block tower in Birmingham designed by James A Roberts, which sits astride the controversial Bullring shopping centre, completed in 1964; while one of 'Swinging' London's most distinctive Space Age landmarks was the Post Office Tower, at 190 metres, the tallest building in the capital when it opened in 1966, complete with revolving restaurant 160 metres above ground level. The same year that the Post Office Tower was completed the Japanese architect Kiyonori Kikutake produced a model of an idealised floating community called Ocean City. Built on man-made circular islands connected by bridges, all the buildings on the islands were also circular, mostly in the form of tall cylindrical towers with projecting circular windows. Although this spatial model was intended purely as a hypothesis, not as a technological possibility, by the mid-1960s many of the ideas being postulated were already becoming a reality in different parts of the world. 'The look' envisaged for Ocean City was, in fact, not dissimilar to the reality of Marina City and the Post Office Tower.

Less well known but equally striking examples of circular buildings include an apartment block in Milan, composed of three linked cylindrical towers, designed by Angelo Mangiarotti and Bruno Morasutti. Featured in *Domus* in February 1962, this building was remarkable for being designed so that each of the three towers was raised off the ground to first-storey level on a single central pedestal column, thus further emphasizing the drum-like nature of the design. Later in the decade a variant on the cylindrical theme appeared in the form of a drum-shaped house in Lombardy with a diagonally sliced monopitch roof. Designed by Enrico Castiglioni, well known for his adventurous and expressive building projects, particularly in the city of Busto Arsizio, this house was featured at length in *Domus* in June 1966. Similar ideas were explored by Peter Womersley, one of the most creative British architects of the decade, in his design for a doctor's group practice at Kelso in Scotland, completed in 1966. In this building, composed of six interlinked cylinders containing a waiting room and individual consulting rooms for five doctors, each funnel is split in two, and the roofs of each half are separate and slant in opposite directions. The resulting complex has a strikingly modern appearance and must have caused quite a stir when it first appeared in the small town in the Scottish Borders in the middle of the decade.

Equally distinctive is Peter Moro's Nottingham Playhouse designed in 1961, which has a low drum-shaped tower above the auditorium, and which combines rectilinear and cylindrical elements in a highly creative way.

The idea of the cylinder as a tower formed the basic premise behind a remarkable house called Stony Tor built by Maurice Metcalfe for his own use at Stony Point, Rockland County, USA, designed in 1962. This astonishing and highly idiosyncratic building, featured in *Interiors* in November 1965, was composed of two four-storey towers linked by a glass passage, the smaller one containing a spiral staircase, the larger one containing the living quarters. This was an extremely original and intriguing building, as the magazine pointed out: 'The form relates to no architectural prototype, hints at no purpose. This is no cottage nor castle nor chapel nor manor nor silo nor barn. The unanswered question catapults you into the unknown.' The house was made even more mysterious by the fact that it was camouflaged in a mature woodland setting through being clad with cross-sawn redwood shiplap siding, vertically aligned. The windows were oval and convex, and projected outwards like giant bubbles; while most of the furniture, fixtures and fittings – tables, chairs, stools, sofa and giant 56-inch diameter bathtub included – were also on a circular theme. As with a number of architects and designers during the 1960s, such as the individualistic Los Angeles-based architect John Lautner, the image of the circle clearly took hold of Metcalfe and became something of an obsession. It was a similar obsessive attention to geometric detail that resulted in 'the look' of Lautner's Reiner Residence at Silvertop in 1963.

One of the most imaginative public buildings of the decade, albeit one of the smallest, was the stunning and meticulously detailed extension to the Dumbarton Oaks Museum in Washington, DC, designed by Philip Johnson in 1963. Earlier in his career Johnson, like Bertrand Goldberg, had been an ardent Modernist and had worked closely with, and in the pared-down rectilinear style of, his hero Mies van der Rohe. By the early 1960s, however, Johnson had clearly begun to tire of minimalism and austerity, and in his New Harmony Church in Indiana of 1960 and his Nuclear Reactor at Rohovot in Israel in 1961, he signified a desire to branch out in a new direction by exploring other geometric forms. Of this shift in direction he remarked: 'There is only one absolute today and that is change. There are no rules, surely no certainties in any of the arts. There is only a feeling of wonderful freedom, of endless possibilities to investigate, of endless past years of historically great buildings to enjoy.' Designed to house an exquisite collection of Pre-Columbian gold, and located in a beautiful woodland setting, the museum was composed of a ring of six small glazed circular drum-shaped rooms, each with a low domed roof. In the centre was a circular courtyard with a fountain. The museum, although highly expressive, was an exercise in pure geometry, and its intimate scale was such that visitors could absorb the building's layout and structure all in one go. In Britain a similar interest in formalism and purity was demonstrated by Chamberlain, Powell and Bon in their design for New Hall, Cambridge, dating from 1962, which, like Dumbarton Oaks, also makes striking use of circular domed forms.

'There is nothing sacred about the square or rectangular in housing', wrote Scott Kelly in *Industrial Design* in

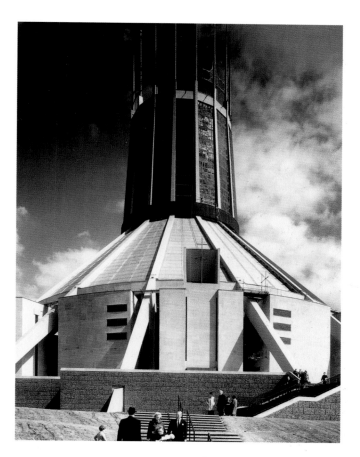

left
Metropolitan Cathedral of Christ the King, Liverpool, designed by Frederick Gibberd, and completed in 1967. Perched on a hillside, the crown of thorns imagery of this building is striking from the outside, while from within the central tower of stained glass is inspirational.
below
It was the Japanese architect, Kenzo Tange, who came closest to transforming fantasy into reality during the 1960s. His Shizuoka Centre in Tokyo, dating from 1969, reflects the clip-on aesthetics of Archigram's Plug-In City and Dessauges's Cylinder House scheme.

July/August 1967. The fact that architects themselves were conscious of the cylinder as a potent new architectural form in the 1960s is indicated by a proposal formulated and patented by the Swiss architect Guy Dessauges in 1967, to create prefabricated capsule-like apartments called Cylinder houses which could be stacked or clustered in various differ-ent arrangements. What was radical about this scheme, how-ever, and what distinguished it from all the other cylindrical buildings of the period, was that the cylinders were horizontal. Each cylindrical unit was flat at one end but sliced diagonally at the other end, thereby creating either a balcony or a canopy as required, depending on the climate. It was envis-aged that they would be made of either wood, concrete or plastics, although the architect himself favoured the latter. Among the models illustrated were Cylinder houses stacked in the same alignment like rolls of fabric, and others set at right angles and raised up on supports. The most radical pro-posal, however, was one where the cylinders were attached at one end to a central column and projected outwards in a spiral. This was what the architect called 'thinking vertically', and it was proposed as a solution to chronic land shortages in the future. Interestingly, although it would appear that this scheme never developed further than the proposal stage (the article records that the Centre for Advanced Study of Science in London was in the process of estimating the unit costs of the cylinders), the model for Dessauges's vertical column arrangement bore a striking resemblance to Kenzo Tange's Shizuoka Centre in Tokyo dating from 1969, built to house the offices of a Japanese newspaper company. In the 1960s the line between fantasy and reality, and between the present and the future, became increasingly blurred. As the work of the radical British group Archigram demonstrated so well, in the 1960s what seemed futuristic one year, such as Archigram's Plug-In City, could often be realized the next.

When a building itself was constructed from circular forms, as with Dumbarton Oaks and Stony Tor, this naturally had a major impact on the design of the interior. Other circu-lar buildings such as the Guggenheim Museum in New York, designed by Frank Lloyd Wright and completed posthumously in 1959, and the Hirshhorn Museum in Washington, designed by Gordon Bunshaft and completed in 1974, illustrate this point well. The same is true of Frederick Gibberd's Metropolitan Cathedral in Liverpool, built between 1960 and 1967, itself inspired by the crown of thorns symbolism embodied in the structure of Oscar Niemeyer's Cathedral at Brasilia, designed in the late 1950s but not completed until the early 1970s. During the 1960s, however, even when the shell of a building itself was not round, cylindrical elements were often incorporated within interiors, normally for self-con-sciously dramatic effect. Staircases were an obvious feature for highlighting cylindrical forms, and were exploited by archi-tects such as Gae Aulenti, in her design for the Paris show-room of Olivetti in 1967. Fireplaces, in particular the exposed chimneys of feature fireplaces, were another obvious target for the attention of the style-conscious architect anxious to capture 'the look' of the early 1960s. A dramatic suspended cylindrical chimney was installed in a house in Michigan designed by Birkerts and Straub, for example, and featured in Interiors in August 1962. Designers of shop interiors, particu-lary fashion boutiques, seldom needed an excuse to co-opt 'the look' and transform it into a dramatic visual statement.

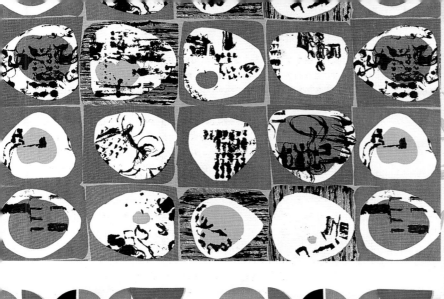

A particularly striking example is provided by a boutique in Milan called Altre Cose designed by Aldo Jacober, Ugo La Pietra and Paolo Rizzatto, which was featured in *Domus* in March 1968, and later in the year by both *Design* and the *Architectural Review*. The interior was dominated by thirty giant clear perspex capsule-like cylinders suspended from the ceiling, inside which the dresses were displayed. These cylinders could be moved up and down at the push of a button by an assistant who sat at a control panel at the side of the room. Altre Cose represented a truly Space Age concept of interior design, therefore, and the commentator in *Domus* drew parallels with the designs of Paco Rabanne in the field of contemporary fashion and Quasar Khanh in the field of inflatable furniture, all related manifestations of 'the look'.

Circles and Op Art

In addition to tubes and cylinders the prevailing shapes of the early 1960s were spheres, domes and discs, while in pattern design the circle itself was the most dominant image. Circular motifs were widely used on carpets during the early 1960s, for example, especially in Britain where strongly patterned carpets were still in vogue at this date. The trend began with an influential pattern called Mandala designed by Audrey Tanner for the Carpet Manufacturing Company, an early recipient of a Design Centre Award in 1959. Even though the textile industry in Britain was entering a decline in terms of its overall output, both the range and the quality of UK furnishing fabrics and carpets was still outstanding. The designs of Olive Sullivan for Stockwell Carpets between the years 1963 and 1966 perfectly

complemented the work of Barbara Brown for Heal Fabrics. A design called Thumbprint dating from 1963, based on oval repeats, was followed by a pattern called Ovoid in 1964, and by January 1966 Stockwell was advertising a range of six 'geometrics' in the *Architectural Review*. Lucienne Day had been designing carpets since 1957 when she produced various small-scale designs in the Contemporary style for Tompkinsons. By the early 1960s she had adapted her aesthetic to meet the needs of the contract market, producing a much larger pattern called Big Circle for I & C Steele in 1963. Her husband, Robin Day, although best known as a furniture designer, also carried out some pioneering work in the field of contract carpets for the Kidderminster-based firm of Grosvenor Carpets during the early 1960s. Designs advertised in 1961 showed the continuing influence of Contemporary design, but in 1962 a series of new striped patterns were marketed, and the adoption of 'the look' was confirmed with the launch of a circular geometric pattern called Discus in 1963. The success of this particular pattern is indicated by the fact that it continued to be featured in adverts in the architectural press right through until 1966.

Pattern designs for furnishing fabrics also moved up a gear during the early 1960s, so that by 1964 very few of the characteristics of Contemporary design persisted. In public buildings double-height lobbies with tall windows requiring long drops of fabrics were now common, while many new houses had large picture windows. For these interiors, curtains were needed with patterns that could match the scale of the architecture. Large-scale bold geometrics, such as those

top left
Cadenza furnishing fabric designed by Lucienne Day for Heal's, 1962. With its irregular outlines and mottled textures, this pattern marks the transition from the Contemporary style to 'the look', but was soon to be superseded by designs composed of precise geometric shapes and flat planes of colour.

above left
Lunette furnishing fabric designed by Dorothy Smith for Heal's, 1961, one of the earliest examples of the use of pure geometric flat patterns in textiles during the early 1960s.

above
Sunflowers furnishing fabric designed by Howard Carter for Heal's, 1962, an example of a short-lived trend for giant floral motifs on textiles.

HEAL FABRICS

'Pansies' by Howard Carter
printed cotton, from 14/11 yd.
'Recurrence' by Barbara Brown
printed cotton, from 17/6 yd.

196 Tottenham Court Road, London W1 Museum 1666

above
Advert for Heal Fabrics,
1963, showing a floral
pattern called Pansies by
Howard Carter, and a
geometric pattern called
Recurrence by Barbara
Brown.

designed by Barbara Brown for Heal's, were ideal as they created maximum impact, while at the same time respecting the abstract geometric qualities of the new buildings. From this type of pattern it was but a short step away to Op Art, the next major influence on pattern design, which represented the culmination of a series of explorations in the field of advanced abstraction during the 1960s.

Like Mandala, many textile patterns of the late 1950s and early 1960s were composed either of radiating lines or disintegrating circular motifs. In the field of furnishing, fabric patterns of this type included Lucienne Day's Ducatoon dating from 1959, Barbara Brown's Intermission, 1960, Fay Hillier's Corona, 1961, and Doreen Dyall's Formation, 1964, all manufactured by Heal Fabrics. Such patterns showed the continuing influence of a loose painterly style of abstraction popular during the late 1950s, although the emerging circles – or Nearing Circles as they were described in the title of a woven textile by William Scott for Edinburgh Weavers in 1962 – indicated that pattern design, like painting, was about to move in the direction of greater definition.

At the end of the 1950s patterns had been strongly influenced by Abstract Expressionism and other forms of dynamic abstraction such as tachism, intended to give the impression of spontaneity and structured disorder. During the early 1960s pattern design was still strongly textural, and printed textiles were often grainy or mottled. A series of evocatively named printed cotton furnishing fabrics produced by Heal's typify the visual effects of the period. They include Osier by Fay Hillier from 1960, inspired by the texture of woven willow; Vibration by Nicola Wood, dating from 1962, a dense shaky abstract pattern; Doreen Dyall's Reflections, evoking the patterns on the surface of rippling water; and Cumulus, also by Dyall, dating from 1961, based on the textures of loose cloud formations. Gradually during the early 1960s, however, this brand of pattern-making began to be displaced by two new types of pattern design. The first grew logically out of the earlier Abstract Expressionist trend, but reintroduced quasi-representational imagery. This was the fashion for large-scale painterly floral designs, typified by Howard Carter's gigantic and impressive Sunflowers for Heal's, winner of a Design Centre Award in 1962. This pattern was very influential and resulted in a number of spin-offs by other firms. Also typical of this trend were Solstice and Sea Holly by the firm of David Whitehead, advertised in 1961 and 1962 respectively; and a series of patterns by Heal's, including Robert Dodd's Flora Bella from 1960; Jane Daniels' Teasle and Wild Orchid, from 1960 and 1961 respectively; Trinidad and Tobago by Althea McNish, both from 1961; and another pattern by Howard Carter called Pansies, advertised in 1963. Although this fashion for recognizable patterns had a big impact initially, its effects were relatively short-lived. The move towards larger-scale patterns, though, was clearly a more general one, the second new trend in pattern-making being for outsize abstract geometric patterns. Although they shared similarities of scale, these two different types of pattern were at opposite ends of the spectrum: one was the embodiment of freedom, the other epitomized the imposition of control. It was the latter that prevailed and came to symbolize 'the look'.

Pattern design was Britain's particular forte during the post-war period, and it was firms such as Heal's, which had been so creative throughout the 1950s, that were responsible for fostering and formulating 'the look' of the early 1960s. A change of tempo was suggested in 1960 with the launch of a geometric pattern called Crescendo designed by Giorgio Bay, composed entirely of ring-shaped motifs. Also significant was Dorothy Smith's Lunette of 1961, a pattern of flat, semi-circular motifs grouped in squares. During the late 1950s Heal's had bought several patterns from Barbara Brown, who was at that time a recent graduate of the Royal College of Art, working in the abstract expressionist style. Within the space of a few years, however, her style changed completely. Suddenly, instead of following an established trend, she was setting a new one of her own. The turning point came around 1960 with a pattern called Country Bunch which, although still expressionist in style, incorporated strong geometric elements in the form of small triangles. This was followed in 1962 by Symmetry which, as the title suggests, was basically a geometric pattern, but one that was still root-ed in painterly abstraction. Finally, in 1963, Barbara Brown broke through the geometric divide completely with Recurrence, a bold pattern on an architectural scale, com-posed of columns of large circles inside squares. Typical of 'the look' was the way in which the pattern was created on a grid, with squares containing four smaller circles alternating with a single large square each containing a circle. The signifi-cance of this pattern was indicated by David Queensberry's suggestion that it should be used as the basis for a printed pattern – renamed Focus – on his newly designed Fine table-ware for Midwinter. Queensberry recognized that Recurrence had exactly the precise controlled 'look' needed to comple-ment his restrained straight-sided vessel form.

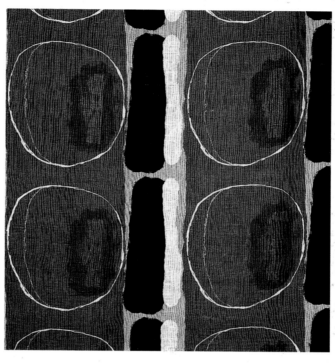

left
Whithorn furnishing fabric designed by the artist William Scott for Edinburgh Weavers, 1962, a pattern which marks the transition from the Contemporary style to 'the look'.
below
Construction furnishing fabric designed by Barbara Brown for Heal's, 1966. By the mid-1960s, Brown's flat geometrics had taken on a three-dimensional effect.

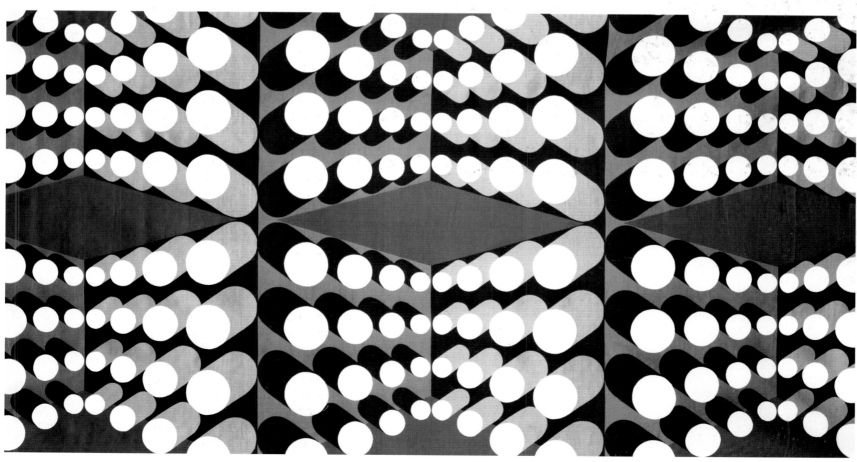

Recurrence was followed in 1964 by two patterns composed entirely of circles and stripes called Piazza and Colonnade (see pages 54 and 56), and a third called Reciprocation constructed from alternating circles and squares. While they shared a similar aesthetic, each pattern had a distinct character arising from the varied scale of the motifs and the specific rhythms evoked by the arrangement of the different elements. From this date onwards, 'the look' gathered its own momentum, and Barbara Brown herself went from strength to strength. Having helped to define 'the look' through her mastery of geometric patterns, circular motifs were to remain a prominent feature in her work right through to the early 1970s. Brown was by no means the only designer working in this idiom at Heal's, however. Other patterns with a related aesthetic included Peter Hall's Abacus of 1964; Counters by Richard Jarvis dating from 1968; Wolfgang Bauer's Hoop-La of 1968; and Aureole by Doreen Dyall, also dating from 1968. The titles of these fabrics all give a good indication of the nature of the design. Tom Worthington, design director for Heal Fabrics, noted astutely in 1968: 'It may take a year or longer for a really advanced design to start selling. And sometimes an avant garde design – although not selling itself – can gain so much publicity it will create a market for similar designs.'

Although it was Heal's that took the lead both nationally and internationally in the development of abstract geometric pattern design during the early 1960s, several other British firms contributed to the development of 'the look'. At Hull Traders, for example, Derek Ellwood's pattern Revo, described in a publicity leaflet as 'a clear formal design of circles and half circles', bore remarkable similarities to Heal's Crescendo; while Peter McCulloch produced a design called Cruachan based on coloured spots, creating a similar effect to the punchmarks used in early computer programs, which was the winner of a Design Centre Award in 1963. Along with Heal's, it was Edinburgh Weavers that helped to establish Britain's reputation abroad in the field of progressive textiles by establishing outlets in the USA. Both companies advertised widely in the architecture and design press, as they realized the importance of marketing 'the look', and Edinburgh Weavers even took the enlightened step of placing adverts in *Domus* during the early 1960s. Four patterns that exploited large-scale circular motifs were Mithras by Fay Hillier dating from 1960; Whithorn and Nearing Circles designed by William Scott, the latter a woven design; and Bocca by Joe Tilson, all dating from 1962. Because of their use of artists, Edinburgh Weaver's designs were often more painterly than precise, and many patterns were overtly textural. In 1965 Edinburgh Weavers embarked on a fruitful partnership with the painter Alan Reynolds, which resulted in the creation of various abstract geometric designs, including one called Megalith based on oblongs, and another called Legend 0700 composed of striped motifs within larger circles.

A new departure at Heal's in the mid-1960s was the introduction of three-dimensionality, a feature that is particularly noticeable in a textile by Barbara Brown called Construction dating from 1966. Brown's earlier patterns had been deliberately flat, and even though the new ones continued to rely on flat planes of colour rather than graduated or textural effects, these were arranged to suggest that the planes were raised above the surface and were casting shadows. In Construction and Chimney Pots, for example, flat

opposite
Blaze 1, Bridget Riley, 1962, emulsion on board (43" x 43"). This painting, and others which followed in its wake during the early 1960s, triggered a wave of media and design interest in Op Art.

above
While Bridget Riley sought to distance herself from commercial associations, Victor Vasarely, another leading artist associated with Op Art, took a more positive attitude, responding to an invitation from Edinburgh Weavers to create textile patterns such as Kernoo, 1962.

left
Koreana two-colour bowl designed by Tapio Wirkkala for Venini, 1968.

circles were transformed into cylinders, and in Alpha, another pattern from 1966, a basic calligraphic motif was repeated three times, with each repeat being slightly offset, suggesting a template casting two shadows. This move from the two-dimensional to the three-dimensional between 1964 and 1966 parallels the rise of Op Art, an important new international development in fine art pioneered by artists such as Bridget Riley in Britain, Hungarian-born Victor Vasarely and the Israeli artist Yaacov Agam in France and Richard Anuskiewicz in the USA. Op Art evolved concurrently with, but as an alternative to, Pop Art. Pop Art fed off and celebrated the aesthetics and energy of commercial art: British artists such as Eduardo Paolozzi and Richard Hamilton freely raided American advertising imagery in their collages and prints of the 1950s, while in the USA Andy Warhol made a strategic career move in 1960 from commercial art to fine art, exploiting the slick techniques and the imagery of the former in his fine art screen prints. Op Art, on the other hand, fed into pattern design and was to have a decisive impact on fashion, textiles, wallpapers, graphics and interiors.

Op paintings created optical effects that confused the viewer's perception, making a flat surface seem literally dynamic, as though it was moving in several directions, and sometimes in several dimensions, concurrently. Riley's early Op Art paintings were entirely in black and white (it was not until 1967 that she began to use colour), two of the most striking being the circular work *Blaze 1* dating from 1962, composed of a spiral of chevrons; and *Fall*, dating from 1963, a vertical pattern of wavy lines, increasing in intensity and in their dizzying effect towards the bottom of the painting. Having succeeded in creating the impression of three-dimensionality purely through flat abstract patterns, Riley went on to experiment with three-dimensionality in a more literal way by creating a maze-like cylindrical painting entitled *Continuum* in 1965 which completely enveloped the viewer. Riley became an international celebrity when her work was shown in a high-profile exhibition at the Museum of Modern Art in New York in 1965 called 'The Responsive Eye', and it was in the immediate aftermath of this that the widespread craze for Op-inspired design set in. Riley's pre-eminence in the art world is indicated by the fact that in 1968, not only was she the first British painter, but also the first female artist to win the International Prize for Painting at the Venice Biennale; while her significance as a reluctant but pivotal figure in the development of 'the look' is confirmed by the fact that in 1967 she was identified by a leading magazine as one of the three most famous women in Britain, along with Mary Quant and Twiggy. Robert Melville, writing in the *New Statesman* in 1971 at the time of a major Bridget Riley retrospective at the Hayward Gallery, declared: 'No painter, dead or alive, has ever made us more aware of our eyes than Bridget Riley.'

Op Art made such an impact on pattern designers that most design-led textile firms found themselves drawn irresistibly towards producing Op-inspired furnishing fabrics during the mid-1960s, partly because this was what the young freelance designers from whom they were buying work were most interested in at the time. While some artists, such as Victor Vasarely, actively collaborated on such initiatives, Bridget Riley was dismayed when she found her work being blatantly plagiarized in other media. As part of its Autumn Collection in 1962, Edinburgh Weavers launched a printed pattern by Victor Vasarely called Kernoo, and the following year they produced

Fabric of unblinking splendour

IMPACT by Evelyn Brooks

This fabric is one of the 1966 range of new designs and is a Cotton Board/House & Garden Award Winner
48 ins/122 cms wide printed cotton, shrink resistant
Pattern repeat 47.3/4 ins/121.5 cms, about 15/11 per yard
Woven and printed in Great Britain.
List of 600 leading stockists available on request

HEAL FABRICS

HEAL FABRICS LTD., 196 TOTTENHAM COURT ROAD, LONDON W1 LANgham 3781
Heal Textil, GmbH, 7, Stuttgart W. Reinsburgstrasse, 171 Stuttgart 62.62.51

DESIGN 2

opposite above
Extension furnishing fabric, a complex three-dimensional geometric pattern designed by Haydon Williams for Heal's. This fabric won a Design Centre Award in 1968.
opposite below
Formula, a wallpaper designed by Edward Veevers for the Palladio 6 collection. It was produced by the progressive Lightbown Aspinall branch of the Wall Paper Manufacturers, 1963.
left
Op Art added a new dimension to the exploration of geometric patterns in the applied arts. Its influence was felt in textile designs such as Impact by Evelyn Brooks for Heal's, 1966.
below
Sphere wallpaper designed by Rosemary Newson for the Palladio 7 collection produced by Sanderson, 1966. This in-situ image highlights the optical qualities of the pattern.

a woven pattern by Vasarely called Oeta. The latter was very much in the Op Art idiom, and was composed of a dynamic arrangement of square and diamond-shaped motifs. Kernoo had a geometric structure but the individual elements – rounded triangular motifs – were more organic. In 1965 Edinburgh Weavers introduced a dazzling black and white Op pattern called Nantucket into their range, purchased from the American designer Bettina. According to a short feature in *Design* magazine in April 1965, this pattern 'clearly derives from the preoccupation of modern painters with geometric patterns and their "kinetic" effects' and was produced in response to 'the recent demand for a small-scale contract pattern'.

The most striking Op Art pattern produced by Heal's was a black and white design called Impact created by Evelyn Brooks in 1966. Winner of a Cotton Board/*House and Garden* Award, this dazzling pattern was composed of overlapping circles, cleverly arranged so that the circles were clustered together to form the outline of larger circles. Along with Impact, Heal's 1966 collection contained another bold black and white Op pattern called Illusion by Barbara Pegg, purchased by Tom Worthington from the designer while she was still a student at Loughborough College of Art. Op Art ideas were also explored in the work of Haydon Williams, who produced two particularly bold designs in 1968 called Suspension and Extension, the abstract nature of which is conveyed by their conceptual titles. Extension won a Design Centre Award in 1968. Williams was an artist and a graphic designer, as well as a textile designer, and he had also spent time working in the USA. This explains why such a keen awareness of contemporary art is reflected in his work. Several of Barbara Brown's later patterns for Heal's explored visual ideas closely related to Op Art in a more direct way, especially Frequency, 1969, and Gyration, 1970, a pattern composed of circular motifs in the form of spirals. Her work took on a quasi-mechanical dimension during the late 1960s and early 1970s, and some patterns even appear to prefigure effects which would be created artificially twenty years later through the use of computer-aided design.

Hull Traders, under the inspired direction of the designer Shirley Craven, followed a strongly independent path during the 1960s. By the middle of the decade, however, even it had got caught up in the Op Art craze, producing a design called Centrum by Molly White, described as a 'circular abstract', which recalled the outline of Verner Panton's spherical banded Visir lampshade; and a pointillist pattern called Diminuendo by Roger Dickinson, which conjured up optical illusions from a pattern composed entirely of graduated dots. Hull Traders were also responsible for producing a remarkable pattern called Mandarin by Linda Harper in their spring collection of 1966, which combined Op, psychedelic and ethnic influences. According to *Design* magazine in April 1966, this pattern 'fits into no convenient category', indicating that 1966 was a pivotal year in British pattern design when a number of disparate trends converged. Interestingly, it was in 1966 that Hull Traders branched out into furniture with the launch of Bernard Holdaway's Tomotom range of Cloverleaf tables and cylindrical seating. Although the high point of Op was 1966, its influence continued for several years, and is reflected in the title of Warner Fabrics' Stereoscopic Collection of 1968, which included pointillist designs such as Sue Palmer's Little Boxes, and Isometric by Eddie Squires.

The medium through which it is perhaps easiest to trace the evolution of straightforward abstract geometric patterns into more complex Op Art patterns is wallpapers, especially via the upmarket top-of-the-range series of Palladio wallpaper collections produced at intervals throughout the decade by various different branches of the Wall Paper Manufacturers Ltd (WPM). During the first half of the decade the Palladio collections were exclusively associated with the progressive Lightbown Aspinall branch of the WPM based at Bredbury near Stockport. The Palladio 4 collection of 1960 contained a bold striped pattern called Ribbon Screen by Fritz Werthmuller, while the Palladio 5 collection of the following year saw the introduction of the circular motif that would dominate design over the next few years. Concentric squares formed the basis of Edward Veevers' Quadrille pattern, while circles and squares were combined in a pattern called Formula by the same designer, both of which appeared in the Palladio 6 collection of 1963. It was in this collection that the first Op Art pattern appeared: Brian Knight's Ancora, a design composed of diamonds and triangles, but with large circular motifs superimposed over the main background, creating the visually disconcerting effect of shifting patterns and perspectives.

In 1965 the WPM was taken over by the Reed Paper Group, which introduced some major organizational changes, including the establishment of a new central design studio, initially overseen by David Queensberry, which supplemented the in-house design work carried out at individual factories. The last two Palladio collections produced during the 1960s were both printed by Sandersons, and it was in the first of these, the Palladio 7 collection of 1966, that Op Art finally conquered the British wallpaper industry. This collection was so radical that it contained wallpapers which could be hung vertically, horizontally, or even upside down, depending on the desired optical effect. Brian Knight produced another bold Op-inspired design called Tambourine, in which quarter segments of circles were contained within a grid of squares. Two other patterns in this collection adopted the by now increasingly common Op formula of superimposing one type of fragmented geometric pattern on to another, thereby causing visual confusion between the two. This device was used in Cymbal and Sphere, the latter designed by Rosemary Newson, both of which had background patterns of stripes with striped circular motifs superimposed over them. In another design called Rondeau, printed in classic Op Art black and white, the optical effects were produced entirely as a result of overlapping circles in a not dissimilar way to Heal's Impact fabric of the same year. Synchro was a straightforward striped pattern, but made use of unusual colour juxtapositions such as orange, pink and grey to create Op effects. Stereo by Deryck Healey, its title suggesting double vision, was another pattern based on stripes, but this time graduated in width and interrupted at intervals to produce a visually disjointed effect. This pattern, along with several others in the range, was printed in various colourways including metallic silver and gold finishes, which added to their other-worldly Space Age quality. Rumba, although more subtle in its colouring, was by far the busiest pattern in the collection, being composed of a background of fine stripes, overlaid with striped chevrons, producing a jazzy pattern full of movement. Not all the Op Art wallpaper patterns in Palladio 7 were strictly geometrical; some had organic features. Concord by Michael Hatjoullis, for example,

above
Rondeau wallpaper from the
Palladio 7 collection printed
by Sanderson in 1966.
right
Concord, also from
the Palladio 7 collection,
produced when the Op Art
craze was at its height. This
distorted linear pattern was
designed by Michael
Hatjoullis.

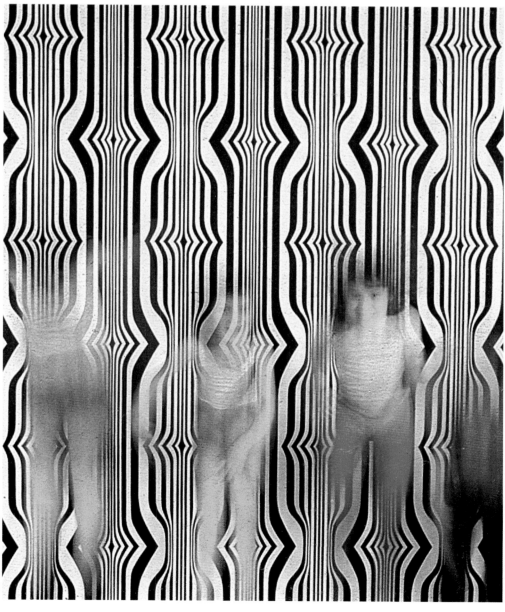

below and opposite
Op Art interiors designed by
Gae Aulenti for the Centro
Fly department store
in Milan, which opened
in 1966.
right
Examples of Italian glass
exhibited at the Venice
Biennale reflected the
influence of Op Art.
Vase and bowl decorated
internally using the *filigrana
stellata* technique, designed
by Archimede Seguso for
his own firm in 1968.
bottom
Op plate designed by
Luciano Gaspari for Salviati,
1966.

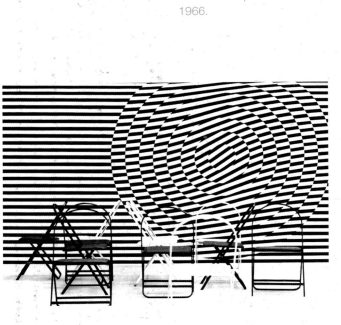

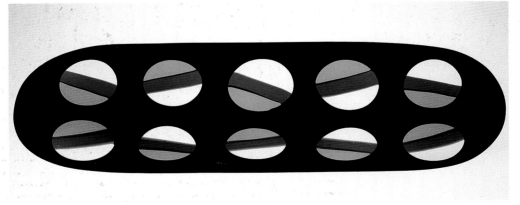

above
Melooni furnishing fabric
designed by Maija Isola for
the Finnish firm, Marimekko,
1963. Like Barbara Brown
in Britain, Isola designed
textiles with dramatic patterns on an architectural
scale. However, although
abstract, her patterns were
freer and less strictly geometric than Brown's.
right
Geometric VII carpet
designed by Verner Panton
for the Danish firm, Unika
Vaev, during the early
1960s. Panton also
designed furnishing fabrics
with similar patterns.

was composed of a pattern of stripes pushed inwards and pulled outwards at intervals to create optical distortions, while Helen Dalby's Harlow introduced giant interlocking chain motifs, dramatically printed in one colourway in gold on a pale brown ground. The influence of Op can still be seen in the Palladio 8 collection of 1968, although by this date designers were taking care not to overload their patterns with too many distortions. Strong abstract patterns from this collection included Compendium by Rosemary Newson, Ziggurat by Margaret Cannon and Gambit by Deryck Healey, all composed of complex geometric motifs, and printed in vivid colourways such as shades of orange and pink. By the end of the decade the fashion for Op Art was on the wane, although echoes of it can still be found in designs such as Stereo One and Stereo Two by Shelagh Wakely from the Palladio 9 collection of 1971.

From the expensive Palladio collections, Op Art filtered down into the cheaper machine-printed ranges produced by the WPM, such as the Crown range of vinyl wallcoverings, for which Deryck Healey designed a small-scale domestic Op Art pattern in 1966. This design was illustrated along with other examples of Healey's work in an article entitled 'The writing on the wall – '66 style' published in *Design* in April of that year. This article was accompanied by specially commissioned photographs showing blurred images of children running in front of wallpapers from the Palladio 7 and Crown ranges, thus further emphasizing the Op-inspired nature of the designs. On a par with the Crown range was Shand Kydd's Focus collection dating from 1968–9, in which a wide selection of popular styles was represented including Op, flower power, psychedelia and historical revivalism. Op Art

patterns included Donald Melbourne's Rondo, composed of striped circles within squares; and an even bolder Op pattern called Pharaoh by Lawrence Corre, which bore some resemblance to the complex three-dimensional geometric abstracts created by Haydon Williams for Heal's Fabrics in 1968.

Op was all the rage in 1966, not just in Britain, but in Europe and the USA. When a new department store called Centro Fly opened in Milan in 1966 selling good quality furniture and furnishings, it was decorated with striking Op Art interiors. In fashion Op Art mini dresses were produced by Biba, and Op raincoats were also enormously popular during the mid-1960s. Typical examples, designed by Scott-Evans and made of cotton printed by the German firm of Württembergishe Cattunmanufaktur using ICI's new Procion dyes, were illustrated in *The Ambassador* in July 1966. Also at the height of its popularity during the mid-1960s was the new wonder plastic fabric, Poly-Vinyl Chloride or PVC, which provided the ideal medium for printing bold Op designs suitable for hats, coats, bags and boots. An advert in *The Ambassador* in September 1965 for a printed PVC fabric by Roger Dickinson of JRM Design, which created an Op Art design out of a fleur-de-lis motif, enthused: 'Take a suit in printed PVC, add a matching print hat, bag and boots, and it all adds up to the Total Look, PVC coordinated from top to toe. Shiny, somewhat sensational, but a Pretty Versatile Capsule.'

In Denmark 'the look' was pioneered by the forward-looking textile firm of Unika Vaev (Unique Weave), which produced both rugs and furnishing fabrics. During the 1950s the company had worked with the graphic artist Rolf Middelboe, who had pursued some interesting experiments combining

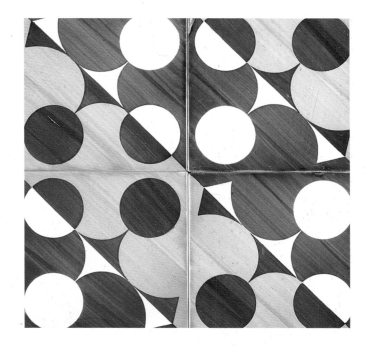

right
Tiles designed by Gio Ponti for Ceramica D'Agostino, 1964, part of a range composed entirely of geometric motifs. The Italians continued to make extensive use of tiles in their buildings during the 1960s, both within interiors and for exterior cladding, which explains why Ponti was so interested in this area of design.
far right
Circular imagery was rife in the field of tile design during the early 1960s. This relief-moulded pattern called Dimex was designed by Michael Caddy for Wade Architectural Ceramics, and won a Design Centre Award in 1962.

colour spectrums and geometric patterns, involving circular motifs with radiating lines. Patterns and shapes based on circles were also central to the work of the furniture designer Verner Panton who collaborated with Unika Vaev during the early 1960s, and who was to have a major impact on its output and its image during the first half of the decade. It was Panton, in fact, who was responsible for creating the Unika Vaev 'look' with the launch of his Geometry patterns in 1960 inspired by the paintings of Victor Vasarely. His partnership with the company resulted in a series of striking carpets, rugs and furnishing fabrics based on compositions of circles, squares and diamonds. These were produced either in stark black and white or in bright two-tone colourways. Like Barbara Brown's Recurrence which followed three years later and may have been inspired by Panton's work, he often placed a circle in the centre of a square, then used the squares as a grid to build up a modular design. Such textiles provided the ideal backdrop for his furniture, which was itself strongly geometrical at this time, particularly his wire-framed Cone chairs produced by Plus-Linje. Panton himself created just such an ensemble in various exhibitions and the new showrooms he designed for Unika Vaev in Copenhagen and New York during the early 1960s, which provide striking early examples of the application of 'the look' to interior design.

In Sweden the firms of Mölnlycke and Claes Håkansson were the acknowledged trendsetters. The latter produced a pattern called Universum in 1962 designed by Brita and Lennart Svefors which was composed of circles inside squares. Finland's foremost textile firm at the time was Marimekko, which specialized in dress fabrics and fashion as well as furnishing fabrics. Recognized as the Scandinavian equivalent of Mary Quant, it played a role of equal importance in terms of fashion and cultural identity. One of the designers who was to take a lead role at the company, Maija Isola, originally designed furnishing fabrics for Printex, the firm out of which Marimekko grew. It was at Printex during the second half of the 1950s that she pioneered the development of bold, large-scale abstract patterns, such as Citrus dating from 1956, based on a cross-section through an orange. Geometric patterns of one form or another, including both stripes and circular motifs, formed the mainstay of Marimekko's production during the mid-1960s, and were an essential component of the Marimekko 'look'.

Another area of pattern-making in which circular motifs featured prominently during the early 1960s was tiles. The Staffordshire firm of H & R Johnson manufactured a range of repeating tiles called Hot Spot during the first half of the 1960s, decorated with a single large circle inside a square. In 1962 Michael Caddy won a Design Centre Award on behalf of Wade Architectural Ceramics for his Dimex tiles decorated with circular indentations. Later in the decade Caddy worked with the Manchester-based firm of Pilkington's Tiles, at this date one of the most progressive tile manufacturers in the country along with Carter Tiles, the tile-making branch of Poole Pottery which had recently merged with Pilkington's. Both firms produced designs in which circular motifs played an important role, and as they were seeking to secure orders from architects working on large-scale public or commercial building projects, several of these designs were for simple abstract motifs which could be juxtaposed in different arrangements so that architects could, in effect,

above
Hand-painted patterns on a range of plates designed by the architect, Gio Ponti, for Ceramica Pozzi, 1967. Ponti had a career in ceramics spanning several decades but, like Susie Cooper in Britain, he updated his style during the 1960s to keep up with 'the look'.
left
Circular tile designed by Ann Wynn Reeves using a blank by H & R Johnson. Reeves and her husband, Kenneth Clark, were two of the most adventurous British tile designers of the 1960s.

create their own patterns. Pilkington's also adopted the new technique of screen-printing in 1961 to produce a series of domino-like tiles in their Chiaroscuro range (pattern numbers SK100–4), decorated with large coloured spots. According to an advert in the *Architectural Review* in July 1961:

This very simple and flexible new development in decorative tiles is composed of five basic elements, all or any number of which will permutate together to create an infinite variety of designs … lending itself particularly well to the creation of large murals.

The way in which these tiles, and another in the Chiaroscuro series decorated with a wavy line motif (pattern number SK85), could be juxtaposed, presaged later Op-related developments. By the mid-1960s Pilkington's had ventured directly into the field of Op Art with their silk-screen printed Zenith and Meridian ranges, decorated with circles, semi-circles, squares or rectangles composed of fine graduated stripes. These tiles could be alternated and set in different alignments to produce bold optical effects.

During the mid-1960s Carter Tiles produced a series of relief-moulded tiles in their Dolphin range with a split circle motif designed by Alfred Burgess Read (pattern number TS18). These reflected the new fashion for textured tiles which were variously described by the industry as 'modelled', 'sculptured', 'profile' or 'surface relief', an important new trend discussed by Lucien Myers in an article entitled 'Variety and vitality in ceramic tiles' in *Design* in March 1965. Other British firms closely associated with this development included Richards Tiles; S G B of Dudley, for which Hans Coper designed a particularly exciting and unusual series of relief-moulded frost-proof tiles in 1963; and Malkin Tiles, the work of which was marketed by the Stoke-on-Trent based H & R Johnson group. Textured tiles by Malkin dating from 1962 were decorated with geometric patterns inspired by Aztec art. Malkin's work became popular not just because of its relief-moulded patterns but because of its rich glazes, which formed an integral part of the overall effect. Particularly successful was the Turinese range designed jointly by James Rushton and Leonard King around 1961, decorated with intricate concentric geometric patterns.

The 1960s marked a highpoint in twentieth-century tile design. As well as mass-produced tiles, there was also a demand for hand-made tiles and tile panels. The latter was the chosen form of expression of the Finnish ceramic artist Rut Bryk. Her creations, which resembled three-dimensional mosaics, reflected two of the prevailing interests of the period: relief-textured surfaces and geometric patterns. The tiles making up these panels were usually square, but were in many different sizes, each one decorated with either raised or impressed geometric motifs, including circles, semi-circles, squares, diamonds and hexagons. Arresting glazes, colours and patterns based on circular motifs formed an essential part of the aesthetic of the hand-decorated tiles made by the Kenneth Clark Pottery in London during the 1960s, designed by Clark himself and his wife, Ann Wynn Reeves. Some tiles were even produced in the form of circles, such as a series designed by Ann Wynn Reeves using H & R Johnson blanks, while Clark himself collaborated with Malkin Tiles. Alan Wallwork was another London-based tile decorator who worked independently in a similar idiom using commercial blanks, circular motifs composed of concentric rings of spots being his particular hallmark.

One of the largest markets for tiles was Italy, where it was taken for granted that tiles should be extensively used as decorative cladding on both the interior and exterior of buildings. The firm of Ceramica d'Agostino of Salerno used simplified abstract geometric patterns in a similar way to Pilkington's. In an article on this company in *Domus*, in May 1964, six different basic tiles were illustrated, along with two panels for each design showing the different ways in which they could be combined. The motifs on the tiles, designed by Gio Ponti, were circles, semi-circles, crescents, stripes and triangles. Ponti had a long history of association with ceramics, having created Art Deco patterns for Richard Ginori during the 1930s and tile designs for Ceramica Joo during the 1950s. He continued to act as a champion for Italian ceramics during the 1960s, and in 1967 he designed a striking series of hand-painted patterns for a range of plates produced by Ceramica Pozzi. Illustrated *en masse* in a feature in *Domus* in September 1967, these brightly coloured patterns were bold in their simplicity, the decoration on some pieces being limited to a solid circle of colour in the centre of the plate, while others were decorated with multi-coloured stripes.

In the ceramics of Ettore Sottsass, form and pattern were completely unified. Ceramics formed a central part of his *œuvre* during the 1960s, and are as important as his other more high-profile achievements in the fields of furniture, product and interior design. It was through the medium of ceramics that Sottsass chose to make some of his most personal statements. The unusual way in which he combined form and decoration was striking and imaginative. Some pieces were small and intimate, some were on a dramatic and architectural scale, as in the group of giant composite ceramic sculptures that he displayed at the Galleria Sperone in Milan, illustrations of which were published in *Domus* in October 1967. Like Hans von Klier's painted wooden children's toys, these sculptures were composed of brightly coloured geometric elements such as discs, cylinders and compressed spheres. Each component was glazed in a different colour or decorated

below
Ettore Sottsass used ceramics periodically throughout the 1960s as a vehicle for making symbolic statements. Some of his creations, such as Menhir of 1967, were composite forms on a huge scale and were used for gallery installations.
below left
In 1969, Sottsass created his Tantra series, followed at the end of the decade by a related group called Yantra. In these works Sottsass moved away from the circular forms and patterns which had dominated his earlier work and began to explore Art Deco-inspired ziggurat forms.

left
The Radomes at RAF
Fylingdales, an Early
Warning Rocket Defence
Station erected on the
North Yorkshire Moors in
1963. As well as being a
potent symbol of the
nuclear age, the 'golf balls'
reflected the prevailing
aesthetics of 'the look'.

with horizontal bands or vertical or diagonal stripes. These were then stacked on top of each other to create tall floor-to-ceiling columns resembling totem poles. Two years later Sottsass created an equally dramatic installation at the Nationalmuseum in Stockholm in which various different media were combined, including ceramics, laminated wood and perspex. Circular columns were the dominant forms once again, along with rectangular towers. In his commentary on this installation Sottsass suggested that these structures were symbolic and had talismanic meanings. Some of these ideas were further explored in Sottsass's two final ceramics series of the decade, Tantra and Yantra. The former was exhibited at the Galleria della Nuova Loggia in Bologna in February 1969, and was featured in *Domus* in September of that year. These pieces were at once the culmination of his earlier works and a new departure. They were still strongly geometric, but now the designer had moved away from composite columns to create one-piece vessels with stepped forms based on cones and ziggurats. In the text which accompanied this feature, Sottsass

made a point of stating that the reason why he was attracted to geometric forms and patterns was not because of their rational qualities, but because of their powerful symbolic resonance and spiritual associations:

Perhaps these ceramic objects have not hit the target at all and someone will come along and say that they belong to the field of pure geometry or pure rationalism, as if the circle belonged only to Euclid, or Leonardo or Descartes, and not also to the Tibetan mandalas, Chinese symbolism and the facade of the Cathedral at Spoleto.

Thus, through his ceramics, Sottsass prefigured the two design revolutions of the 1960s, bridged the divide between the ideas and aesthetics of the early and late 1960s, and prefigured the thinking behind future design developments of the 1970s and 1980s.

Spheres

Whereas cylindrical forms were fairly widespread in 1960s architecture and design, the sphere was less commonly used because of its more limited practical applications. Nevertheless it was the sphere, more than any other three-dimensional form, that was to become the most resonant symbol of the decade, and which invariably attracted attention when architects and designers did succeed in exploiting it. One only has to think of the strange potency of the white spherical Radomes, built by the Ministry of Defence as part of their Early Warning Rocket Defence Station at RAF Fylingdales on the North Yorkshire Moors in 1963, to recognize the link between spherical forms and Space Age design. Known locally as the 'golf balls', the three 46-metre high Radomes were one of three international outstations built to house sophisticated American-developed radar equipment, the other two being in Greenland and Alaska. An ominous but compelling symbol of the Cold War, the Radomes were constructed of hexagonal panels joined by aluminium bolts, the panels being made of 15-centimetre thick fibreglass filled with a honeycomb of reinforced paper. The radars they housed were intended not only to enable the USA to track objects in space, such as satellites, but to provide early warning of any Soviet-launched Inter-Continental Ballistic Missiles, although the maximum amount of warning would only be a matter of minutes. Although there were protests against the intrusion of these huge structures into the wild landscape of the National Park, in December 1963 the *Architectural Review* compared their impact to 'the dream-like quality of Paul Nash's vision of objects in the landscape', and noted that the radar station development as a whole had 'positive qualities and furnishes a quite exhilarating example of the additions science is making to our aesthetic experience'.

Whereas spheres attracted a lot of attention but were actually quite rare, hemispherical forms were more common in architecture and were thus more likely to be taken for granted. Partly this was because the dome was an established form of architectural expression; partly because it was assumed that domes were easier to construct from an engineering point of view. The fact was, however, that until engineer designers such Pier Luigi Nervi mastered the use of prefabricated reinforced concrete construction during the 1940s

and 1950s, there were severe limits on the size of the span to which unsupported shell structures could be extended. Through his work on air hangars, exhibition halls and sports stadia, Nervi overcame these problems, and devised methods for creating large concrete shell structures, where the dome itself was self-supporting and formed the actual building rather than just the roof. Apart from Italy, the other country where hemispherical forms were used in a particularly novel way was Brazil. In its new capital, Brasilia, hemispheres were chosen for two of the most important state buildings: the domed Chamber of the Lower House and the cup-shaped Senate Chamber. Designed by Oscar Niemeyer, they were constructed between 1957 and 1960, and together created a Space Age juxtaposition. The cup-shaped form of the Senate Chamber was particularly unusual and presaged the adoption of spheres later in the 1960s.

The Radomes at Fylingdales were clearly based on ideas developed by the radical architect-engineer Richard Buckminster Fuller, the inventor of the geodesic dome. Geodesy is a branch of mathematics dealing with the measurement of the earth's surface, a geodesic line being the shortest line between two points on a surface. A geodesic dome, therefore, is a dome built of short struts along geodesic lines, the struts forming a skeleton with a triangular or hexagonal framework. Fuller had developed and refined his ideas about geodesic domes over the course of several decades. One of the first to be built was a 50-foot dome clad with cardboard constructed at the Milan Triennale of 1954. This was followed by a much more ambitious project, the Union Tank Car Repair Shop at Baton Rouge, Louisiana, in 1958. Hemispherical in shape and built using a hexagonal honeycomb structure, this dome was 116 feet high and 384 feet in diameter, at the time the largest clear-span enclosure in the world. After this came Fuller's own house in Carbondale, Illinois, 1960, and on a larger scale, the Climatron, a giant glasshouse built using a triangular grid structure to house the Botanical Gardens at St Louis, Missouri, in 1960. What was unusual about Fuller's domes, and the reason why they, and space-frame structures in general, were to exert such a strong influence on high-tech architects of the 1970s, was the way in which their framework was exposed on the exterior like an exoskeleton. During the 1960s there was growing interest in

right
Oscar Niemeyer's cup-shaped Senate Chamber and dome-shaped Chamber of the Lower House in Brasilia, designed and constructed between 1957 and 1960, presaged the wider adoption of hemispherical forms in the 1960s.

Fuller's ideas, partly because of a fascination with this new system of architectural engineering from a technical point of view, but also for purely aesthetic reasons, because the structures that Fuller had engineered captured the desired 'look' of the period. Although Fuller himself was not motivated by formal or aesthetic concerns – he had much wider philosophical preoccupations – that did not stop his work from being co-opted by the media and the architectural fraternity of the day as a symbolic expression of its age.

Fuller's greatest triumph came at the Montreal Expo in 1967 when he was commissioned to design a giant three-quarters globe for the American Pavilion. The largest and most complex geodesic dome ever constructed – large enough to house a twenty-storey building – the American Pavilion attracted the attention and the admiration of the world, and was to become one of the most powerful visual images of the decade, just as Skylon had been at the Festival of Britain in 1951 and the Atomium at the Brussels World Fair in 1958. The monorail which ran around the site entered the pavilion by penetrating the wall of the dome. Constructed of steel, glass and acrylic, the pavilion had an inner hexagonal structure, overlaid with an outer triangular grid exoskeleton. Thus the two main types of structural framework that Fuller had explored in the past were combined. The inner skeleton and the outer exoskeleton, both steel framed, were themselves held together by a structural steel mesh, and the hexagonal windows of the dome, instead of being flat, were convex and projected outwards like bubbles. Walter Eijkelenboom, the designer of another space-frame construction at the Expo, The Netherlands Pavilion, said of Fuller's dome: 'It is a masterpiece of technology, and it is beautiful to look at. But it is not designed intentionally to look beautiful – it is a piece of pure technique.' From a purely formal point of view, what fascinated people was the way in which Fuller used straight-sided geometric forms to create a circular building. Beyond that it was the sheer scale and intricacy of the structure that caught the imagination. In a commentary on the Expo in the American design magazine *Interiors* in June 1967, the dome was praised in eulogistic terms:

It rests like a thistle above the waters of the Le Moyne Channel, an object dream-like and out of another world, an object that tells us that the space age might be an age of poetic contemplation and absolute tranquility. Its bubbles are transparent and are said to expand and contract with temperature and atmospheric changes … The bolted clusters look like lace pinwheels which can be seen twice – large in the foreground and small in the background as one stands outside and looks through the dome. The rays of the sun and lights of the night converge on the bubbles like multiplied stars, changing with every movement of the clouds and of the observer's eye.

Fuller's work on geodesic structures spawned many offshoots, such as the Dome house designed by Bernard Judge in Los Angeles in 1960 (see pages 12 and 103), which used a triangular grid structure and was closely indebted to Fuller's ideas. In 1966 a group of young people seeking to establish an alternative lifestyle in a semi-agrarian community called Drop City in Arizona built *ad-hoc* temporary homes for themselves in the form of geodesic domes constructed from used car bodies and other found materials. Other spin-offs, such as tents, were created, an example being a marquee

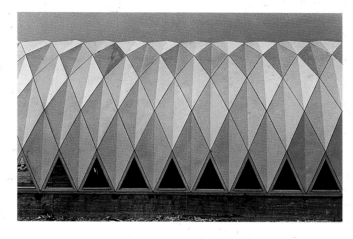

opposite and below centre
The Climatron in St Louis, Missouri, designed by Richard Buckminster Fuller 1960, was a large low-lying dome housing the city's botanical gardens.
left
Temporary shelter for sulphur production equipment at Pomezia, Italy, designed by Renzo Piano, 1966. Like Buckminster Fuller, Piano experimented during the 1960s with lightweight structures composed of geometric elements, which could be quickly and cheaply erected.
bottom
Buckminster Fuller's American Pavilion was constructed for the Montreal Expo in 1967. A giant three-quarters globe more than twenty storeys high, it is seen here with the Expo monorail entering its side.

designed by David Stabb in Britain in 1967 made of triangular components, its light steel framework exposed on the exterior. Some ideas were more quirky and esoteric, such as a feature fireplace in a villa on the Costa Brava in Spain designed by Peter Harnden and Lanfranco Bambelli, which was featured in *Domus* in July 1965. The chimney for the open fire was a geodesic sphere composed of triangular sections. Also loosely related to Fuller's work were the experiments carried out by another pioneering and influential architect, Renzo Piano, during the 1960s. Piano is best known today for his high-tech Pompidou Centre in Paris, designed in conjunction with the British architect Richard Rogers. Completed in 1977, the Pompidou Centre is an all-purpose arts centre cum fun palace, the philosophical concepts behind which are rooted in the cultural ideas of the late 1960s. Prior to this, however, Piano had spent several years refining his techniques for assembling temporary structures made of synthetic materials and composed of faceted geometric elements. In 1966, for example, he designed a temporary shelter for sulphur production equipment on a site at Pomezia. Constructed by four men in the space of four days, the arched tunnel-shaped structure was 24 metres long with a 10-metre vault, and was made of diamond-shaped reinforced polyester components bolted together.

From a practical point of view cylindrical forms have limited applications, spheres even more so, which is why the latter have usually been limited to experimental, prototype or temporary structures. The Radomes at Fylingdales, for example, disappeared in 1993 as rapidly and mysteriously as they had arrived exactly thirty years before. The most widespread use of spherical forms has been in exhibitions, particularly World's Fairs. Another sphere on show at the Montreal Expo, this time in the Children's Creative Centre in the Canadian section, was a prototype for a children's climbing frame called a Playsphere, designed by V Hubel for a firm called Protective Plastics. Made of reinforced plastics and pierced with large ovoid organic holes, the Playsphere stood about 2 metres high and was raised off the ground on a concrete pedestal. Three years earlier at the New York World's Fair in 1964, the Germans had mounted a futuristic display using perspex spheres in their Berlin Pavilion which, according to *Industrial Design* in July 1964, had an 'other worldly quality'. Designed by Ludwig Thuermer, their display cases were composed of two hemispheres held together by an iron belt, supported on metal pedestals. More common at this date were domed Perspex display cabinets of the type used by Joe Colombo in his design for a camera shop in Italy, illustrated in a feature in *Domus* in June 1965. Among the most striking outdoor features at the New York World's Fair were the Brass Rail snack bars designed by the architect Victor Lundy, each sales outlet being surmounted by a huge inflatable canopy composed of a cluster of translucent spheres resembling a bunch of giant balloons, lit internally at night. Also on a circular theme was Charles Eames and Saarinen Associate's IBM Pavilion. Designed in the form of a compressed sphere balanced on top of a grove-like open canopy, the sphere actually contained a theatre and was intended to resemble a cloud.

In addition to exhibition structures, experimental and prototype houses were another rich field of exploration for architects interested in spherical forms, such as Verner Panton's Spherical House in Copenhagen of 1960. In 1968

above
IBM Pavilion at the New York World's Fair, 1964, by Charles Eames and Saarinen Associates. This pavilion and the Brass Rail snack bars were the visual highlights of an otherwise undistinguished Fair.
right
Brass Rail snack bar, New York World's Fair, designed by Victor Lundy, 1964.
opposite above
Dome House, Los Angeles, designed by Bernard Judge, 1960. Although many architects fantasized about living inside a bubble during the 1960s, very few actually achieved it. Buckminster Fuller, in his house in Carbondale, Illinois, was one who did, and Bernard Judge, clearly indebted to Fuller, was another.
opposite below
Futuro House designed by Matti Suuronen for the Finnish plastics firm, Polykem, 1968. Like the IBM Pavilion (above), this spaceship-like capsule house is in the shape of a compressed sphere with matching elliptical windows.

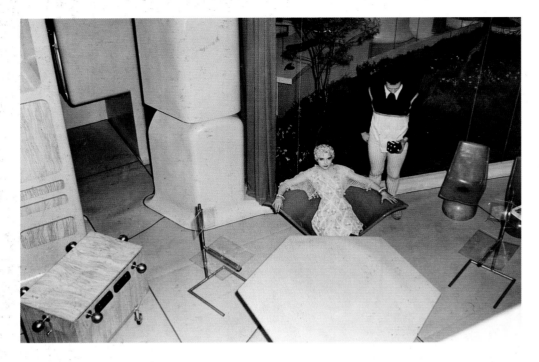

above
House of the Future designed by Alison and Peter Smithson, 'Ideal Home' Exhibition, 1956. This interior, with its rounded skirtings and hexagonal table, was ahead of its time, although by the 1960s plastics technology was more sophisticated and furniture designers were no longer limited to fibreglass and perspex.

above right
Fifth Dimension Fun Palace, Girvan, Ayrshire, designed by Keith Albarn, 1969. The shell of this seaside amusement centre was created from multi-coloured moulded fibreglass panels. The interior was described by

Alastair Best in *Design* magazine in November 1969 as, 'A womb-like enclosure which bombards its victims with patterns of light, colour and sound; walls are lined with exotic "feelies" and floors have a habit of changing, suddenly and without warning, from hard concrete to soft sponge.'

opposite
Stevens Residence, Malibu, California, designed by John Lautner, 1968. In cross section this house is a quarter segment of a circle, and the circular theme is echoed in the domed hood of the fireplace.

the Finnish designer Matti Suuronen created a temporary structure called the Futuro house in the form of a compressed sphere. Designed for the plastics firm Polykem AB of Helsinki, the Futuro house was described in *Domus* in April 1969 as:
… a glass fibre sandwich shell, insulated on the inside by polyurethane foam, which is supported by a steel ring around the base. The ring is attached to four legs which are then bolted to concrete pillars set in the ground beneath … It is made of sixteen sections, and eight of these, which form the upper part of the shell, incorporate two double elliptical windows made from acrylic sheet.

The Futuro house was the latest in a long line of capsule-like experimental houses dating back to the 1920s, few of which progressed beyond the fantasy prototype stage apart from John Lautner's Chemosphere of 1960. One of the earliest was Buckminster Fuller's circular Dymaxion house of 1927, which had a shell of aluminium and glass, and a central mast housing the trunking for all the services. This was followed in 1946 by the Wichita house, another circular building designed by Buckminster Fuller. Sheathed in metal, with pre-moulded and pre-installed services, the Wichita house was designed so that it could be transported in its entirety inside a narrow cylinder. Like the Dymaxion, however, the Wichita house never advanced beyond the prototype stage. By the 1950s, the chemistry and technology of plastics had advanced to such a degree that architects began to abandon metal cladding in favour of lightweight synthetic materials. Although a fantasy rather than a reality, Alison and Peter Smithson's House of the Future at the *Ideal Home* exhibition in 1956 posited the idea of the house as an organic capsule, and of plastics as the primary material for both its structure and its furnishings. Exploiting the latest technology, in terms of both materials and electrical gizmos, Joe Colombo pushed the idea of the house as a capsule to its logical conclusion in the interiors he created for the 'Visiona 69' exhibition installation for Bayer in 1969. Using geometric rather than organic forms, Colombo explored ideas previously thought to be limited to the realms of science fiction, and transformed fantasy into reality. At the same time as Colombo was designing this futuristic domestic interior, a Swedish architect, Staffan Berglund, built an experimental house called the Villa Fjolle near Stockholm. In a feature on the two projects in *Mobilia* in August 1969, it was noted that there were interesting parallels between them: 'There is much similarity between the two experiments. They have much in common, the use of plastics, especially fibreglass, the dividing up of the interiors into closet-like cubicles, and technology, lots of technology.' As well as the technical similarities, however, there were also significant crossovers in the choice of aesthetic vocabulary, as these were both circular houses, and the writer noted that: 'One of the most interesting points of resemblance of the two projects is the use of round forms.' In Colombo's interior the solid cast-plastic bathroom cabin projected like a bubble into the room, and the circular theme was taken up again in the form of the spherical television suspended above the circular bed.

The trend during the 1950s had been to flood the interior with natural light and to reduce the barriers between the interior and the exterior of buildings. Although this fashion continued (in the work of Richard Meier, for example), another trend emerged during the course of the 1960s which was the exact reverse of this earlier movement. In some cases there

were practical reasons for this, such as climate, which made it more sensible to plan for inward-looking rather than outward-looking designs. This was the thinking behind Ralph Erskine's indoor shopping centre in Lulea, built during the early 1960s in the sub-arctic north of Sweden, which was one of the first large community and shopping complexes to be designed with indoor heated streets. However, the idea of the house as a fortress rather than an open pavilion was a concept that began to emerge more generally during the early 1960s. It can be seen in a mild form in the inward-looking courtyard houses of Michael Manser in Britain, and is demonstrated in a more extreme way in a house designed by John Johansen in Westport, Connecticut, in the USA, completed in 1962. Although built in a beachside location, the windows of this house were deeply recessed, thus restricting the view. Constructed from poured concrete with strong vertical striations, the house was Brutalist in the extreme on the exterior, resembling a fortified labyrinth. It was not far from a design of this sort to Marcel Breuer's Whitney Museum in New York of 1966, or to the Hayward Gallery/Queen Elizabeth Hall/National Theatre complex on London's South Bank.

Even houses or apartments that were not overtly fortress-like on the exterior were made to seem more enclosed and inward-looking as a result of the way in which the interiors were designed, and in particular how they were lit. Rather than working from light to dark, as designers had done during the 1950s, the trend during the second half of the 1960s was to control the entry of light from outside, and to work instead from dark to light. Therefore artificial rather than natural light came to be regarded as the major light source, which may explain why the 1960s was such a fruitful and creative period in the history of lighting. A leading exponent of the house as a sealed container was Joe Colombo who, five years before his 'Visiona 69' installation, created a series of domestic interiors that were self-consciously insular, even claustrophobic, such as the two apartments in Milan illustrated in *Domus* in December 1965. The disturbing colour tones and colour contrasts used in these interiors further highlighted their self-conscious artificiality. It was as though they had been chosen with the quasi-sadistic intention of giving the architect pleasure in making the occupant feel queasy. Even when natural materials were used in interior design, as in the Scandinavian-style interiors created by Andrew Powers in a group of apartments in San Marino in 1965 where all the exposed surfaces – walls, ceilings and floors – were bare wood, this sense of cloying oversaturation was often still extremely strong.

Apart from experimental and prototype installations at exhibitions, one of the main avenues for architects to create truly Space Age capsule-like interiors was through innovative interior design projects, particularly shops. A candle shop and a boutique designed by Hans Hollein in Vienna during the late 1960s illustrate the way in which circular imagery formed an integral component of such designs, as does the boutique for Mary Farrin designed by Wilkinson, Calvert and Gough in South Moulton Street, London, towards the end of the decade. The idea of the shop or showroom as a capsule was widely explored, as people were prepared to accept a much greater degree of fantasy in this kind of environment than in a bank, for example. The French fashion designer Jean Cacharel developed these themes in his new showroom and

above
'The look' was embraced by the highest echelons of British society during the late 1960s. Dress Circle restaurant at Harrods, London, designed by Maurice Broughton and Associates, 1968.

left
Exhibition installation in Zurich by Verner Panton, 1961, featuring circular wire furniture designed by Panton for Plus-Linje, 1958–60, and geometric carpets and furnishing fabrics for Unika Vaev, 1960. Like Ettore Sottsass in Italy, Panton embraced the geometric 'look' completely. The combined impact of his furniture and textiles together is as powerful as the Op Art paintings of Bridget Riley and Victor Vasarely; Panton acknowledged the latter as a source of inspiration.

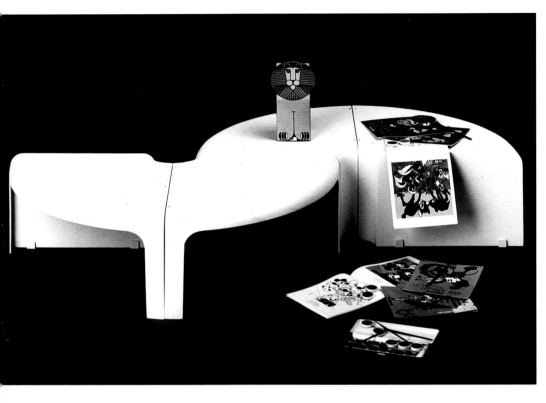

left
700 Quattroquarti plastic table/shelf unit designed by Rodolfo Bonetto for Bernini, 1969. Circular forms were widely used as a source of inspiration for furniture designers during the 1960s, sometimes in segments, sometimes in stacks.
below left
Stacking wooden tables (model 780) designed by Gianfranco Frattini for Cassina, 1966.
below
Advert for London Combination modular seating range designed by Geoffrey Harcourt for Artifort, 1967.

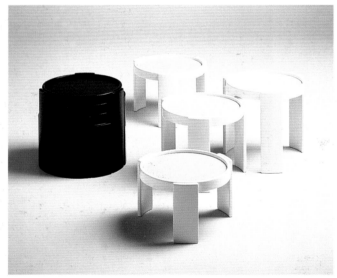

offices in Paris in 1969. The showroom was a giant sealed capsule, containing individual pod-like offices, or office cabins as they were known. Basements were ideal for creating capsule-like interiors. The complete exclusion of daylight, which might otherwise act as a limitation, was a distinct advantage in this situation, as the French designer Annie Tribel of Atelier d'Urbanisme et d'Architecture was to discover when designing the atmospheric interior of a café at the Theatre de la Ville in Paris in 1969. This interior was dominated by a series of forty-three giant seating capsules made of bright orange fibreglass-reinforced polyester. Each capsule, or niche as they were described in an article in *Design* magazine in September 1969, provided not only built-in bench seating and a table, but the walls and hood of a complete alcove. A similar mood of artificiality and enclosure pervaded the two interiors created by Maurice Broughton and Associates for Harrods during the late 1960s, the Way In boutique of 1967, and the Dress Circle restaurant of 1968, demonstrating how, by this date, 'the look' had been assimilated into the heart of the commercial Establishment. Another apparently conventional project, the fitting out of the British cruise liner the *QE2*, provided a vehicle for the exploration of fantastical futuristic ideas of the kind normally limited to film sets. The Queen's Room, designed by Michael Inchbald as a lounge for first class passengers, had a back-lit perforated ceiling made of fibreglass-reinforced plastics, while the support columns were sheathed in trumpet-shaped plastic casings. The room was dominated by a cluster of white plastic shell pedestal armchairs, also designed by Inchbald, their circular bases intended to mirror the flared form of the columns. Further continuity was provided by the use of

plastics for the rounded rectangular window surrounds, which reinforced the visual impression of the ship as a capsule.

Interiors such as these underline the importance for the designer of being able to draw upon furniture, the forms and aesthetics of which complement those of the room itself. One chair design that epitomized 'the look' of the sixties, and which, if bought off the peg, could always be relied upon to create maximum impact on an interior, was Eero Aarnio's Ball or Globe chair of 1965, produced by the Finnish firm Asko. Significantly, this chair was chosen for the interior of a Mary Quant shop in New Bond Street, London, designed by Jon Bannenberg in 1967, perfectly complementing the drum-shaped changing room capsules. Perhaps the best known example of the adoption of the sphere in 1960s design generally, the spherical seat of the Globe chair was created from a moulded fibreglass shell, and like Saarinen's Tulip chair of 1956, the shell seat was raised on a circular pedestal base made of metal, in this case aluminium, with a revolving mechanism. As with the Tulip chair, the replacement of conventional legs by a single circular pedestal base and stem naturally suggested that the seat itself should be curved, the logical extension of this being to make it perfectly round. The interior of the globe was generously padded and upholstered, with additional cushions in the centre. The reason why the Globe made such a dramatic impression was partly its shape, partly its colour (monochrome black, white, red or orange), and partly its size. It was considerably larger than the average armchair, thus enabling the user to curl up inside the sphere as if it were a womb or a cocoon. Some chairs were even equipped with telephones or stereo speakers, suggesting that

below left
Product designers embraced 'the look' by creating spherical metal and plastic casings for electrical appliances. Record player with spherical speakers, designed by Hugh Spencer and John Magyar for the Canadian company, the Clairtone Sound Corporation, c1963. In the advert illustrated the Canadian jazz musician, Oscar Peterson, sits in an Egg chair, right, designed by Arne Jacobsen.
below
Spherical television designed by Arthur D Bracegirdle for Keracolor, c1969.

opposite
Globe chair designed by Eero Aarnio for the Finnish firm, Asko, 1965. It is capacious enough to curl up inside. Used in Mary Quant's new Bond Street boutique in 1968, in the cult television series 'The Prisoner' (from 1967), and in films such as *The Italian Job* (1969) starring Michael Caine, this chair was immediately recognized as an icon of 1960s design, as evocative as the mini skirt or the Mini Cooper.

left
Sunball easy chair designed by Günter Ferdinand Ris and Herbert Seildorf for Rosenthal, 1969–71. Designed for outdoor use, (hence its name) the chair's hood could be completely closed by rotating one of the two spherical fibreglass segments from which it is composed. The seat, which was wide enough for two people, could be converted from a chair to a day bed. Accessories included clip-on trays, a built-in lamp and a speaker system.

the user could retreat into a self-contained environment. The Globe chair achieved quasi-iconic status in Britain after it was used in the futuristic television series 'The Prisoner' from 1967, where it was associated with the enigmatic character, Number 2. Interestingly, whenever the Prisoner, played by Patrick McGoohan, tried to escape from the Village to which he had unaccountably been taken, he was menaced by a giant plastic bubble which bounced across the sea, forcing him to return. The programme, therefore, highlighted the 1960s preoccupation with spherical forms in two ways, and suggested that such shapes, because they were 'perfect', were somehow intrinsically sinister, like the Radomes at Fylingdales.

Trained as an interior and industrial designer at the School of Industrial Design in Helsinki between 1954 and 1957, Eero Aarnio was one of the new generation of designers to emerge in Finland during the early 1960s who, like Panton in Denmark, challenged the fundamental principles of Scandinavian Modern design. After establishing his own office in 1962, his fascination with plastics and the unconventional forms they suggested led him to experiment with radically new furniture shapes. In an interview in the *New York Times* in December 1970, Aarnio stated his conviction that geometric shapes were 'the most comfortable forms to hold up the human body'. The Globe was followed in 1965 by the Bubble chair, and by a range of furniture that Aarnio designed for the Italian firm Cassina, shown at the 6th Selective Exhibition at Cantu in 1965, and illustrated subsequently in *Industrial Design* in April 1966. Aarnio continued to explore circular themes in this range, which included a disc-shaped leather upholstered stool with a circular metal pedestal base, complemented by a matching low-backed chair.

Although spheres were relatively rare in furniture design because of the complicated logistics of sitting inside them or on top of them, hemispheres and cones, being better adapted to this function, were more common. One of the earliest attempts to design strongly geometrical furniture using basic forms such as cones, cylinders and hemispheres was a range designed by Verner Panton for Plus-Linje during the late 1950s and early 1960s. When speaking of his work in 1970 Panton said:

I try to forget existing examples even though they may be good, and concern myself above all with the material. The result then rarely has four legs, not because I do not wish to make such a chair, but because the processing of materials such as wire and polyester calls for new shapes.

Of Panton's early designs the Cone chair of 1958 was the most dramatic. Two different versions were produced, both equally striking: the more restrained one had a simple semicircular seat back; the more flamboyant was flared and wing-shaped. In both its basic shape (like a giant ice cream cone on a cross-shaped stand) and its materials (open wire mesh with a single disc-shaped cushion, or foam covered and upholstered in brightly coloured fabric), the Cone chair marked a turning point in modern furniture design, not just in Denmark but internationally. It was also one of the earliest designs in the 1950s to presage the design revolution of the 1960s, and to suggest an association between geometric shapes and 'the look'.

One version of the Cone chair had an open wire structure. In this form it was clearly related to a group of wire furniture designed by Panton for Plus-Linje in 1960, including

stools and tables made of cylindrical wire mesh, and the T2 easy chair, composed of a hemispherical wire basket seat balanced on a cylindrical wire ring base, the seat being lined with loose disc-shaped foam cushions. The idea of a hemispherical seat balanced on a ring-shaped base was later used by other designers working in different materials, particularly plastics, with several different variants being produced in Italy, such as the Eco chair designed by Cesare Leonardi and Franco Stagi for Bernini in Florence in 1969. In the USA the firm of Thornton and Sandberg produced a design called the Bowl chair, illustrated in *Industrial Design* in February 1966. According to the magazine, the reasoning behind it was that:

The designers discovered that very few people sit in one position in a chair for any length of time. Rather, small changes of position occur regularly at short intervals – these changes are limited by the static chair's construction. The Bowl chair attacks this problem by providing a comfortable seat and then making it completely free to follow the sitter's movements. The chair is also provided with a separate ring base of laminated plywood with a padded edge, which restricts mobility while allowing complete adjustability.

In Italy at the end of the decade Studio Rossi Molinari designed the Toy chair for the Vicenza-based firm of Totem di Ganni, which consisted of a hemispherical shell set into a cube-shaped frame. Illustrated in *Domus* in March 1969, the contrasting geometric forms used in this design were highlighted by the fact that it was made of clear perspex.

Another way in which geometric imagery was expressed was through circular modular stacking furniture. This was the case with the London Combination modular seating range designed by Geoffrey Harcourt for Artifort in 1967, the various elements of which could be combined to form banks of square, rectangular or circular seating. In the case of the latter, each seat formed a quarter section of a circle. A similar idea was used by Rodolfo Bonetto in his plastic 700 Quattroquarti tables for Bernini dating from 1969, each of which formed a quarter segment of a circle. The way in which this system was designed meant that the units could be combined in various different arrangements, both horizontally (to form either a circle or a wavy line) or vertically (to form a corner stacking shelf unit). More common still were small circular stacking tables, where the stacking facility was intended to reduce the bulk of the units when stored rather than to create shelving. Two Italian systems of this kind were Gianfranco Frattini's three-legged wooden stacking tables for Cassina (model 780) dating from 1966, which formed a compact cylinder when stacked together in groups of four; and the plastic stacking tables designed by Giotto Stoppino for Kartell in 1968 (models 4905 and 4907), produced in groups of three.

Spheres, somewhat limited in their application to furniture, were more successfully and widely adopted in the fast-developing field of electrical appliances, where they were used for the casings of various products, from radios and televisions to vacuum cleaners and stereo speakers. In most cases, however, spherical forms were adopted not because of their practical or functional advantages, but because of their specific association with Space Age modernity, a fail-safe marketing ploy in an age obsessed with scientific progress. The use of spherical forms immediately gave a product 'the look', which as well as being visually attractive, was clearly

112

intended to convince the consumer that, technically as well as aesthetically, this product was at the cutting edge, whether of vacuum-powered suction, sound reproduction or image transmission. As stand-alone stereophonic sound systems began to replace built-in mono speakers, manufacturers had to devise casings to house this new technology. Whereas most opted for the predictable solution of a rectangular box, one manufacturer, the Clairtone Sound Corporation of Canada, produced a system with spherical speakers (see p109). Designed by Hugh Spencer and John Magyar, this remarkable and memorable system, featured in *Domus* in April 1964, had two large spherical metal speakers supported on steel bars on either side of a rectangular unit containing a combined radio and record player. The designers' justification for the use of this form was that sound was emitted from the spheres in all directions.

Spherical forms were also adopted by television manufacturers during the late 1960s, again largely for visual and symbolic effect. At this time television, particularly colour television, was still regarded as something of a technical novelty, so consumers were keen to highlight the fact that they owned the latest model. In August 1965 Verner Panton designed a futuristic three-level sound and television system for Wega-Radio GMBH of Stuttgart which was shown at the German Radio Exhibition. The system, a prototype intended as an illustration of the future of home entertainment, included a hi-fi composed of various cylindrical elements resembling a drum-kit, and a suspended spherical television screen. A classic spherical television of the period was the white plastic console designed by Arthur D Bracegirdle for the American firm of Keracolor (see p109) which, like Eero Aarnio's Globe chair, sat on a circular pedestal base. Even the humble vacuum cleaner assumed the Space Age aesthetics of 'the look', an example being the spherical model produced by Hoover called the Constellation. Originally introduced as early as 1952, variants of the Constellation were sold right up until the late 1960s. Later models were said to float on air because their exhaust was emitted downwards under the metal ring on which the machine rested. In theory this created a cushion of air which made the vacuum easier to pull around, but the down side of this was that it reduced the suction power of the machine, and had the unfortunate effect of blowing dust out rather than sucking it in when the machine was lifted off the floor.

Modernism did continue to hold sway during the 1960s, and function was not always treated as a secondary consideration. Sometimes, by happy coincidence, geometric form followed technical function. This was the case in the field of lighting where, in addition to tubular and cylindrical forms, domes and spheres were also widely adopted and often proved the ideal solution for casing bulbs and diffusing light. In Britain hemispherical forms were successfully exploited by Robert Welch in his pendant and floor lamps dating from 1966 for the futuristically named firm Lumitron, a small company which had hitherto specialized in contract lighting for architectural purposes. Of this range Robert Welch has written in his autobiographical work *Hand and Machine*: 'I have never known a design concept appear, as this one did, in the proverbial flash of inspiration; it fell into place as if it were pre-ordained, and not just one lamp but a series of different types, each closely related to one another.' The materials for the range, which included eight related designs, were as

futuristic as the name and the aesthetic: the underside of the lamp through which the light was diffused was made of opal perspex, surmounted by a domed cover made of smoked grey perspex, with fittings made of satin-finished anodized aluminium.

The alternative to using opal perspex or glass to diffuse the glare from a naked bulb was to have a louvered cover, a formula widely adopted during the 1960s. In 1966 Merchant Adventurers produced both wide cylindrical and hemispherical pendant lampshades with enamelled metal shades, which had either single or double louvers in a pattern of concentric rings. Along with Merchant Adventurers, one of the most forward-looking British lighting manufacturers of the 1950s had been Rotaflex, established in 1953, for whom the architects John and Sylvia Reid acted as consultant designers until the early 1960s. It was the Reids who had been responsible for introducing geometric forms into British lighting towards the end of the 1950s, signalling a move away from the prevailing organic trend which they themselves had also been instrumental in establishing. This shift in aesthetic was first indicated by a range of floor and table lamps dating from the late 1950s that had open drum-shaped pierced and enamelled aluminium shades. By 1960 Rotaflex were marketing the D range of cylindrical pendant and ceiling lamps with circular louvred diffusers. It was characteristic of the free-ranging and flexible approach adopted by Rotaflex that it produced a wide variety of fittings concurrently, some in the pared-down Modernist idiom, such as the cylindrical Multigroove downlighters advertised in the *Architectural Review* in June 1964; and others in a more sculptural and expressive style, such as the ribbed plastic egg-shaped, spherical and tear-shaped lampshades advertised in *House Beautiful* in January 1962. The latter were described in this advert as the 'exciting shape of lighting', but in fact it was through a more understated form of expression that the 'look' of 1960s lighting came to be embodied.

In 1959 Rotaflex decided to branch out from the domestic market into contract lighting, and shortly afterwards it signed an agreement with the American firm of Lightolier that gave it access to greater technical expertise in this field. Its first range of recessed incandescent fittings, designed by Derek Phillips and Associates, was launched in 1961. Another new area that Rotaflex made a strategic decision to enter at the end of the 1950s was spotlighting, and this too became increasingly important for the company during the course of the ensuing decade. Their first spotlight, the Universal, designed by John and Sylvia Reid, was launched in 1959, and won a Design Centre Award in 1961. This fitting was internationally successful, and was produced under licence in the USA by Lightolier. Subsequently Rotaflex engaged the experienced industrial design team of Robert Heritage and Partners to develop their spotlight range, as well as to design fittings for fluorescent bulbs. This resulted in two further Design Centre Awards, one in 1966 for the Quartet Major range of display lighting, and a second two years later for the Silverspan range of fluorescent lightfittings. The attachments for the latter were designed by Luciano Zucchi, who later became their design manager. According to Zucchi in an article entitled 'Spotlight on Rotaflex' in *Design* magazine in November 1969, the firm's philosophy was: 'We don't sell lightfittings – we sell lighting.' Its final triumph of the decade,

top
Advert for louvered pendant lamps (MA 3460) designed by Paul Boissevain for Merchant Adventurers, 1966. Spherical, domed and cylindrical forms dominated 'the look' of light-fittings during the 1960s.
above
Advert for the Superjet spotlight and the Supermini table lamp by Concord Rotaflex, 1969.

however, somewhat belies this assertion, as the company became the recipient of yet another Design Centre Award in 1969 for one of its most stylish and fashion-conscious spotlight designs to date, the spherical Superjet. Rotaflex recognized that lighting was a field in which the 'look' of a product could not be assessed in isolation from its function: progress had to be made on both fronts at the same time.

In Denmark the firm of Louis Poulsen displayed a similar commitment to the functional aspects of lighting design, but were equally conscious of 'the look', and it was this company that produced perhaps the single most inventive and memorable spherical lighting design of the early 1960s, the Visir (Visor) or Moon lampshade designed by Verner Panton. Composed of a series of circular metal bands positioned concentrically on a central pivot, the Visir offered complete flexibility as to how the graduated strips were arranged: either fully open to form a sphere, closed to form a circle, or partly fanned out to form a hemisphere. Because of its shape, the Visir had a genuinely Space Age aesthetic, a feature emphasized when it was used in interiors created by the designer himself, such as the Unika Vaev showroom in New York designed in 1961. When used by others, such as Olive Sullivan in a domestic interior created for *House and Garden* in June 1965, the Visir lamp was exploited to dramatic effect as a signifier of ultra-modernity. A pendant lamp designed by Panton for Louis Poulsen later in the decade embodied a later

interpretation of 'the look', and has since also been recognized as a design classic of the 1960s. This was Panton's hemispherical Flower Pot series dating from 1968, made of brightly coloured enamelled metal, and possibly produced in response to the flower-power craze. In this design, as with Robert Welch's pendant lamps for Lumitron, the dome of the lampshade was suspended over an inverted hemisphere, also made of enamelled metal in this case, which diffused the light from the bulb.

One of the most innovative Contemporary lighting designers in the USA during the 1950s had been George Nelson, working in conjunction with the Howard Miller Clock Company. It was Nelson who had designed the widely imitated ribbed plastic Bubble lamps during the 1950s, made in a variety of organic ovoid shapes. During the 1960s Nelson continued his alliance with this firm, but gradually left behind the Contemporary style in favour of 'the look'. By the mid-1960s his designs had become at once more geometric in their forms and more textural in their patterns, the new trend being for shades constructed from interwoven leaves of plastic or copper. Also in the USA was the New York-based firm of Habitat Inc, which produced some of the most avant-garde American designs for lighting and furniture during the 1960s, and which exploited the archetypal forms of 'the look' most fully. In a feature on 'Lighting's New Look' in *Industrial Design* in November 1967, two dramatic works by Habitat were

opposite
Visir or Moon pendant lamp designed by Verner Panton for Louis Poulsen, 1960. It is suspended above three wire Cone chairs by the same designer for Plus-Linje, 1958.
above right
Advert for lampshades designed by George Nelson for Howard Miller, 1962. In the 1950s, Nelson had set the trend with his organic plastic-coated Bubble lamps. During the early 1960s, he evolved a new aesthetic which emphasized textures rather than forms.
right
Flower Pot pendant lamps designed by Verner Panton for Louis Poulsen, 1968. They combine the hemispherical forms of 'the look' with the vibrant colours of pop.

illustrated: a tall cylindrical floor lamp, 30 centimetres in diameter and 130 centimetres tall, made of translucent plastic; and a huge spherical lamp, 90 centimetres in diameter, which was described as 'the largest one-piece plastic globe in existence'.

The Italians, who had already developed considerable expertise in the field of lighting during the 1950s, created a vast array of new designs during the 1960s, many of which adopted the circular motifs of 'the look'. In 1962 Tobia Scarpa designed two spun-metal pendant lamps for Flos called Nictala and Nelumbium, composed of domed, spherical, ring and disc-shaped elements. Pierced dots further emphasized the circular theme. Flos, one of the most creative of the new generation of Italian lighting companies, was founded in 1960 by the owners of two leading furniture manufacturers, Dino Gavina and Cesare Cassina, with the specific objective of producing lighting that would complement the modern aesthetics of their furniture. Gavina brought in two designers who were already involved in his furniture business, Achille and Pier Giacomo Castiglioni, who had a major impact on Flos over the next decade. In 1962 they designed the Arco floor lamp, which rapidly became recognized as a classic of 1960s design, and which had a dome-shaped perforated aluminium shade attached to the end of a long arched stainless steel arm set into a marble block. Thus, in this design hemispherical forms were twice repeated, once in the hood of the lampshade, once in the arc of the stem, making it doubly dramatic. That the Castiglioni brothers realized that 'the look' of 1960s lighting was integrally linked to the exploration of hemispherical forms is suggested by another design from 1962, the dome-shaped Relemme pendant lamp.

Another leading lighting manufacturer in Italy was the Milan-based firm of Artemide, also known as Studio Artemide. Founded in 1960 by Ernesto Gismondi, Artemide also made a major contribution in the field of furniture where it excelled in the use of plastics. Vico Magistretti, one of its leading designers, designed both furniture and lighting, his single most famous creation being the Eclipse bedside lamp of 1966. Made of enamelled aluminium, the Eclipse perfectly captured 'the look' of the mid-1960s through its unusual form: a spherical casing surmounting a hemispherical base. The key point about this design, however, was that, like Panton's Visir lamp, it had a visor in the form of a revolving cover which could be pulled around the front of the lamp to screen the light. Other designers who created lighting for Artemide during the course of the decade included Sergio Mazza and Emma Schweinberger Gismondi. In a feature on the company which appeared in Domus in April 1964 to mark the opening of its new Milan showroom designed by Sergio Mazza, a wide selection of ultra-modern appliances was illustrated. Made of a combination of metal and plastics, many of these fittings were either dome-shaped or spherical, although most of the basic forms were either compressed or extended in some way, the latter resulting in egg-shaped forms. In the commentary that accompanied this article, strong emphasis was laid on the way in which these curved forms contrasted with the rectilinear nature of the interiors for which they were intended, and of the importance of the creative tension arising from this juxtaposition.

Another seminal Italian manufacturer of the 1960s, which produced both furniture and lighting, and was equally influential in both fields, was Kartell. Like Artemide it manufactured goods in a variety of materials but was closely associated with plastics in particular. Founded in 1949 by Giulio Castelli, Kartell came to prominence slightly later than Studio Artemide, having concentrated during the 1950s on the production of a modest range of domestic accessories designed by Gino Columbini. It was not until the early to mid-1960s that it moved up a gear and expanded the range and scale of the objects it produced, and a key factor in Kartell's success was its adoption of the aesthetics of 'the look'. An advert for Kartell lighting in Domus in March 1967, followed by a short feature in November 1967, showed a variety of pendant and floor lamps based on spherical and dome-shaped forms. Achille and Pier Giacomo Castiglioni designed several dome-shaped pendant lamps, produced in different coloured plastics, while Joe Colombo designed a ceiling lamp in the shape of an inverted dome, and a series of table lamps in which a pierced cylindrical metal casing acted as a support for a compressed opal plastic sphere. The Kartell family of circular lighting forms at this date also included two floor lamps: one designed by Gae Aulenti, composed of interlocking circular discs of clear perspex slotted together around a central bulb to create a sphere; and another designed by Marcello Siard, in which an opal perspex ball sat on a perspex ring, so that the light radiated in all directions.

Other Italian lighting manufacturers that were similarly committed to modern design and allied themselves closely with the aesthetics of 'the look' included Arteluce, Stilnovo, Guzzini, Martinelli-Luce and O-Luce. Joe Colombo created a number of designs for O-Luce during the early 1960s, all with strong curvilinear or circular elements, a group of which were illustrated in a feature in Domus in December 1964. These included a helmet-shaped pendant lamp made of aluminium; a table lamp constructed from an inner cylinder of translucent opal plastic and an outer cylinder of opalescent plastic pierced with a pattern of circles; and a spherical table or floor lamp which could be swivelled in order to direct the light. The Milan-based firm of Stilnovo had established their reputation for avant-garde lighting during the 1950s, and continued to produce ultra-modern designs during the following decade. The sphere was the ultimate expression of allegiance to the 'look', and it was fundamental to a group of lamps produced by Stilnovo featured in Domus in April 1968. One particular range of floor lamps, table lamps and wall lamps all shared a distinctive spotlight head, housed in a compact spherical enamelled metal casing. Whereas these proto high-tech designs were clean cut and geometric, other spherical lamps produced by Stilnovo at the same date were more organic. One design, which could be used either as a floor or table lamp, was composed of three spheres, one inside the other, the inner globe being translucent, the outer two being transparent, all three sitting on a curvilinear pedestal ring made of enamelled aluminium.

Among the first purely spherical lamps were those designed by the inventive Gino Sarfatti for his firm Arteluce in 1963, which were featured in Domus in June of that year. Made of anodized aluminium, the series included both table lamps and wall lamps, a novel feature being that the spherical casing could be swivelled to alter the direction of the light. In 1965 Sarfatti launched another flexible spherical light fitting, the Ondulux table lamp. In this lamp, featured in Industrial Design in June 1965, half the sphere was made of metal, half

opposite
Arco lamp designed by Achille and Pier Giacomo Castiglioni for Flos, 1962. Minimalist but luxurious at the same time, this floor lamp embodies the hemispherical 'look' of lighting design through its domed shade and arched stem.

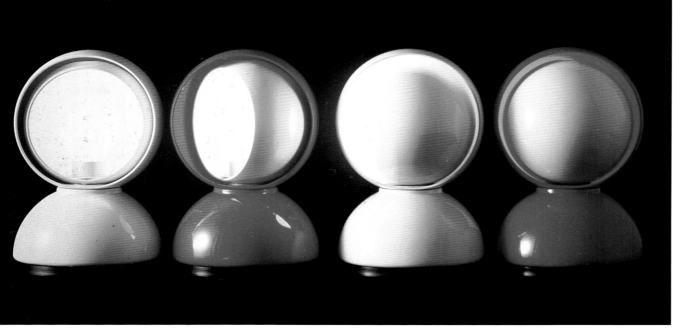

above
Jucker table lamp designed
by Tobia Scarpa for Flos,
1963.
left
Eclipse bedside lamp
designed by Vico Magistretti
for Artemide, 1966. Both
the Jucker and Eclipse
lamps work on the principle
of being able to direct and
control the amount of light.
While the domed shade of
the Jucker swivels up and
down, the Eclipse lamp can
be rotated through 180°
within its spherical casing.

of clear plastic, and the globe rested freely on a ring-shaped base, thus enabling the light source to be pointed in different directions. Spheres, hemispheres and compressed spheres dominated the aesthetics of Italian lighting during the late 1960s and were clearly linked to the contemporary fascination with space exploration. The firm of Guzzini produced a striking range of lamps in 1968 called Disco designed by Cesare Casati, the organic plastic shades of which resembled the planet Saturn, with an inner globe encircled by an outer ring. The Disco lampshade could be either suspended from the ceiling or supported by a floor-standing metal cylinder in a horizontal or vertical position. Space Age aesthetics were also exploited in a radical table lamp designed in 1968 by Ugo La Pietra for Zema Elettronica of Milan called the Globo Tissurato. This was a clear perspex sphere pierced with small circles, which was suspended on the rim of a cylinder above a pierced inverted hemisphere. A dimmable bulb illuminated the latter, the upper sphere serving as a reflector.

Although cylindrical forms dominated the lighting industry during the first half of the 1960s, tableware that combined spherical and cylindrical elements also began to appear during the second half of the decade, such as the MQ2 range designed by David Queensberry and Roy Midwinter for Midwinter in 1967. In ceramics it was the Italians who created some of the most adventurous forms. One particularly outstanding firm was Gabbianelli, which produced simple but striking accessories decorated in monochrome glazes, not dissimilar in their appearance and aesthetic appeal to contemporary Italian plastics. A feature on the firm's latest work in *Domus* in April 1967 illustrated the DA range of spherical vases and boxes designed by Roberto Arioli, along with cylindrical umbrella stands, cylindrical mugs with double ring handles, and a circular hors-d'œuvres tray. An interesting variant on the circular theme was the OPI range of vases, bowls, ashtrays and cigarette holders, where the basic form was cylindrical, but the vessel became concave at the centre and square at the rim.

Not dissimilar in its approach was the firm of Ceramica Pozzi, founded by Franco Pozzi and run by his two sons, Carlo and Ambrogio Pozzi. Like Gabbianelli, Ceramica Pozzi produced families of forms rather than stand-alone pieces. In a feature on the company in *Domus* in September 1967, the veteran designer Gio Ponti wrote admiringly of the way in which these families of forms were conceived. 'It would seem that Ambrogio Pozzi's design grows above all out of the pleasure of turning useful objects into toys. Objects that hook onto each other, that fit into one another, that form a new object when placed on top of each other, that have another function when turned upside down, that look different when the arrangement of their parts is changed.' The use of geometric shapes as building blocks for the creation of composite forms recalls the toys of Hans von Klier, a comparison which makes Ponti's reference to 'the pleasure of turning useful objects into toys' all the more pertinent. At the end of the decade Ambrogio Pozzi designed another distinctive family of forms based on cubes, circles and spheres which, although still made by Ceramica Pozzi, were specifically created for the fashion designer Pierre Cardin. The range was called Environment, and the idea was that these accessories would complement Cardin's clothes, and thus extend the influence

below
Advert for the Italian firm, Studio Artemide, 1967. Together with Kartell and Flos, Artemide was one of the leading manufacturers of plastic furniture and lighting during the 1960s. The Giano drum table on the left was designed by Emma Schweinberger Gismondi in 1967; the square Demetrio tables were designed by Vico Magistretti in 1964; and the Nesso lamp was designed by Gruppo Architetti Urbanisti Città Nova in 1965.

Besides being beautifully designed and made, easily erected, endlessly adaptable and extremely economical, the Hille Storage Wall System actually saves floor space. How?

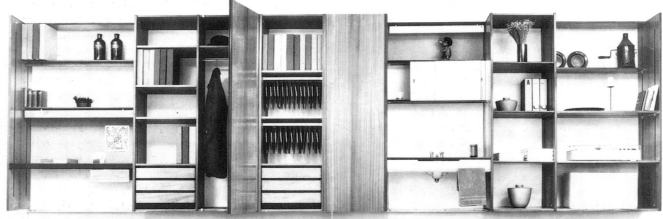

Look, no feet!

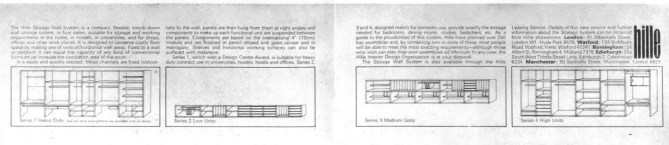

of 'the look' into the office and the home. According to an article in *Domus* in September 1969, the range was conceived as 'a way of creating the possibility of a formal unity between "the things we wear" and "the things we use" or look at: from attire to ambiance.' Thus the imagery in Cardin's outfits, such as a circular PVC raincoat decorated with a target pattern, was directly reflected in the forms of Pozzi's accessories. The name Environment recalls Terence Conran's Habitat, and the suggestion in both cases was of a total design package. 'The look', it was implied, was so comprehensive that it could shape every aspect of one's lifestyle.

Cubes, Checks and Stripes

During the early 1960s forms became chunkier, and the spindly, tapering and splayed furniture legs of the 1950s were abandoned in favour of straight, solid blocks or square-section steel bars. Some aspects of the Tulip Phenomenon still persisted, but gradually the tendency for vessels to be exaggeratedly thick or thin, or for forms to flare and taper from one extreme to the other, was largely abandoned in favour of greater regularity. Square and rectangular shapes and patterns became widespread during the early 1960s, and an important new geometric form that entered the design vocabulary at this date was the cube. Closely linked with the cube was an interest in modular design, an idea that spread from architecture to three-dimensional design. Various local authorities in Britain had grouped together during the 1950s to develop prefabricated modular building systems for schools, such as CLASP, which was later used extensively on the new campus buildings designed by Robert Matthew, Johnson-Marshall and Partners at the University of York. During the 1960s it was increasingly common for blocks of flats to be constructed from prefabricated units or clad with prefabricated modular panels, initiatives that grew out of pressure on local authorities and developers to build quickly and cheaply. The SFI panel system, made of foamed concrete, reinforced concrete and glass, was developed by the Department of Architecture and Civic Design in the Greater London Council in the mid-1960s, for example, and by 1967 was being used in twenty-five building schemes, a fact recorded admiringly in an article called 'The British Face-Up to the Module' in the American magazine *Industrial Design* in July/August 1967.

Even before the start of the decade there had been a growing interest in modular furniture, an idea prompted by the development of unit furniture in the USA during the 1940s. Pioneered by George Nelson, design director of Herman Miller, unit furniture was designed so that different items within a range could be combined in a flexible arrangement. Modular furniture was based on the same basic principles, but the system was more highly codified and the units were more regularized. By the early 1960s two basic types of modular furniture were being promoted, modular seating and modular storage, cube forms being important to both. Modular storage was widely adopted in the home, especially in kitchens and bedrooms, whereas modular seating was mainly associated with public buildings.

Important and pioneering research was also undertaken in the field of domestic storage in Scandinavia after the war, particularly in Sweden and Denmark. In their choice of materials, particularly their use of high-quality wood finishes, the Scandinavians laid great emphasis on aesthetics even in the field of storage, whereas for the Americans the primary concerns were flexibility and functionalism. The Scandinavians were just as interested in functionalism, but they adopted a more pragmatic approach to domestic planning which presaged their later interest in ergonomics. For example, in wardrobe storage they measured the average dimensions of different types of clothing in order to calculate the optimum dimensions for hanging space and drawer size. In 1952 the Danish designers Børge Mogensen and Grethe Meyer collaborated on the development of a radical new storage system based on sectional units. Designed to meet every conceivable domestic storage need, their system was formulated on a detailed analysis of the average measurements of common domestic objects needing to be stored. This resulted in the Boligens Byggeskabe system, known as the BB series, first produced in 1954, and named after the firm for which it was originally designed, although it was later produced by other manufacturers. Although formulated on the principles of modularity, all units being based on multiples of 6.6 centimetres, the BB series was built-in rather than freestanding, and was most suitable for wall-to-wall or floor-to-ceiling storage installations. Ahead of its time when it first appeared, the BB system remained in production throughout the 1960s. It still looked ultra-modern in 1968 when the firm of Cox began to import it into Britain.

British furniture design of the early 1960s combined concepts from both America and Scandinavia, taking the idea of no-nonsense functionalism and total flexibility from the former, but aspiring to the refinement and quality of finish of the latter. This combination of influences can be seen in the designs by Robert Heritage for the firm of Archie Shine, in particular his Heritage range of wall storage units, the recipient of another Design Centre Award in 1963. Another firm which seamlessly melded the American and Scandinavian approaches was Hille, where the chief storage designers were Alan Turville and John Lewak. Their Wall Storage System, inspired by George Nelson's Comprehensive Storage System of 1959, also won a Design Centre Award in 1965, indicating the penchant of the Council of Industrial Design for understated functionalist design solutions. Designed to suit the needs of the contract market, particularly the study bedrooms required in the halls of residence at the many new universities being built at this date, the Wall Storage System had a steel frame which could be wall-mounted without legs, on to which a variety of plastic laminate or flush teak, beech and mahogany veneered wooden panels could be fixed. The system was designed so that it could be used in a variety of different domestic, office and institutional situations, and components included a washbasin, a fold-down bed, and attachments for filing systems, as well as drawers and cupboards. Four different series were created, including a heavy-duty floor-to-ceiling system suitable for study bedrooms; low units for use as sideboards; medium units appropriate for television and hi-fi storage in living rooms; and high units suitable as wardrobes. From this date onwards the idea of fitted wardobes, in particular, became very popular in Britain. The Stag Cabinet Company of Nottingham, for example, advertised a neat Scandinavian-inspired system called Opus 22 in the *Architectural Review* in February 1967. Described as 'beautifully designed wardrobe units with the built-in look', the range was designed by Walter Muller in Germany and was produced under licence in the UK by Stag.

top
Common Room at Falmer
House, University of
Sussex, designed by Sir
Basil Spence, 1960. On
view is the H range of mod-
ular furniture designed by
the architect and manufac-
tured by John Higgin
(Furniture) Ltd.
above
Advert from 1967 for the
Forum range, designed by
Robin Day for Hille, 1964.

left
Action Office range
designed by George Nelson
for Herman Miller, 1964.
Intended to meet the
changing needs of the modern office, this range was
developed following
ergonomic research by
Robert Propst at the
Herman Miller Research
Corporation. A 1966 advert
proclaimed: 'Foot bars and
arm rests, bumper edges
and recessed legs encour-
age relaxed, active posture.
A variety of working attitudes evolve from co-
ordinated equipment of
different heights, widths
and functions. Preserving
independent work
situations, forming open
sided work areas, and
supporting the attainment
of meaningful activity, Action
Office provides a new world
in which to work.'

Apart from the bedroom, the room most likely to be infiltrated by modular storage furniture was the kitchen. The fitted kitchen had grown out of Modernist ideology about the house as a machine for living in, closely related in turn to the idea of the kitchen as a laboratory for the preparation of food. This concept was enthusiastically adopted in the USA after the Second World War, although closer attention to cosmetics resulted in the repackaging of the idea in a more palatable form as the housewife's 'dream kitchen'. In Britain the firm of Wrighton became market leaders with the launch of their colourful Californian range designed by Nigel Walters in 1958. Ten years later they were to win a Design Centre Award for their newly launched International range, also designed by Walters. In this carefully conceived and thoughtfully detailed range, based on a 10 centimetre (4 inch) module so that it could be sold in Europe as well as Britain, all the basic characteristics of the flexible modular fitted kitchen which are taken for granted today were first established.

It was in the field of modular seating that the association between furniture and the cube was most obvious. As with modular storage, the rationale behind the idea was originally developed in the USA, and once again the man behind it was George Nelson. Nelson's Modular Seating Group, made under licence in the UK by Hille from around 1963, gave consumers the choice of combining upholstered bench seating, sofa seating with back rests and optional arm-rests, low wooden storage units, and low plastic laminate-topped tables, all supported on a framework of satin chrome finished square-section steel bar. It was Nelson's ideas that inspired Robin Day's Form Group of 1961 and his later, heavier and more block-like Plus Group. Contemporary adverts emphasized that 'The scope for different arrangements is prodigious.'

As the fashion for tapering turned wooden legs and spindly legs made of steel rod declined during the early 1960s, they were replaced with forms and frameworks that were much more regular and overtly geometric. Influenced by the aesthetics of modular seating, many stand-alone armchairs and sofas began to take on squarer proportions, a feature that would become an important expression of 'the look'. Once again this move had been prefigured in the USA, this time by Florence Knoll at Knoll International. During the 1950s Florence Knoll had carried out the less high-profile design work undertaken by the company in the field of office furniture and public seating. Ultimately these designs, which she referred to as the 'meat and potatoes' of Knoll's output as a whole, were to become as influential as Saarinen's eye-catching white plastic Tulip chair and Bertoia's intriguing wire-grid Diamond chair. Florence Knoll pioneered the use of square-section steel bar as a frame for chairs, sofas, desks, tables and cupboards, a simple but highly effective idea which had an enormous influence on the mass-market American furniture industry throughout the 1960s. However, whereas at Knoll these materials had been adopted as an expression of precision and finesse, in the hands of other manufacturers they became simply a crude construction formula. Where the use of tubular steel during the 1930s had led naturally to the development of curved forms for furniture, so the use of square-section steel bar during the 1960s led equally naturally to an aesthetic based on square and rectangular forms. Robin Day's Club chair of 1960 typifies these trends with its square-section stainless-steel frame, its square cushions, and the

square pattern of its buttoned upholstery. Later, in 1964, came Robin Day's Forum range which had chromium-plated steel-bar legs attached to a comb-jointed solid afrormosia frame, with thick square and rectangular cushions. The Forum range was the ultimate expression of the chair as cube and the sofa as double or triple cube, and it was described in an advert in the Architectural Review in December 1967 as being 'beautifully designed, precision-built, luxuriously comfortable'. Similar materials and aesthetics were adopted in the Concave modular seating range by Westnofa, advertised in Design magazine in April 1968. Westnofa was the name of a consortium of furniture manufacturers in West Norway who were very active in marketing their products in Britain during the 1960s. Having concentrated initially on furniture that reflected the Scandinavian Modern style, particularly that of the Danes, by the late 1960s the Norwegians were abandoning their 'native' style in favour of a more international corporate aesthetic reflecting the influence of the Americans.

The adoption of solid block-like forms and the transition from metal to wood were phenomena by no means limited to the work of Robin Day. By 1963 such features had been assimilated as an essential expression of 'the look' of British furniture design in general. In addition to the role of modular furniture in determining this trend, another important external factor was the contract market, and in particular the growth in demand from the public sector, especially in the field of higher education. According to Gillian Naylor in an article written for the American magazine Industrial Design in March 1965:
The new hospitals and universities that are springing up throughout Britain have provided the stimulus for a growth of experimentation. The architects of these establishments demanded furniture of high standards, both in appearance and functional efficiency, but which was inexpensive, easy to produce and simple to install.
The burgeoning university market was a particularly lucrative one because not only were numerous new academic buildings being erected, but considerable resources were also being invested in residential accommodation. As most of the new universities and colleges were campus-based, the demand for modern institutional furniture to complement the confidently modern architecture was considerable. The prevalence of strongly geometric buildings, normally rectilinear but sometimes triangular or hexagonal, appears to have fostered the geometric aesthetic in furniture, while the widespread use of exposed brick, concrete and wood within the interiors of these buildings may have prompted the adoption of wood as a standard material for furniture.

A typical British furniture firm of the early 1960s was Design Furnishing Contracts which produced the Combination range of study-bedroom furniture for university residences, advertised in the Architectural Review in October 1963. Designed by Roland Gibbard, the range included beds, wardrobes, cupboards, desks, armchairs and chests of drawers, and was complemented by the Plus range of modular seating, a flexible knock-down range designed for public spaces. Earlier that year the firm had won a Design Centre Award for their square-shaped interlocking and stacking chairs designed by Clive Bacon, the adverts for which made a point of mentioning that the chairs met the requirements of British Standard 3030 for school furniture, and were therefore guaranteed as practical and hardwearing. Also specifically

Campus competes

designed to suit the needs of universities was the H range of modular furniture by the architect Sir Basil Spence, who was responsible for designing Falmer House and the Physics Building at the University of Sussex and St Aidan's College at the University of Durham. Produced by the Lancashire firm of John Higgin (Furniture) Ltd, the H range, as advertised in 1964, included chairs, desks, tables and settees, with thick rectilinear H-shaped wooden frames.

Another manufacturer that clearly had its sights on the university market was LM Furniture, which marketed a new range called the Campus Group in 1967. Specifically targeted at the needs of the new universities, the Campus range was adopted by a host of academic institutions, including the Universities of Essex, Leicester, Strathclyde and Warwick. LM Furniture was taken over by Ryman Conran in June 1969 (itself a new company formed as a result of a merger between Ryman and the Conran group), and later that year the Campus range appeared in the first full-colour Habitat *Creative Living* catalogue. Somewhat less heavy and slab-like than the H range, this series had a square plan but the supports for the tables and seating were round rather than square. Even Henry Rothschild's firm, Primavera, which had craft shops in London and Cambridge at this date, moved away from commissioning individual items of furniture to contract design for the university market. By the mid-1960s the Primavera Design Group was carrying out an increasing amount of work in the university sector, including furnishings for the new Students Union and Refectory building at the University of Newcastle designed by William Whitfield in 1964; and for Duryard Hall at Exeter University in 1965–6, a contract which resulted in the creation of the Exeter chair and the masterful Exeter dining table designed by Martin Tallents. In 1966 adverts appeared in the architectural press for Primavera's square-shaped beech Aberdeen chairs, designed the previous year by Cuthbert Conn for the new Science Library at the University of Aberdeen. A group of woven upholstery fabrics known as the University Collection had also been launched in 1965, while the previous year the striped University blanket came on the market. Originally designed for the Wolfson Building at St Anne's College, Oxford, and intended to complement a plain low wooden bed also produced by Primavera, the blanket was the recipient of a Design Centre Award in 1965.

One British manufacturer that penetrated both the contract market and the domestic retail market was Conran Furniture. Its success was due in part to the company's close relationship with the Conran Design Group, which both designed the furniture and often specified its usage in the interiors it designed. In the domestic market the reason for its success were the sales opportunities provided by Habitat, the interiors of which were also designed by the Conran Design Group, thus presenting the public with a complete package. Wooden construction and geometric shapes of the most basic and simple kind formed the essence of the Conran style during the mid-1960s. Slab-like bunk beds and benches, and cube-shaped storage units which could be stacked together at random were available in 1966, for example, and proved enormously popular. What was radical about Habitat was that it made no-nonsense knock-down contract-style furniture available to the proverbial 'man in the street'. Thus the division that had previously existed between the domestic and the

contract market was finally broken down, and the public were able to take advantage of the cost savings resulting from simplified design and bulk furniture production. This meant that the young people passing through the new universities were afterwards able to go out and buy furniture in a similar style to the furnishings in their study-bedrooms.

While the Italians' love affair with plastics triggered off a new interest in circular and organic forms, the Americans remained wedded to the concepts of rationalism through rectilinearity in the field of office furniture. Throughout the 1960s rectilinearity remained the dominant aesthetic in American office furniture, whether embodied in steel-framed furniture, such as that produced by Art Metal (the company to which Knoll International was eventually sold in 1959), or whether combined with the Scandinavian Modern style and given expression in wood, as in the work of Jens Risom. In a feature in *Industrial Design* in February 1966, Barbara Allen noted:
In discussing the use of different materials for office furnishings, Risom's strong prejudice for wood and fabric is evident. He feels that their 'live' qualities add necessary warmth to an office whose exterior is constructed largely from 'dead' materials. Although he realises that wood and fabric are considered more luxurious than steel and vinyl, Risom says 'you are not designing for a reform school'.
The link between rectilinearity and rationalism in American office design, and the idea of geometric forms as an expression of control systems, were not just fanciful interpretations by sociologists during the 1960s. Similar conclusions were reached by professional design commentators, who suggested that there was a direct connection between corporate philosophies, corporate systems and corporate aesthetics. In an article entitled 'Office Design in the USA' written by Claud Bunyard in *Design* magazine in May 1964 the writer pointed to the potential risk of designers exerting too much control over every visual detail:
There is a danger that such absolute control may become authoritarian to an objectionable degree, especially when it excludes all expression by individual staff members of their personal tastes … When artistic discipline becomes tyranny there is something wrong with it. Designers are not infallible in their judgement.
However, although critical of some aspects of American office design as an expression of corporate control systems, the author concluded that the positive characteristics of American office furniture in the mid-1960s outnumbered these disadvantages:
American office furniture is essentially American in feeling and inventiveness. Its main characteristics are integrity, clean lines, classic proportions and sturdiness. The production quality of the best is very good indeed. This applies to both wood and steel furniture. There are several makes of furniture in the lower price brackets which also achieve a high standard of design and quality.
Of the two firms that had led the field during the 1950s, Knoll and Herman Miller, neither managed to sustain the same level of creative intensity during the ensuing decade, and both, to a certain extent, relied on their earlier achievements to carry them through. However, although the pace was slower – a reflection to a certain extent of the size of these two companies, both of which now operated on a global level, and of the rigorous but slow-moving systems of research and

development now in place – there was still progress. At Herman Miller, for example, George Nelson and his team developed the concept of the Action Office in 1964, a series of flexible units that could be configured in various ways to produce desks, tables and storage systems tailored to individual needs. Modularity was still the key, but the purpose of the system was to create a flexible working environment that could be adapted to the specific needs of the individual, rather than to produce a system that dictated how an individual should work. Herman Miller's Action Office range, therefore, signified an important shift in thinking, and it is significant in aesthetic terms that this move away from rigidity and control should have been embodied in a design which, while continuing to rely on basically rectilinear forms, introduced rounded elements. Similarly, although the basic structural framework was still metal, square-section steel bar was abandoned in favour of aluminium supports cast in rounded rectangular C-shaped forms. This marked the start of a rejection of strictly rectilinear design during the second half of the 1960s as part of the counter-revolutionary reaction against 'the look', which was also closely linked to the new interest in ergonomics.

Other areas of design in which cube forms were adopted included lighting, ceramics, glass and plastics. In Britain, for example, an enterprising company called Staples and Gray marketed a do-it-yourself flat-packed paper lampshade called the 'Cubelight' in 1968 made of translucent coloured card. In ceramics, Bristol Pottery produced a range of square and rectangular flower bricks during the second half of the decade with printed patterns designed by Lucienne Day. Brick-shaped forms were also an important part of the repertoire of shapes in the textured mould-blown glass range designed by Geoffrey Baxter for Whitefriars Glass in 1966, launched early the following year. One vase even earned the nickname of the 'Drunken Bricklayer' because it was composed of three cubes, the middle one being offset. Another vase in the Textured range, as well as being rectangular in form, was decorated with square-shaped indentations.

Although less common than circles, the square, the rectangle and the diamond formed the basis of many patterns during the early 1960s, and were a particularly important part of 'the look' of British furnishing fabrics and wallpapers. The scene was set in 1960 with the strongly geometric and rectilinear patterns of the Palladio Magnus range. Produced by the Wall Paper Manufacturers, this range was specifically targeted at architects designing modern interiors, as the patterns were much bolder and on a much larger scale than those being produced for the domestic market. One particularly important wallpaper from this range was Pannus, an abstract design composed of rectangular motifs designed by Humphrey Spender, winner of a Design Centre Award in 1960. Geometric patterns also formed an essential part of the main Palladio wallpaper collections, such as the striped Ribbon Screen by Fritz Werthmuller from Palladio 4 in 1960; the diamond-patterned Zeus by Natalie Gibson, and the square-grid patterned Quadrille designed by Edward Veevers, both from Palladio 6 in 1963. Geometric rectilinear patterns were also popular in textiles during the early 1960s, especially in woven furnishing fabrics. Many of the woven textiles produced by Conran Fabrics during the early 1960s were simple large-scale check patterns. Cawdor Check and Cawdor Stripe were

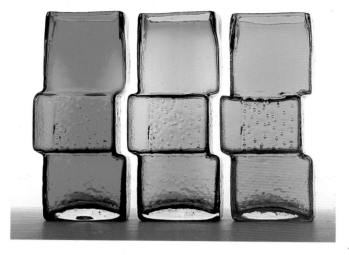

left
Drunken Bricklayer vases from the Textured range designed by Geoffrey Baxter for Whitefriars Glass, 1966. New colours were introduced periodically until the early 1970s.
below left
Quadrille wallpaper designed by Edward Veevers for the Palladio 6 collection, and produced by the Lightbown Aspinall branch of the Wall Paper Manufacturers, 1963.
below
Advert for the American furniture and lighting company Habitat Inc., showing a cube-shaped armchair and lamp, 1968.

right
Advert from 1969 for
Hexagon modular seating
designed by Peter Murdoch
for Hille, 1967. Hexagonal,
octagonal and decagonal
objects and buildings were
another offshoot of the
geometric 'look'.
far right
Banjo vase from the
Textured range designed by
Geoffrey Baxter for
Whitefriars Glass, 1966,
produced from 1967.
below left and right
Exterior and interior of the
Chemosphere (Malin
Residence), Los Angeles,
designed by John Lautner,
1960. Of this house the
architect said, 'I wanted it
to work like a penthouse
overlooking the valley. I
purposely sloped the glass
inwards, so that when you
stand up against it, you
can't look straight down;
you are forced to look at
the magnificent view.'

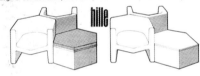

Hille Hexagon gives
Total Seating Flexability

A new concept in Public Area Seating—the Hille Hexagon range of tables,
stools and extra lightweight rigid plastic foam chairs provide an almost endless
permutation of layouts and groupings on a honeycomb grid—result—instant transformation
of interior atmosphere without tears. Hille contract personnel have wide experience in the planning of
large public areas such as air terminals, hotel lobbies, libraries and would be pleased to
discuss the layout and installation problems of any type of interior scheme.
Hille of London Limited 41 Albemarle Street, London W1X 4DD. 01-493 9576
50 Sackville Street, Manchester 1 061-236 6929 | 24 Albert Street, Birmingham 4. 021-MID 7378
9-11 St Stephens Street, Bristol BS1 1EE. 0271-28311 | 25a South West Thistle Street Lane
Edinburgh 2. 031-225 6234 | Hille S.A., 4-6 Grand Rue, 1204 Geneva, Switzerland

hille

two woven linen furnishing fabrics designed by Peter Simpson for Donald Brothers, and these too were the recipients of a Design Centre Award in 1962, thus confirming that this new trend in pattern design met with the approval of the British design Establishment. Tibor also manufactured various woven geometrics, including Cymbeline and Twelfth Check dating from 1960. Bold striped and banded patterns were also a feature of 'the look' of British printed furnishing fabrics, an example being the two brightly coloured complementary geometric patterns designed by Shirley Craven for Hull Traders in 1965 called Straight Six (a pattern of wide horizontal bands) and Angle Six (composed of chevrons), which were intended to be used in juxtaposition. Chevron and Simplicity, the latter being a square-grid pattern, were two bold geometric designs by Lucienne Day for Heal's from 1968, showing how Day had radically updated her style from the earlier Contemporary aesthetic with which she had been so closely associated during the 1950s.

Hexagons, Octagons and Ziggurats

Although hexagonal and octagonal shapes and patterns were not as prevalent as either circles or squares during the 1960s, they were a distinct feature of the period. A significant proportion appeared during the later part of the decade, and as such they can be seen as a belated manifestation of 'the look'. An early example was a carpet designed by Lucienne Day called Octagon, produced by Wilton Royal Carpets as part of their Architects' range in 1964. Large hexagonal motifs formed the basis of a wallpaper design called Parti by Pat Albeck for the Palladio 8 collection in 1968. In glass Geoffrey Baxter designed a decagonal vase as part of his textured range produced by Whitefriars Glass from 1967; while in furniture Jean-Claude Barray and Kim Moltzer designed the

right
An advert for Heal Fabrics celebrating their Design Centre Award in 1968. It shows the continuing prevalence of geometric patterns towards the end of the decade. From left to right: Extension by Haydon Williams, Complex by Barbara Brown and Chevron by Lucienne Day, 1968.
below
Interior of the Festival Theatre, Chichester, designed by Powell and Moya, 1961. The steel tension cables which brace this hexagonal structure can be seen criss-crossing the auditorium below the lighting rig.

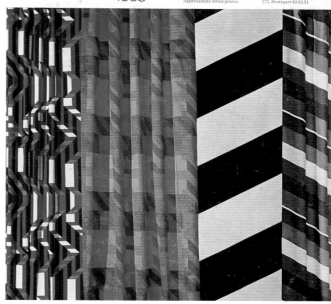

HEAL'S WIN IT

CoID
design
award
1968

Left to right
EXTENSION by Haydon Williams, 6 colourways on plain cotton, 17s 6d per yard.
COMPLEX by Barbara Brown, 4 colourways on satin cotton, 26s 11d per yard.
CHEVRON by Lucienne Day, 5 colourways on plain cotton, 17s 6d per yard.
All fabrics 48 in. wide. Approximate retail prices.

Heal Fabrics are available from over 600 leading stockists throughout the U.K.

Write for samples and address of your nearest stockist.

HEAL FABRICS LTD.
196 Tottenham Court Road London, W1 01-580 3781
Heal Textil, GmbH.
7 Stuttgart W., Reinsburgstrasse
171, Stuttgart 62.62.51

above
Trevelyan College, University of Durham, designed by Stilman and Eastwick-Field, 1964–7, was composed of a series of hexagonal residential and amenity blocks set around hexagonal courtyards.
left
Sunderland Civic Centre designed by Sir Basil Spence, Bonnington and Collins, 1968.

Penta chair for the German firm of Wilhelm Böfinger in 1969, composed of a zinc-plated steel-rod open hexagonal frame with a slung canvas seat. Hexagonal forms were also used as the basis for the design of modular units in interiors, including seating and display cases. An article entitled 'Deception via Hexagon' in *Interiors* in September 1962 drew attention to their potential in this respect. The subject of the feature was an interior remodelled by Gerald Luss for the Norelco Electric Shaver Service Center in the USA, in which hexagonal forms were used in every aspect of the design in order to maximize space:

The partitions are hexagonal, the seating, service counters, and lighting wells are hexagonal. Luss has strengthened the hexagonal shapes by use of shiny and startling colours: purple, red, black, white – also in hexagonal patterns, and his use of glass, mirrors, and polished plastic laminates.

In 1968 Kazuhide Takahama designed the ESA system of modular hexagonal foam stools for Gavina, while the following year Hille launched a new range of modular public seating designed by Peter Murdoch called the Hexagon range, which could be used in a similar way, but in a more formal environment, to create seating clusters which formed larger composite groupings.

It has already been noted that hexagons formed a vital component of the structure of Buckminster Fuller's geodesic domes. Hexagonal and octagonal forms also influenced the shape of interiors and the form of buildings. John Lautner's Chemosphere of 1960, a house resembling a space ship designed for an aircraft engineer, provides a perfect if somewhat idiosyncratic example of an octagonal construction. Perched on a column high on the hillside above Los Angeles, each room in the Chemosphere is wedge-shaped, with the open-plan kitchen/dining/living room taking up approximately half the building, and the bedrooms forming smaller wedges. Hexagons were used on several occasions during the 1960s as the basis for individual buildings or groups of buildings. An early example was Powell and Moya's Festival Theatre in Chichester designed in 1961. This was the first theatre in Britain to be built with an open stage and without a proscenium arch, and it was its hexagonal shape that enabled it to be designed in this way, so that the audience could sit on three sides of the stage. The auditorium was supported on six concrete ribs, one at each corner. Structurally as well as aesthetically this was a particularly interesting and inventive building, the roof being supported by a hexagonal ring girder made of steel tubing. The girder rests on steel tension cables which brace the main structure, and which are visible below the lighting gallery in the main auditorium. An example of the use of multiple hexagons in architecture is provided by Trevelyan College at the University of Durham by Stilman and Eastwick-Field, 1964–7. Built as a residence for 250 female students, the college has an introverted plan, and is composed of a series of hexagonal buildings set around hexagonal courtyards. Some of these contain study bedrooms (twelve on each floor around a central staircase and kitchen); while others contain common rooms and a dining room. Another building designed entirely on a hexagonal plan was Sunderland Civic Centre by Sir Basil Spence, Bonnington and Collins, dating from 1968. Built on a much larger scale than Trevelyan College, it has three main hexagonal sections: the largest, with a courtyard in the centre, containing the

above
Self-conscious angularity
was a feature of many buildings during the 1960s, not
just in plan but in cross
section too. The Japanese
architect Kenzo Tange created a dramatic effect with
the soaring concrete roofscape of his Cultural Centre
at Nichinan during the first
half of the 1960s.

right
On a smaller scale,
Raymond Reed created
a dynamic counterpoint
between the planes of
this house in Iowa in 1968
through his use of diagonal
wooden cladding. Inside,
there is a hexagonal
skylight.

administrative offices for a thousand council employees; the second containing a large car park; and the third containing the council chamber and civic entertaining suite.

Other buildings of the 1960s, while avoiding regular geometric forms, were often self-consciously angular, another distinctive feature of 'the look' in 1960s architecture. Although this trend was less marked in the USA, except in the work of Paul Rudolph and John Johansen, it was strongly defined in Britain, and in Japan it was integral to the aesthetic of Kenzo Tange and can be seen in his Cultural Centre at Nichinan, for example. Coventry Cathedral by Sir Basil Spence, completed in 1962, was an important transitional British building in this respect, providing a link between the Contemporary style and 'the look'. Originally designed during the early 1950s when the organic style was all-pervasive, Spence's design gradually became increasingly angular in its aesthetic and in its detailing as the project progressed. The two masterpieces by James Stirling and James Gowan from the early part of the decade, the Engineering Building at Leicester University dating from 1959, and the Institute of History at Cambridge dating from

1964, provide the best examples of the asymmetrical geometric trend in its mature form, and are almost perverse in their wayward angularity. The Economist Buildings by Alison and Peter Smithson, 1962–5, although to a certain extent influenced by the irregular shape of the site, use angularity to make a subtle statement about the need for architects to move on from the design of rectilinear glass boxes to create buildings which are more expressive in their forms and surfaces, whilst still being highly controlled. Equally pertinent in this context, although in an even more extreme and subversive way, was the Aviary at Regent's Park Zoo in London designed by Cedric Price in conjunction with Lord Snowdon and Frank Newby in 1962. Another example of the controlled use of angularity to create a deliberately dynamic effect is provided by a concrete transport exchange and signal box in Birmingham designed in 1963 by Bicknell and Hamilton with its distinctive zigzagged profile. A sense of dynamism in architecture was also frequently expressed during the 1960s through stepped or terraced forms. Mostly these were triangular or pyramidal in some way, although in the case of

above
United Convent Church,
Danville, Illinois, designed
by Crites and McConnell,
1967. The severe angularity
of this building lends it a
special intense quality, as
though the structure
has been pared down
to essentials.
right
St Matthew's Church, Perry
Beeches, Birmingham,
designed by Robert Maguire
and Keith Murray, 1959–62.
This church reflects how
ecclesiastical architecture
was used during the 1960s
to enable the clergy to be
closer to their congregation.

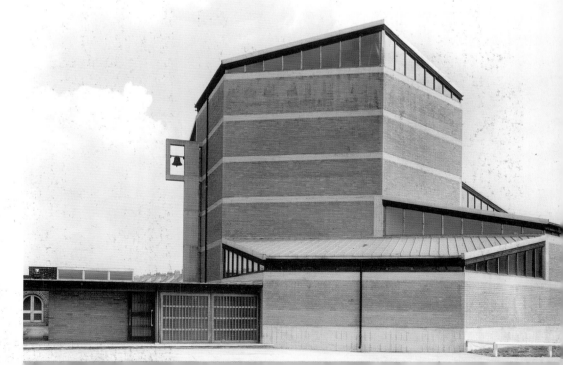

Moshe Safdie's Habitat at the Montreal Expo, the basic components were rectangular. Perhaps the most famous ziggurats of the decade were the halls of residence at the University of East Anglia designed by Denys Lasdun in 1964. Built as an urban landscape but in a rural setting, the terraces were not only triangular vertically, each block was set at an angle to the next, so that viewed from above the pattern of the terraces formed a series of projecting triangles. Tiered housing became increasingly popular during the 1960s, one of the best examples being the Brunswick Centre, a double bank of flats in the Bloomsbury district of London designed by Patrick Hodgkinson between 1959–70, completed in 1972. In this case the tiered balconies were originally intended as glazed winter gardens.

The culmination of 'the look'
At the beginning of this exploration of the key shapes of the 1960s, reference was made to a range of painted wooden toys designed by Hans von Klier, and it was suggested that the geometric components of these toys represented in miniature a visual vocabulary of the decade. At the other extreme in terms of size, the pavilions erected for the Montreal Expo in 1967 could be said to perform a similar function, reflecting on an exaggerated architectural scale the family of forms that had characterized 'the look' of design up to this point in the decade. Even the excitement of Op Art was embodied on a giant scale in the painted decoration of a pavement outside the Ontario Pavilion. It could be argued, in fact, that the Expo was the culmination of 'the look' of the early 1960s, and that 1967 marked at once a high point and a turning point in design. James Acland of the University of Toronto School of Architecture was one of the many commentators on the Expo who realized its wider symbolic significance: 'Though monotonous cubes towering into our skies have threatened to destroy every vestige of amenity and delight in our cities, the wave of protest against them has now bred a moving exultation of form and structure.' Robert Fulford, in his book *This Was Expo* written in 1968, noted that 'a good world's fair is a nursery, in the sense that it's both a playground where architects can lose their inhibitions and a learning place, where they can grow up by developing or discarding behaviour patterns in preparation for a more exacting world.' The metaphor of the nursery provides another link to the toys of Hans von Klier, and suggests a specific association in the 1960s psyche between creativity and childhood. Many of the pavilions at the Expo were like giant children's toys, while play itself was encouraged in many of the displays, as well as in the Children's Creative Centre and the other attractions at La Ronde.

The success of the Montreal Expo as a celebration of design was in stark contrast to the failure of the New York World's Fair three years previously. According to Paul Sargent Clark writing in *Industrial Design* in July/August 1967: 'The 1964–5 New York World's Fair was gaudy, commercial, preposterous, empty-headed … Expo is tasteful, progressive, intelligent, instructive and all the rest, but is also quite a lot of fun.' Before visiting the Expo, Sargent had been concerned that it could not possibly live up to expectations:
Not since the coming of Christ has any public occurrence received quite so much favourable advance publicity as Expo 67; the build-up in the press was sufficient, in fact, to convince me that my first encounter would almost certainly prove

to be disappointing. So it came as a particularly pleasant shock to discover how thoroughly, and at the same time how unpretentiously, Expo lives up to all the nice things that have been said about it.
One of the things that design commentators found particularly satisfying about the Expo, in addition to the obvious attractions of the individual national and thematic pavilions, was the planning and layout of the site itself, and the graphics, transport systems and street furniture by which it was served. Every detail had been carefully thought through, right down to the triangular litter bins and planters, the elegant streetlamps with their cylindrical uplighters and domed reflectors, and the telephone kiosks with their eye-catching domed acrylic covers. In fact a whole new system of street furniture was specially created for the Expo by the Colombian designer Luis Villa, and it was Villa who introduced the essential element of coherence into what might otherwise have been a potentially chaotic celebration of cultural diversity. Of his task he commented: 'At Expo every building is totally different, and the only way you can put them together is by planning and reinforcing the planning with design.'

Whereas the New York World's Fair had failed to receive the endorsement of the Bureau of International Expositions, and thus failed to attract contributions from many of the most important design nations, including Britain, Italy, France and most of the Scandinavian countries, the Montreal Expo attracted participation from seventy countries, representing more than two-thirds of the world's population. Extensive reference has already been made to Buckminster Fuller's monumental geodesic dome, which was compared at the time to a modern cathedral because of the feeling of awe it inspired. Moshe Safdie's Habitat, intended as an experiment in urban design, was another landmark construction which attracted worldwide attention. The overall theme of the Expo was Man and his World, which explains the context in which Habitat was created. Its name has a particular resonance, and the ideas by which it was motivated – especially the desire to create capsule-like apartments which could be mass-produced, complete with built-in appliances – are potent reminders of the moral and technological idealism of the time. Originally planned as a scheme for one thousand apartments, with shops and a school as part of the proposed development, only 354 units were actually erected, varying in size from a one-bedroomed apartment to a four-bedroomed house, each with its own private roof garden complete with automatic irrigation system. Most of the bathroom fittings and a large proportion of the kitchen fittings were made of pre-moulded plastic, with all the latest appliances built-in, including cookers, food mixers and dishwashers. Of the thinking behind the scheme Safdie himself explained: 'We have to talk in terms of a million human beings at a time, and in terms of how they want to live. We cannot continue to design homes as if there were still a landed aristocracy.' In reality, however, the Habitat system of building proved somewhat impractical. The boxes were so heavy that an entirely new type of crane had to be developed to lift the units into place, which added greatly to the overall cost. Safdie himself was undeterred, however; he considered Habitat as just the first stage in a much larger experiment which needed to be taken further before it could be proved to be economically viable:
The existing patterns could be broken if we were able to pour

opposite
View of Habitat, the experimental housing complex designed by Moshe Safdie, and built for the Montreal Expo in 1967. Each concrete box in the structure was prefabricated, then crane-lifted into position. Habitat attracted worldwide attention and triggered heated international architectural debate.

left
German Pavilion at the Montreal Expo, designed by Frei Otto: a multi-pinnacled tented structure. Pyramidal forms and space frame structures of all shapes and sizes were recurrent themes of the Montreal Expo, 1967, which provided a feast of forms and materials for architectural enthusiasts.
below and opposite above
Man in the Community Pavilion designed by Massey Erickson Associates. The building was constructed from a series of tapering offset wooden hexagons.
opposite below
US Pavilion. Detail of the hexagonal space frame structure from which Buckminster Fuller's geodesic dome was constructed.

hundreds of millions of dollars into large-scale prototypes. Unions would be forced to assume a new attitude to their role in the building industry. Private industry would become interested in bringing forth its best men and total resources. Local governments would be forced to revise dated building codes and municipal legislation. It would also force architects, engineers and contractors to recognise that the present relationship – the traditional, linear, non-overlapping approach – is as outdated as the piano roll.

Although critical of Habitat's failings, James Murray, the editor of *Canadian Architecture*, admitted that: 'Habitat is a phenomenon most heartening in a nation unmarked by housing innovation since the disappearance of the wigwam … Housing design will never be quite the same.'

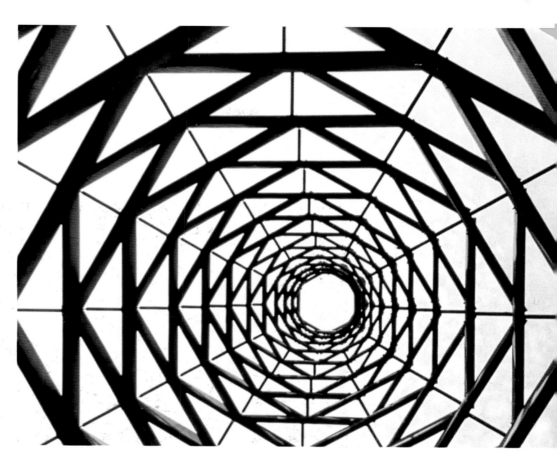

Also important, apart from the economics of the Habitat project, were the aesthetics of its construction: a set of rectangular building blocks stacked together apparently at random, producing formal and textural variety out of geometric monotony. As Scott Kelly pointed out in an article entitled 'Expo's Promising Pile of Boxes' in *Industrial Design* in July/August 1967, Habitat provided 'proof at last that cluster housing is possible and that industrialized building does not have to mean either dreary houses or tract homes.' It is worth pointing out the parallels between this creative exercise and Charles Eames' 'House of Cards', Hans von Klier's totemic wooden toys, and several other children's toys of the period, such as the Playplax kit of coloured interlocking perspex rings and squares produced by the British firm Trendon Toys.

The pyramidal theme expressed in Habitat was a recurrent motif running thoughout Expo and can be seen in the forms of a number of pavilions on the site, such as the forest of pyramids that made up the roofscape of the dramatic Pulp and Paper Pavilion. Although each pavilion was highly individual – this was, after all, a place to make grand visual statements – viewed as a whole, there were a number of common visual themes. Triangular forms of one sort or another, both pyramidal and conical, were central to the Expo, for example, and were highlighted at the point of arrival, the Place d'Acceuil on the Mackay Pier, which had a triodetic space-frame roof surmounted by a series of underlit pyramids. The overall theme of the Expo, Man and his World, was broken down into a number of sections, the main ones being Man the Explorer, Man the Producer, and Man in the Community. The Man the Explorer and Man the Producer pavilions, designed by Affleck, Desbarats, Dimakopoulos, Lebensold and Sise, had heavy space-frame structures based on tetrahedrons, and were constructed from rusted steel. More elegant and ethereal was the Man in the Community Pavilion, designed by Massey Erickson Associates, composed of a series of cones constructed from a stack of offset hexagons, tapering upwards, made of British Columbia fir. Thus one geometric shape – in this case, the hexagon – was used to create another entirely different geometric form. This was exactly what Buckminster Fuller had done with his geodesic dome, the exoskeleton of which was also constructed from hexagons. The hexagon theme was continued inside the Man in the Commmunity Pavilion, which was composed of seven chambers, including a water garden with hexagonal walkways. Frei Otto's German Pavilion also drew on the image of the cone, but in an entirely different way, presaging a revival of interest in neo-organic forms. Otto was the director of the

above
Pulp and Paper Pavilion at
the Montreal Expo, 1967.
left
The Netherlands Pavilion,
Montreal Expo, 1967,
designed by Walter
Eijkelenboom and
K Middelhoek, was an
impressive, tubular-steel,
space-frame structure.
The domed reflectors of
Luis Villa's streetlamps
were a prominent feature
of the Expo, as seen in
this night image.

Institute of Lightweight Structures in Berlin, and the pavilion he created was a giant flexible tent constructed from steel mesh with a heavy translucent plastic fabric covering, propped up at intervals by huge masts, thereby creating a dramatic roofed landscape. For architects and engineers, it was this pavilion along with Fuller's dome which were the highpoints of the Expo. Dr Karl Schanzer, the designer of the Austrian Pavilion, described the Expo as a whole as: 'The most exciting collection of buildings I have ever seen.'

Apart from these two show stoppers, one of the most eyecatching and intriguing pavilions was the Canadian Katimavik (meaning 'meeting place' in Inuktitut), which was in the shape of a giant inverted pyramid. The British Pavilion, designed by Sir Basil Spence, was more conventional, being crowned by an angular cone with its top lopped off. However, along with the Czech pavilion, it attracted some of the largest crowds because of the quality of its displays. The aquarium and dolphin pool were both cylindrical in form, the latter being topped by a spiralling cone-shaped aluminium roof. The Israeli Pavilion, designed by Sharon, Reznik and Sharon, was composed of a huge cluster of white plastic polygons. Creative exploration of geometric forms was another theme running through the Expo, with angular space-frame structures being particularly prevalent. The Austrian Pavilion was irregularly angular and had a triangular framework of aluminium with glass cladding. The Gyrotron, designed by Sean Kenny, was a glorified high-tech fairground pavilion, complete with amusement rides. Intended as a 'compact travel package from inner earth to outer space', the Gyrotron was constructed in the form of a skeletal pyramid, its open space-frame structure composed of a triangular grid resembling scaffolding. In addition to the space frames used in the Gyrotron, the Place d'Acceuil and Buckminster Fuller's 'geodesic skybreak bubble', as he called it, a giant triodetic space frame was used as the skeleton for The Netherlands Pavilion designed by Walter Eijkelenboom and K Middelhoek. Robert Fulford described this pavilion as 'not so much a building, more of a building set', and compared it to the educational children's game Meccano. Made from 57,000 sections of aluminum tubing slotted together, it was constructed without the need for either welding or riveting, and it demonstrated how flexible space-frame architecture could be.

Tented structures, both organic, as in the case of the German Pavilion, and angular, as in the case of the Ontario Pavilion, were another recurrent feature. Angular forms were more common than organic ones, although in several cases, such as the geodesic dome, a rounded form was created from an angular framework. One of the most colourful pavilions was the Canadian Kaleidoscope, a multi-coloured ribbed cylinder resembling a giant slide carousel. The performance it ran, sponsored by a group of Canadian chemical companies, was on the theme of Man and Colour, and was itself called *Kaleidoscope*. Combining filmed images and mirrors with electronic music, *Kaleidoscope* was the ultimate celebration of psychedelia. At the opposite end of the spectrum, one of the most restrained pavilions was that of the Scandinavians which was in the shape of a rectangular box with an openwork steel frame painted white. Co-designed by a team of architects from the five different countries that shared the pavilion – Finland, Denmark, Sweden, Iceland and Norway – it was generally thought to be disappointing by comparison with those

of other countries, although it did contain some wonderful exhibits, such as Tapio Wirkkala's monumental *Ultima Thule* sculpture. Writing in *Interiors*, the conclusion of Paul Sargent Clark was that, overall, the Expo was a resounding triumph: 'There is so much to see and to hear at the Expo that I would judge it to be worth nearly any amount of trouble for you to get there before it closes … it may be decades before anything like its equal will again be set up.' Concluding his book *This Was Expo* in 1968, Robert Fulford wrote: 'Expo was the greatest birthday party in history, but for those willing to learn it was also an education. For one beautiful and unforgettable summer, Expo took us into the future that can be ours.'

These, in short, were the principal aesthetic departures of the 1960s which, together, combined to create 'the look'. By comparison with Contemporary design, what made 'the look' exciting was that it represented a further advance on what was already, by conventional standards, a progressive style. This is what gave 'the look' its special edge. It was daring; it was thrilling; it signified a breakthrough for the next generation and the start of a new age. Like contemporary science, it seemed that design was overcoming barriers and

pushing forward into completely new territory. In 1963 Harold Wilson had proclaimed his vision of progress forged in 'the white heat of technology'. For designers this was a similarly exciting time to be working, because what was emerging was a vision of progress forged out of 'the white heat of creativity'. 'The look', therefore, was much more than merely a style of clothes and home furnishings: it represented a creative attitude and a wholeheartedly positive vision of the future. Although by implication the displacement of Contemporary design by 'the look' symbolized a rejection of an earlier pattern of life and accepted codes of behaviour, the mood was not negative but forward-looking. People were too engrossed in the present to dwell on the past.

design superpowers of the sixties

four

opposite
Finnish Pavilion, Milan
Triennale, designed by Tapio
Wirkkala, 1954. Having
established an international
reputation in the applied
arts during the 1950s,
Finland retained its position
as one of the design superpowers of the 1960s.
above
Detail of Whirlpool, a pattern
designed by Vuokko
Eskolin-Nurmesniemi for the
Finnish firm, Vuokko, 1964.
right
Detail of Dondolo rocking
chair, designed by Cesare
Leonardi and Franca Stagi
for Elco, 1969.

The Second World War prompted a fundamental shift in the balance of power within the international design community. Throughout the 1920s and 1930s Western Europe had been the undisputed centre of influence, with France reigning supreme in the field of decorative art, and the Bauhaus acting as a creative powerhouse for the development of Modernist architecture and design in Germany until the closure of the school in 1933. Important contributions to the development of modern design were also made by neighbouring central European states during the inter-war period, notably Holland, Austria and Czechoslovakia, reflecting the importance of the well-established communication network between architects and designers in these countries at this time. All this came to an end with the outbreak of the Second World War.

The physical devastation caused by the war in central Europe, and the disruptive impact on traditional centres of manufacturing, created a situation ripe for exploitation by countries that had hitherto been overshadowed by the dominant powers, or that had previously been considered on the margins of mainstream development. Because there was no established mainstream anymore – it had been virtually wiped out – completely new patterns of trading could be developed and new forms of design marketed. The first countries to take advantage of this situation and move in to fill the void were the three newly emergent Scandinavian nations, Sweden, Denmark and Finland. Through a combination of independent and joint initiatives they worked swiftly and effectively during the 1940s to develop and promote what became known as the Scandinavian Modern style. The early success they encountered when they displayed their work at the Milan

Triennales from 1951 onwards provided a further boost, and throughout the 1950s their confidence continued to grow. This in turn had an invigorating effect on their designers, who were inspired to produce ever more interesting and inventive designs; and it also gave reassurance to manufacturers who had taken the risk of investing in modern design, and who could now see that this was paying off in terms of both sales and national and international prestige.

Up until the Second World War the USA, although it had begun to make a major contribution to the development of modern architecture through the school of Frank Lloyd Wright, and although it had been highly successful in establishing efficient mechanized methods of production in its factories, remained a net importer of European culture. Until the 1940s most of the USA's home-produced visual culture, including both art and design, was overtly influenced by stylistic trends and innovations that originated in Europe. A new wave of European immigrants during the 1930s, including leading artists, architects and designers, only served to reinforce this pattern. Even Art Deco, which was embraced so energetically and developed so convincingly by American architects and industrial designers during the 1930s (so much so that it almost appeared to be a home-grown style) had in reality developed out of a design trend that originated in France during the 1920s. The Moderne or 'jazz modern' style, America's commercialized version of Art Deco, had been co-opted from Europe and shipped over to the USA following the Exposition Internationale des Arts Décoratifs et Industriels Modernes in Paris of 1925. Nevertheless, the enthusiastic adoption of Art Deco by the Americans during the 1930s, and its subsequent application to everything from the ornamentation of skyscrapers, to the design of cinemas, to the styling of office equipment, gave an enormous boost to the American design fraternity. This, combined with the USA's increasing political confidence and economic prosperity after the Second World War, made it inevitable that by the end of the 1940s the tide would have finally turned, and the Americans would have begun to export their own visual culture back to Europe.

Already by the 1930s the Americans had begun to exert a considerable influence abroad in the field of cinema. After the war they moved up a gear and set their sights even higher. By the 1950s the cultural package the USA was offering had been expanded to include all aspects of visual and popular culture, from Abstract Expressionism to youth fashion, advertising, car styling, soft drinks and domestic accessories. The war enabled the Americans to gain vital political and commercial footholds abroad, notably in Europe and Japan. First came the military forces; then the economic investment and the growth of political influence; and finally the most important and widespread development of all, the exploitation of new markets for American products and ideas. Although some countries, such as Britain, were concerned about the threat of invasion by American culture, the pressure was so great and the public response so overwhelmingly enthusiastic (whether in relation to James Dean, Elvis Presley, Jackson Pollock, commercial television, Coca Cola or dream kitchens) that resistance was useless. The war left Europe vulnerable and made the American invasion unstoppable. The result was an inversion in the pattern of cultural exchange. After the war the Americans were in the ascendant, and would remain so in cultural terms until the early 1960s.

By the second half of the 1950s, however, Western Europe was finally getting back on its feet, and it was at this stage that a fifth new design superpower – Italy – began to emerge. Italy had been in a state of arrested development during the 1930s as a result of the Mussolini dictatorship, and the country was one of the most badly affected by the war. Nevertheless, in spite of this, Italian architects, designers and manufacturers responded in a particularly energetic way to the new freedom of expression and the new economic opportunities that opened up during the early post-war period. A vigorous programme of rebuilding was undertaken, along with the modernization and expansion of the country's manufacturing base, so that by the end of the decade the situation had been transformed from one of devastation to one of thriving productivity. The emergence of Italy as a fifth dynamic and new creative force in design, an appropriate host for the increasingly spectacular Milan Triennales completed the transformation of the international design community as a whole. No longer was design in Europe dominated by France, Germany and Austria; the Scandinavian triumvirate had marched in from the north; the USA had sailed in across the Atlantic; and Italy had risen up from obscurity within the midst of the continent. These were the five new design superpowers of the 1950s.

Unlike the 1940s, there was no major world event during the 1950s to precipitate any radical shifts of power within the international design community at the start of the 1960s. The lowering of the Iron Curtain, the consolidation of the Eastern bloc and the onset of the Cold War, all had an effect, but as these Communist states were outside the newly established mainstream, the impact of their isolationism was relatively insignificant in design terms. The exception was Czechoslovakia where, ironically, isolation appears to have fostered increased creativity in one specific field – glass – so that by the end of the 1950s the Czechs had established themselves as world players in this particular area. The Czechs had made a significant impression on the international design community when they had shown their new art glass at the Milan Triennale of 1957 and at the Brussels World Fair the following year. After this they went quiet again for a time, re-emerging with a ground-breaking exhibition at the Museum of Contemporary Crafts in New York in 1964, and a stunning installation in the Czech Pavilion at the Montreal Expo in 1967, where they showed works, the freedom and creativity of which presaged subsequent developments in American studio glass. Because of the Cold War, however, international cross-fertilization of this type was rare between communist and capitalist countries, and any patterns of cultural exchange that might have developed out of this initiative were shattered by the Soviet invasion of Czechoslovakia in 1968. Thus what might have developed into a creative East–West partnership was brought to an abrupt halt; a turn of events that only served to foster the status quo in the development of national design characteristics. This is not to suggest that the international design community was static during the 1960s, but there was a much greater degree of continuity than there had been fifteen years earlier. None of the newly established design superpowers of the 1950s disappeared from view during the ensuing decade, although Italy developed at such a prodigious rate that, by the mid-1960s, it was in danger of eclipsing the others altogether. This was not because standards in Scandinavia or the USA had slipped in any significant

way; simply that, as Andrea Branzi has recognized, there was a hot-house atmosphere within the Italian design community at this time, and by the second half of the decade the intensity and volume of their creative output was almost overpowering.

At the start of the 1960s the balance of power within the international design community was also affected by the introduction (or in some cases the re-launch) of several new players on to the scene. This was particularly the case once the economies of Britain, France, Holland, Germany and Japan, which for obvious reasons had all suffered from a slow start after the war, finally began to boom. Of these, Britain was arguably the most significant, although a particular feature of British design was its inconsistency, with dynamic and cutting-edge activities co-existing alongside the mediocre and the downright poor. In this respect it was very different to Italy, where there was an astonishingly high level of both activity and creativity. While the eclectic Italians took what they wanted from British design, enthused about it and paid no heed to the rest, Britain's inconsistency was a major cause of concern and puzzlement to the Scandinavians, whose achievements ever since the war had been a byword for high standards and consistency. In the January/February 1969 issue of the Danish design magazine *Mobilia*, for example, Jørgen Kastholm described British efforts in the field of modern furniture design as 'energetic' but 'sporadic', while expressing his dismay at the derivative nature of the output of most British furniture producers and their low overall standards:

Just one visit to the Earl's Court in London is sufficient to make one draw the conclusion that one might just as well have stayed at home. You literally wade through horrors without end which, as regards both quality and design, are far below the things we are used to seeing at home in Scandinavia.

The previous year, however, in a special feature on British design in *Mobilia* in March 1968, the Danish designer Rolf Middelboe had commented: 'One must not generalize when speaking of a city like London. It is too varied. It is a jigsaw puzzle you will never be able to finish, so you will never have the complete picture; it will forever be a jumble of pieces, each of them with a character of its own.' The more perceptive foreign critics, therefore, realized that inconsistency and unpredictability were essential ingredients of Britain's cultural make-up. While standards of design were poor in many factories, they were outstandingly high in others (examples being Heal Fabrics, Race Furniture, Midwinter Pottery and Whitefriars Glass). It was therefore as misleading to judge the latter by the former, as it was to make generalizations about the former on the basis of the achievements of the latter. This point was reaffirmed by Michael Webb in his article 'Action in England' in *Industrial Design* in October 1967: 'What is the face of British design in the mid-sixties? Overseas observers have exaggerated the abruptness and the extent of the shift from traditional stodginess to Mod frivolity.' Nevertheless, having carried out a detailed survey of 'the look' in British design, and having identified designers such as Terence Conran, William Plunkett, Bernard Holdaway, Peter Murdoch, Max Clendinning, David Mellor and Robert Heritage as being central to the new developments that were taking place, the author concluded that while 'it would be absurd to pretend that these younger talents, and more established names, are representative of the British design scene … compared with

style had stood out as being exactly what was needed after
the cathartic effects of the Second World War. By the late
1960s, however, the situation had changed both culturally and
economically. In the age of Pop, idiosyncrasy and irreverence
were openly encouraged (as in the zany displays by James
Gardner in the 'Britain Today' section of the British Pavilion at
the Expo), and the cool restraint of the Scandinavians was in
danger of seeming old-fashioned and 'square'.

France, even more than Britain, displayed an openly
schizophrenic attitude towards modern design during the
1960s. After the war interior designers such as Jean Royère
had tried unsuccessfully to revive the outmoded concept of
the 'artiste décorateur' with a fey and highly self-conscious
version of the Contemporary style. French textiles and
wallpapers remained rooted in traditional styles of pattern-
making, however, and throughout the 1950s and 1960s
the French furniture industry continued to be dominated by
historical reproductions. At the same time, however, out of
this unpromising environment a number of exceptionally
creative individuals emerged who were to make some of the
most radical, revolutionary and influential contributions to
furniture design. The 'new wave' included the talented Pierre
Paulin through his work for the Dutch firm Artifort; the
brilliant Olivier Mourgue in his innovative designs for Airborne; the
maverick mystic of inflatable furniture, Quasar Khanh, born in
Vietnam, and French by adoption; and Bernard Govin and
Roger Tallon, two unconventional figures who emerged
towards the end of the decade and made the creative crossover between furniture and sculpture. While it can hardly be
argued that France was one of the design superpowers of the
1960s, it was undoubtedly important in nurturing the geniuses
of these five individuals, much as it has fostered the talent of
the inimitable Philippe Starck during the 1980s and 1990s.

This wide-ranging input into international design led
to much greater diversification during the 1960s, particularly
towards the end of the decade. Although the number of players in the superpower league was arguably increased by only
one, Britain (Germany and Japan did not really achieve full
design superpower status until the 1970s), the critical mass of
international design activity as a whole was greatly intensified
due to the concentrated but selective input from other countries such as France and Czechoslovakia. The fact that there
was greater input from a wider range of sources meant that,
with the exception of Italy, no one group dominated the
scene. Furthermore, because there were more countries playing an active role in design, competition was greater. Rather
than having a negative effect, however, design flourished in
this competitive atmosphere as each country strove to excel
in its own particular field. It was this spirit that made the
Montreal Expo such a success.

the situation of native whimsy and imported gentility that was
current only ten years ago, the prospects are encouraging.'

It was perhaps partly as a result of pressure to conform that Norway entered the Scandinavian Modern design
fold during the early 1960s, becoming particularly active in the
export of furniture and ceramics. In 1967 it was significant
that all five Scandinavian countries (the fifth being Iceland) collaborated on the design of a shared pavilion at the Montreal
Expo, although ironically what should, in theory, have been a
great triumph, turned out to be something of a disappointment. Paul Sargent Clark's view, expressed in *Industrial
Design* in July/August 1967, was that conformity had stifled
individuality: 'It's all very neatly done, of course; nearly everything these people put their hands to is in some way excellent. But the overall effect of the pavilion is surprisingly sterile,
and I had hoped to see more of Scandinavia than what is
contained in the five minimal displays.' During the 1950s,
when Sweden, Denmark and Finland had won international
design acclaim at the Milan Triennales, they had done so as
individual countries, each with a distinctive character of its
own, particularly Finland. By grouping them together, and by
showing their work alongside that of two countries who were
not in the same design superpower league, the individual
identities of each country were weakened and the overall
impact of Scandinavian design watered down. Ultimately it
seems to have been a mistake, therefore, for five such different countries to have banded together as a region. What the
Scandinavian Pavilion at the Expo also demonstrated,
however, was that by 1967 the Scandinavians had got 'out of
sync' with the rest of the international design community.
During the early 1950s their cool, controlled, ultra-restrained

Britain

The role of Britain within the international design community was highly significant during the 1960s. Admittedly much of its influence arose indirectly, not from the design mainstream, but as a result of Britain's dominance in the field of pop music, art and associated manifestations of popular culture and consumerism such as fashion, Pop Art, Op Art, graphics and retailing. Nevertheless its importance should not be underestimated. Because many of these areas of creativity were so ephemeral and, in many cases, overtly commercial, it would be easy to dismiss them as lightweight, but 'the look' associated with the British 'youthquake' during the mid-1960s – music, clothes, hair-styles, album covers, posters, shop fronts and interiors – represented a potent and dynamic combination of forces, the impact of which was unmatched in any other country. One of the prime-movers on the British 'scene', Mary Quant, wrote in her autobiography in 1965:

London led the way in changing the focus of fashion from the Establishment to the young. As a country, we were aware of the great potential of this change long before the Americans or the French. We were one step ahead from the start; we are still one step ahead and we have simply got to stay that way.

No doubt some of Britain's and London's reputation arose from mass-media hype, but as serious foreign design magazines such *Domus* and *Mobilia* recognized, the phenomenon of the Swinging Sixties was not just a myth; there was a lot of substance to it. *Mobilia* identified the Beatles and Mary Quant as two of the primary catalysts responsible for transforming Britain from a country associated with drabness, post-war austerity and Victorian conformity to a place that was vibrant, stimulating and fun. British visual culture, particularly youth culture, was deliberately 'provocative', they noted in March 1968. What appealed to, and at the same time slightly horrified, the Scandinavians was the extreme eclecticism, both historical and cultural, of British fashion and furnishings, typified by the clothes sold through the 'happening' boutique of the moment, Biba. In their lightning survey of British design *Mobilia* focused on the lively, eclectic and commercial graphics-based work of firms such as Dodo Designs (which made ornamental accessories described as 'pop-style play-things for adults') and the plastics firm Xlon (which made domestic products such as trays, tablecloths and boxes, decorated with brightly coloured, highly patterned surfaces). Along with the British flair for pattern-making, another phenomenon that intrigued foreign commentators was the irreverent and iconoclastic approach of young British furniture designers such as Peter Murdoch, Max Clendinning and Terence Conran. In each case it was as much due to their entrepreneurial spirit as their design talents that they were successful, even to the point of going out and finding manufacturers for their designs, or, in the case of Conran, taking the risk of setting up a factory of his own. Along with Bernard Holdaway at Hull Traders, it was these energetic youthful designer-entrepreneurs who revolutionized the perception of British furniture abroad. Like Mary Quant and Barbara Hulanicki in the field of youth fashion, they created a brand new image which united design and popular culture, and which brought design bang up to date.

One of the reasons for the success of Britain on an international level was the 'balanced and integrated relationship' between art, architecture, music and fashion, which

left
Interior of the Chelsea Drug Store, King's Road, London, designed by Garnett, Cloughey, Blackmore and Associates, c1970. This practice, which also designed the Just Looking boutique on the King's Road, created flamboyant facades and interiors which embodied the aesthetics of Swinging London.

below
Interior of a flat in Belfast designed by Max Clendinning showing furniture related to the Maxima range he created for Race Furniture in 1966. The pieces were made from preformed laminated timber with polyether foam cushions. Clendinning's sculptural furniture, designed to be seen from all sides, was described as 'Mackintosh taking a trip'.

were often lumped together as part of the British cultural package. British art enjoyed a deservedly high reputation internationally during the 1960s; the acclaimed works of Op and Pop artists such as Bridget Riley, David Hockney and Peter Blake ensuring that the international spotlight was turned on Britain during the middle years of the decade. Enlightened commentators from abroad also appreciated the importance of Britain's achievements in the field of architecture during this period. New buildings by James Stirling, John Winter and Team 4 were all written up on the pages of *Domus*, for example, while the avant-garde architectural group Archigram was to have a major influence on Italian design during the second half of the decade, prompting the formation of radical design groups such as Archizoom and Superstudio. Less appreciated internationally, however, were Britain's achievements in other fields of mainstream domestic design, particularly ceramics, glass, metalwork, textiles and wallpapers. During the 1960s Britain still had a significant manufacturing base in most fields of the applied arts, from carpets through to tableware and, although the overall standards of design in Britain could not be said to be high (there was still far too great a reliance on traditional design), in each branch there were at least three or four progressive manufacturers with a high level of commitment to modern design. Employing designers of the highest calibre, it was these manufacturers that took the initiative to lead the market forward, and without their contribution to enhance that of Quant and Hulanicki in fashion, and Conran, Race and Hille in furniture, Britain would never have achieved design superpower status during the 1960s.

In ceramics the leading firm was Midwinter, where Roy Midwinter, in addition to collaborating with David Queensberry on the design of a series of new shapes, drew upon a combination of in-house and freelance design talent to generate a diverse range of ground-breaking new patterns. As in the 1950s Midwinter's strength lay in the way its shapes and patterns complemented each other, with the latter being used to update the former so that together they captured the changing moods of the time. Barbara Brown's abstract geometric Focus and Nigel Wilde's Diagonal both capture 'the look' of the mid-1960s; while Jessie Tait's stylized floral Spanish Garden and Eve Midwinter's psychedelic Tango evoke the flower-power aesthetic of the late 1960s. All were used on the same shape, Fine, and it was the patterns that kept the shape up to date. Another leading British ceramics manufacturer, Poole Pottery, reflected a similar awareness of the need to keep moving forward in design. Its approach was more radical than Midwinter's, however, as it went against the prevailing trend of the early 1960s by introducing a hand-decorated Studio range. Although printed decoration was adopted in both its tablewares and cookwares (such as the Lucullus oven-to-table ware designed by Robert Jefferson in 1961), in the Studio range of ornamental bowls and vases, developed between 1961 and 1963, Poole took its lead from a combination of studio pottery, sculpture and painting. There were two distinct aspects to the Studio range: firstly, a series of pieces called Delphis, launched in 1963, which were hand-painted with bold quasi-psychedelic designs in brightly coloured glazes; secondly, the Atlantis range, produced from 1969, consisting of hand-thrown stoneware vessels which were impressed, carved and incised with rich textural patterns

and partly decorated with unusual mottled glazes. The latter were similar to the glazes on two production tableware ranges, developed during 1967–8, called Sea Crest and Blue Lace. These initiatives were driven forward until 1966 by the firm's chief designer, Robert Jefferson, working in conjunction with the thrower, Guy Sydenham, who was later responsible for developing the Atlantis range. Jefferson and Sydenham were joined in 1963 by the talented Tony Morris, a recent graduate from Newport School of Art, who refined the glaze-painting technique used on the Delphis range and contributed to many other aspects of design. It was also part of the Poole ethos to encourage individual decorators in the Craft Section (which was established in 1966 and drew on graduates from local art schools) to give free rein to their creative imaginations, each individual being identified by his or her own monogram.

In the field of glass, in addition to the award-winning designs for cut glass by David Queensberry for Webb Corbett, the leading British factory was Whitefriars Glass. During the 1960s the firm was managed by William Wilson, whose background was as a designer, and who continued to contribute to the pool of designs put into production. His Knobbly range of 1964 was particularly important as it presaged the move towards textural surfaces and streaky colouring in glass design during the second half of the decade, itself a response to the studio glass movement. The chief designer at Whitefriars during the 1960s, however, was Geoffrey Baxter, and it was he who was responsible for most of the main innovations at the factory during the course of the decade, such as the introduction of thinly blown angular shapes in 1962, and the development of the highly influential mould-blown Textured range in 1966, launched to great acclaim and commercial success the following year. The latter was a range of thick-walled underlay glass (coloured glass encased in a layer of clear glass) which took its shapes from richly textured deep-relief moulds. The most well-known pieces in this range were the cylindrical Bark vases, the original mould for which was lined with actual tree bark. Other pieces had more unusual and irregular forms, and their surface patterns were created from textures such as rough nail heads, gouged wood, and stapled scrolls of copper wire. Initially produced in three dark Scandinavian-inspired colours, cinnamon, willow and indigo, the Textured range was revitalized two years later by the introduction of two new psychedelic colours, tangerine and kingfisher blue. The direct influence of the studio glass movement was overtly acknowledged in 1969 with the creation of the limited production Studio range. Techniques first used here, such as random strapping (the application of uneven molten trails of glass in a band around the vessel) were later used in a simplified form on a mass-production range during the early 1970s (see page 223). Although other new firms such as Caithness, King's Lynn and Dartington all made a positive contribution to modern glass design in Britain during the 1960s, it was the established firm of Whitefriars that deserves credit as the most important centre of innovation within the industry as a whole.

In pattern design the major contributions made by the Wall Paper Manufacturers, Heal Fabrics, Hull Traders and Edinburgh Weavers have already been mentioned. As in the 1950s Heal's dominated the quality end of the furnishing textile market, while the Wall Paper Manufacturers catered to a wider range of decorative tastes through the work of their various different branches. The two industries drew on a pool of freelance designers, many of whom worked in both fields. This explains some of the cross-overs in design between the two media, although the very different applications of their products meant that at times they developed in parallel and at times they diverged. The reasons for the success of the two industries were, firstly, because of the wealth of design talent in Britain at this date and, secondly, because of the vision of the individuals procuring or commissioning their work. Tom Worthington at Heal Fabrics was described in *Design* in July 1965 as 'the most brilliant and dynamic impresario/converter in the business'. An article entitled 'Tom Worthington – patron and salesman' in *House and Garden* in November 1962 stressed his vital role and, in particular, the importance of his intuition about the market and its potential:

Tom Worthington's preoccupation is staying up with the new generation. To sell modern design to young people – and they are always the most important customers, he says – you must lead a catholic life. It means keeping in touch with fashions in every branch of the arts. Looking to haute couture for new colours, to the art schools for new talent.

These comments are significant because they highlight one of the primary reasons why Britain excelled in the field of design during the 1960s: the quality of the young designers who had been coming up through the art college system ever since the 1950s. Britain benefited from what was perhaps the best art and design education system in the world at this time, at both graduate and postgraduate level. The Royal College of Art was the jewel in Britain's educational crown, and almost all the leading designers of the period either went to it or became involved in teaching there at some point in their careers. Creativity flourished as a result of the encouragement that young people were given at art colleges throughout the country. Although only a relatively small proportion of this creativity was channelled through conventional established outlets, there were enough opportunities for entrepreneurialism for designers either to pursue successful freelance careers, or to branch out into manufacturing themselves. This is what happened with both Terence Conran and Mary Quant: they started out as designers, then became manufacturers, and in both cases this led to an involvement in retailing. In 1960s Britain these three areas were inextricably linked, and the phenomenon of design cannot be detached from new patterns of making, marketing and selling.

left
Northwestern National Life Insurance Company Offices, Minneapolis, Minnesota, designed by Minoru Yamasaki, 1964–5. Like the work of Philip Johnson and Wallace K Harrison at the Lincoln Center in New York, this building, with its overt gothic references and lavish interiors, was criticized at the time for its formalism and neo-historicism. Its exaggeratedly slender arches were 85 feet tall.

above
Metropolitan Opera House, Lincoln Center for the Performing Arts, New York, designed by Wallace K Harrison, completed in 1966. The classical inspiration behind this building, and the Lincoln Center complex as a whole, is very much apparent in this view of the arcaded Opera House.

right
With its richly-carpeted serpentine staircase, hammered bronze stair-rail, gold-leaf lobby ceiling and crystal cluster Lobmeyr chandeliers, the interior of the Opera House was extremely luxurious. Ada Louise Huxtable, architectural critic of the *New York Times*, described the Center as 'lushly decorated, conservative structures that the public finds pleasing and most professionals consider a failure of nerve, imagination and talent.'

USA

During the 1950s the USA had embraced both the home-grown American Modern version of Contemporary design as well as imported Scandinavian Modern design. High standards of living, combined with widespread acceptance of Contemporary design as the embodiment of American Establishment values, meant that most consumers saw no need to reject what they were comfortable with in favour of something more risqué and unsettling the following decade. It was not until the tide turned against the Establishment with the anti-Vietnam War protests of 1968 that people began to question seriously the aesthetic merits, as well as the moral values, of their material culture. For most of the 1960s American architecture and design represented a consolidation of earlier stylistic trends but expressed in a more expansive and opulent form. The Lincoln Center arts complex in New York provides a good example of this, suggesting that in spite of the obvious sophistication, an element of vulgarity had begun to creep in. The influence of the first generation European Modernists who had settled in the USA before the Second World War was becoming watered down by the 1960s; there was less resistance to historical revivalism, classical forms in particular, and the crucial element of in-built austerity and self-imposed self-restraint, which both Modernism and the war had fostered, were lost as a result. The 'corrupting' influence of greater prosperity was also an important factor in the changes that took place. Because there was so much more money swimming around in the economy, successful businessmen were attracted by the idea of making their buildings – whether corporate headquarters or homes – an obvious manifestation of their wealth. Sometimes this was expressed through scale, sometimes through the choice of lavish materials, sometimes through the choice of the artworks – usually large abstract paintings – selected to adorn an interior. Together these were used as a vehicle for making statements about the dominance of American culture on an international level. So although this was not a period of such obvious creativity for the Americans as the 1950s had been, this is not something which would necessarily be deduced from an examination of the interiors of the time, which projected very different messages.

Two unique geographical factors determined the complexion of American design in the sixties. The first and most important was the scale of the country and the size, diversity and distribution of its population. In European countries it was normally the case that one city emerged as the leading centre of design activity and creativity. In the USA, however, the capital was most definitely not the centre of design activity, which instead of being concentrated in a single centre, was dispersed through various cities, including New York, Los Angeles and Chicago. In addition, the diverse cultural make-up of the population, combined with the long distances between different markets, meant that, as in pop music, it was less likely that a single dominant idea would take hold across the whole country. When a new trend did become established, however, it was likely to be widely copied, as a result of which, even though the design was popularized, the work of the original innovator was often obscured. The effect of this was to slow down design progress even further, as Barbara Allen noted in an article on American office furniture in *Industrial Design* in February 1966:

'Another reason for this standstill is that, too often, manufacturers put their engineers (not designers) to work copying good designs which are then mass-produced at low cost. This serves merely to flood the market; it hardly stimulates new thinking.' That the Americans themselves realized that they had failed to capitalize on the design advances of the 1940s and 1950s is indicated by the conclusions reached in a survey of American design between the years 1954 and 1968, published in *Industrial Design* in April 1969:
Industrial design has reaped wealth and prestige in the last fifteen years, and has become very businesslike in the process … Yet, despite all our sophistication and design acumen, we haven't really come as far as one might have hoped in 1954.
The second factor that fundamentally affected the complexion of American design during the 1960s was its physical isolation from Europe. Even in an age of increasingly advanced technological communication systems, there was still a gulf between Europe and the USA, philosophically as well as geographically. After the war, American culture was imported back from the New World to the Old World, along with many American business ideas and business interests, but in reality very few actual American-designed products made the transition. This was partly because the cost of shipping goods across the Atlantic made them prohibitively expensive, but also because at this date the USA, because its economy was still growing, was its own readiest market and had an apparently insatiable appetite for almost any home-produced goods. While this was a healthy situation commercially for American industry, it was an unhealthy situation artistically, as prosperity did not in itself stimulate innovation. Furthermore, astute manufacturers in Britain, Italy and Scandinavia, realizing that there was still room within the American market for expansion, began targeting some of their output at the United States. This explains why, when advances were made in American design, they were often stimulated by innovations originating in Europe. The net result of these two factors – size and isolation – was that, on the one hand, home-produced American design was fairly homogenized but, on the other hand, the range of products available on the market was free-ranging and eclectic.

Having experienced a period of rapid evolution during the 1940s and 1950s, the pace of change in American design slowed down noticeably during the 1960s. American designers and manufacturers were coasting and their approach was becoming formulaic. This was a point made in the February 1966 issue of *Industrial Design*, in a report on the American furniture designer Paul McCobb:
… he feels that designers, having reached a certain point in office design, have been content to remain there too long. Beyond this point, many directions are open, yet few have been investigated. Although cautious of extremes in designs, McCobb feels that an extreme move in some direction is necessary to force designers to apply their creative imaginations.
For most of the 1960s the USA seemed to be lodged in a time warp. Technologically great advances continued to be made, most obviously in the area of space travel, which led people to believe that there was similar progress on all fronts. Aesthetically, however, although high overall standards were maintained, there were considerably fewer breakthroughs in architecture and design than during the previous decade. *Industrial Design* noted in April 1969 that by the end of 1961 the USA seemed to have reached a 'design plateau'; while by

1964 'commercialism and design clichés seemed to dominate a variety of products for the home.'

This sense of a design hiatus, as if the country was in a state of suspended animation, was particularly apparent in the fields of furniture (especially by comparison with the Italians) and pattern design (by comparison with British textiles and wallpapers). In pattern design, in particular, there was a noticeable lack of impetus during the 1960s, even among manufacturers that had been strongly design-led during the 1950s. Some of the most progressive American manufacturers retreated from outright pursuit of the avant-garde and, at most, perpetuated the Contemporary formula into the ensuing decade with only slight and superficial variations. Ben Rose, for example, one of the most adventurous textile and wallpaper designer-manufacturers of the early post-war period, and a leading proponent of the linear whimsical Contemporary style, carried on largely in the same idiom. It was as though, having once discovered a successful design formula, American manufacturers were loath to move on, in case their new ideas were not as successful. This in turn had a sluggish effect on the market, conditioning consumers to become more conservative and less receptive to change. The American rug manufacturer, V'Soske, for example, began the decade in an apparently confident mood with a range of bold abstract and textural designs. Within the space of a few years, however, its commitment to modern design began ebbing away, and its work became increasingly bland during the remainder of the decade. Another rug manufacturer, Wunda Weave, advertised a range of brightly coloured rugs in 1962, which self-consciously reflected design idioms

associated with the previous decade. As late as 1968, when Europe had already moved on into a new cycle of design, American firms were only just starting to promote patterns, such as the Ambla collection of vinyl wall coverings by Winfield, the aesthetics of which had been an essential part of 'the look' of British design in 1962, but which had long since been overtaken in Britain by patterns in a newer idiom.

Mainstream American textile and wallpaper manufacturers struggled to develop a 'look' for the sixties and eventually, having exhausted the Contemporary style, many began to fall back on traditional sources of inspiration. Two leading textile and wallpaper companies, Schumacher and Greeff, both beat a retreat during the early 1960s by re-adopting the formula of floral patterns in traditional styles. Greeff's American Legacy II collection of 1962 was typical of these more retrogressive trends. This was not self-conscious historical revivalism, a fashion that would not emerge until later in the decade, it simply reflected a shortage of ideas and a lack of certainty about the way forward. Whereas in Britain the adoption of large-scale floral patterns during the early 1960s was a short-lived fashion arising out of the vogue for painterly textural abstraction, in the USA the return to representational patterns in traditional styles marked a more decided and longer term shift away from Contemporary, or any other form of wholeheartedly modern design.

There were exceptions to this trend, however, such as Herman Miller where the furnishings division was steered by Alexander Girard. Reference has already been made to Girard's Palio range of 1964, patterns based on simplified versions of Italian heraldic motifs. Raised and educated in Italy,

far left
Advert for printed fibreglass fabrics by Ben Rose, 1964.
centre left
'Designs that challenge the imagination': advert for the American textile manufacturer, David and Dash, 1961.
left
Palette '61 Collection, 1961 by Jack Lenor Larsen, whose fabrics were described as having 'the heady color, sensuous form and rich velvety texture of Art Nouveau'.

Girard's father was Italian and his mother American, which explains the inspiration behind these designs, although the range of different cultural ideas that he drew upon was very much international. In 1961 Herman Miller marketed two new stylized flat floral patterns by Girard called Flores and April. Although possibly referring back to the quasi-botanical floral textiles and wallpaper patterns produced in Sweden and Denmark during the late 1940s, Girard's patterns looked forward in their ultra-simplicity to the trend for Pop Art-influenced flower-power patterns popular during the second half of the decade. Girard, along with another innovative American textile designer, Jack Lenor Larsen, also revealed himself to be ahead of his time in the range of ethnographic sources from which his ideas were derived. Girard himself was a collector of South American folk art, and it is not surprising, therefore, that some of his designs should reflect the imagery and patterns of Mexico, Peru and Colombia. Because of their angularity these patterns also complemented the prevalent geometric trend in design at this time.

The main new identifiable trend in American furnishing fabrics during the early 1960s was for increasingly simple patterns based on coloured stripes, a fashion reflected in the work of both Knoll and Herman Miller, as well as in the popularity of imported Thai silks, such as those marketed by Isabel Scott Fabrics. Striped patterns were also adopted in carpets, where they can be seen in the Grand Stripes range by Berven of California advertised in 1963. In November 1962 *Interiors* announced that Knoll was 'striping its fabrics this season each with its matching or related colour'. Designed by Suzanne Huguenin, the range included strongly geometric

woven patterns with names such as Quartet and Linea. The latter was designed so that the vertical stripes formed a continuous repeat when sewn together in panels, an idea utilized the previous year by Ben Rose in a set of modular striped panels, including one called Mojave Stripe, which, according to *Interiors* in April 1961, was intended to solve 'the nagging contract problem of giving visual life to a large expanse of windows'. The colour schemes for these panels were conceived by Helen Stern, a partner in the firm, and the patterns were printed on either a textured fibreglass fabric or Belgian linen. Three years later Ben Rose launched the Skyline collection, which included matching vinyl wallcoverings as well as printed drapery textiles. With evocative names such as Caissons, Monolithic and Mullions, the new patterns were based entirely on squares and stripes. According to a commentary in *Interiors* in March 1964 at the time the collection was launched, they were inspired by 'the forceful new architecture of the Chicago skyline'.

Another significant development in American textiles was the emphasis on purely textural effects in woven fabrics. Simple geometric patterns and subtle textural effects, both of which exploited the strengths of the weaving process, formed the mainstay of the Bauhaus-inspired approach to textile design exemplified by the hand weaves of Marianne Strengell, and the production designs of Dorothy Liebes for Stroheim and Romann in 1963. Like the fashion for striped patterns, this trend reflected the prevailing penchant for simplicity and understatement. Two fibres commonly used for woven textiles were fibreglass and linen. Fibreglass represented the ultimate triumph of synthetic fibres during the early 1960s, and was

below
Jack Lenor Larsen's Samarkand, a hand screen-printed velvet upholstery fabric, 1968. This fabric belongs to a collection called The Pleasure Dome of Kublai Khan, which was inspired, according to *Interiors* magazine, by 'the legendary and remote trade routes of the silk caravans which Marco Polo followed to Tibet and Peking'.

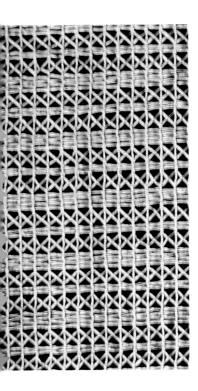

above
Interplay by Jack Lenor
Larsen, 1960. A durable,
fade-resistant, fire-retardant
casement fabric made from
woven saran, which was
heat-set after production
to make it dimensionally
stable.

described by Ben Rose in one of his adverts in November 1963 as 'the finest filaments ever made by man or nature'. At the other end of the spectrum linen was considered important because of its naturally textural qualities, making it ideal for semi-translucent casement fabrics, which were very much in demand because of the increased use of glass in modern architecture. The texture of the material on to which the patterns were printed, or into which they were woven, increasingly took precedence over the pattern itself, as translucent or sheer casements replaced traditional patterned curtains. This trend was astutely exploited by Knoll which, by February 1964, had launched its Casement Collection, a wide-ranging and aesthetically varied group of woven cottons, linens and synthetics with pierced and sheer effects. Although linen had an ancient pedigree, it was as though it was rediscovered by American designers in the 1960s and revitalized through being re-used in a modern context. Imported Belgian linens, like Danish furniture, were also highly revered and symbolized 'the look' of modern textile design in the USA.

While linens were the most popular choice for casements, the innovative Jack Lenor Larsen introduced a fabric resembling crochet called Bobbin Cloth in his Palette '61 collection, woven from bleached white cotton on a Nottingham lace loom. The Tivoli collection of 1962 included a widely spaced open-weave casement fabric called Illusion made of ivory mohair. Designed by Sue Goldberg, the threads of this fabric were so loosely woven that a wavy pattern was created both vertically and horizontally. Although he fully appreciated the subtleties of natural fibres, Larsen, like Suzanne Huguenin at Knoll with her Nylon Homespun upholstery fabric, was just as likely to make use of the latest synthetic fibres if they served his purpose. Other textile manufacturers were also experimenting widely with synthetic fibres at this time. Early in 1963 Herman Miller introduced a medium-weight upholstery fabric called Nylomix. Among Knoll's casement collection of 1964 was a fabric imported from West Germany called Filigree, made from a polyester fibre called Diolen. Diolen was popular because it was easily washable and dimensionally stable, an essential characteristic of loose-weave or sheer fabrics.

Along with Herman Miller and Knoll, the third main American textile firm working outside conventional parameters was Jack Lenor Larsen, led by the designer himself. Larsen's eclectic approach to pattern design stands out as being in a totally different vein to that of his competitors. There was a fearlessness about his choices and a level of drive and commitment uncommon in the American design scene of the time. Whereas other manufacturers played safe and either inched forward or resorted to tried-and-tested formulae, Larsen, although commercially astute, was quick off the mark, and was prepared to take risks and go off in new directions. Although his work is difficult to characterize because it is so wide-ranging in character, two areas that were clearly important during the 1960s were textured weaves and flat stylized printed patterns. Larsen's work was eclectic in a positive and creative way rather than in a negative and reactionary way. As with Alexander Girard, his eclecticism was a reflection of his historical and ethnographic interests: Larsen was constantly seeking out and absorbing visual ideas from textiles of the past and from other countries. He found Europe just as inspirational as Africa, and the Middle Ages just as interesting as

the nineteenth century. Although his collections often focused on particular themes reflecting his latest design discoveries, it is a tribute to his creativity that it is not always self-evident what the original source of inspiration was. His Palette '61 range, for example, was described in a contemporary advert as 'a new collection with the heady colour, sensuous form and rich velvety texture of Art Nouveau', although in reality the patterns were so different from genuine Art Nouveau that it seems perverse to place them in a historical revival category. Whereas other manufacturers exploited historical sources in an increasingly unimaginative way, Larsen used them as catalysts rather than as templates, and his firm's work was characterized by a restless and dynamic search for something genuinely new. In March 1964 *Interiors* described Larsen's Africa 2 collection, which was inspired by the Moorish designs of North Africa, as 'a refreshing contrast to the watered down versions which have filtered through into the Mediterranean style popular in our country today'. At the end of the decade in November 1969 an article in the Danish magazine *Mobilia* summarized Larsen's achievements:

For quite a number of years Jack Lenor Larsen has held the position of one of the most interesting textile designers of the USA. His aptitude for renewing himself is linked together with his interest in the cultures of other countries and his contacts with designers in all parts of the world.

By the mid-1960s Larsen had become associated in the public mind with the latest visual phenomenon to hit America, Op Art. In a feature in *Interiors* in June 1965 entitled 'The Eclectic Eye', produced in response to the Museum of Modern Art's definitive exhibition, 'The Responsive Eye', various patterns from Larsen's Baedeker collection were illustrated, the title of the range suggesting the importance of world travel. Although the inspiration for these designs was clearly ethnographic (two of the patterns were created using wax batik dyeing methods), they were included in the magazine's Op Art survey because of their visual dynamism. According to the commentary in 'The Eclectic Eye':

The world is tuned in on Op. The big revolt from pallid traditionalism can be seen in the art galleries, in the haute couture, and now in the interiors field. A free-wheeling exuberance has taken over with patterns on fabrics and rugs which are eclectic with rhythm and colour.

Among the Baedeker collection was a flocked casement fabric in white polyester voile called Marmara, first shown at the Milan Triennale the previous year, and composed of what *Industrial Design* referred to as 'a series of undulating lines worked into subtle swirls and eddies'. A second swirling linear pattern, evocatively named Hellespont, was made of jacquard woven reversible cotton, and was designed to complement Marmara, with the latter being intended for curtains and Hellespont for upholstery. It was these designs in particular that appeared to demonstrate Larsen's allegiance to Op Art.

As well as being interested in pattern and texture, Larsen was also fascinated by the sculptural potential of textiles. This was something he explored in the award-winning display he designed for the American section of the Milan Triennale in 1964. Exploiting the full height of a high-ceilinged room, this serene and magical installation used long lengths of loose suspended and taut stretched fabrics, some printed, some translucent, to create sculptural canopies through which visitors wandered, as if in a sanctuary or a chapel.

The introduction of stretch fabrics into the Baedeker range was to presage a further important development in the firm's work towards the end of the decade, also linked to Larsen's interest in sculpture. Intrigued by European 'new wave' furniture design of the mid-1960s, particularly that of Pierre Paulin and Olivier Mourgue, Larsen was prompted to rethink his approach to the design of upholstery fabrics. Conventional woven textiles were too bulky and inflexible to be used as coverings on this new type of fluid and ribbon-like frameless furniture, so instead he asked the question in *Interiors* in February 1968:

Why cut and sew to fit fabric on a chaise or around a human body? Why limit furniture design to contours compatible with straight-line, tailored upholstery? Why work with fabric patterns whose clearly defined repeats and directions make them inapplicable for covering flow-lined shapes?

Coming up with a solution to these questions, Larsen produced his first stretch fabric, 'Milestone', in 1965. According to a feature in *Industrial Design* in June of that year: 'The elasticity of this woven fabric anticipates furniture forms that are difficult or impossible to upholster. With such stretch fabrics, tufting and channelling are simplified, and much of the expensive hard labour required to cover sculptural furniture forms is eliminated.' Larsen's stretch fabrics were featured again in the February 1968 issue of *Interiors*, this time in patterned form as part of the Butterfly collection. They included a group of stretch-nylon foam-backed fabrics printed with dynamic overtly psychedelic patterns, some (such as Momentum and Labyrinth) resembling animal patterning, others (such as Firebird and Bojangles) loosely inspired by the exaggerations and visual distortions of Art Nouveau. When Jack Lenor Larsen launched the Butterfly collection, and examples of these remarkable and revolutionary new stretch fabrics on furniture by Paulin and Mourgue were published in *Mobilia*, there was a rare moment of harmony between American and European design.

Although Larsen only designed a proportion of the firm's output (Tony Ballatore was one of their chief designers during the 1960s), the company was very much shaped by his energetic personality and idiosyncratic taste. While he ran a company based on the premise of mass production, what Larsen was really interested in was individual expression.

His approach to design was summed up in *Interiors* in February 1966 in an editorial which accompanied a feature on his house. As with the houses of both Charles Eames and Alexander Girard, Larsen's home was full of miscellaneous objects collected on his travels, some functional, some purely decorative, a fact that led the magazine to conclude:

Aside from the individual charms of each of these things, and their effectiveness in the context of the total environment Larsen has designed for them, they constitute a passionate refusal to abide by the dictates of a world run by and for machines. By insisting on a house as personal as his own fingerprint, Larsen has reminded us that the real sin – in art and life – is the denial of humanity.

The dichotomy between the personal need for individual expression and the economic need for mass production is something that Larsen himself commented upon in an overview on post-war textiles he contributed to a catalogue called *Design Since 1945* produced by the Philadelphia Museum of Art in 1984:

The 1960s was a period of the new Establishment, of the rise of contract design, of the International Style ... There was considerable interest in controlling the glare and the 'night blackness' of the vast new windows of the modern houses and the curtain walls of the new high-rise towers ... We saw, too, a schizophrenic split between a youth-oriented, free-wheeling residential market and the growing contract market, staid and Establishment in its point of view.

The comments made by Larsen about 'the new Establishment' of the 1960s apply equally well to the field of furniture. Furniture produced for the American home market was just as wide-ranging, but in many ways just as limited, as textiles. It encompassed everything from straightforward historical reproduction (such as the 'authentic reproduction' furniture made by the firm of Craftique in North Carolina), to American Modern versions of the Scandinavian Modern style (typified by the restrained designs of Paul McCobb, Jens Risom and the firm of Helikon), to the industrial aesthetic of steel-framed office furniture (exemplified by the work of firms such as Steelcase of Grand Rapids, Michigan, and CI Designs of Boston). In the regular surveys of new furniture published in *Interiors* it appears to have been accepted that there was a pool of styles upon which furniture manufacturers were at

right
Circle Sections, a printed fabric panel designed by Alexander Girard for Herman Miller, *c*1971, similar in style to his patterns for furnishing textiles created during the 1960s.

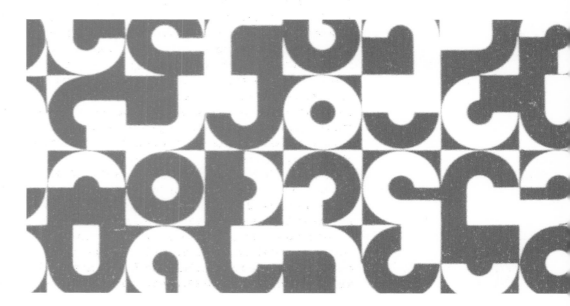

liberty to draw, and that each was equally valid. The adverts and editorials in *Interiors* would suggest that most American interior designers made no moral distinction between revivalism, plagiarism and innovation, although the editorials in the more rigorous *Industrial Design* magazine (which equated to the Council of Industrial Design's *Design* magazine in Britain) were more judgemental. For example, in a feature called 'Looking into Lighting' in June 1965, the magazine lamented: 'There is a superabundance of Early American designs replete with eagles and fluted brass, Miami Beach baroque fixtures laden with cupids and rosebuds, and bland Woolworth modern units – but only a very few well designed pieces scattered in their midst.'

The liberal (some might say, lax) editorial policy of *Interiors* was certainly very different to that adopted by the editors of *Design* magazine in Britain, *Mobilia* in Denmark and *Domus* in Italy, where reproduction furniture received no coverage at all. This reflected the fact that the American furniture industry – and the American design profession in general – was more openly and unapologetically commercial than that in Europe. This was noted with surprise and dismay by John E Blake, writing in *Design* in August 1965 about an exhibition of American Design that had recently taken place at the US Trade Centre in London. Blake suggested that the American designer 'is untroubled by the pangs of conscience that afflict at least some of his European colleagues', concluding, 'What is disturbing about this frankly commercial approach is that it appears to leave little room for the upgrading of design standards.' During the 1950s a powerful mystique had grown up in Europe around American design. This was partly due to the personae of leading figures such as Charles Eames and Eero Saarinen, and partly to the fact that greater affluence had fuelled a much earlier consumer boom in the USA, while Europe was still in the grip of post-war austerity. It took some time before the bubble burst and this mystique began to be questioned. It was not until the mid-1960s that designers in Europe began to realize that they had, in fact, caught up with the USA, and that in terms of innovation, they had actually taken the lead. John Blake concluded:
What emerged from this venture of American design and designers into Britain was a slight sense of disappointment that there was less to tell us than we had hoped, less to show us than we had expected, more common ground, perhaps than we had imagined, yet an uncomfortable suspicion that common words disguised subtle differences of meaning.
In the case of furniture there were, on the surface, many similarities between Britain and the USA during the mid-1960s. Both had healthy markets for reproduction furniture as well as furniture in a restrained Modern idiom. What was different, however, was the design climate in which the industry operated. In Britain reproduction furniture was strongly disapproved of by the design Establishment. Not allowing its coverage or adverts in the pages of *Design* was a way of denying that it had a right to exist. The American design profession was apparently much less severe. In spite of all the proselytizing carried out by institutions such as the Museum of Modern Art through its Organic Furniture and Low-Cost Furniture design competitions of the 1940s and its 'Good Design' exhibitions of the 1950s, the 'design police' did not have such a strong foothold in the USA as they did in Britain and Scandinavia. The more inclusive attitude that prevailed in the USA during

the first half of the 1960s was celebrated by *Interiors* in February 1966 in an editorial entitled 'Sinful Design':
In an era when the design community can shrug off camp, take Op in its stride, and look forward to the next fad with amused tolerance, the Museum of Modern Art's 'Good Design' exhibitions, discontinued more than ten years ago, seem as ancient as the Book of Genesis. How thoroughly we have abandoned the moralistic approach to design which in those days made us apply the language of moral values to aesthetics – when we asked whether design was good or bad, honest or dishonest, rather than whether it was beautiful or ugly! Outdated though it seems today, MOMA's erstwhile fanaticism swept though the design world like a fresh wind through a smoke-filled room. It captured the attention of the public, jerked builders and manufacturers out of a long, nostalgic reverie, and reconciled us all to the machine age. 'Good Design's' very success set us free to appraise its foibles coolly and objectively – its grumpy disapproval of ornament, its Bauhaus obsession with machine production, its shrill insistence on Spartan economy. These were useful ideals to a world repairing itself after a war. 'Good Design's' sumptuary laws prevented waste. But it allowed few luxuries. It was all function and no fun, all work and no play. In the end 'Good Design's' own prophets grew bored – its high priest Edgar Kaufmann Jr. collecting curlicued art nouveau and Victoriana, Miesian architect Philip Johnson designing neoclassical manoirs and sculptural temples, and machine-made chair designer Charles Eames turning to the production of free-wheeling movies.
Already by this date, therefore, a significant shift in attitude was emerging which presaged the second design revolution of the 1960s, and which hinted at the fragmentation of the ideals on which the Modern Movement was based.

While the American design media was conscious of these stirrings, the American public was apparently quite satisfied with the range of goods it was being offered. Increasingly, however, manufacturers in Europe recognized the commercial potential of the American market, and became more proactive and opportunistic in their attempts to secure exports, either directly by finding an agent for their goods, or indirectly by arranging for their products to be made in the USA under licence. These imports added to the eclecticism of the American market. The Finnish firm Finnrya arranged for its rugs to be distributed in the USA by the New York based company Simon Manges and Son, while the Scandinavian Marketing Association, recognizing the potential of the American market for the sale of *rya* rugs, launched a range by Scandinavian designers in 1962. The following year a new marketing organization called the Danish Interior Group, representing six major Danish furnishing fabric and rug manufacturers producing work by leading designers such as Arne Jacobsen, and Nanna and Jørgen Ditzel, established a showroom in New York selling directly to interior designers, architects and furnishing stores. Later that year another group of Danish manufacturers, this time ten different firms in the fields of furniture, lighting and textiles, established the Danish Design Centre on Long Island. Among the goods they sold were furniture by Børge Mogensen and lighting by Ib Fabiansen and Jo Hammerbog. Also in 1963 a Swedish architect, Hans Lindblom, opened a showroom in New York called Scandinavian Design selling a variety of Finnish and Swedish

left
1705 lounge chair and
1709 ottoman designed by
the architect Warren Platner
for Knoll, 1966. Made from
electronically welded,
copper-coated or nickel-
coated steel wire, this
complex design required
1,400 separate welds,
and took several years to
develop. Like Harry
Bertoia's wire Diamond
chair for Knoll, 1952, it
combined functionalism
with sculptural form.

right
Advert for square-section
steel bar furniture by the
American firm, CI Designs
of Boston, 1962. This type
of furniture, widely produced
in the USA during the
1960s, was a spin-off from
the earlier designs of
Florence Knoll for Knoll.
far right
Ribbon chair designed by
Pierre Paulin for Artifort,
1966, covered with a
stretch fabric called
Momentum from Jack
Lenor Larsen's Butterfly
Collection, 1968.

furniture, including classics from the 1930s by Bruno Mathsson and Alvar Aalto, as well as furniture by younger designers such as Sven Kai Larsen and Pirkko Stenrose.

This penetration of the American market by entrepreneurial companies from Sweden, Denmark and Finland had been happening since the early 1950s, when it was first recognized that Scandinavian Modern design perfectly complemented the spaces in American Contemporary interiors, but during the early 1960s the Scandinavian Modern 'look' became more popular than ever, prompting an increase in commercial activity. This gave companies such as the Swedish furniture firm Dux the confidence to establish an American manufacturing base at Burlingame, California, in 1959, followed by a large showroom in the Merchandise Mart in Chicago in 1961. The Danish manufacturers Fritz Hansen and Unika Vaev opened high-profile showrooms at the Decorative Arts Center in New York in 1961 designed by Baard Henriksen and Verner Panton respectively, which were featured in the February 1962 issue of *Interiors*. Also significant was the increased activity among import-retailers such as Frederik Lunning (the man behind the prestigious annual Lunning Prize awards to Scandinavian designers), who offered a range of top quality Danish furniture during the early years of the decade, including a selection of chairs designed by Hans Wegner. Not all import companies ran their own retail outlets; some, such as Dansk Form, simply acted as suppliers to established shops. Sometimes import arrangements resulted from American rather than Scandinavian initiatives, as in the case of the firm of John Stuart, which promoted its Danish Craftsmen Series of chairs during the early 1960s, sold through outlets in New York and Philadelphia.

Also important in America during the 1960s was the firm of Dansk International Design, established by the American entrepreneur Ted Nierenberg in 1954 to sell tableware, kitchenwares and domestic accessories by leading Scandinavian designers such as Jens Quistgaard and Gunnar Cyrén. Produced in a range of materials including ceramics, glass, wood and metal, the goods sold under the Dansk name were not necessarily even manufactured in Scandinavia, and were themselves exported to various other countries, as well as being produced to supply the American market. Although only tenuously connected with Denmark itself, Dansk Design nevertheless played an important role in marketing the Scandinavian Modern image abroad, particularly through the shops and concessions bearing its name in the USA. A similar role was played in Britain by the wholesale import company Danasco, although somewhat more indirectly, as the firm acted as a supplier to shops around the country selling Scandinavian design rather than selling goods directly through its own stores. Among retailers, however, the name of Danasco, run by Palle Glitre, along with that of Finmar, run by Paul Stemann, had great resonance and exerted considerable influence as a tastemaker. Having originally been set up during the 1930s to market the work of Alvar Aalto in Britain, Finmar re-established its reputation during the late 1940s by importing Danish furniture and lighting, and it continued to import furniture designed by Arne Jacobsen, and Peter Hvidt and Orla Mølgaard Nielsen into the UK during the 1950s and 60s.

The New York firm of Stendig played a central role in raising awareness of both Scandinavian and Italian design, in the case of the former by importing furniture from Finland representing the 'new wave' of younger designers such as Eero Aarnio. Thus it was that the European 'look' was introduced to the American market, its impact being particularly striking when compared with the often staid Establishment designs being produced by American manufacturers. Stendig pulled off a major marketing coup when it advertised the imminent arrival of Eero Aarnio's Globe chair at the end of 1965.

Because the Scandinavians had been so keen to establish lucrative commercial outlets in the USA, they had taken the trouble to bring their products to the door of the Americans. Thus Scandinavian design was effortlessly absorbed into the American market, and adopted as painlessly as if it was produced on American shores. Italian design suffered initially simply because of its low profile. Because of the paternalistic role that the USA had played in the liberation and rebuilding of Europe after the war, the Americans saw themselves as the dominant cultural force, and it took them some time to realize that, although so much smaller, and insignificant internationally in political terms, the Italians had more power to infiltrate and influence American design than vice versa. The realization that, culturally, the USA had been overtaken by Swinging London, and in design terms by the upstart Italians, came as something of a shock to the Americans, and initially they found it difficult to accept. After the war they became used to being at the centre of things, and to having their ideas taken seriously. Twenty years later they were in the uncomfortable position of having to keep up with Europe. It was Italian domestic products that contrasted most starkly with those created by the Americans, and it was the arrival of Italian furniture on the American market that demonstrated how far the Americans had fallen behind in creative terms during the first half of the 1960s.

When compared with Scandinavian furniture, American design had seemed to be keeping pace. The revolutionary new furniture of Eero Aarnio imported by Stendig from 1965 had suggested that things might be about to change quite dramatically, but the Americans were totally unprepared for the assault that they were about to receive from the Italians. When *Interiors* illustrated Bruno Munari's

STENDIG 457 Park Avenue, New York City 10022 / Shown: #905 MUSHROOM rattan lounge chair. Designer: Eero Aarnio of Finland. / Write on your letterhead for our new 1964 catalogue.

From Finland
---with Love!
Our new additions can be seen in Chicago, at Space 1156 The Merchandise Mart. Why not visit us soon?

Falkland lamp in November 1966 in a feature on new domestic lighting, the article was called 'Something familiar, something fanciful', the Italian contribution clearly being the 'fanciful' component. The same issue included a feature on Joe Colombo, characterized as 'a young Italian iconoclast [who] delights in stirring up the old controversy between form and function'. Colombo's opinions about the mismatch between technology and aesthetics, cited in this article, were as much a critique of the American dilemma as of the situation in Europe: 'People are confused ... because intellectually they embrace the world of science and modern technology in which they live, but emotionally they still insist on surrounding themselves with familiar objects which have outgrown both time and function.' This dichotomy was particularly apparent in the USA, which prided itself on its scientific and technological achievements, especially in the field of space travel, but which seemed to be suffering from a mounting identity crisis when it came to the issue of domestic design.

As with Scandinavian furniture and textiles during the early 1960s, Italian design achieved a higher profile through being featured in advertisements by leading importers such as Stendig, George Tanier (who acted as an agent for Joe Colombo and Olivier Mourgue) and Atelier International. Atelier International, which had exclusive US distribution rights for the work of Cassina and Flos, established a showroom in New York in 1967 where it featured, among others, designs by Vico Magistretti, and Afra and Tobia Scarpa. Within a short space of time Italian design began to exert a positive influence on American design, just as Scandinavian design had done seven or eight years earlier. The impact of Italian design was clearly recorded in a feature entitled 'Way-Out Lighting' in *Interiors* in September 1968. Whereas twelve months earlier

there had been a noticeable gap between Italian and American lighting design, the arrival of the latest Italian lighting on to the American market had prompted a burst of design activity among American manufacturers. Although several of these designs were somewhat derivative, manufacturers were clearly making an effort to be more visually inventive, recognizing the importance of the relationship – so central to Italian design – between the fine and applied arts. During the last two years of the decade the American design fraternity finally acknowledged how far behind they had fallen, and began to make a concerted effort to catch up. On the whole, though, it was only small firms such as Habitat Inc. and Neal Small that managed to be really innovative; the latter's imaginative use of plastics, acrylics in particular, had a natural affinity with Italian design.

Italy

The character of Italian design itself during the 1960s was coloured by the close interrelationship established since the Second World War between the three main branches of the visual arts: architecture, fine art and the applied arts. Because there was no specialist design education system in Italy as such, most designers were trained as architects, which prompted a free crossover of ideas between these two disciplines. What was unusual about Italy in comparison with other countries was that there was no obvious hierarchy between the three different branches, whereas in most other countries a ranking system was in operation, with the fine arts at the top, architecture in the centre, and the applied arts at the bottom; making value judgements about the relative aesthetic merits of different disciplines had the detrimental effect of driving a wedge between them, and thus of discouraging the

free flow of ideas. This process was accelerated by the increasing specialization and isolation of practitioners. Architecture and industrial design, for example, became increasingly technical during the course of the 1960s, while craftspeople sought to establish a separate identity for them- selves through the creation of a breakaway movement. Although for some this isolation served to liberate the imagi- nation, there were negative effects too, as practitioners became more inward-looking. The Italians were largely untrammelled by such false divisions, however, and *Domus* provides an impressive testament to the benefits of the free flow of creative ideas between art, architecture, craft and design during the 1960s. Not only is this evidenced by the range of subjects tackled in the magazine – a new art exhibi- tion was just as likely to be featured as a new building or a new chair – but in the unselfconscious way in which it was accepted that ideas from one field could feed into another. It was assumed that readers of the magazine had open minds, and that they would judge the material with which they were presented on its own merits, rather than on the basis of an artificial, externally formulated value system.

The free-ranging approach to design in Italy is demonstrated by the work of leading practitioners such as Ettore Sottsass and Gio Ponti. A new range of lamps designed by Gio Ponti for the firm of Lumi, and featured in *Domus* in December 1961, could quite easily be mistaken for relief wall sculptures, while the patterns on Ettore Sottsass's enamels, also dating from 1961, bore a strong resemblance to the paintings he displayed two years later. Sottsass in par- ticularly clearly felt there were no boundaries to the scope of his activities and interests. It was less a case of trying his hand at something, than of applying his mind. Thus during the 1960s the gamut of his activities encompassed writing, photography, ceramics, enamels, jewellery, architecture, furniture, painting, sculpture and product design. Similarly, in the field of fine art, Lucio Fontana and Fausto Melotti, two key figures of the 1960s, ranged freely between different media, and what is striking about their work from a foreign perspective is the ease with which they encompassed both the two-dimensional and the three-dimensional, or combined elements of both within a single object. Giò Pomodoro, a sculptor and painter who, with his brother Arnaldo, also designed sculptural jewellery during the 1950s and 1960s, was another example of an artist who was uninhibited about applying his talents to different branch- es of the fine and applied arts. During the 1950s he had designed abstract printed textiles, but with his jewellery he immersed himself in pure ornamentation. The resulting works were rich and jagged, composed of clusters of multi-textured jewels and precious metals.

Unlike the Americans, the British and the Scandinavians, all of whom were still largely preoccupied dur- ing the first half of the 1960s with the idea that form should follow function (a concept that imposed many false restraints), the Italians were driven less by the head than the heart. Their guiding precept could be characterized as 'form follows emo- tion'. Although a supra-rational element did come to the fore in Italian design towards the end of the decade, embodied in the late work of Joe Colombo and the Radical Design move- ment, what enabled the Italians to make such significant advances during the first half of the 1960s was that they set their own agenda, and did not feel compelled to play by the

same rules as the other design superpowers of the day. Significantly, when the Americans and the Scandinavians reached an impasse during the mid-1960s, it was to the Italian model that they were obliged to turn in order to free their imaginations.

Whereas in the field of pattern design the interrela- tionship between the fine and the applied arts is easy to trace, the correspondences are not so obvious with everyday domestic objects. One Italian designer who clearly approached the design of such objects with the creative intensity and inventiveness of an artist, however, was Enzo Mari in his wide-ranging work for the Milanese firm of Danese. Mari was an artist by training and had studied at the Accademia di Bella Arti in Milan during the mid-1950s. He was also a theoretician, and carried out extensive research into the psychology and perception of colour, space and vol- ume. Like the maverick designer Piero Fornasetti, although in a less self-conscious and more thoughtful way, Mari focused his mind on a particular object, such as a vase, then allowed his imagination free range, and conceived a collection of designs that were like musical variations on a theme. In some ways his approach resembled that of the fashion designer, who each season faces the challenge of producing an entire collection rather than just a one-off individual outfit. One of the benefits of such an approach is that it encourages lateral thinking. Rather than tackling the design of an object directly, the designer stands back, and by distancing himself from the problem in hand, arrives at a variety of novel solutions. Mari's work demonstrates that it is possible to be both functional and imaginative at the same time; in fact, in many instances it was by allowing himself to be freely and uninhibitedly imagina- tive that he arrived at an ingenious breakthrough in practical terms, as in the case of his conical Pago-Pago plastic vases of 1969, which can be inverted to accommodate either small or large bunches of flowers.

Another Italian designer whose work was idiosyn- cratic and original, and encompassed various media, including ceramics, glass, metalwork, furniture and lighting, was Sergio Asti, who had trained as an architect at the Milan Politecnico. Although he started out in an apparently conventional mode with the ceramic plant pots he designed for Gabbianelli in 1963, Asti's work took on a weird other-worldly quality when he first began to design in glass. Working in opaque white glass for the Murano firm of Salviati in 1964, Asti developed an entirely new range of forms in a neo-organic vein, which, although soft in outline, were utterly unlike the biomorphic organic designs of the 1950s. Asti's forms took on the smooth appearance of Space Age plastics, although he aban- doned the hard and precise geometrical forms that others were using at this time in favour of melted but still highly con- trolled forms. Such was the strangeness of his designs that they gave the impression of being designed not in a studio but in a laboratory, as if created by genetic engineering.

The concept of the artist-scientist working in his studio-lab was an idea that took hold in Italy during the mid- 1960s and strongly influenced the course of both object design and interior design over the next few years. Its chief exponent was Joe Colombo, and the culmination of his experiments was the 'Visiona 69' installation that he created at the Cologne Furniture Fair in 1969, a capsule-like Habitat of the Future where most of the basic elements were made of plastics. In an article in the Danish magazine *Mobilia* in August 1969, comparing Colombo's futuristic interior to a flying saucer-shaped experimental house called the Villa Fjolle near Stockholm designed by the young Swedish architect Staffan Berglund, it was noted that: 'Both Colombo and Spies have every imaginable kind of radio-stereo and TV device … Close to the beds are ingenious control panels from which the mechanical arrangements of the house are controlled.'

Although Colombo was one of the most outstanding Italian designers of the decade, he was by no means alone. Italy was bursting at the seams with talent. In creative terms the situation had been encouraging during the 1950s – the period of 'riconstruzione' – but now it was even healthier. Industry was expanding, many adventurous new applied art manufactures were being established, and the demand for exports was growing. Because the Italian economy was back on its feet, this meant that, unlike during the early post-war period, it was actually possible to ensure that good design ideas went into production. Without an expanding manufacturing base, and without a receptive market, there would have been no boom in Italian design during the 1960s and very few designs would have left the drawing board.

There were also major changes taking place in many industries. Although manufacturing methods in traditional crafts such as glass-making changed little, the Italian furniture industry was revolutionized during the 1960s. Prior to this it had been almost entirely workshop-based, the basic material had been wood, and most production had been in the form of high-quality joinery. New or newly industrialized furniture firms such as Arflex and Tecno had introduced far-reaching changes. Arflex, which was a subsidiary of Pirelli, had been responsible for developing and popularizing new forms of suspension in the form of rubber webbing, and new forms of padding for upholstery in the form of rubber foam. The 1950s had also witnessed the rapid expansion of the chemicals industry in Italy, dominated by Montecatini. This trend continued in the 1960s, and led to the widespread application of plastics within the Italian furniture industry, particularly via firms such as Kartell and Artemide. For established companies such as Cassina the 1960s was a time of consolidation and expansion, which led to the increased mechanization and rationalization of production processes, and the growth of professional administration and marketing. It was noticeable, for example, during the course of the decade how much more effort firms such as Cassina began to put into marketing as a way of expanding their operations.

As well as the dramatic increase in the number of firms, particularly in the fields of furniture and lighting, and the growth in the size of the leading manufacturers, the other development that was particularly noteworthy in Italy during the second half of the 1960s was the expansion of joint marketing initiatives via specialist trade fairs. This was where the design media was important, with *Domus* playing a particularly dynamic role. In 1966, for example, the first 'Eurodomus' trade fair was held in Genoa, bringing together many leading Italian applied arts manufacturers. Unlike the Triennales, which during the 1950s had been aesthetics-led and during the 1960s were increasingly issues-led, 'Eurodomus' was a more straightforwardly commercial venture, albeit one at which the overall standards were high, and where there was a basic guarantee of design quality. This was a celebration of Italian

Charlie Towsend, from Cardiff, letterato, se la porta al week-end si siede e scrive con Valentine nel prato.

valentine
olivetti

design by the Italian design media, a blowing of Italy's trumpet at home and later abroad, when an exhibition called 'Domus Formes Italiennes' was shown at the Galeries Lafayette department store in Paris in 1967, followed by 'Domus Design' in Zurich in 1969.

What other countries noticed about Italy was how forward-looking its designers were, and the unusual way in which Italian design was allied with the visual arts on the one hand, and bound up with a futuristic vision of society on the other. In a feature on Italian lighting in *Mobilia* in April 1968 the writer noted: 'In recent years the Italian designers' inborn sense of the dramatic has become more clarified … The vision of things to come, and of what can be done to make them come, influence many of the Italian designers' and artists' conceptions of their surroundings.'

In addition to technical experimentation, what distinguished Italian design was the way it was used as a forum for intellectual debate. According to Andrea Branzi in his history of post-war Italian 'new wave' design, *The Hot House*, published in 1984:

The avant-garde of Italian architecture, unlike those of England, Austria and America, assumed that its own works of cultural revival had a political content. Triumphalism and analysis of the alternative uses of capital allowed pop culture to be used as a 'Trojan horse' within the limited and partial setting of bourgeois culture with its fragile reformist equilibrium.

Radical discussion about the purpose of architecture and design had been an important thread running through Italian design right from the start of the decade. Ever since 1960, when a specific theme was first adopted for each Milan Triennale, it was natural that debate should be focused on this event, which was why it evolved from being a straightforward celebration of aesthetic achievements into a forum for questioning the state of design in the modern world. There was

a certain inevitability that the Triennale itself would finally be used as a vehicle for expressing protest about the design Establishment. This was largely because it had an ambiguous role as a showcase for design and a promotional tool for the latest products, as well as a catalyst for critical debate.

At the end of the decade, in October 1969, a perceptive article appeared in *Mobilia* on the Furniture Fair in Milan, which provides an apt conclusion to this discussion of Italian design. Like Andrea Branzi, the Danes had recognized that there had been a unique but artificial hot-house atmosphere in Italy during the 1960s, and they linked the Italian design revolution specifically to the alliance between the Italian furniture industry and the Italian plastics industry:

The Italian furniture boom, progressive, untrammelled, and refreshing, must be ascribed to the implicit belief of these factories that their chance lay with investment in [the] development of synthetic materials products in close co-operation with the very best designers. This was a happy gamble – courage brought them conviction right from the beginning.

While admiring the achievements of the Italians, however, the Danes found it hard to believe that they could sustain this level of activity much longer: 'This year's Italian furniture fair had the effect of a climax to a number of years of intensive efforts in the field of the new plastic materials … The near future will probably show a calmer picture of Italian furniture design with meditation and closer study of designs …' Because the Danes had been made to feel so keenly aware of the creative and commercial edge that Italian design had over the Danish furniture industry, it was perhaps not surprising that an element of wishful thinking should creep into their judgements. This was evident in their suggestion that the momentum of the Italians was unsustainable, and that the frenzy of creative activity witnessed in Italy during the second half of the 1960s would inevitably be succeeded by a lull.

above
Marco vases designed by Sergio Asti for Salviati, 1962. During the 1960s the Italians increasingly dominated international design, assuming premier position in the superpower league. Italian supremacy came about partly because of the talent of individuals such as Ettore Sottsass and Joe Colombo, but also because of the sheer volume of Italian designers and the intensity of their activities.
right
Pago-Pago plastic vases designed by Enzo Mari for Danese, 1969.

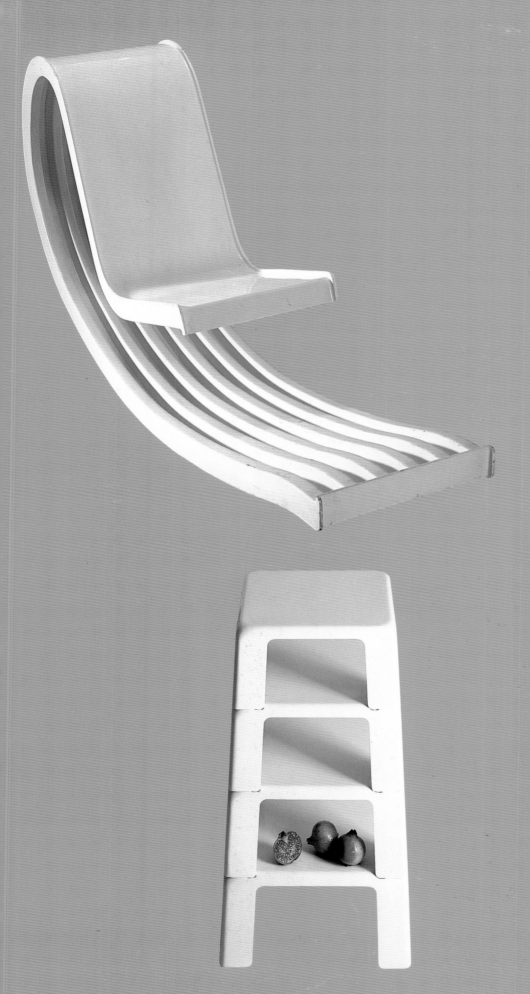

above left
Dondolo rocking chair
designed by Cesare Leonardi
and Franca Stagi for Elco,
1969, made of ribbed fibreglass. Plastics dominated
Italian furniture design during
the 1960s: designers and
manufacturers were much
quicker to appreciate and
exploit the potential of these
materials than their competitors in other countries.

above
Bacco Mobile Bar designed
by Sergio Mazza for
Artemide, 1969.
left
Quattro Gatti (Four Cats)
fibreglass stacking tables
designed by Mario Bellini for
C & B Italia, 1966.

Denmark

Denmark had established a similarly high profile in modern design, particularly in high-quality furniture during the 1950s, but by the 1960s it had lost some of its momentum and proved less of a powerhouse for generating new ideas. Apart from the mass-produced bent plywood furniture of Fritz Hansen, Danish furniture tended to be associated with high-quality woods and fine craftsmanship. Manufacturers such as J L Møller, which specialized in elegant teak-framed dining chairs, typified this aspect of the industry. Although Møller in fact relied almost as heavily on industrialized production techniques as Fritz Hansen, the image it projected was one of hand craftsmanship rather than mechanization, because of the superb finish that the firm achieved. The widespread promotion of the quality assurance mark of the Danish Furniture-Makers' Control Association reaffirmed this commitment to excellence, an image that was further reinforced by articles in the media, such as a feature in *House and Garden* in March 1961 entitled 'Some of the furniture that has made the Danes' renown'. During the early 1960s there was a clearly identifiable visual character and a reassuring consistency about the Danish Modern style. Later, although standards were to remain high, some designers such as Verner Panton, Jørn Utzon and Grete Jalk made a self-conscious attempt to dissociate themselves from this restrictive image, and thus, as the decade progressed, Danish design developed more of a split personality.

An exhibition of Danish design held at the Design Centre in London in 1968 provided the occasion for Richard Carr's interesting analysis of 'The challenge that faces Danish design', published in *Design* in May 1968. Carr noted that in recent years Denmark had appeared to be suffering from 'a lack of design innovation', and ascribed this in part to the fact that 'Danish furniture has become almost synonymous with the 1950s – and, in consequence, just as dated.' Carr proposed, as one explanation for this, that Danish designers may simply have burnt themselves out during the 1950s following a frenzy of activity in the early post-war period, and that it was because manufacturers had been so successful during the 1950s that they were now 'disinclined to move with the times'. Carr concluded his analysis by querying the economic viability of the industry in the future unless it addressed the vexed issue of cost: 'The previous strength of Danish furniture – its craft tradition geared to making high quality pieces on comparatively short runs – has become a drawback in a world where the emotional value attached to furniture, and the price people are prepared to pay for it, is rapidly changing.' Here Carr exposed the real problem: by the late 1960s the world was rapidly changing but Danish design had not evolved quickly enough to keep pace. The Danes themselves were not unaware of the dilemma they faced in trying to compete with their recent glorious past. In her commentary on the Scandinavian Furniture Fair, Grete Jalk wrote in *Mobilia* in May/June 1968 that the fair 'gave an impression of much vacillation, of uncertainty which is widespread in the world today in general, and in the Danish furniture field in particular after the "great" years.' Jalk warned, however, that it was unwise for the Danes simply to co-opt ideas from Italy, where the furniture industry was very obviously thriving, as this approach was not necessarily appropriate to the character of Danish design. Jalk noted with concern that at this year's fair 'Many

furniture people had been "inspired" a little too much by excellent Italian products', but questioned 'why run after others?'

Although truly innovative work was limited to a relatively small number of Danish designers, the influence that they exerted was nevertheless quite considerable, particularly the visually inventive Verner Panton. After working as an associate of Arne Jacobsen during the early 1950s, Panton established his own architectural and design practice in Denmark in 1955. In 1962 he moved to France, and the following year he settled in Switzerland. Recognizing that his ideas about design did not fit into the established pattern of thinking in Denmark, Panton clearly felt more comfortable working in a wider European, rather than a specifically Danish or Scandinavian, context. Apart from his work for the Danish lighting manufacturer Louis Poulsen and the furniture firm Plus-Linje, he worked mainly with European furniture manufacturers during the 1960s. His single most important design, a one-piece cantilevered plastic stacking chair designed in 1960, was eventually produced as the Panton chair by Vitra in Germany on behalf of Herman Miller from 1968. Originally conceived in advance of the plastics technology required to make it – indicating how far ahead of his time Panton often was – the Panton chair rapidly became an icon of modern design in the same way as Saarinen's Tulip chair for Knoll had done during the 1950s.

Panton's profile on the international design scene is indicated by the fact that he was twice invited by the chemicals company Bayer to create a special installation as part of the Cologne Furniture Fair, first in 1968, and again in 1970. As with the showrooms he had designed earlier in the decade for the Danish textile manufacturer Unika Vaev, in his first installation Panton exploited the colours, textures and patterns of the textiles at his disposal. In this case the material was Bayer's synthetic fabric, Dralon, specially printed for the occasion with giant enlarged photographic images of lips, hands, feet, eyes and ears. Draped from the ceilings and walls, Panton's installation created a dreamlike ambiance, with the textile-lined interior being complemented by examples of the designer's remarkable furniture and lighting. Svend Erik Møller described the installation in *Mobilia* in February 1968 as 'a firework of light and colours; sound and fragrance, furniture, lamps, and thrilling experiments in textiles. His furniture was no common furniture but visions of a future more emancipated way of life, sculptures made in air and foam.' The furniture on display included the Panton chairs, some upholstered foam-slab furniture made by the German firm of Metzeler-Schaum and Alfred Kill of Stuttgart, and a group of giant rubber balls upholstered with Dralon towelling, made specially for the installation, while among the lighting was Panton's new dome-shaped pendant Flower Pot lamp designed for Louis Poulsen.

Whereas Verner Panton used his designs to offer radical alternatives to conventional lifestyles, the architect Jørn Utzon was less concerned with making grand statements through his furniture, and more with refining an aesthetic that offered an alternative to the self-consciously hand-crafted look associated with Danish furniture. In the Floating Dock range of modular seating and tables which Utzon designed for Fritz Hansen in 1967, he used U-shaped hoops of beech plywood in triangular cross-section as the interchangeable parts of a flexible framework. Such ideas were the legacy not of Danish design but of the work of the Finnish designer Alvar Aalto

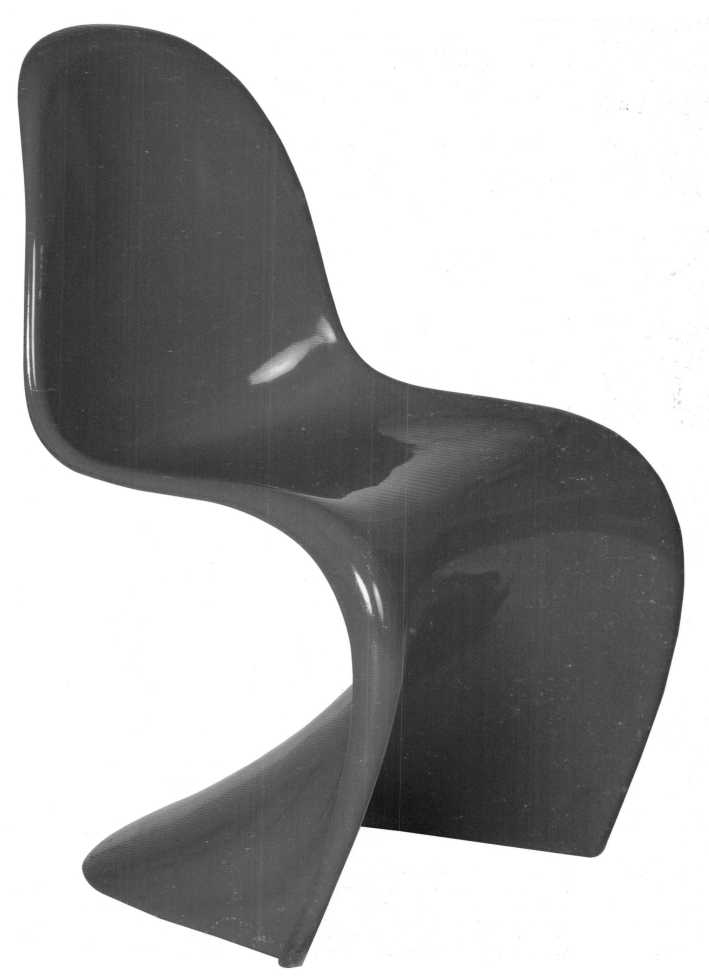

during the 1930s, although as used by Utzon this structure was simpler and more flexible. Described by *Mobilia* in July 1967 as 'a coherent furniture landscape', Utzon's Floating Dock system was in keeping not only with the functionalist concept of modularity, but with the contemporary idea of rooms as evolving habitats.

Towards the end of the decade Utzon's work became increasingly sculptural, his forms reflecting the revival of interest in neo-organic shapes. One low-level stacking chair designed in 1968 for the Danish firm Bramin, and produced under licence in Italy by Casala, was called Fallen Beech Leaf, and attempted to capture in an abstract way the outline and curvature of a dead leaf. Utzon's 8101 chair for Fritz Hansen, which came with the accompanying 8110 footstool, had a sling-like bent tubular steel frame with a billowing seat of bent plywood lined with upholstered polyfoam. Utzon's most memorable design of the decade, however, was the sculptured polyfoam public seating system he designed for Ken Muff Lassen in 1968. Made of expanded moulded polystyrene, the liquid plastic used to make each section was enlarged under forced air pressure to forty times its original size. The system consisted of three basic multi-curved elements that could be joined together, one behind the other, to create a seat, a low seat back and a high seat back. Each section was cut at an angle of 22.5 degrees, so that when placed side by side the units created a natural curve. In this way Utzon combined modularity with sculptural form, producing a range that was comfortable and visually dramatic.

Gradually, as a result of the contributions made by designers such as Utzon and Panton, it came to be accepted in Denmark that there was more to furniture design than the Wegner approach of exploiting beautiful woods and harnessing fine craftsmanship; more even than the Jacobsen approach of the inventive use of bent plywood and steel. Furniture design, the Danes discovered, was also about exploring the potential of synthetic materials, and about experimenting with pure sculptural forms, both geometric and organic. Often during the later 1960s these two new areas of interest were united. As in Italy new materials prompted a new philosophy of design which liberated the creative potential of the designer. The exploration of frameless sculptural upholstered forms, with a foam-rubber or plastic core, was one of the wider international trends that astute Danish designers such as Grete Jalk adopted towards the end of the decade. Jalk herself provides an interesting example of a Danish designer who responded positively to the dramatic changes taking place in international design during the 1960s. Originally trained as a cabinetmaker's apprentice between 1940 and 1943, she then studied furniture design at the Copenhagen School of Arts, Crafts and Design until 1946. During the 1950s, while teaching, she established her own design office in 1954. Most of her furniture was produced by the firm of Poul Jeppesen, her earliest pieces being hand-crafted in the Danish Modern style, although by the early 1960s, inspired by the work of Charles Eames, she had begun working with bent laminated plywood to produce simpler and cheaper designs for chairs and nests of tables. A ribbon-like side chair designed in 1963 was ingeniously created from two pieces of bent laminated plywood, while an armchair from the same year had a barrel-shaped frame composed of a single strip of plywood folded back on itself, into

which a flat seat was slotted. These ribbon-like forms suggest comparisons with the work of Pierre Paulin for Artifort and, like Joe Colombo's bent plywood chair for Kartell dating from 1965, Jalk's chairs presage the design ingenuity that would later be applied to plastics. During the second half of the decade, it is not surprising to learn that Jalk did indeed move in this direction. At the Danish Furniture Fair in 1969 she exhibited a range of modular seating designed for the firm of Erik Jørgensen, based entirely on velvet-upholstered soft polyether-foam cushions. These were cut into two shapes, with a cube for the base, and a semi-circle cut out of a triangle serving as the seatback.

One of the most adventurous furniture manufacturers in Denmark during the 1960s was the company run by Paul Cadovius, the creator of the successful Abstracta metal space frame display system. So unique was his contribution that Torben Schmidt lamented in *Mobilia* in May 1969: 'One might wish that there were more furniture manufacturers who had Paul Cadovius' courage and intrepidity.' Cadovius himself was an architect and a designer, as well as being the owner and manager of the firm that bore his name, which explains why his company was so strongly design-led. Drawing on the talents of a wide range of freelance designers, the firm's output was diverse. While some designs were relatively conventional and made use of traditional materials such as wood, most had some unusual feature that distinguished them from the mainstream. A feature on the company in *Mobilia* in May/June 1968 included illustrations of several startling but somewhat contrived designs made of moulded fibreglass-reinforced polyester, including a set of low three-legged chairs designed by Aage Egeriis, a cantilevered armchair by Steen Østergaard, and a prototype for a stacking chair with an adjustable seat designed by Peter Karpf. Also striking was the upholstered foam furniture designed by Johannes Larsen, composed of linked geometric forms that folded out to produce seating in various flexible arrangements. Only a year later, a whole new set of innovative designs was on show in the inspiring setting of Cadovius's converted barn showroom in the Christianhus at Horsholm. Illustrated in a second *Mobilia* feature, the new range included an unusual set of tubular steel chairs designed by the architect Preben Dal, which had swivel seats and seat backs in the form of foam rubber balls covered in synthetic stretch fabric. Also revolutionary were the vacuum-pressed stackable PVC chairs designed by Gjerløv Knudsen and Torben Lind. Shaped like a large flared bucket and intended to be similarly inexpensive, these cheap and cheerful chairs came with a loose disc-shaped cushion, and could be stacked very compactly, just like buckets. As with Terence Conran in Britain, the importance of Cadovius in Denmark was as a design-led entrepreneur rather than as a designer *per se*.

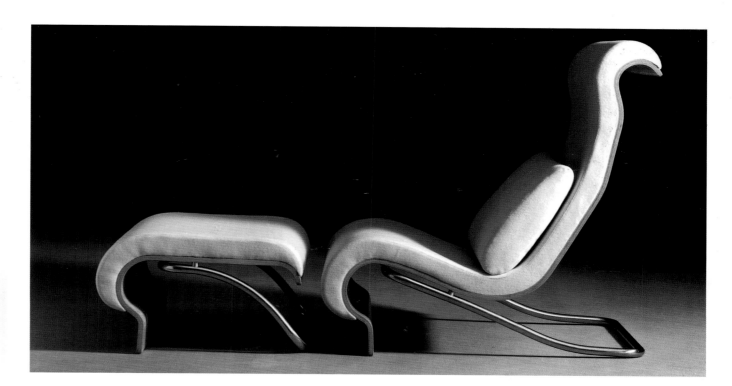

Sweden

Individualism and innovation were qualities somewhat lacking in Swedish furniture design. The Swedes were popularizers rather than initiators of new trends in furniture; they tended to look to their neighbours – Denmark in particular – for ideas, then quietly and efficiently produce and market their own versions. For this reason much Swedish furniture is virtually indistinguishable from Danish furniture of the same period, an example being the teak desks produced by the firm of Sandslätts of Alsterbro, which were very much in the Danish Contemporary style, and the blond oak sideboards produced by Hugo Troeds to designs by Nils Jonsson during the early 1960s, which could easily be mistaken for work in the same material and with a similar aesthetic being produced concurrently in Denmark.

Sweden's design strengths were in other areas of the applied arts such as ceramics, glass and metalwork, and it was in these areas that the Swedes made original contributions at an international level, as in the case of the metalwork designer Sigurd Persson. By way of demonstrating this point, Swedish designers who won the Lunning Prize during the 1960s included the studio potter Hertha Hillfon in 1962; the ceramic designer Karin Björquist in 1963; and the glass designers Gunnar Cyrén in 1966, and Ann and Göran Wärff in 1968. Sweden's glass industry was particularly buoyant during this period; there were many different firms and each projected a distinctive image through their adverts in the Swedish design magazine *Form*. In 1961, for example, Flygsfors advertised a range of mould-blown vases decorated in relief with primitive patterns inspired by carvings on ancient Viking graves at Birka designed by Victor Berndt. Boda meanwhile continued with the Brutalist aesthetic developed by Erik Höglund during the 1950s, producing stocky vessels in which impurities and blemishes were deliberately left untreated in the glass. At Johansfors during the early 1960s, Bengt Orup designed finely blown angular tableware decorated with engraved geometric line patterns. Of the factories that had dominated the industry during the 1950s, Orrefors continued to produce work of the highest quality both technically and aesthetically, supplementing the proven talents of Ingeborg Lundin with the colourful and playful designs of Gunnar Cyrén. Works by Lundin using the Ariel technique were accompanied by blown vessels used as a vehicle for bold painterly engraved abstract designs. Responding to the prevailing Pop aesthetic, Cyrén explored the potential applications of colour in glass. His two most important designs were the cartoon-like enamelled patterns on his Sweden bowls, 1967–8, and his Pop goblets, 1967, decorated with bands of enamel colouring within the stem. The other leading Swedish glass manufacturer of the 1950s, Kosta, having recently recruited a new designer, Mona Morales-Schildt, was assertive in promoting a completely new image. Schildt designed thick-walled vessel forms with multiple layers of coloured underlay, the surfaces of which were decorated with large circular or oval mirror cuts creating optical effects. Adverts for the new Kosta 'look' began to appear in 1962, and continued the following year with the launch of the cylindrical Granados range.

Other designers who contributed to the diversity of the Swedish glass industry during the early 1960s included Folke Walwing and Britt-Louise Sundell at Målerås; Bengt Edenfalk at Skruf; Tom Möller and Paul Kedelv at Reijmyre;

Kjell Blomberg at Gullaskruf; and Gunnar Ander and Christer Sjögren at Lindshammar. During the mid-1960s, however, there was a sudden upsurge of creativity as the Swedes began to be infected by the dynamism of the international studio glass movement. The second half of the decade was a particularly exciting era in the history of Swedish glass, dominated by the work of Lars Hellsten at Skruf; Erik and Margareta Hennix at Johansfors; Göran and Ann Wärff at Pukeberg and Kosta; and Bertil and Ulrika Vallien at Åfors. Whereas during the first half of the 1960s most designers had perpetuated the familiar aesthetics of the Scandinavian style, the younger generation of designers who emerged in the middle of the decade rejected refinement and elegance in favour of spontaneity and vigour. As in Finnish glass, mould-blown and free-blown vessels with irregular forms and rough uneven textural surfaces were created, but the imagery that the Swedes developed, such as the flamboyant Red Square sculpture of 1965 inspired by the Kremlin and designed by Lars Hellsten at Skruf, was highly idiosyncratic and personal.

In ceramics the industry was dominated once again, as it had been during the 1950s, by the firm of Gustavsberg. The main difference now was that Stig Lindberg, who had completely dominated the firm's output during the 1950s, was no longer the company's artistic director. Although he remained involved with the factory throughout the 1960s, his work was now supplemented by a host of other designers. The younger artists working in the Gustavsberg studio introduced many new ideas from studio pottery and, as in Swedish glass, textural effects became particularly important. Relief textures were created either by making marks in the clay or through applied decoration on the surface, a typical example being the spherical vessels with impressed patterning designed by Karin Björquist for an installation at the Georg Jensen shop in New York in 1964. Björquist had taken over Wilhelm Kåge's studio at Gustavsberg in 1961, and as well as producing one-off stoneware vessels, she also designed production wares such as the Marmite tableware range of 1964, decorated with an impressed circular motif. Gustavsberg regularly advertised in *Form* throughout the 1960s, and these images provide a good record of the firm's creative output during this period. In *Form* (no 2) in 1962, for example, Britt Louise Sundell's Mykene tableware was illustrated, a thickly potted stoneware range decorated with bands of impressed circles and dots. Later in the year the large-scale stoneware vessels of Lisa Larson were featured, decorated with impressed and incised striations in loose painterly arrangements. Hitherto such a free and uninhibited style of decoration had not been common in Swedish ceramics, the work of Lindberg himself being extremely varied and imaginative but highly controlled. Clearly Gustavsberg was a place where creative expression was actively fostered during the 1960s, and because artists were encouraged to explore their own ideas, this resulted in some remarkable creations, such as Bengt Berglund's robot-like sculptures of 1963. Gustavberg's main competitor, Rörstrand, also continued to play a leading role during the 1960s, with active input from two designers who had helped to create the firm's image during the post-war period, Hertha Bengtson and Carl-Harry Stålhane. As at Gustavsberg the rougher and more varied textures of studio pottery were increasingly influential. For a range of vases produced in 1962 called Klitt, for example,

above
Vases designed by Mona Morales-Schildt for Kosta, early 1960s, in which layers of different coloured glass have been exposed by cutting. Swedish glass took on a Jekyll and Hyde character during the 1960s: some designs were cool and restrained; others were gaudy and extrovert.

far left
Pop goblets designed by Gunnar Cyrén for Orrefors, 1967, inspired by tropical fish and the brash colours of Carnaby Street.

left
Crystal Fruits, designed by Ann and Göran Wärff for Kosta, 1967. The Wärffs took a hands-on approach to the design of glass, and their work was very much in tune with the pioneers of the studio glass movement in the USA. Their sense of freedom is apparent in this exotic sculpture.

Hertha Bengtson used a rough grainy chamotte stoneware body in order to create a richer surface. A range of unique pieces made by Sylvia Leuchovius for Rörstrand in 1962, decorated with jewel-like incised and applied decoration, was also made of chamotte stoneware. Rörstrand continued to achieve world-wide success during the 1960s with their distinctive tableware, some designed the previous decade, particularly the ranges decorated with patterns in deep cobalt blue, such as Swedish Blue designed by Carl-Harry Stålhane.

Swedish textiles represented another area of design strength in the applied arts, and added to the body of work which ensured that Sweden maintained its design superpower status during the 1960s. By comparison with firms such as Heal's in Britain, Marimekko in Finland, and Jack Lenor Larsen in the USA, however, the Swedish approach to furnishing fabrics was much more restrained. Striped and linear geometric printed patterns were common at the start of the decade, such as San Remo by Lisa Gustafsson and Brooklyn by Inez Svensson, both produced by the firm of Wäfveribolaget Borås, and both winners of Svensk Form's Good Design Awards in 1961. Two other prevalent types of printed design during the early 1960s were stylized leaf patterns (such as Göta Trägardh's Mexicana pattern for Stobo Textil, and Bladguld by Annika Malmström for Mölnlycke) and mandala-type radiating circle patterns (such as Himmelsbloss by Birgitta Dahlström for Farma Textiltryck, and Tivoli by Inez Svensson for Borås Wäfveri). All these designs appeared in adverts in *Form* during 1962. Similar motifs had first been introduced by the Finnish designer Viola Gråsten, who worked in Sweden from the 1950s onwards designing for both Mölnlycke and Nordiska Kompaniet. Another designer who had been associated with Nordiska Kompaniet during the post-war period was Stig Lindberg. A significant transitional design incorporating elements of both Contemporary design and 'the look' was Lindberg's pattern Tallyho, composed of rows of apples with tiny leaves and stalks, winner of a Gold Medal at the California State Fair in 1962. Although representational, the pattern presaged the widespread use of circular motifs in the 1960s. The first Swedish firm to embrace 'the look' wholeheartedly, however, was Claes Håkansson of Kinna in its Universum fabric, 1962, designed by Brita and Lennart Svefors, which had a bold geometric pattern of circles inside squares. Woven fabrics were as important in Sweden as printed textiles, and one of the leading firms was Borås Jacquardväfveri which produced patterns using the jacquard weaving technique. A typical design was Speglar by the handweaver Alice Lund, a pattern of squares within a grid, which was advertised in *Form* (no 1) in 1962. Later in the year the firm advertised a pattern called Diamant by Göran Hammargren which incorporated the same bold mandala-type motifs used on printed fabrics at this date. By comparison with Britain, therefore, the range of styles and motifs used in Swedish textiles was quite limited, and it appears that Swedish designers were not encouraged to be as freely inventive as their counterparts in the UK.

Although the Swedes themselves were content with their subdued version of the Scandinavian Modern aesthetic, some foreign commentators were critical of its predictability. The English journalist Patience Gray wrote in *Form* (no 10) in 1961: 'To be perfectly honest I (a barbaric Englishwoman) am bored to death with the Swedish emphasis on domestic perfection … I long for the casual uncalculated element, which is not a feature of Swedish life.' However, following a trip to Sweden itself, which involved taking a train journey through the Swedish countryside, Gray felt that she had developed a better understanding of the reasons behind the Swedish obsession with consistency and control:

As I travelled by train through Sweden I felt I was beginning to understand more about the Swedish approach to life. I detected the monotony which is a recurrent theme reflected in Swedish artifacts. This might explain the compelling search for form, a basic longing, the persistent groping for identity, snatched as it were from an endless sameness. I felt I understood the lack of tonal interest in Swedish textiles (birch against fir) and the emphasis on sparkling freshness conjured from the transparent air. The source of that blonde subtlety hard for a foreigner to grasp is the feathery grass fringes on the mirror lakes.

This is an illuminating interpretation of Swedish design, but as Gray pointed out at the end of her commentary, it was important for the sake of Sweden's future role as a design superpower that inconsistent and even iconoclastic forms of creative expression should be encouraged to develop alongside the 'monotonous'. At this stage Gray identified the studio potter Hertha Hillfon, the ceramics manufacturer Gustavsberg, and the Orrefors glass factory as producers of exciting work. She would no doubt have been pleased to witness the extent of the creative flowering that took place in the Swedish glass industry during the second half of the 1960s and, as in the field of ceramics, the way in which the studio movement gave creative impetus to the factory system.

Finland

Because Finland was more out on a limb than Sweden and Denmark, and because its population was, in any case, a lot smaller, its designers and manufacturers had to make more of an effort to ensure that their voices were heard outside Scandinavia. Another hurdle that the Finnish design profession faced during the 1960s was competing with the dauntingly high standards and the distinctive image of 1950s Finnish Contemporary design. Finnish glass and ceramics in particular had been so successful abroad, and leading designers such as Tapio Wirkkala, Timo Sarpaneva and Kaj Franck had received so many accolades at international exhibitions, that initially during the 1960s it was difficult for new talent and new voices to attract attention. Eventually, though, a number of younger designers did emerge, and they made their names not by emulating the style of their predecessors, but by developing a new voice and a 'look' unmistakably associated with the sixties. The most important of these were the furniture designers Eero Aarnio, Yrjö Kukkapuro and Esko Pajamies; the glass designers Oiva Toikka and Nanny Still; the textile designer Marjatta Metsovaara; and the textile manufacturer Marimekko.

The link connecting Finland's three leading furniture designers was their commitment to developing a 'look' for Finnish furniture in the 1960s that signified a complete break with the past. For Aarnio this meant embracing the potential of plastics and exploiting it to create new furniture shapes that reflected, first, the geometric trend in design, perfectly captured in his Globe chair of 1965, and later, the fashion for neo-organic forms, encapsulated in his Pastilli chair of 1968. The work of Esko Pajamies was less flamboyant: and in his use of tubular steel as a framework for his furniture, and in the clean-lined industrial aesthetic he developed, his work is more closely allied with the international Modernist tradition. The work of Yrjö Kukkapuro, one of the youngest ever winners of the Lunning Prize in 1966, was much more idiosyncratic. Kukkapuro was clearly uninterested in conventional ideas of beauty and good taste, as there was an apparently deliberate awkwardness to some of the forms he created. What he was interested in was comfort and practicality. Typical of his work is the Carousel chair of 1965 for Haimi Oy with its plastic pedestal base and its upholstered plastic shell seat, suspended on a steel spring so that it could be rocked backwards and forwards. An indication of the new philosophy influencing the direction of his work is given in comments made by the designer in an article on Finnish furniture in *Industrial Design* in May 1967, which reveal a distinct shift in emphasis away from aesthetics towards ergonomics: 'The relationship of the human being to an object is important, especially in the design of a chair. The basis is always the human being, and his physiological demands of the chair. The object creates the milieu, not vice versa.' The Lunning Prize awarded to Kukkapuro was a recognition of the fact that the character of Scandinavian design in general, and Finnish design in particular, was changing in quite a radical way during the second half of the 1960s, and that this was essential for its long-term survival as a potent force within the international design scene.

Like Verner Panton who left Denmark to live and work in Switzerland, one way in which Finnish designers established an independent voice and identity was by moving abroad and developing links with other manufacturers. Both Marjatta Metsovaara and Nanny Still established roots in Belgium, the latter as a result of marrying an American sculptor who was based in Brussels. In the case of Metsovaara, as well as designing for both hand and machine production for her own firm, Metsovaara Oy, based at Urjala in Finland, she also arranged for her textiles to be woven by firms abroad, including Van Havere – Van de Velde in Belgium, where she established a studio. Some of her designs were also produced under licence by Jack Lenor Larsen in the USA. Metsovaara, who was described by *Form* magazine in 1965 as 'a new star in Finland's textile heaven', designed both woven and printed textiles (although mainly the former), some of which were intended as upholstery fabrics, some as suit fabrics. She also designed traditional Finnish long-pile *rya* rugs, machine-produced by a company called Finnrya, which were extremely popular during the first half of the 1960s. As with Marimekko, Metsovaara became associated with 'the look' through her use of geometric patterns. The pattern on a hand-woven *rya* rug entitled Nukka which dates from 1965 was, for example, based on spirals. Because of the nature of her work, many of her woven textiles were striped or chequered, but patterns from the early 1960s also included huge circular motifs.

Metsovaara had made her name earlier in the decade with richly textured tweed fabrics produced in ravishingly bright colours – pink, orange and blue especially – where the visual interest was in the colour and in the depth and textures of the weave. In 1960 she won a Gold Medal at the Milan Triennale, the first of many honours she would later receive. Metsovaara also designed jacquard woven textiles. For her Primavera collection of 1967 she used this technique to incorporate stylized floral patterns into the weave. The same bright colours were used as earlier in the decade but the patterns were now closely allied with contemporary printed fabrics and revealed an interest in psychedelia and flower power. In a feature on Metsovaara in *Mobilia* in January/February 1969, the designer was described in glowing terms as a 'glittering star in present-day European textile design', a 'Titan of the textile world', and a 'dynamic glutton for colour and a bold experimenter with new types of textile'. By this date her output included rugs, wall coverings, curtain fabrics, and both smooth woven and coarse tweed furniture upholstery fabrics, as well as patterned jacquard weaves. All these different textile ranges were produced in interrelated colours so that they could be easily co-ordinated and combined, possibilities which were demonstrated to clients when they visited Metsovaara's impressive showroom in Helsinki.

The most potent symbol of the dynamism and freshness of Finnish design during the 1960s was the firm of Marimekko. Run by the autocratic but inspiring Armi Ratia, Marimekko grew out of and later subsumed a company called Printex, originally a manufacturer of oilskin clothes, which was revitalized by Ratia during the early post-war period and transformed into a factory for making hand-printed furnishing and dress fabrics in a bold modern style. Ratia herself, along with Maija Isola (who was recruited in 1949), and Vuokko Eskolin-Nurmesniemi (who joined in 1954), were the chief designers at Printex during the 1950s, and Isola continued to design hand-screen-printed furnishing fabrics for Marimekko throughout the 1960s. Eskolin meanwhile went off and established her own firm, Vuokko, in 1964, which was also very successful.

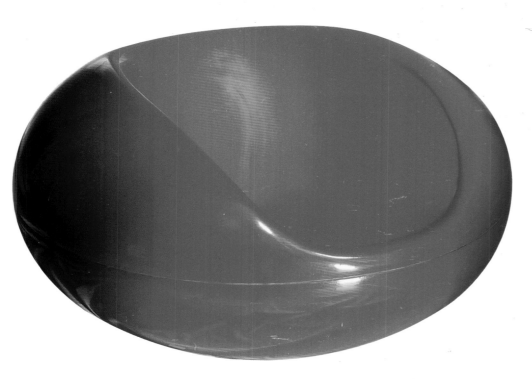

left
Pastilli or Gyro chair designed by Eero Aarnio for Asko, 1968. Aarnio was the most high-profile Finnish furniture designer of the 1960s, and his work was internationally acclaimed. This chair shows the designer successfully harnessing plastics to explore the type of seamless neo-organic forms he had previously created from natural materials such as rattan.

below
Bonanza armchair and sofas designed by Esko Pajamies for Asko, 1968. Towards the end of the decade there was a new trend in Scandinavia for sofas of this type with plank-like rectilinear wooden frames and leather- or fabric-covered cushions.

below
Carousel 412 armchair designed by Yrjö Kukkapuro for Haimi Oy, 1965. At first sight this appears to be a conventional pedestal chair, but in fact the plastic shell seat is suspended from a steel spring, thus enabling the chair to be rocked. The leather-covered cushions are attached with press studs so that they can be removed for cleaning.

top and left
Marjatta Metsovaara was Finland's leading designer and manufacturer of woven textiles during the 1960s. Her work combines technical ingenuity with a vivid sense of colour and texture. In addition to tweeds (left), Metsovaara also designed patterned jacquard-woven textiles, such as the Primavera range for her company Metsovaara Oy, seen here in an advert from 1967 (top).

During the first year it produced a printed design called Pyörre (Whirlpool), a giant calligraphic swirling motif which could be used to dramatic effect on both dress fabrics and furnishing fabrics. An image of a bare-foot model wearing a dress made from this fabric, photographed in triple exposure, became an icon of the 1960s Scandinavian Modern 'look'. Although Isola, who had trained as an artist rather than as a textile designer, is best known for her bold large-scale daubed painterly patterns, some of her textiles from the early 1960s were small-scale, intricate and highly detailed patterns inspired by Karelian folk art. A group of designs illustrated in a feature on Isola in Form (no 6) in 1963 included several pieces with an overtly Slavic character. Three others, called Nooa, Noitta and Joonas, were totally different in character, composed of wavy line patterns with a quasi-biological character. It is the endless variety and complete originality of Isola's work at this date that make it significant; her ideas were quite unlike those of any other designer in the 1960s. Classic large-scale patterns designed by Isola during the first half of the 1960s, which were responsible for establishing the company's international reputation, included Silkkikuikka of 1961, a wavy line pattern printed in bands of bright colours; Melooni of 1963, a pattern of giant ovals; and Kaivo of 1964, a vibrant pattern of compressed concentric spheres.

Marimekko was originally established as a subsidiary of Printex in order to produce dresses from printed fabrics to popularize the new style of patterns being produced by Printex. What happened, however, was that Marimekko was a runaway success in its own right, and eventually the furnishing fabrics produced by Printex were marketed under the name of Marimekko instead, as the latter was recognized as the most powerful and effective brand name. The first Marimekko shop opened in Helsinki in 1957; by 1964 there were ten. Unusually at this date, Marimekko offered an aesthetic that encompassed a complete lifestyle. While it became increasingly common during the course of the 1960s and 1970s for fashion designers such as Mary Quant and Pierre Cardin to branch out into other areas of the applied arts, it was unusual for a textile manufacturer to move from furnishing fabrics to dress fabrics, and more unusual still for a fabric manufacturer to move across into designing and manufacturing dresses, the firm of Horrockses in the UK being a notable exception. Marimekko was remarkable in a number of ways, not least for the complete originality and endless creativity of its printed designs, but also for the daring simplicity of its dresses. Observers noticed that a special aura permeated the company, which they ascribed to the unique personality of its managing director, Armi Ratia. In a feature on Marimekko in Form (no 1) in 1964 Susanne Frennberg wrote admiringly: Joy in the beautiful permeates the company in a totally unique way. A factory always graced with fresh flowers is not exactly common. Moreover, Marimekko is really a vision of a way of life. The garments are the result of a democratic dream of clothes for most women and occasions. But also for a new type of woman – aware, active, proud, independent. Clothes which serve without demanding too much time and attention. Marimekko means 'a dress for all girls', more or less. But still, due to its unconventional and informal style, it has exclusiveness. Export deserves much of the credit for the fact that the distinctiveness can be maintained – they do not cater to the *tastes of as many women as possible in a small area but rather go out to find those who want just what Marimekko has to offer anywhere in the world.*

It was largely because of active marketing by firms such as Marimekko, which were not content to restrict themselves to the home market but took active steps to consolidate their position abroad, that Finland maintained its position as a design superpower during the 1960s.

International recognition, although not always an accurate or full reflection of a nation's achievements, at least provides an indication of the scale of a country's aspirations. This is why the Montreal Expo was so important, because it reflected the healthy spirit of competition that characterized the 1960s. The Expo confirmed that the international design climate was extremely buoyant during the mid-1960s, and it suggested that, not only design professionals, but also the general public, had a high degree of curiosity concerning design on a global level. This infectious curiosity had been reflected in the international design media since the start of the decade. Although it had its work cut out keeping on top of the flourishing Italian design scene, *Domus* was always on the lookout for information about interesting new developments abroad. A similarly alert attitude prevailed in the Danish magazine *Mobilia*, where great efforts were made, not only to ensure detailed coverage of developments in Scandinavia, but to keep the magazine's readers abreast of activities in the rest of Europe and the USA. The Swedish magazine *Form* and the British magazine *Design* were both somewhat more constrained in their remit as a result of being published by official government bodies, although both contained regular features on international developments, as did the *Architectural Review*, which had a monthly feature on world architecture at the beginning of each issue. *Interiors* magazine in the USA was rather more insular in its coverage, except in the case of imported foreign furniture and furnishings, whereas the editors of *Industrial Design* were more proactive in their efforts to feature the work of designers and manufacturers from abroad. What everyone was forced to recognize by the end of the decade was that in the field of furniture and lighting the Italians were in a different league, a fact belatedly but handsomely acknowledged in New York through the landmark exhibition 'Italy – The New Domestic Landscape' held at the Museum of Modern Art in 1972.

right
Multiple-exposure of model wearing a dress made of Whirlpool, a fabric designed by Vuokko Eskolin-Nurmesniemi for Vuokko, 1964.
Printed textiles for furnishings and dresses were among Finland's great strengths during the 1960s. The industry was dominated by two firms, Marimekko, run by Armi Ratia, and Vuokko, run by Vuokko Eskolin-Nurmesniemi. The latter originally worked for Marimekko, but left in 1960 and established her own company in 1964.
below right
Great Crested Grebe furnishing fabric by Maija Isola for Marimekko, 1961.

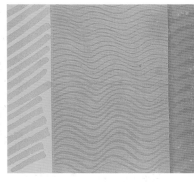

left
Monrepos dress designed by Annika Rimala for Marimekko, 1967, made from Oasis fabric, 1966.
far left
Minuet furnishing fabric designed by Anneli Qveflander for Marimekko, 1968.

design in revolt

opposite
Large Psychedelic Spheres designed by Giusto Toso for Fratelli Toso, 1970. The imagery of psychedelia, originally inspired by hallu-cinogenic drugs, spread from discothèques, posters and record sleeves to all areas of the applied arts during the late 1960s, including furnishing fabrics, wallpapers, ceramics and even glass.

above
Jane Fonda in the film, *Barbarella*, 1968.

right

Soviet tanks roll into Prague in August 1968 crushing the liberal Dubcek regime. The Summer of Love in 1967 was quickly followed by 'the year of the barricades' in 1968. Both movements had a direct impact on design.

Our homes are like so many cubes, square boxes of the same sort that are being piled up in Rome, Tokyo, Rio, New Delhi, Paris, Accra or London. This world-wide anonymity, this universal urbanization toward taller and more impersonal sugar-cubes, has touched off an enormous revolution in people. Half the battle today is our drive toward individuality.
Emily Malino, 'Speaking of Colour', *Industrial Design*, April 1967

Until 1967, the year of the Montreal Expo, the future of international design seemed clear and there was a general consensus about the way forward. Shortly after this, however, the mood began to change, and architects and designers started seriously questioning the assumptions that had moti-vated them up until this date. There was less agreement about what the future held, and a growing interest in exploring individual ideas rather than imposing blanket solutions, a trend very much in evidence, for example, in Ralph Erskine's Byker Wall housing scheme in Newcastle built from 1969 onwards. Although this re-evaluation produced many positive outcomes – design was much more varied and less pre-dictable – there were some negative side-effects as well. Whereas the first half of the decade was characterized by convergence and mounting confidence, the last quarter of the decade was marked by divergence, fragmentation and doubt. In 1968, 'the year of the barricades', as it has been described by the writer David Caute, many issues came to a head, and the widespread social discontent that erupted was reflected by an acceleration in the process of disintegration in design. The latter part of the decade was a period of counter-revolution, a time when numerous radical design theories and

often contradictory design alternatives were put forward, and everybody was determined to have their own say.

In many ways 1967 was a remarkable year, with the achievements of international architects and designers being celebrated with unparalleled enthusiasm at the Montreal Expo, with Italian design reaching an all-time high in terms of creativity and critical mass, and with the spread of the peace movement and flower power culminating in the Summer of Love. During the first seven years of the decade Italian design had been riding on an incredible tide of success, the creative momentum of which had been entirely positive. During the last two years of the decade, however, established and emergent figures within the Italian design fraternity began to call into question some of the fundamental tenets on which their success was based. In 1968 Italian architects, designers and students got caught up in the growing international protest movement that was beginning to sweep through Europe and North America. This protest movement is easy to understand in relation to the Civil Rights and anti-Vietnam War demonstrations in the USA; the invasion of Czechoslovakia by the Soviet Union in Eastern Europe; and even the more intellectual arguments behind the anti-Establishment student demonstrations and the General Strike in Paris. It is also easy to see how these diverse issues could be rolled together into a multi-faceted anti-Establishment protest movement. However, it is less easy to comprehend why the design fraternity in Italy should have been so vocal in its protests given that, in many ways, things appeared to be going so incredibly well. However, it is an irony of the human condition that when worn down by failure, people are motivated to fight back; but they are just as likely to tire of success, and to react against it in an apparently irrational and destructive way. There is

only so long that any regime, repressive or creative, can expect to continue in power before arousing murmurs of dissent and calls for change.

What happened in Italy in 1968 at the time of the Mila Triennale was that these murmurs of dissent erupted, and the design Establishment suddenly found itself confronted by the questioning of the avant-garde. On 30 May 1968, the day the Triennale was scheduled to open, a group of demonstrators occupied the exhibition and locked the doors, a sit-in which lasted for ten days. According to *Domus* in its commentary on the event, there was little resistance when the protesters moved in as many of the exhibitors sided with them, and agreed with their accusation that the organizers were both cliquey and fascist. The magazine concluded that this 'internal malfunction' indicated 'a desire for renewal', and suggested that this ground swell had, in fact, been growing throughout the decade: *Perhaps the doubts which this explosion brought out into the light had already been present, noticeably in the last two or three 'editions' of the Triennale – which were increasingly focused on social criticism, translated into visual spectacle – a 'spectacle of problems' with no solution proposed, justified, however, by its formal brilliance.*

What the writer was suggesting was that it was an excess of self-consciousness that had prompted the revolt in the end. By raising difficult issues and highlighting the impossibility of solving them through design alone, the Triennale called into question the very validity of design as an activity. To the protesters it seemed that in its present form design could only generate problems and then analyse the problems it had created for itself; it was incapable of providing solutions without being radically overhauled.

One of the reasons why the design protest movement emerged so strongly in Italy, as opposed to Scandinavia or the USA, was simply the intensity of creative activity that had taken place there during the decade. Significantly, the other country where an identifiable protest movement took place in relation to the visual arts was Britain, and it seems that it was partly because the art and design education system was so well developed, and because students had such high expectations, that they were so ready to express their dissatisfaction. In an article in *Design* in August 1968 called 'The sit-ins and beyond', the editor was of the opinion that: 'It is not surprising that the frustration of students, and many staff members, has bubbled over. The growing feeling of futility and aimlessness cannot be exaggerated.' What the protesters were drawing attention to was the complacency and authoritarianism of the design Establishment (including the educational Establishment), and what they were seeking to do was to stimulate a freer and wider debate about contemporary design, and a recognition of the value of greater diversity. The ideas of Victor Papanek were widely discussed during the late 1960s, as was the new theory of ergonomics. Papanek criticized American designers for wasting their time designing useless gadgets for the wealthy when they could apply their talents much more fruitfully for the benefit of the poor, the sick, and the disabled. In an article in *Industrial Design* in April 1969, he warned apocalyptically 'Only by using design as a political tool, design as a tool for the survival of mankind, shall man himself prevail.' The related interest in ergonomics grew out of approaching design from a primarily scientific, rather than aesthetic, point of view. Furniture was the first area to which ergonomics was applied, particularly domestic storage systems, an area of study pioneered by the Swedes and the Danes. Subsequently office furniture came under the spotlight, prompting articles such as the one that appeared in *Design* in April 1966 by Dorothy Meade entitled 'The odd ergonomic inch and why it matters in the office'. Later in the decade other areas of design were scrutinized, such as tools and cutlery, in an effort to match the shape of implements to the shape of the hands which operated them.

However, as well as prompting positive initiatives such as these, another effect of the student protests and social unrest of 1968 was to trigger off destabilizing forces and to make the situation as a whole more fragmented. The design climate at the end of the decade was summarized by Emilio Ambasz in the preface to his catalogue of the exhibition *Italy: The New Domestic Landscape* held at the Museum of Modern Art in New York in 1972. With the benefit of hindsight Ambasz was able to put the events of 1968 into context and into perspective:

Design in Italy today does not present a consistent body of ideas, with respect to either form or ideology. Its complex marches and countermarches made it necessary to develop what might be called 'provocation' techniques that would result in an exhibition revealing the contradictions and conflicts underlying a feverish production of objects, which are constantly generated by designers, and which in turn generate a state of doubt among them as to the ultimate significance of their activity.

Ambasz then went on to explain in more detail what he believed these different factions to be, grouping them into three categories: conformist, reformist and contestational. The conformist group, by far the largest, were those designers who accepted the existing structure and purpose of applied art industries and were happy to work within this framework. The reformist group were those who questioned both their own role as designers and that of industry, but who continued working within this framework in an ironic or subversive way. As Ambasz points out, there was a large degree of crossover between these two groups:

The distinction between the two main approaches so far discussed, the conformist and the reformist, is in reality not so clear-cut. The oscillations of designers between these two attitudes reflect the contradictions and paradoxes that result from simultaneously doubting the benefits of our consumer society, and at the same time enacting the role of voyeurs of the technological dream.

The third approach, the contestational, was very much a hard-line minority movement, but one that became

opposite top left
Prairie Chicken House, Norman, Oklahoma, designed by Herb Greene, 1961. The work of Greene and another idiosyncratic Mid-West architect, Bruce Goff, prefigured some of the eclectic alternatives that other architects would begin to explore towards the end of the decade.
opposite top right
Byker Wall Housing, Newcastle-upon-Tyne, an early example of 'social architecture' designed from 1969 onwards by Ralph Erskine. This scheme, developed following extensive consultation with the local community who were to be rehoused in it, reflects a desire on the part of the local authority to adopt a more humane approach to high-density low-cost housing.
opposite bottom
The hippy movement of the late 1960s was just one of the reflections of the fragmentation of society and design towards the end of the decade.

right
Student protests in Paris, 1968.
far right
Protesters at the Milan Triennale in 1968, who forced the closure of the exhibition.

increasingly vocal during the late 1960s, encouraged by the general climate of anti-Establishment protest, and it was to this group that the direct action taken at the 1968 Triennale can be ascribed. These designers refused to collaborate with industry, and confined their action to political protest or awareness-raising through philosophical discussion. Ambasz recognized the validity of all three groups, which is why his survey exhibition encompassed conventional, unconventional and radical forms of expression, and included written manifestos as well as individual objects and installations. He also pointed to the wider significance of the events in Italy during the late 1960s, suggesting that they were symptomatic of fragmentation on an international level:

Italy has become a micromodel in which a wide range of the possibilities, limitations, and critical issues of contemporary design are brought into sharp focus. Many of the concerns of contemporary designers throughout the world are fairly represented by the diverse and frequently opposite approaches being developed in Italy.

Radical Design

The closure of the Milan Triennale was the most visible symbol of the fact that the design revolution of the early 1960s had been overtaken by a counter-revolution. On a broader level, the growing international fragmentation was reflected in the divergent paths pursued by various individuals and alliances within the Italian avant-garde during the second half of the 1960s. It was not that they were necessarily all opposed to each other; but increasingly they had different priorities, expressed through distinct aesthetics, each with their own coded messages. In 1966, for example, Ettore Sottsass collaborated with the plastic laminates manufacturer Abet to create a series of mysterious striped wardrobes, Katalogo Mobili, which were shown on Abet's stand at the first *Eurodomus* exhibition, variants of which were subsequently manufactured by the radical furniture firm Poltronova. Sottsass had begun his career by designing imaginative individual objects isolated from any wider context. Through his exploration of two-dimensional pattern-making (both oil paintings and surface-decorated applied arts such as enamels and ceramics), he had expanded his repertoire and increased the scale of his ambition. This led to the design of interiors, complete environments in which Sottsass exerted control, not just over the form and layout, but over the surface decoration of

floors and walls as well. In many ways, therefore, his alliance with Abet can be seen as a natural progression from these other activities, as was the application of plastic laminates to furniture design to create his Katalogo Mobili, and the idea of using these wardrobes in a symbolic way to suggest a new kind of environment. Like his self-consciously decorative ceramics, Sottsass used this furniture as a vehicle for transmitting moods and meanings. Tommaso Trini remarked in *Domus* in April 1967: 'These new wardrobes are both more and less than furniture. They erupt into the centre of the interior, liberating the domestic space at their leisure and creating a concentric movement of expansion. Isolated in the middle of the room and banded with colours, they eliminate, as it were, the presence of the walls.' Trini also meditated on the designer's fearless attitude towards decoration, and on his relationship to Op Art and the Modern Movement:

For twenty years, now, Sottsass has been working in terms of planes rather than in terms of structures; in form that becomes colour, and therefore sign, he has searched for a means of communication that goes beyond the rational ... The primitivism of this new electrical and spacial era is the context to which Sottsass's work is connected. But Sottsass, expanding into the mythical, works in counterpoint to the situation, unlike the others who magnify its technological aspect.

The Katalogo Mobili was years ahead of its time when it appeared in 1966. Many of Sottsass's ideas would not receive widespread acceptance until they were repackaged fourteen years later under the guise of Memphis, and officially re-classified as manifestations of Post-Modernism.

Sottsass became a guru for young avant-garde Italian designers, and he, in turn, drew attention to the work of the younger generation. When the radical design group Archizoom Associati emerged and their work was featured in *Domus* in October 1967, it was Sottsass who wrote the accompanying commentary. He particularly valued Archizoom's contribution to the debate about contemporary design because of the fearless way it questioned and subverted the ideas of the design Establishment:

I am very pleased to have been picked to present these 'Archizoom' gentlemen and their products to you because I find these products of theirs most conducive to spreading panic among those with vested interests in a country like ours, where things cultural and ideological are so highly organized, stratified, stereotyped and sedimentary.

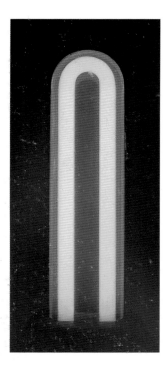

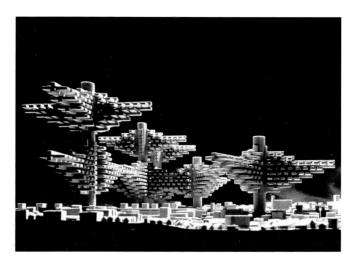

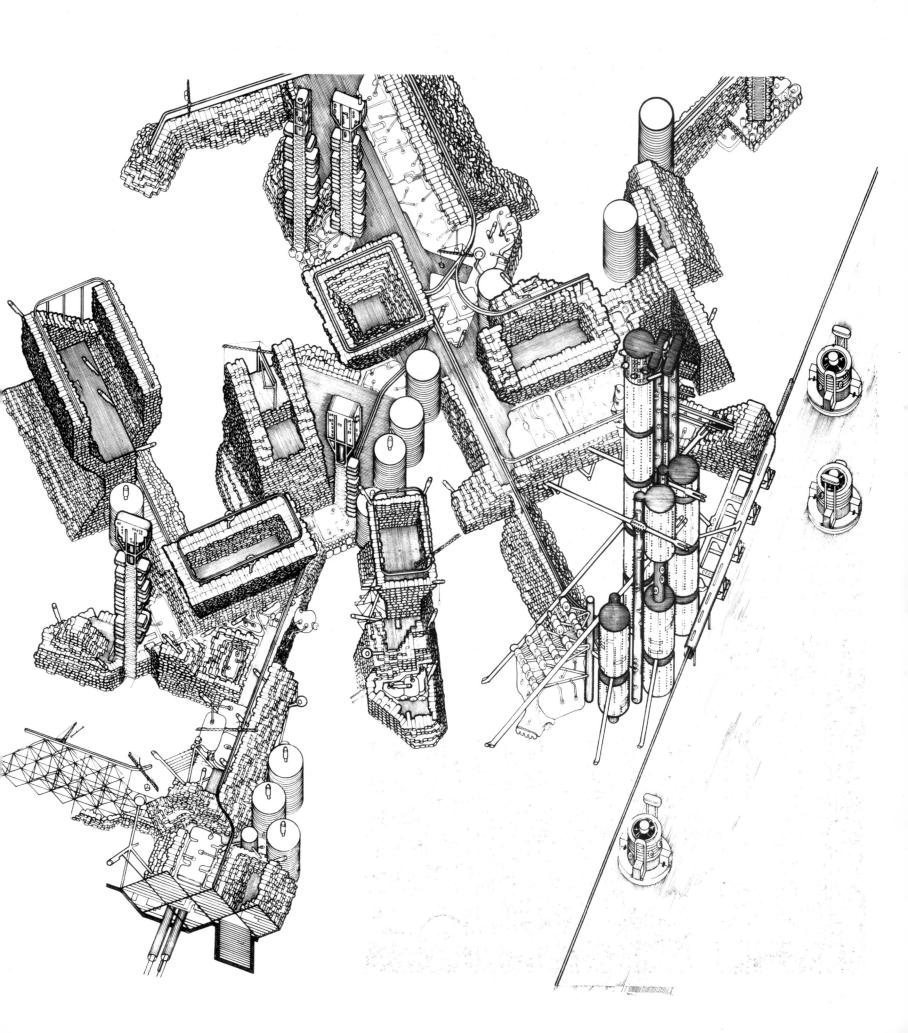

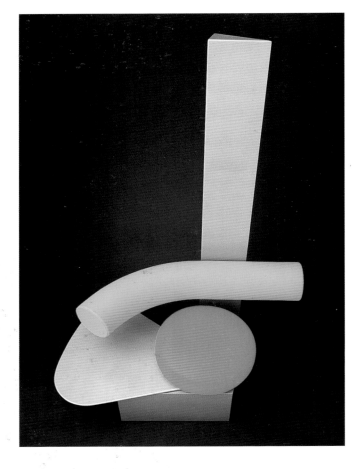

Formed in 1966, and active as a group until 1974, Archizoom was a Florence-based alliance of six designers, all in their twenties, whose polemical ideas were as important as the actual objects they created. In this respect they were following in the footsteps of the radical British architectural group, Archigram, which sent its first architectural telegram to the world in 1961, and continued to publish manifestos in comic book-style throughout the course of the decade. The members of Archigram were Warren Chalk, Peter Cook, Denis Crompton, David Greene, Ron Herron and Michael Webb. Archigram's work was deliberately provocative but amusing, very much in the spirit of contemporary Pop Art (particularly its 'Living City' exhibition of 1963), and thus an interesting and revealing reflection of the changing concerns of the time. Its Plug-In City of 1964, for example, was devised in response to the concept of built-in obsolescence, each building being designed so that it could be unplugged and disposed of after it had come to the end of its useful life. Archigram achieved notoriety and international media coverage with the publication of high-tech sci-fi proposals such as this, along with Computer City and the tank-like Walking City of 1964, its inflatable Blow-Out City of 1965, and its Instant City of 1969, the latter composed of hot air balloons, travelling cranes, robots, and light and sound equipment – all the prerequisites of a giant pop festival.

The work of Archizoom – its name a clear Pop Art comic book reference and an open homage to Archigram – was similarly difficult to interpret. Sottsass himself proposed no answers and, like Archigram, it was hard to know quite how seriously they intended their work to be taken. Originally composed of four architects (Andrea Branzi, Gilberto Coretti, Paolo Deganello and Massimo Morozzi), and two industrial designers (Dario Bartolini and Lucia Bartolini), Archizoom's work included architecture, interiors, products and exhibition installations. At the Milan Triennale in 1968 they organized a Centre for Eclectic Conspiracy, a deliberately provocative project very much in tune with the confrontational spirit of the time. Prior to this they had made their name with an exhibition held in Pistoia in 1967 entitled 'Superarchitettura', and later in the decade, between 1969 and 1971, they worked on a project called No-Stop City. The culmination of their collaboration was the essay they contributed to the catalogue of 'Italy: The New Domestic Landscape'.

Archizoom was the voice of Italian counter-culture. Its aim was to raise questions by subverting ideas of functionalism and conventional notions of good taste. Its ideas, although closely related to Pop Art, were expressed with a more hard-edged intellectual slant. In its written contribution to 'Italy: The New Domestic Landscape', for example, the group asserted: 'the right to go against a reality that lacks "meaning"' and 'to act, modify, form and destroy the surrounding environment'. Like the French furniture designer Olivier Mourgue, they questioned an Establishment where the fertile human imagination was repressed, but whereas Mourgue came up with a series of practical and commercially viable alternatives, Archizoom's creations were largely ironic. The most commercially viable of its furniture designs, and one which draws on contemporary neo-organic forms, was the undulating Superonda sofa manufactured by Poltronova from 1966. This was composed of two blocks of foam with wavy profiles, upholstered in shiny vinyl fabric; the two sections

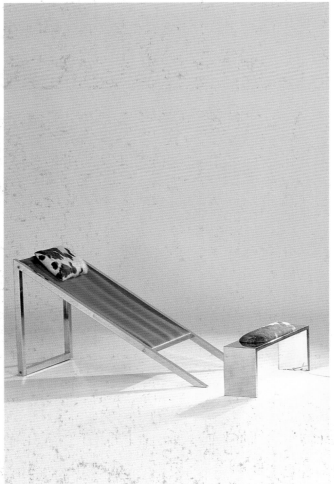

above
Chair designed by Jane Dillon in 1968 for her degree show at the Royal College of Art. After graduating Dillon went to work with Ettore Sottsass at Olivetti in Italy.
left
The radical Italian design collective, Archizoom, were at the forefront of the Anti-Design movement during the second half of the 1960s. The Mies chair and footstool, produced by Poltronova, 1969, deliberately challenged conventional Modernist orthodoxies.

could be used singly or in a pair, and could be combined in various arrangements with the undulating edge facing upwards or outwards. Several designs from Archizoom's furniture collection of 1967 were overtly camp or Pop-inspired, including a series of fantasy beds (only ever produced in model form), such as the Naufragio di Rose with its giant rainbow bedstead and its bedcover emblazoned with a giant image of Bob Dylan. Other pieces made reference, either through their shapes or decoration, to the glamorous era of Art Deco. An arched lighting unit called Grande A was dotted with numerous individual lightbulbs, conjuring up associations with make-up consoles in Hollywood dressing rooms. A monumental chaise-longue called Rosa d'Arabia was crowned with two spherical lamps, and had an exaggeratedly streamlined form and a large circular bolster.

Vibrant surface decoration was another recurrent feature. Leopard-spot patterning was used for the cover on the Presagio di Rose bed, complete with Art Deco-inspired ziggurat bedstead; while tiger-stripe patterning was used for the upholstery on the Safari sofa. Unlike the bed and the chaise-longue, however, which were characterized by self-conscious historical pastiche, the organic shape and modular construction of the Safari seating unit were very much contemporary, and like the Superonda sofa this design was put into production by Poltronova in 1968. Designed in four sections, the Safari unit could be transformed from an object on which one sat and looked outwards, to a self-contained environment which one sat inside, the seating area being cut in a clover-leaf shape from within a square frame. All these designs were deliberately larger than life, symbolizing excess rather than restraint. A later design of 1969, the Mies chair, poked fun at the Modernist idea of 'less is more', typified by the minimalist aesthetic of Mies van der Rohe. The wedge-shaped Mies chair made reference to Modernist furniture via its chromed metal frame and its pony skin cushions, but turned this idea on its head by using these materials to create a piece of furniture that had deliberately frivolous associations (its deck chair-like form, for example). This suggestion of subversion was compounded by the taut latex rubber seat, and the accompanying foot stool lit from below by electric light bulbs. The late 1960s, as well as being the period in which Art Deco was rediscovered and celebrated in furniture, fabrics and wallpapers, also witnessed a revival of interest in Modernist furniture by architects such as Mies van der Rohe, Marcel Breuer and Le Corbusier, with several leading firms, such as Knoll, Cassina and Thonet, entering the reproduction market. This development was seen by 1960s designers as both a threat to, and a critique of, contemporary furniture, and a trend that could stifle future development if it were to get out of hand. The Mies chair can, in part, be interpreted as a comment on this situation.

Another radical architecture and design group formed at the same time as Archizoom was Superstudio, which was also based in Florence, and which collaborated on Archizoom's first exhibition, 'Superarchitettura'. The five members of Superstudio, who were all architects, were Adolfo Natalini, Cristiano Toraldo di Francia, Piero Frassinelli, Alessandro Magris and Roberto Magris, and the group specialized in architecture and interior design. Like Archizoom, they were regularly invited to participate in exhibitions, including the fifteenth and sixteenth Triennales, and 'Italy: The New

right
Safari sofa, produced by Poltronova, 1968, a four-part modular design which could be arranged so that the seating faced either inwards or outwards. Archizoom's furniture celebrated pop culture and some of the overtly decorative anti-Modernist trends in contemporary design, such as Art Deco revivalism.
below
Presagio di Rose bed, by Archizoom, 1967, was only ever produced in model form. The ziggurat form of this bed, and the use of faux patterns such as marble and leopard skin, were deliberately intended to outrage the design world.

Domestic Landscape'. They also produced publications, ran courses and made films. A feature on their recent work in *Domus* in April 1969, which included a bookshop and a nightclub in Florence, indicated the degree to which radical architectural solutions were now being accepted in Italy. The bookshop was used to make symbolic statements about the rarified intellectual pursuit of reading. The nightclub was an exercise in state-of-the-art Space Age design, and made extensive use of synthetic materials, experimental lighting and lurid colours to create a self-consciously artificial environment.

Joe Colombo was another designer whose *œuvre* embodied virtually the full spectrum of design. Like Sottsass, Colombo was at once conformist and reformist, but also latterly, with the production of his *Anti-Design* manifesto, contestational as well. As with many Italian designers, Colombo's priorities shifted during the course of the decade from a concern with individual objects to an interest in the human environment. Like many designers of his generation, he was motivated by a desire to design for mass production in order to make his products widely available at a reasonable price. During the first half of the decade he designed a series of highly innovative and original chairs. These included the Roll armchair of 1962, the Sella and Elda armchairs of 1963, and the Supercomfort armchair of 1964, all for the Milanese firm of Comfort; the Nastro armchair, of 1964 for Bonacina made from curved malacca canes; and a bent plywood armchair of 1964 and the all-plastic Universale chair of 1965, both for Kartell. He also produced a series of important lighting designs during this period, mainly for O-Luce. However, at the same time as designing these stand-alone objects, Colombo began to develop a series of multi-functional products. These marked a new departure, not just in aesthetic and engineering terms, but philosophically and psychologically as well, and were conceived outside the accepted traditions of furniture-making and furniture consumption. The design equivalent of a sophisticated high-tech one-man-band, Colombo's multi-functional compact appliances – such as the 'Mini-Kitchen' for Boffi dating from 1963, and his multi-purpose flexible and transportable storage systems, such as the Combi-Centre for Bernini of 1963, and the Man-Woman Container of 1964 for Arnolfo di Cambio (which combined wardrobe and dressing table facilities) – were both radical and revolutionary. Through these experimental designs Colombo initiated debates that,

by the end of the decade, would become central issues within the Italian avant-garde, and that would have a major influence on the emergent design philosophies in other countries, particularly France.

As the decade progressed Colombo became increasingly ambitious about the range of different functions that could be incorporated within a single design. Eventually he came to believe that the future lay in highly condensed self-contained environments, rather than in complementary independent objects. In 1968 he designed the Box 1 day-and-night facility, a bedroom storage system that combined a wardrobe, cupboards, shelving, drawers and a bed. The following year he produced Visiona 69, an installation intended as a Habitat of the Future, for Bayer at the Cologne Furniture Fair; this was a futuristic apartment-within-a-capsule, which combined facilities for sitting and sleeping with those for cooking and eating. In this open-plan design, all the main functions were condensed into three distinct 'blocks': an air-conditioned Kitchen-Box for cooking and eating; a Central-Living block for leisure activities such as listening to music, watching television, reading and entertaining; and a Night-Cell, also air-conditioned, containing bedroom and bathroom facilities. For his own apartment Colombo designed two multi-functional systems that were subsequently put into production by Sormani in 1969. These were the Roto Living System, a daytime unit combining kitchen and living room facilities, including an electrically operated rotating table; and the Cabriolet bed, equipped with a variety of electronic gadgets and storage facilities, and covered by a tent-like electrically operated hood. These ideas were clearly related to the Visiona 69 installation and show that the latter was by no means as fantastical as it seemed. Finally, in his Total Furnishing Unit of 1971, a prototype designed shortly before his death for the exhibition 'Italy: The New Domestic Landscape', Colombo achieved the ultimate uni-block system, one which combined all the different domestic functions in a single coherent design.

Colombo's ideas about seating developed along parallel lines during the second half of the decade, with flexibility and compactness becoming primary considerations. In 1967 he designed the Additional seating system for Cassina, composed of a row of upholstered foam cushions, vertically aligned, fastened together by means of a pin. Depending on

below left
Elda armchair designed by Joe Colombo for Comfort, 1963.
below right
Colombo shifted his attentions during the course of the 1960s from the design of individual items of furniture to the creation of multi-functional living systems. His Cabriolet Bed was originally designed for his own house in 1969. The hood over the bed was electrically operated, and the bed itself was equipped with a variety of appliances.

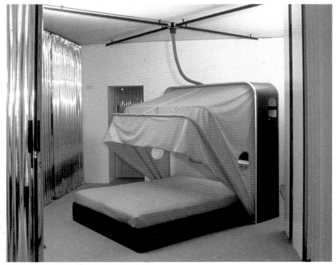

the number of cushions used and the order in which they were arranged, this system could be adapted to create a variety of chairs, sofas and chaise-longues. His compact Tube chair of 1969 for Flexform was followed in 1970 by the Multi-Chair for Sormani which, like the Tube chair, dispensed with legs and brought the sitter down to ground level, and was composed of two elements that could be strapped together to accommodate different body positions. Finally, in his Living Centre for Rosenthal, dating from 1970, Colombo created a trolley-like sofa with a combined foot-rest and head-rest, pull-out trays and built-in storage, accompanied by another wheelable unit containing a bar and a music centre.

In the catalogue to the exhibition 'Italy: The New Domestic Landscape', Emilio Ambasz noted of Colombo: *Although the objects he designed were acclaimed both in Italy and abroad, during the last years of his life he concentrated particularly on problems relating to man's habitat. His researches in ecology and ergonomics led him increasingly to view the individual habitat as a microcosm, which should serve as a point of departure for a macrocosm attainable in the future by means of coordinated structures created through programmed systems production.*

This analysis draws attention to the fact that the reason why Colombo and other radical designers of the late 1960s were interested in the creation of 'habitats' or 'domestic landscapes' was because their view of society was essentially optimistic and idealistic. They genuinely believed that they could improve the human condition by controlling the environments in which people lived. Unlike the modern-day ecology movement which has evolved as a reaction against the failure of society to protect the environment, Colombo was being proactive rather than reactive, trying to pre-empt problems in the future by keeping one step ahead. His Visiona 69 installation was accompanied by a manifesto called *Anti-Design*, and although this might suggest an element of reaction, Colombo was actually using the word 'anti' in a positive rather than a negative way. In a feature on the designer in *Mobilia* in November 1969, it was noted that Colombo now earnestly rejected (the word actually used was 'denounced') the individual pieces of furniture he had previously created. According to Colombo, a more 'methodical' way of thinking was now required:

We have overcome the pseudo-cultured furniture that is only a product of bourgeois taste and in its development follows only fashion, ie. it is a product of capitalist industry whose only purpose is to exploit the consumer by refining its products, with functionalism and technology secondary considerations. Modern research into architecture must necessarily begin with ecological study of modern human beings and, especially, of the microcosmos in which they live.

Although *Mobilia* found much to admire in Colombo's high-minded ideals, and in the application of these concepts within the Visiona 69 installation itself, the magazine nevertheless felt obliged to warn its readers that there was something potentially sinister in the path that Colombo was proposing. The irony was that in seeking to liberate the individual, Colombo was in danger of imposing a completely authoritarian state, and the writer concluded with a warning:

To me he stands as an exponent of a technocratic society where there is nothing but formulas, schedules, index cards etc. Goodness gracious, the end will be that the times of our

left
Pool Living Pad designed by
Luigi Colani for Rosenthal,
1970–1. Made of polyfoam
with removable fabric
covers, this design was produced as a response to the
desire for informal, comfortable, communal seating,
and represents the culmination of trends which had
been emerging during the
late 1960s.
below
Additional seating designed
by Joe Colombo for
Cassina, 1967, used as
public seating at the Milan
Triennale in 1968. According
to the designer: 'The
problem today is to offer
furnishings that are basically
autonomous, that is
independent of their
architectonic housing and
so interchangeable and
programmable that they
can be adapted to every
present and future spatial
situation.'

above
Living Centre designed by
Joe Colombo for Rosenthal,
1971. One of Colombo's
last designs, the system
consists of low-level
daybeds on castors, sup-
plemented by two service
units, one with plate warmer
and refrigerator, with pull-
out flaps for dining; another
with cupboard space and
built-in stereo. Headrests
doubled as upright seats
and a trolley desk could be
wheeled into position.

visits to the privy are to be data processed, and even if Colombo intended his Visiona 69 *as a contribution to the standing debate, I feel it is my duty to point out the dangerous tendencies it contains, and of the idea he expresses in his* Anti-Design.

Whereas during the 1950s leading furniture designers such as Charles Eames and Eero Saarinen had worked comfortably as part of the design mainstream, in the following decade, because of the diversity of ideas, there was a more obvious divide between the mainstream and the avant-garde. Some designers, such as Colombo and Panton, made regular forays between the conformist and the reformist camps, and this open-mindedness and flexibility was a key element in their creative character. At the end of the decade, however, particularly from 1968 onwards with the emergence of a hardline avant-garde movement, the gulf became wider and harder to cross. Increasingly, it was more an issue of design principles than of aesthetics. At the time he formulated his *Anti-Design* manifesto in 1969, Joe Colombo clearly felt that he had crossed over from one camp to the other for the last time. Until that date Colombo, like Panton, had expressed his allegiances through his designs rather than through written theory, and the fact is that, at heart, both men were fundamentally avant-garde. Although they both worked within the framework of the established furniture industry, they never allowed themselves to be constrained by it. They always showed themselves to be free spirits committed to experimentation as a purely creative and liberating exercise.

Neo-Organic Design

By contrast with the intensity of Colombo, there was something playful about Verner Panton's approach to design. Like Sottsass his inventiveness seemed to spring from a quality of child-like innocence (in the Blakean sense). Panton had challenged conventional approaches to design ever since establishing his own practice in 1955. He sought to get to the root of design by identifying fundamental issues and tackling them from different angles. Although by no means all his experiments were successful, they were invariably interesting and valid in one way or another. Panton always rose to the challenge of an exhibition. In 1964, for example, he created an installation in which most of the seating was either suspended by ropes from the ceiling, or raised at different levels on a scaffolding rig. This idea of a Living Tower would later evolve into his Pantower concept of 1968–9. The Pantower produced by Herman Miller was one of the most evocative designs of the period and provided a physical embodiment of flexibility and relaxation. When launched, it was variously described in the media as a 'living room honeycomb' and a 'seating cave'. Like the communal seating units developed by Joe Colombo, Olivier Mourgue and Bernard Govin, and the huge seating pools produced by Rosenthal during the early 1970s, the Pantower was meant to influence people's behaviour. By encouraging varied postures the designer hoped to stimulate more relaxed social intercourse. Through the idea of the sofa as a tower Panton was also exploring the possibilities of vertical rather than horizontal seating. The theory behind this was the impulse to save space by aligning furniture upwards rather than outwards, although in practice the Pantower was extremely bulky and required an above average-sized living room. It also proved expensive to produce as

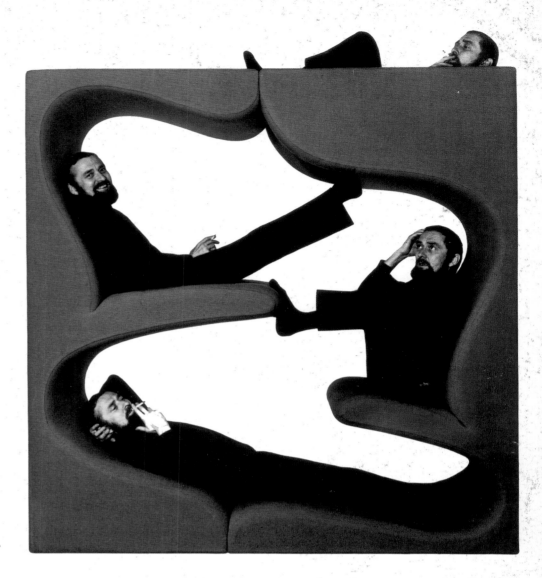

above
Verner Panton demonstrating the different positions which could be adopted in his Pantower, produced by Herman Miller from 1968–9, subsequently made by Fritz Hansen from 1970–5.

opposite
Visiona II at the Cologne Furniture Fair in 1970, designed by Verner Panton. This psychedelic, surreal, quasi-biological installation, resembling a cluster of Pantowers, was filled with neo-organic fabric-covered frames. The Pantower itself was as much a piece of organic interactive sculpture as an item of furniture.

left
Visiona installation designed by Panton for the Bayer ship at the Cologne Furniture Fair in 1968, showing a model sitting on a suspended shell, and a cluster of soft spherical sculptures complemented by low-hanging domed lamps.

it required a complex wooden frame in order for the structure to retain its shape, and the frame itself, with its multiple curves, was difficult and time-consuming to upholster. As with the jigsaw-like Malitte cushion system designed by Sergio Matta for Gavina in 1966, however, the Pantower was as much a piece of sculpture as a piece of furniture, and any assessment of the rationale behind it must encompass the psychological impact of physically and mentally engaging with the object as a work of art. As an example of neo-organic sculpture, its full potential was demonstrated by the designer himself in his Visiona II installation for Bayer at the Cologne Furniture Fair in 1970. In this futuristic furniture 'happening' an entire room was filled with Pantower-like structures, the surreal effect being heightened by the use of coloured lights.

One of the most important designers to emerge in France after the Second World War was Pierre Paulin. Although he never achieved the quasi-celebrity status of Panton, Colombo or Mourgue, his significance as a pioneer of radical furniture design should not be overlooked. It is not surprising to discover that Paulin's background was in sculpture (he trained at the École Camondo in Paris during the early 1950s). From the outset his work had a naturally expressive quality which, like Panton's, manifested itself increasingly freely and confidently as the decade progressed. Paulin broke free from the restrictions of the French *artiste décorateur* tradition by building an alliance with the Dutch manufacturer, Artifort. He teamed up with Artifort during the late 1950s, and his fruitful partnership with the firm lasted throughout the ensuing decade. His earliest designs for the company, such as the 437 easy chair dating from 1959, had the narrow spindly metal legs and organic shell seats typical of the early post-war period. A radical change of aesthetic occurred in 1966, however, when Paulin created his Ribbon chair. From this date onwards his work became increasingly fluid, and as there were such close parallels between his aesthetic and that of Olivier Mourgue, it is likely that they were both stimulated by each other's work. The Ribbon chair was a sinuous all-in-one design supported on a flat wooden base, the ribbon-like seat being created from a frame of tubular steel covered with foam and stretch fabric upholstery. A similar technique was used initially in Paulin's minimalist 577 low stacking easy chair produced from 1967, although later this was replaced with a fibreglass shell. Sometimes known as the Tongue chair because of its expressive undulating form, this design was masterful for the way in which its contours enabled the chair to be stacked. The lowness of the Tongue chair presaged the trends of the later 1960s, when more informal codes of behaviour were adopted by young people, and reclining was favoured instead of more upright postures. Like Mourgue's Djinn range, the Tongue chair continued to look ultra-modern for many years after it was designed, and it was by no means out of date when it was used by the designer in the French Pavilion at the Osaka Expo in 1970.

Neo-organic and undulating forms remained a feature of Paulin's work until the end of the decade. His later designs included the 300 easy chair dating from 1967, which had a fibreglass shell lined with polyfoam upholstery, and the 305 easy chair dating from 1969, a not dissimilar form but made entirely of polyester. The same year saw the launch of an undulating easy chair and matching sofa which, unlike Paulin's earlier designs, were formed in three distinct sections,

opposite
Ribbon chair, designed by Pierre Paulin, for Artifort, 1966. To the right is the Chimera lamp designed by Vico Magistretti for Artemide, 1966. The neo-organic trend in design during the second half of the 1960s is illustrated by Paulin's work for the Dutch company Artifort.
right
Easy chair (model 305), 1969, made from moulded polyester. To the right is the Giano table designed by Emma Schweinberger Gismondi for Artemide, 1967.
below
Tongue chair (model 577), 1967, a low-level reclining chair designed to suit the informal lifestyles of the young.

above

Lombrico sofa designed by
Marco Zanuso for C & B
Italia, 1967. Created in
modular units which could
be combined to any length,
the base of this sofa was
made from moulded fibre-
glass, and the seat from
upholstered polyfoam.
Snake-like ribbed modular
seating of this type was produced by several designers
at the end of the decade,
including Pierre Paulin and
Jørn Utzon.

joined together and mounted on castors. Made of polyester
and upholstered in polyfoam, not only did the seat itself rise
and fall, but the seat back had a wavy profile as well. Like
Bernard Govin's wave-like Asmara seating unit for Roset
launched the previous year, Paulin's design was extremely
comfortable, and the psychological impact of the shape was
to encourage a feeling of calm and relaxation. Working with
Mobilier International in Paris, Paulin produced some even
more radical designs towards the end of the decade, illustrated in an article in *Domus* in July 1968. Among these was a
remarkable undulating canopied *chaise-longue* described as
an 'articulated carpet'. Constructed from fabric-covered
wooden slats which could be joined together in varying
lengths, articulated joints between the slats meant that the
angles at which the seat could be set were also fully
adjustable. This unusual piece of furniture provides a clear link
between the later work of Paulin and Mourgue, whose output
during the 1960s culminated in the creation of a 'flying carpet'. Meanwhile a design for a long snake-like tripartite sofa
by Paulin dating from 1969 for Mobilier International provides
a crossover to the work of other designers in different parts of
Europe such as Jørn Utzon in Denmark and Marco Zanuso in
Italy, illustrating the cosmopolitan nature of his work, and suggesting how effectively he crossed the divide between the
mainstream and the avant-garde.

Whereas Paulin was already established as a major
figure in furniture design at the start of the decade, Olivier
Mourgue did not achieve recognition until the mid-1960s,
when he became an instant celebrity with the launch of his
ribbon-like Djinn easy chairs and *chaises-longues,* produced
by the Paris-based firm of Airborne from 1965. The futuristic
quality of the Djinn range was recognized by Stanley Kubrick,
the director of *2001: A Space Odyssey*, released in 1968,
where Mourgue's chairs provided the furnishings for an imaginary space station. Trained in interior design at the École
Boulle and École Nationale Supérieure des Arts Décoratifs
between 1954 and 1960, Mourgue's unconventional approach
to furniture was apparent in his Tric-Trac armchair of 1963, in
which a padded upholstered seat was suspended in a steel
wire cage frame. In the mid-1960s Mourgue found himself
hungering to create furniture that was not only practical but
expressive, and he began to use the curves of the human
body as the inspiration for the contours and forms of his
designs. However, although there was something reassuringly
humanoid about much of Mourgue's work, it was also decidedly abstract. What made Mourgue's seating so distinctive
was partly its unconventional construction methods – in the
case of the Djinn range, a bent tubular steel frame covered
with foam and upholstered with stretch fabric – but also its
weightless, airy quality. Gentle fluidity was the over-riding feature, expressed through pure free-floating forms. Although
organic, however, there was no hint of regression to the biomorphic shapes of the 1950s in Mourgue's designs which,
like those of Paulin, should more correctly be described as
neo-organic rather than organic, presaging a trend that would
become increasingly important in French furniture during
the late 1960s. A quirky design from the late 1960s was
Mourgue's Bouloum chair of 1968, made of polyester
moulded in the shape of a flattened stylized human being,
then covered with foam and upholstered in nylon jersey
fabric. This was the ultimate Pop Art object: a chair shaped
to fit the human form by mirroring its shape directly. To intro-
duce such an item into the home was to people it rather
than to furnish it.

Mourgue wrote of his philosophy in an essay for the
Philadelphia Museum of Art's 1984 exhibition catalogue,

Design Since 1945: 'Functionalism and rationalism cannot be the goal of design, an end in themselves; they are simply part of the honesty required for the construction of an object. I have the feeling that one must pursue other paths, and the condition of visual poetry interests me.' Following a feature on his apartment in Paris published in *Domus* in June 1966, Mourgue became a cult figure, particularly among young designers. They admired him because he appeared to have scrapped all recognizable design conventions, and to be completely rethinking and reinventing the relationship between furniture and the interior. What Mourgue was seeking to evoke through his designs was not just a domestic interior but a revolutionary new habitat. Mood and ambiance were all-important, hence his choice of white and beige for the furniture and furnishings in his own apartment, as bold a statement in its way as that made by Charles Rennie Mackintosh in his interiors at the turn of the nineteenth century. This serene mood provided a counterpoint to the colourfulness and playfulness of contemporary Pop Art, the frenzied pattern-making of Op Art and, later, the artificially heightened visual sensations and stimulations of psychedelia. Mourgue's habitat suggested alternative interests which would become increasingly important during the second half of the 1960s, such as meditation and Eastern mysticism.

The furnishings in Mourgue's apartment were, in fact, co-opted from a bedroom which he had exhibited in 1965 at the Salon des Artistes Décorateurs in Paris. This was described in *Industrial Design* in April 1966 as follows: *The bedroom designed by Mourgue has no openings except a doorway. All four walls are covered with white curtains; the floor and furniture (including a round bed in the centre) are covered in beige jersey. The large fan on the back wall in the shape of a flower rotates slowly to provide ventilation for the*

above
Djinn chairs and sofas designed by Olivier Mourgue for Airborne in 1965. They were chosen by Stanley Kubrick for his film *2001: A Space Odyssey* in 1968.

right
Olivier Mourgue's all-white apartment in Paris, 1966, with furniture from the Djinn range in the foreground. The French designer became a cult figure among students during the second half of the 1960s following the publication of his neo-organic furniture designs for Airborne on the pages of *Domus*. Items from this interior had been exhibited at the Société des Artistes Décorateurs in Paris in 1965. The large flower-like object on the wall, originally used as a fan, was subsequently converted into a lamp.

room. According to Mourgue the 'only connection with the outside world is represented by a hanging television and telephone'.

This room drew attention to Mourgue's desire to create a special atmosphere by isolating the interior from the outside world. In this respect his work was similar to that of Joe Colombo who also treated the domestic interior as a self-contained capsule. What was different about Mourgue's work, however, was that, unlike Colombo, who apparently revelled in the artificial, Mourgue adopted ploys that distracted attention from potential feelings of claustrophobia. Although completely enclosed and lit entirely by artificial means, Mourgue's interiors had a lightness and an openness to them to which Colombo never aspired.

The Americans and the Italians were both clearly fascinated by Mourgue's work, and continued to pay close attention to it for the remainder of the decade. In July 1967 *Domus* featured Mourgue's new studio, including illustrations of some of his latest furniture prototypes. The most striking of these was a circular rocking chair in the form of a large wheel, inside which the user reclined. In September 1967 *Domus* illustrated some of the new furniture shown by Mourgue at the Salon des Arts Ménagers in Paris in March of that year. Here the main focus of attention was a communal seating unit variously described as a 'raft' and a 'flying carpet'. Designed to accommodate up to eight people, the unit was covered with a long-pile fabric resembling a *rya* rug, suspended above the floor across a scaffolding-like rig. Each side of the unit was set at an angle so that people could comfortably recline, and a low table was built into the centre for food and drinks. The 'raft' was designed to minimize human need for exertion, and to encourage communal relaxation. As such it was completely in tune with the laid-back hippy culture of the late 1960s and was the ideal piece of furniture on which to celebrate the

Summer of Love. Commenting on this design in 'An Interview with Olivier Mourgue' in *Industrial Design*, October 1968, the writer noted:

The current trend in French interior design is focused on the total 'environment' rather than on individual pieces. Mourgue is part of this trend. His most recent interior design is a complete seating environment – it's not a couch, sofa or porch swing – rather it's a carpeted square upraised on two sides and supported on a metal frame … Mourgue says: 'They can be built in almost any size and they can function for all the pieces of furniture most people have in their living rooms or elsewhere – couch, end tables, foot rest, and coffee table all in one.' Eventually he hopes to plug in entertainment and lighting units to make it even more complete.

As the work of Mourgue and Paulin demonstrates, the counter-revolution of the late 1960s marked a departure from the geometrical correctness of 'the look' in favour of neo-organic design. Organic design had dominated the late 1940s and the 1950s but had gone out of favour around 1960. Although the term neo-organic might suggest a revamp of early post-war styling, it was, in fact, quite different. A celebration of the artificial and the synthetic, neo-organic design evolved out of a completely new investigation into the idea of the organic, fully informed by the latest technology and materials. This trend was outlined in some detail in an article called 'Free-Form Furniture' by José Manser in *Design* in December 1968, where a direct link was made with the counter-revolutionary 'youthquake':

From Italy, France, Scandinavia and Great Britain, the news is the same: chairs are to be lain in rather than sat upon, preferably en masse, but almost certainly à deux, and the lower the user's centre of gravity, the better. Youthful moeurs and a boom market in furniture are stimulating designers to stretch, remould and rethink the conventional shapes of chairs and

sofas; at the same time, the plastics industry is providing new materials to make their ideals possible. *Throughout Europe, the furniture shown at this year's exhibitions has had a common, undulating theme. It has been curvaceous and comfortable, a blatant invitation to relaxation and ease. It is young furniture which will be admired by those who are still able to contort rheumatic-free limbs into unwonted positions, and still have the urge to flop about in erotically motivated heaps.* Not surprisingly, it was young furniture designers who responded most enthusiastically to the neo-organic trend. Manser concluded her survey with the following observations: *Already, in exhibition rooms and even in one or two esoteric apartments, conventional furniture has been replaced by soft lounging pads or cushioned or carpeted shelves, and it seems entirely predictable that many rooms will have their corners softened and their seating levels nearer the ground over the next few years.*

The neo-organic trend in interior design had, in fact, already been realized earlier in the decade by Nanda Vigo in an apartment in Milan, designed as a controlled and completely artificial environment for housing a group of works by leading contemporary artists such as Lucio Fontana. Illustrated in *Domus* in June 1964, this interior suggested the idea of the room as a self-contained cell or a capsule, and contained unusual features such as floors which curved up seamlessly into the walls or melted into pieces of built-in furniture. This idea, and the inspiration for some of the other neo-organic trends in furniture and interiors which followed, may well have been influenced by the organic slit and pierced canvases produced by Fontana, known as *Spatial Concepts*, which challenged conventional perceptions of three-dimensionality. Interestingly, Nanda Vigo and Lucio Fontana had collaborated on the Utopia section of the introductory displays at the Milan Triennale in 1964, an installation that relied exclusively on the

impact of artificial lighting in a blacked out interior. In lighting, the neo-organic trend was taken to extremes in the Boalum light designed by Livio Castiglioni and Gianfranco Frattini for Artemide in 1969. Described in *Domus* in December 1969 as 'an endless snake of light', the Boalum was entirely flexible and perfectly illustrated the concept of lighting as a form of habitat; it could also be extended to any length and arranged in any position, making it ideal for sculptural installations.

In furniture it was plastics that were most closely associated with neo-organic design. Extremely flexible in their application, plastics could be used to suggest either crisp geometric forms or fluid neo-organic forms. Some plastics were literally organic in that they were actually soft, a characteristic exploited in inflatable PVC furniture and polyurethane foam furniture. Other plastics, such as polyester and polypropylene, were moulded into forms that could be used to suggest fluidity, although the material itself was rigid, while acrylic could be either moulded or reheated and bent into shape. The neo-organic trend was closely associated with French design during the late 1960s, and was embodied in a range of storage furniture shown at the International Furniture Show in Paris in January 1967 by the firm of Doubinski Frères of Montreuil. The DF range of sideboards and cupboards, developed in collaboration with CEI-Raymond Loewy, had rosewood frames with moulded plastic fronts, distinguished by their integral handles in the form of Fontana-esque soft bulges. The trend away from the geometric towards the neo-organic was also captured in the work of the Finnish designer Eero Aarnio during the late 1960s. Although Aarnio continued working with rigid rather than soft plastics, notably fibreglass-reinforced polyester, the forms of his later furniture were much more fluid than his earlier designs. Characteristic of the new trend was the Pastilli chair of 1968, a pod-like shape with a sunken seat moulded into the all-in-one form. The subtle

above left
Boalum lamp designed by Livio Castiglioni and Gianfranco Frattini for Artemide, 1969, an example of neo-organic lighting design.
above right
Olivier Mourgue's studio in Paris in 1967, showing an experimental reclining chair.

above
Bouloum stacking lounge
chairs designed by Olivier
Mourgue for Airborne, 1968.

above
Toga chair designed by
Sergio Mazza for Artemide,
1968. The Italians exploited
their mastery of plastics to
produce both rigid and soft
synthetic forms which
embodied the neo-organic
trend in design.

right
In chair designed by Angelo
Mangiarotti for Zanotta,
1969.

far right
Jumbo chair designed by
Alberto Rosselli for Saporiti,
1969.

bottom right
Seating range (model 932)
designed by Mario Bellini for
Cassina, 1964, a rectilinear
design made using soft
materials.

right
Sea Urchin designed by
Roger Dean, produced by
Hille, 1967, a precursor of
the Sacco chair in its soft-
ness and formlessness,
although made of soft foam
rather than polystyrene
balls.
below
Bobolungo chair designed
by Cini Boeri for Arflex,
1969. Arflex was set up as
a subsidiary of Pirelli during
the early post-war period in
order to exploit the company's rubber webbing and
foam rubber products. The
Bobolungo chair makes full
use of the sculptural potential of foam.

left
Sacco chair designed by
Piero Gatti, Cesare Paolini
and Franco Teodoro for
Zanotta, 1968. This chair,
which can be used length-
ways or propped upright, is
also known as the Anatomic
chair because it has no
fixed form of its own and
adjusts itself to the contours
of the human body.

difference between the organic designs of the 1950s and the
neo-organic designs of the 1960s is highlighted by another of
Aarnio's works, the Kantarelli table of 1965. Although inspired,
like the famous Kantarelli glass vase by Tapio Wirkkala of
1947, by the form of a chanterelle mushroom, Aarnio's table
was a completely and unaffectedly artificial creation made of
smooth plastic, whereas Wirkkala's vase had textural markings that accentuated its organic qualities in a literal way.
Neo-organic forms were also at the heart of the aesthetic of
the American designer and craftsman Wendell Castle, who
expanded his repertoire during the course of the decade from
hand-crafted wood to mass-produced plastics, including a
range of chairs and sofas resembling giant molars dating from
1969–70. Towards the end of the decade Italian designers
enthusiastically adopted neo-organic design too, its influence
being very much in evidence at the Milan Furniture Fair in
1969. Featured in this display were Alberto Rosselli's fibreglass chairs for Saporiti, which included a neo-organic low-
level semi-reclining garden chair called Moby Dick, a follow-up
to Rosselli's earlier Jumbo design. The work shown by
Zanotta at the Milan Furniture Fair in 1969 also reflected the
neo-organic trend, exemplified by the moulded polyurethane
foam In chair by Angelo Mangiarotti. Interestingly it was
Mangiarotti who had been one of the early pioneers of the
neo-organic trend ever since the creation of his polystyrene
1110 chair for Cassina in 1961.

Foam began to be widely used in furniture after
Pirelli set up Arflex in 1951 as a subsidiary company making
furniture that exploited rubber-based products. These products included rubber webbing instead of metal springs, and
foam-rubber padding instead of horsehair or feathers. During
the 1960s a wider range of synthetic foams became available,
each with a unique character and density. Polyfoam was
widely used as padding for lining hard plastic shells, and later
in the decade, as designers sought to free themselves from
the constraints of rigid shells and frames, polyfoam was used
on its own as an independent medium. As early as 1964,
Cassina had launched the 932 seating range designed by
Mario Bellini, composed of leather-covered foam blocks held
in position by means of straps. Sculpted blocks of firm foam
were used for the Bobolungo chair designed by Cini Boeri for
Arflex in 1969, which resembled a small section of one of
Verner Panton's Pantowers. The increasingly widespread use
of foam as a primary material in furniture spread from Italy to
other countries during the late 1960s, and can be seen in the
'sitting system' designed by Grete Jalk for Erik Jørgensen in
1969. Made of soft polyether foam, upholstered with corduroy
fabric, the system was composed of a series of geometric
blocks that could be strapped together in a variety of flexible
seating arrangements.

When designers wanted to create furniture that was
overtly structureless, softer foam was chosen. This was the
case with Roger Dean's dome-shaped Sea Urchin chair of
1967, composed of twelve sections of soft polyurethane foam
stuck together with contact adhesive then covered in fur
fabric. Also designed to be intentionally soft was the Ciprea
armchair by Afra and Tobia Scarpa for Cassina in 1968. A
series of images in *Domus* in March 1968 showed this chair
being contorted to illustrate how malleable it was. The Sacco
chair, the most influential soft chair of the 1960s, was marketed in a similar way by using photographs of models in different

above
Publicity image for the UP
series designed by Gaetano
Pesce for C & B Italia, 1969.
Made of self-supporting
moulded polyurethane foam
covered in nylon jersey,
the UP range was supplied
vacuum-packed. When
unwrapped the foam
expanded to ten times its
original size.

opposite above
Cube-shaped plastic inflatable stools designed by Verner Panton for Unika Vaev, 1960: the earliest recorded example of blow-up plastic furniture. Inflatable furniture became a major international craze during the second half of the 1960s, and, along with paper furniture, represented the ultimate pop lifestyle accessory.
opposite centre left
Christo and Jeanne-Claude, *42,390 Cubic Feet Package*, University of Minneapolis, Minnesota, 1966. With the assistance of 147 students, the artists completed an air package using four US Army high altitude research balloons and 2,800 coloured balloons. However, due to air turbulence, the Aviation Agency forbade the planned airlift and the helicopter lifted the package only six metres off the ground.
opposite centre
Blow armchair designed by Scolari, Lomazzi, D'Urbino and De Pas for Zanotta, 1967: the most well-known inflatable chair of the 1960s.
opposite centre right
Quasar and Emmanuelle Khanh, sitting inside their inflatable house on blow-up furniture sold through Quasar Khanh's Paris shop. This photograph was taken during an exhibition called 'Structures Gonflables' at the Musée des Arts Décoratifs in Paris in 1968.
opposite below right
Sofa in the form of an inflatable tyre, designed by Atelier Eta 1 for Mobilier International, late 1960s.

poses. Basically a large fabric bag containing a mass of tiny plastic granules, the Sacco – the chair that launched a thousand bean bags – was designed by Piero Gatti, Cesare Paolini and Franco Teodoro for Zanotta in 1969. A potent symbol of the rejection of conventions and embodiment of total informality, the Sacco could be used in clusters and was ideal for impromptu communal gatherings. Zanotta also produced the evocatively named and suggestively sculptural Bottom chair shown at the Milan Furniture Fair in 1969, made entirely of soft foam, which was designed by De Pas, D'Urbino, Lomazzi and Decursu. Also shown at the Milan Furniture Fair that year was the UP series designed by Gaetano Pesce for C & B Italia in 1969. This range caused a sensation when it was launched because of the fact that, before being packed, the chairs were compressed to one tenth of their original size, so that when their outer packaging was removed, they expanded dramatically to their original size and shape. The ultimate soft furniture of the decade, there were six different chairs in the UP series, all strongly organic, some overtly sexual in their imagery.

Inflatables and Paper Furniture

Along with neo-organic design, one of the most important concepts of the late 1960s was expendability, and it was this idea that led to the development of 'throwaway' paper furniture and inflatable furniture. Verner Panton, one of the most creative minds of the decade, was responsible for designing the first example of inflatable furniture. Intended for outdoor use in a garden or on a terrace, this was a simple square stool made of blue plastic, produced by the Danish textile firm Unika Vaev in 1960. By the time other manufacturers began to produce inflatable furniture six years later, however, Panton's earlier contribution appears to have been virtually forgotten, as it is barely mentioned in any of the survey articles on inflatables published in the design press during the late 1960s. A feature in *Domus* in December 1967 drew attention to the recently launched Blow armchair designed by Carla Scolari, Donato D'Urbino, Paolo Lomazzi and Jonathan De Pas for Zanotta, made in both transparent and coloured PVC. Unique at this time in having a suspended seat and a head-rest, each chair had five different valves for inflation. The Blow chair was part of a wider international trend that had begun the previous year. It was predated in Italy by a chair created by the set designer Piero Poletto for the film *La Decima Vittima* by Elio Petri in 1966, while in Britain Arthur Quarmby designed a circular pouffe in 1966, inflated by means of a central perforated tube. Also highlighted in this *Domus* article was a series of chairs designed by three young New York artists, Phil Orenstein, Dorian Gody and Sujan Souri, for a firm called Mass Art. These had clear perspex or tubular steel frames with inflatable seats, pumped up using a vacuum cleaner. In London the design wholesaler Goods and Chattels marketed inflatable chairs and sofas produced by Incadinc, which were sold in a range of colours. These were accompanied by a selection of inflatable cushions decorated with vibrant Pop patterns, designed by Eric Victor. Patterned blow-up cushions were also made from around 1967 onwards in Italy by Kartell. The trend for inflatables also spread to Sweden at this time where it was successfully employed by Stephan Gip in a range of furniture for Hagaplast, distributed in Britain by Conran and Company. Made of opaque red, yellow, blue and white PVC, this range was supplied with a puncture repair kit in case of accidents.

Apart from Zanotta, the other large-scale manufacturer of inflatable furniture during the late 1960s was Quasar Khanh in France, who built up a whole empire centred on this specific area of production, and who was himself the designer of the furniture that bore his name. Vietnamese-born Khanh was the husband of the fashion designer Emmanuelle Khanh, the French equivalent of Mary Quant. This perhaps explains why he was so adept at marketing his work, as he exploited techniques learnt from the fashion industry. Khanh became obsessed with inflatables and the concept of transparency during the late 1960s. To him inflatables were more of a philosophy, or what he called a 'morality', than merely a lifestyle accessory. His idiosyncratic views were recorded in an article called 'The World is Transparent' in *Mobilia* in October 1968: *I am a materialist, and there is nothing immoral in enjoying things. Nothing can be kept hidden today. The world is constantly becoming more open, and human need of contact is constantly growing. I do not want to keep things hidden 'inside'. I want to be open in this ever more transparent society. I believe in the lightness and airiness of things. I am more of a moralist than an engineer, and I want to prove my philosophy by creating things.*

Khanh's work was made available in various countries as a result of licencing arrangements. In Britain, for example, his chairs were manufactured by a firm called Ultralite. In spite of his views on transparency he used both transparent and opaque materials for his furniture, including chairs with a mock leather finish. In 1969 he set up a shop in Paris called Quasar, with ambitious plans for a multi-national chain of up to two hundred outlets around the world. His Paris shop on the Rue Boissy d'Anglais was entirely fitted out from floor to ceiling in transparent materials, including mirrors and acrylics as well as inflatables. By the end of the decade Khanh had expanded his range of production to include a whole family of inflatable forms, from chairs, beds and *chaise-longues* to floating inflatable houses. A cylindrical house made of transparent PVC and weighing only 95 kilograms was illustrated in *Design* in May 1968. The cylindrical walls were composed of a ring of vertical tubes encircled at the top and bottom by two inflatable belts.

Khanh was not alone in using inflatables to create cylindrical forms. Mobilier International produced a sofa in the form of an inflatable tyre designed by Atelier Eta 1 during the late 1960s, a horizontal cylinder inside which the user reclined, which was wedged in position by two inflatable bolsters. Another French inflatables firm was A J S Aerolande, founded by three architects, Jean Aubert, Jean-Paul Jungmann and Antonio Stinco, who designed an inflatable armchair not dissimilar to the Blow chair around 1967. Inflated in two separate sections, the round seat of the chair could be used separately as a pouffe. The same trio also designed a divan composed of a series of tubular and square cushions that could be buttoned or laced together in various arrangements to create either beds or settees. Another emergent talent on the French experimental furniture design scene at this date was Bernard Quentin, who created a pod-shaped inflatable armchair in 1966 which was used in the bar of the French Pavilion at the Montreal Expo the following year. Quentin also designed various inflatable installations during the late 1960s, including one called the *Blow-Up Club* in Milan, an environment completely dominated by a mass of inflatables. Quentin's work in this field continued to attract attention until the end of the decade. In

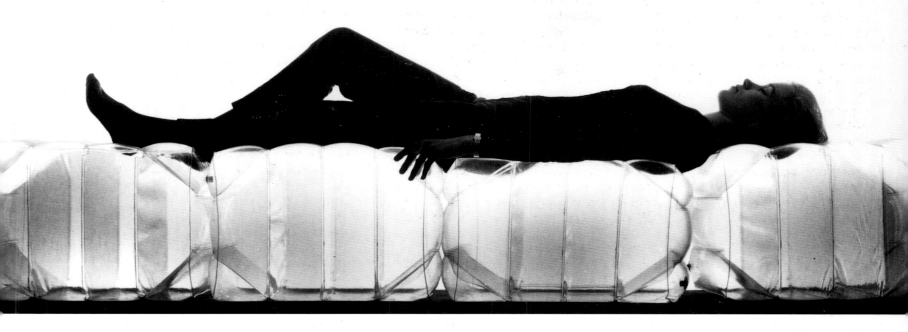

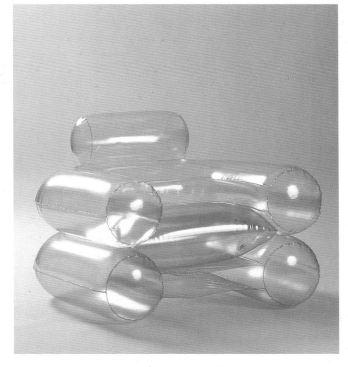

February 1969, for example, there was a feature in *Domus* on his latest inflatable chairs for the firm of Interdesign. Whereas most other designers used tube-shaped sections, Quentin created 'molecular' furniture from clusters of giant inflatable balls. In one way his obsession with spheres can be seen as a continuation of 'the look' of the early 1960s, although it appears that Quentin only discovered its virtues after dabbling with neo-organic forms. In choosing to create whole environments and installations rather than stand-alone pieces of furniture, Quentin was very much of his time.

The vogue for inflatables was by no means confined to furniture: similar ideas were explored with equal relish in the fields of architecture and sculpture. Through the work of the artists Christo and Jeanne-Claude, inflatable architecture and sculpture were combined. Internationally renowned for their installations involving the wrapping of entire buildings, Christo and Jeanne-Claude collaborated with students at the Minneapolis School of Art in October 1966 to create a giant inflatable polythene sculpture. Other artists and architects who experimented with inflatables during the second half of the 1960s included Archigram, Andy Warhol, Les Levine in an exhibition in Philadelphia called 'Air Art', and Hans Hollein and Walter Pichler in Vienna. In March 1968 an important exhibition called 'Structures Gonflables' was held at the Musée d'Art Moderne de la Ville in Paris, organized by the Groupe Animation Recherche Confrontation. It was in this exhibition that Archigram's proposal for an inflatable living capsule was presented, while Aubert, Jungmann and Stinco put forward a design for an inflatable house, and exhibited an inflatable structure called Utopia which visitors were able to sit inside. Quasar Khanh made the dream of an inflatable house a reality, and took the idea even further by furnishing it with his inflatable furniture and lamps. While the craze for inflatable furniture proved appropriately short-lived once the inevitable punctures started to appear, inflatable architecture proved more enduring, and was used for a variety of industrial, commercial and leisure applications. These included a winter cover for a swimming pool at a sports centre at Montfleury, Cannes, designed by Roger Tallibert; a temporary store for Vauxhall Motors at Dunstable, Kent, produced by the Gourock Ropework Company; and temporary offices for a computer company at Hemel Hempstead designed by Foster Associates in 1970. The latter, made of nylon reinforced PVC, was inflated in less than an hour and was created at a cost of less than £1 per square foot.

In an article called 'Plastic and Cardboard Alter the Scene' in *Form* (no 9) in 1967, Lena Larsson wrote: 'Maybe pretty soon our whole household can be moved in a big bag – when inflatable plastics and folding cardboard have become popular as furniture materials.' Paper was first adopted in non-traditional areas such as furniture and clothing during the mid-1960s. The earliest paper furniture was a fold-out cardboard children's chair designed in 1963 by Peter Murdoch while still a student at the Royal College of Art, which was subsequently manufactured by an American firm called International Paper between 1964 and 1965, but was only ever produced in small quantities. Ahead of its time when first conceived, Murdoch's idea was successfully redesigned, repackaged and relaunched in Britain in 1967 by a firm called Perspective Designs, which described it as 'Fibreboard furniture for the young – Designed to last!' Manufactured by a

paper company called New Merton Board Mills, marketed under the slogan 'Those Things', and sold flat-packed in a box with eye-catching graphics by Paul Clark, this time round Murdoch's designs for the Chair Thing, Stool Thing and Table Thing achieved the wide-scale commercial success they deserved both in Britain and abroad. Perspective Designs had been established by Philip Bidwell in 1966 to market the work of young British designers, and its other products included stationery, giftware, mugs and kitchen accessories. In an article in *Design* in May 1968 after the announcement that Those Things had won a Design Centre Award, Philip Bidwell was quoted as saying:

We decided to produce fibreboard furniture not only because it has particular advantages for the customer, but also because low development costs made it possible to launch the range in small quantities to test the market. We try to avoid gimmicks which use novelty for novelty's sake rather than producing an object that is an improvement on its predecessors.

Significantly, in view of the intrinsic importance and far-reaching influence of Pop culture in Britain during the 1960s, the second most famous range of paper furniture produced in the 1960s, Tomotom (see page 73), was also British. Manufactured by Hull Traders from 1966, it was widely exported, and was sold through Macy's in New York. Although described generically as paper furniture, the actual materials utilized were rather more substantial. Compressed cardboard tubes and wood-based chipboard were coated with a tough enamel paint, which increased the furniture's durability and made it washable, non-flammable and resistant to alcohol, acids and alkalis. Originally conceived as a product geared specifically to children, it soon became apparent that Tomotom furniture was just as saleable within the adult market. By the end of the decade, the range had been extended to include over a hundred items.

Compressed paper tubes were also exploited as the basic framework for a range of furniture, including chairs, stools and a cylindrical stacking storage unit, designed by Jean-Louis Avril in 1966 and produced by the firm of B Marty of Paris. More common, however, was folded cardboard furniture; a successful range, sold internationally during the late 1960s, being the Papp series by the German designer Peter Raacke dating from 1967–8, manufactured by Faltmöbel Ellen Raacke. Designed for mass production, this furniture was punched out of cardboard by rolling cylinders and, like Those Things, was supplied flat-packed for self-assembly by the customer. The range included furniture for both children and adults, the latter mainly based on a hexagonal structure and including chairs, tables, stools and shelf units; while the children's range consisted of boxes of various shapes that could be made into chairs and tables, or combined to create other forms of play furniture. More ambitious larger pieces were also produced, including easy chairs, sofas, desks, bookcases and cupboards, some of which were made of corrugated cardboard and lined with plastic laminate. Paper furniture was particularly popular in the USA and Canada, a fact highlighted in an important exhibition organized by the Museum of Contemporary Crafts in New York in 1967 called 'Made with Paper', which was featured in an article in *Interiors* in November 1967. Ingenious North American products included a stool with a corrugated cardboard base by Design

opposite top left
Spotty chair designed by Peter Murdoch in 1963, produced in the USA by International Paper, 1964–5. Paper furniture, mainly intended for children, was the perfect embodiment of expendability, a concept which fascinated society in the 1960s. It was cheap but stylish; it could be bought flat-packed; and if it got damaged or was no longer required, it could simply be thrown away. Murdoch's first paper chair, designed while he was still a student at the Royal College of Art, was ahead of its time when it first appeared.
opposite top right
Cartoon by Léon which appeared on the front cover of the Danish design magazine, *Mobilia*, in 1968, satirizing the fashion for paper furniture, and making specific reference to Peter Murdoch's Spotty chair.
opposite bottom left
Chair Thing, a later commercially successful design by Peter Murdoch, produced in Britain from 1967 by Perspective Designs. It is shown here with its packaging, prior to construction, and in its completed state.
opposite bottom right
Papp furniture range designed by Peter Raacke for the German firm Faltmöbel Ellen Raacke, 1967–8.

below
Advert from 1964 showing
(left) Catena designed by
Mo Sullivan, an abstract
geometric pattern reflecting
'the look' of the early
1960s, and (right) Pastoral
by Regina Moritz-Evers, a
stylized floral pattern looking
forward to the pop aesthetic
of the mid-1960s. This and
the bottom advert for Heal
Fabrics illustrate the type of
patterns described as 'flat
florals'.
bottom
Tivoli designed by Peter
Hall, a full-blown quasi-
psychedelic flat floral
pattern, 1968.

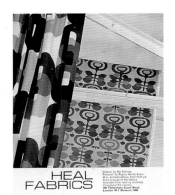

Workshop of Detroit; a chair and ottoman made of a cluster of cardboard tubes glued and riveted together by the Canadian designer Donald Lloyd McKinley; and a stacking child's chair by Yarme/Beckman, produced by the Container Corporation of America. As with inflatables, some designers combined paper with other materials in order to give it greater strength and rigidity. This was the principle adopted by the young Swedish designer Michael Björnsterna in his unusual multi-purpose zig-zag-shaped table/stool/storage unit system designed for Bejra Möbiler of Tibro. The sides of the units were made of cardboard but all the edges were lined with strips of aluminium.

Pop patterns and psychedelia

Because inflatable and paper furniture was so closely linked to the concept of expendability, and because they were often produced in bright colours, they are sometimes classed as Pop design. This term can also be usefully applied to a certain field of pattern design during the mid-1960s, although in a somewhat different context. An article in *The Ambassador* in January 1964 highlighted the refreshing contribution being made to British textiles at this date by the many young female designers emerging from Britain's art colleges. These designers introduced a new mood of light-heartedness and fun into pattern design, characterized as Pop. Typical of the new breed of designers was Gillian Farr, who had trained at Harrow School of Art, and was now working freelance for forward-looking firms such as Conran Fabrics. The stylized floral pattern of her Gilliflower furnishing fabric, 1964, for Conran perfectly captured the upbeat mood of the day. Farr also designed dress fabrics, and an indication of how successfully she managed to capture the *Zeitgeist* of the 1960s is provided by the fact that her work was used by both Establishment couturiers such as Digby Morton, and anti-Establishment fashion designers such as Mary Quant. Another typically ebullient British pattern designer of the mid-1960s was Natalie Gibson, a graduate of the Royal College of Art. Her clients included the design-led firm of Danasco, for which she created a high Pop design called My Love, composed of giant hearts, in 1964. Subject matter of this kind would have been taboo at the end of the 1950s, and the fact that it was now in such demand emphasized the impact of the 'youthquake' and the new mood of buoyancy that now prevailed. One of the most successful pattern designers of the 1960s was Pat Albeck, who worked in a variety of media, including ceramics, wallpapers and textiles. Through her dress fabrics, furnishing fabrics and tea towels, in particular, Albeck's designs reached a mass audience. Her work was modern but commercial at the same time, and it was because she was so eclectic in her sources that Albeck was the archetypal 1960s Pop designer.

The aesthetics of Pop Art itself appear to have influenced the stylized flat floral patterns so characteristic of the mid-1960s. Examples among the furnishing fabrics produced by Heal's at this date include Pastoral by Regina Moritz-Evers from 1964, Rhapsody by Michael Griffin from 1965, and Verdure by Peter Hall from 1966. Styles of pattern design were evolving at such a rapid rate during the mid-1960s that buyers had to be extremely energetic in order to keep on top of the latest trends. As the decade progressed, the range of styles became increasingly diverse, a fact acknowledged in a feature called 'Hip Hip Heals!'

in *The Ambassador* in April 1966:
Year after year Mr Tom Worthington, the eminence anything-but-grise of Heal Fabrics, states his credo that colour and design sell fabrics. Stimulating, encouraging, prodding and persevering in his search for designers, he produces each season a collection which draws on talent from both recognized and new sources. To young designers Heal's spells hope and many established textile design names got their first chance under the Worthington wing. The 1966 collection covers several design styles – Op is recognized, abstracts in clear, bright colours are included, but the crop of flat florals are an indication that designers are recovering from their recent graphic indigestion.

This trend for 'flat florals' continued at Heal's into the late 1960s, with some designs taking on ethnic overtones, and others becoming increasingly cartoon-like in the spirit of the Beatles' film *Yellow Submarine*. Heal's 1968 collection included two strikingly bold cartoon-like quasi-psychedelic patterns by Peter Hall called Petrus and Tivoli. Flat florals were also widely used in Britain to decorate domestic accessories such as trays and tins. Pauline Butler's patterns for Xlon in 1967 were typical, with their stylized floral designs, strongly defined outlines and bright colours. The fashion for simplified and stylized flat patterns was not confined to Britain, but was also reflected in fabrics produced by Scandinavian firms, such as Mölnlycke and Borås Wäfveribolaget in Sweden, and Marimekko in Finland. Although difficult to define precisely, one of the essential characteristics of Pop pattern design was the reduction of images to their simplest elements, as in a furnishing fabric with a scrolling pattern called Pop Baroque designed by Douglas Binder, Dudley Edwards and David Vaughan for Sanderson in 1967. Interestingly, this design trio had made a name for themselves through their customized hand-painted Pop furniture and cars for celebrities such as the Beatles. Another type of pattern design that could just as validly be described as Pop, in the Paolozzi/Warhol sense of the word, were the photographic reproductions used on Pop memorabilia. This type of literal Pop aesthetic spilled over into mainstream design at the end of the decade when Eddie Squires designed a garish fabric called Lunar Rocket for Warner in 1970, produced to celebrate the landing of the Apollo spacecraft on the moon.

The rapidly changing face of pattern design in the mid-1960s, as well as being a reflection of a throw-away society, was also an expression of the desire for ever more heightened sensations. 'The look' of the early 1960s had been encapsulated in abstract geometric patterns of a highly controlled nature. During the second half of the decade, however, two new trends emerged – Op and psychedelia – both of which explored the idea of artificially enhanced stimulation. In Op design, patterns composed of static geometric forms such as squares, rectangles, circles, dots and stripes were manipulated to suggest the impression of being three-dimensional and kinetic. While in one way Op patterns were fun, in another way they were subversive because they deliberately manipulated sensory perceptions, evoking distortions that were not really there, and simulating optical breakdown. Through Op, science and art were amalgamated. This was like computer-aided design before it had been invented, an idea also suggested by the Pop prints of Eduardo Paolozzi from the mid-1960s, with their obsessive interest in electrical circuitry.

right

The Beatles' feature-length cartoon, *Yellow Submarine*, 1968. The film's graphics, designed by Heinz Edelmann, were of a similar style to contemporary textiles and wallpapers.

far right

Circuit, a furnishing fabric from the Programmed Pattern collection designed by Eddie Squires for Warner Fabrics, 1967, inspired by a copper-foil printed circuit. By this date geometric patterns were melting down to become neo-organic or psychedelic.

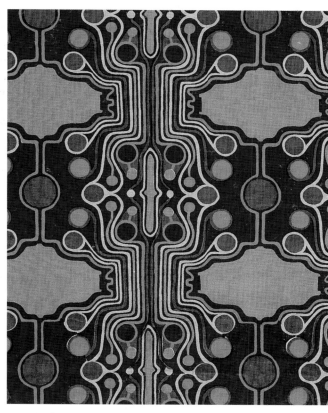

left

Frequency, a psychedelic Op Art fabric designed by Barbara Brown for Heal's, 1969. Pattern design was one of the most dynamic fields of British creativity during the 1960s. Towards the end of the decade, textile and wallpaper designers freely mixed ultra-modern and retro sources to produce a rich and complex mélange of styles.

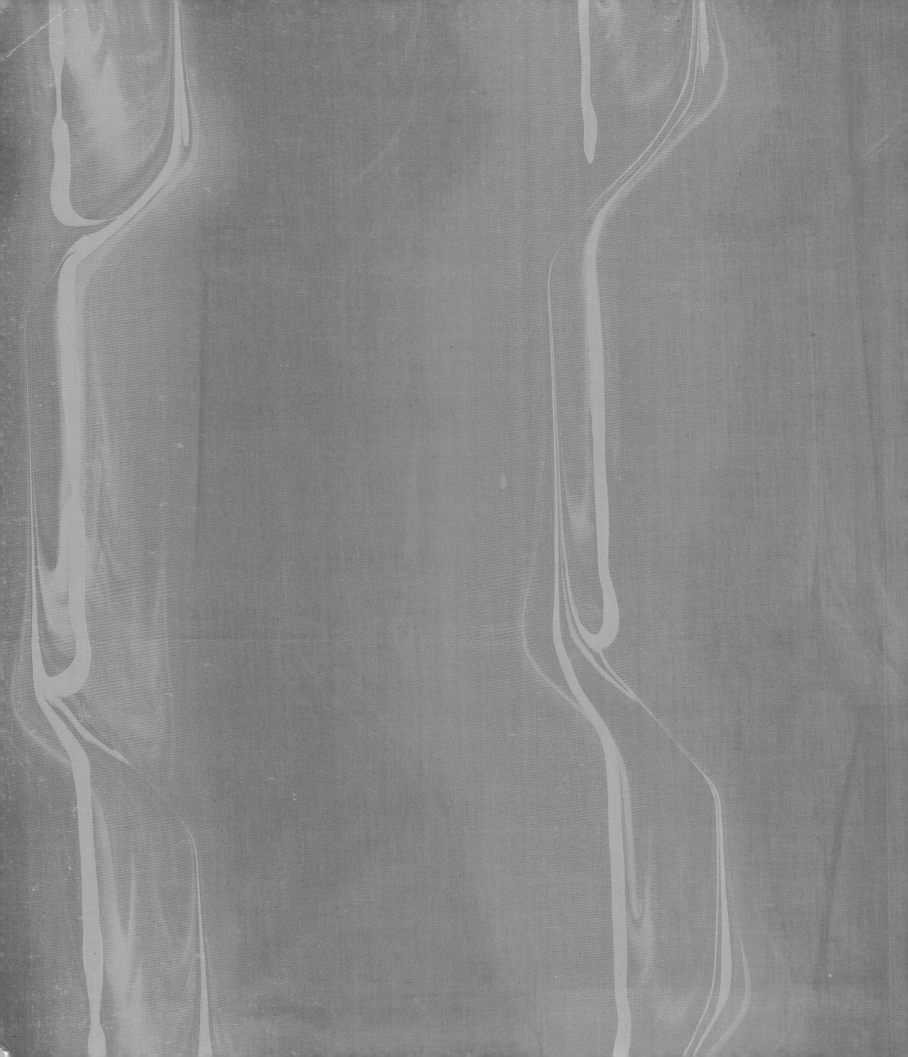

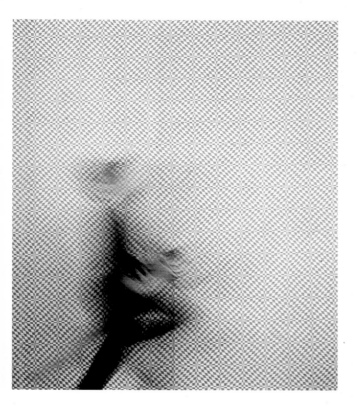

opposite
Shade Print 208, a double-sided psychedelic fabric designed by Timo Sarpaneva for Jack Lenor Larsen, 1969, manufactured in Britain by Danasco.
above
Op-inspired wallpaper (L80795), designed by Deryck Healey for the Crown Vinyl range produced by the Wall Paper Manufacturers, 1968.
right
Simple Solar furnishing fabric by Shirley Craven for Hull Traders, 1967.

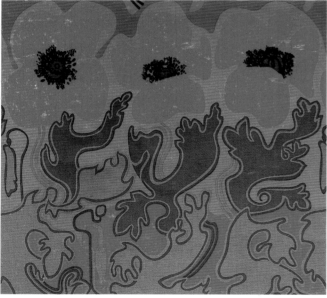

above
Shape, a bold collage-like abstract fabric designed by Shirley Craven for Hull Traders, 1964.
left
Floppy Poppy, a textile overtly inspired by hippy drug culture, designed by Diana and Derek Collard for Sanderson, 1967.

Later the idea of the designer as computer programmer was explored by Eddie Squires at Warner Fabrics in a series of printed textiles for the Programmed Pattern collection of 1968. Among these were the evocatively named Circuit, Colourtron and Univac, which had strong psychedelic over-tones in their vibrant colouring and the frenetic quality of their patterns. Circuit was inspired by a copper-foil printed circuit, while Colourtron was named after an integrated silicon circuit device used in colour television sets. The third pattern, Univac, was named after an American digital computer, and the design was based on shapes seen in a computer-drawn map. At the end of the decade in 1969 Barbara Brown designed a pattern called Frequency for Heal's which was a vibrant evocation of pulsating sound waves. Printed in bright tonally related colourways, such as reds, yellows, oranges and blues, this design, like the Programmed Patterns of Eddie Squires, made the crossover from the total control of Op to the total release of psychedelic design.

One of the earliest signals that designers were start-ing to feel constrained by the strict geometry that had governed their work during the first half of the 1960s came from the much freer designs of Shirley Craven at Hull Traders during the middle of the decade. In 1964 Design Centre Awards were presented to three bold, colourful, painterly patterns by Craven called Sixty-Three, Division and Shape. Although clearly related to Abstract Expressionism and colour-field painting, these patterns do not fit neatly into either category, and have an energetic and liberating quality all of their own. As well as designing for Hull Traders, Craven was also responsible for buying in patterns from freelancers, and in 1965 she chose to put into production a proto-psychedelic design called Spindrift by Margaret Cannon, the scrolling motifs of which prefigured trends during the last quarter of the decade. In 1967 Hull Traders produced a new series of pat-terns by Craven herself which were freer still and which were no longer based on flat planes of colour, but were instead cross-hatched with crayon-like linear shading. The outlines of these patterns, which included Simple Solar, Five and November, were apparently completely random and chaotic – in a word, trippy – and thus they were a perfect reflection of the spirit of the time. Craven's choice of colours was also highly distinctive, including colourways combining yellow, orange, red and brown for Five, and pastel shades of orange, pink, green and blue for Simple Solar.

'The look' of the early 1960s had been sharp-edged, precise and controlled. The counter-revolution of the later 1960s introduced neo-organic furniture and psychedelic pat-terns. In other words, there was a general melt-down of forms and a loosening of control over patterns. In 1967 Sanderson introduced a vibrant pink, red and green psychedelic furnish-ing fabric called Floppy Poppy designed by Diana and Derek Collard, composed of giant drooping flowers. Both the flow-ers themselves and the way in which they were depicted sug-gested an association with drugs, as did the title of the fabric. Whereas Op patterns arose from the imposition of control over the conscious rational mind, psychedelic patterns devel-oped out of an exploration of the subconscious. Originally inspired by the experience of using hallucinogenic drugs such as LSD, once psychedelic patterns had evolved as a genre, they were freely co-opted by graphic and pattern designers for purely commercial applications. Although psychedelic design evolved initially as an anti-control and anti-Establishment form of expression, therefore, it was rapidly co-opted by the Establishment and put to work in a highly effective but purely commercial way. As with Op, it was not actually necessary for designers to hold any particular artistic theory or philosophical belief system in order to harness the visual impact of psychedelia for decorative purposes.

Patterns of the later 1960s were dense, dynamic and convoluted. Floppy Poppy was by no means an isolated example of psychedelic design within Sanderson's output. In 1968 the firm produced a free-swirling abstract pattern printed in shades of pink and orange. The impact of psychedelia spread far and wide. In Finland Timo Sarpaneva designed a range of textiles called Shade Prints for the American manufacturer Jack Lenor Larsen at the end of the decade, which were produced in Britain by Danasco. The freedom of these patterns (as if different coloured paints had been allowed to mingle freely together) and the vividness and intensity of the colours (including infusions of yellow, pink and orange) reflected the influence of psychedelic design. Psychedelia, although easily identifiable as a style in its own right, was also in part an amalgamation of other styles – Pop and Op, for example, with elements of Art Nouveau and Art Deco.

The way in which Pop, Op and psychedelic patterns were accepted as part of the mainstream visual language of the period is indicated by their widespread adoption in fashion, and their influence on the decoration of domestic accessories, packaging and printed ephemera. In November 1969 the Canadian firm Arborite advertised a range of plastic laminates called Myriad in the Architectural Review. Described as 'six specially designed contemporary patterns' which could be overlaid like tracery on top of any plain coloured ground, the range included a Pop-inspired pattern called Cipher, composed of juxtaposed enlarged letters; two bold Op patterns called Ariola and Rhythm; and a psychedelic pattern called Cirius.

Historical Revivalism

From the mid-1960s onwards, not only was Modernism called into question, but the validity of a debate centred on this issue. Designers were beginning to tire of the Western concept of 'the modern' altogether. This explains why, as part of the counter-revolution of the late 1960s, they began to seek alternatives in the traditions of other cultures and in the inspiration of the past. Suddenly, after being out of vogue for almost twenty years, people began to rediscover and revel in the richness of Victorian design, particularly late nineteenth-century pattern design, but also Victorian and Edwardian ephemera and antiques. For those brought up on the pared-down aesthetic of Contemporary design and the cool control of 'the look', Victorian textiles and wallpapers came as a revelation. The revival of interest in Victorian design in general, and Art Nouveau in particular, started during the first half of the decade and was associated almost exclusively with textiles and wallpapers. At first Art Nouveau was just one of a medley of sources that designers began to dip into for inspiration. In the Palette 61 collection produced by Jack Lenor Larsen, for example, Art Nouveau was simply one element within an extensive repertoire of historical and multi-cultural influences, and had no particular significance in its own right. It was not until several years later that Art Nouveau took off in a more

significant way and became accepted as a mainstream historical revival style. A survey feature in The Ambassador in July 1963 hinted at this forthcoming transition:
The aesthetic in furnishings is slowly changing direction. Whilst abstracts will continue to be valid, there is a definite feel for the more natural decorative impulses. Pop Art through its more representational aspects is beginning to approach Art Nouveau – the other extreme of the prevailing decorative mood.
Although Art Nouveau was mentioned in this context, however, none of the fabrics illustrated supported the assertion that it was a significant influence, and it appears to have been erroneously associated with any form of elaborate patterning at this date.

Signs that the Victorian revival was becoming more established began to appear in 1964 at the 'Inprint' exhibition held at the Cotton Board's Colour Design and Style Centre in Manchester. A feature on the exhibition in The Ambassador in July 1964 called 'Floreat Habitat' drew attention to a Morris-inspired design by Bernard Wardle called Pandora, a printed cotton satin simulating a Victorian brocade by David Whitehead, and an Iznik-inspired pattern called Persia by the Manchester firm of William O'Hanlon, all reflecting Victorian taste. Also in 1964, John Line produced a wallpaper pattern book Epoch, which, as its title suggests, consisted of groups of self-consciously historical revival designs, placed in different categories such as 'Victorian Style', 'Art Nouveau Style' and '19th Century English Style'. Although produced in colour schemes that were unmistakably of their own time, these designs revealed a new awareness and appreciation of the work of leading Victorian pattern designers such as William Morris, Christopher Dresser, C F A Voysey and Lewis F Day. In May 1966 The Ambassador recorded in its 'Fabric News' section that 'the modest Victorian flower designs which sparked off the print stampede have blossomed into bold, vigorously designed prints reflecting the current preoccupation with Art Nouveau and Geometrics, in vivid Byzantine colours.' Pattern design had clearly reached a crossroads, and designers now had various options to choose from: the modern in the form of Pop, Op and psychedelia; the traditional in the form of historical revivalism; or the ethnic in the form of Asian, African and South American design.

For those who opted for historical revivalism, two main choices were on offer: Art Nouveau (loosely interpreted at this date to encompass late Victorian design) and Art Deco (incorporating both the Modern and the Moderne). Within the Art Nouveau category, two different approaches were apparent. One was literal and took the form of what were, in effect, reproductions of original designs, or adaptations of the work of a particular designer, such as Charles Rennie Mackintosh. This was the case with a wallpaper called Marlborough produced by Cole and Son in 1966, which was printed from original blocks dating from 1910. According to a commentary in Design in April 1966, this wallpaper 'amply demonstrates how much more satisfactory the genuine Art Nouveau article is than most modern re-vamped versions.' However, with hindsight it is the latter, the 'modern re-vamped versions', that are more interesting to the design historian because of the element of creative intervention by the contemporary designer. What Design referred to as 'revamped' designs were, in fact, contemporary designs with Art Nouveau overtones, rather

than vice versa. An example of this category of pattern is provided by a vinyl wallpaper designed by Evelyn Erlbeck for the Wall Paper Manufacturer's Scene collection in 1968, which in stylistic terms was precariously balanced on the border between Art Nouveau and psychedelia. The Palladio 8 wallpaper collection of 1968 contained some even more daring psychedelic Art Nouveau concoctions, two of the most extreme being Hecuba by David Bartle and Pomona by Erica Willis. Also dating from the late 1960s was Marbella, a wallpaper designed for Shand Kydd's Focus collection, composed of Victorian-inspired scrolling motifs, but printed in turquoise, purple and bright green. This made the pattern appear more psychedelic than historical because the colours heightened the latent dynamism of the design, a feature that would have seemed much less obvious had the paper been printed in a more subdued colourway.

Most Art Nouveau revival wallpapers of the 1960s can be easily identified. Colouring was the most decisive factor, with many patterns being printed in vivid, artificially heightened, quasi-psychedelic colourways, such as pinks, blues and purples. The fascination with Art Nouveau continued into the early 1970s, although by this date it was being challenged in the field of wallpapers by the new fashion for Art Deco. A late Mackintosh-inspired wallpaper, Cranston, designed by Clare Hartley Jones, appeared in the Palladio 9 collection of 1971, its title referring to the chain of Glasgow tearooms run by Miss Cranston, the interiors of which were designed by Mackintosh. Less directly derivative, but still heavily reliant on Art Nouveau sources, was a wallpaper called Gandalf by David Bartle in the same collection. The adoption of lurid psychedelic colourways, such as purple and green, suggested associations between the extravagant swirling patterns of Art Nouveau and the visual impact of hallucinogenic drugs.

By the mid-1960s the obsession with Art Nouveau was becoming a cause of concern to designers such as Stuart Durant who worked at Edinburgh Weavers; he considered the craze as 'mindless and frenetic', according to an article in *The Ambassador* in November 1966. In spite of this, of all the new trends in pattern design that surfaced during the mid-1960s, ultimately it was the fashion for Victorian design that was to prove the most enduring, significantly influencing the course of mainstream design throughout the 1970s and 1980s. What was different about this fashion during the 1960s, however, was the novelty factor and the fact that it was not aimed at the older generation, many of whom would have had less than fond recollections of the original, but was specifically targeted at young people. In 1969, for example, Sanderson launched a new collection of inexpensive washable wallpapers called Tempo, subtitled 'the young Sanderson set'. Among these were several Art Nouveau and Mackintosh-inspired designs presented in the accompanying publicity shots in a modern context, complete with plastic chairs and acrylic hemispherical lamps. In fact these patterns were presented not as something old at all, but as something as modern as Op, Pop and psychedelia. Although the 1960s interest in Art Nouveau was a form of historical revivalism, it was initially driven by a genuine thrill for rediscovery rather than by nostalgia, as it was during the ensuing decades. In contrast to the situation twenty-five years later, the 1960s approach to Victorian design, even the Laura Ashley version, seems almost refreshing. Furthermore,

top
Pomona, a hallucinogenic wallpaper from the Palladio 8 collection, 1968, designed by Erica Willis, printed by Sanderson.

above
Hecuba wallpaper designed by David Bartle from the Palladio 8 collection, 1968, combining flower-power imagery with Art Nouveau forms.

because other overtly contemporary forms of design were still so strong at this date, they exerted a decisive influence on the way in which Victorian design was interpreted. The use of vivid artificial colours, for example, and bold colour combinations put an entirely different slant on otherwise familiar forms of expression, and transformed them into something completely new. It was less a case of 'Grannie takes a trip', than 'William Morris takes a trip'.

Some historical revival influences were specific, and some were generalized, as in the case of a pattern called Grannie by Natalie Gibson for Hull Traders of the mid-1960s, based on the hexagonal motifs of a patchwork quilt. It was this more free-ranging historical revivalism that was the making of Laura Ashley, a designer and manufacturer turned retailer who exerted a powerful influence over the course of British design from the late 1960s onwards. Laura Ashley and her husband Bernard began silk-screening fabrics on a small scale in 1953, producing designs strongly influenced by Liberty. Ten years later they established a workshop and began to achieve wider commercial success, initially through accessories, and subsequently through clothes, furnishing fabrics and wallpapers. After opening a shop in London in 1969 the business grew rapidly; by 1974 there were two factories in operation and a chain of shops around the world. Although Laura Ashley's mainstream commercial success falls largely outside the chronological parameters of this book, the ideas behind the business had their genesis in the 1960s, and in many ways the company was very much a product of its time. This was the irony of the 1960s, that new ideas initially

exploited in a positive way would eventually end up exerting a negative influence on design. The Laura Ashley phenomenon was so successful and was copied by so many other firms that, by the end of the 1970s, historical revivalism had swamped modern design completely, prompting the public to turn their backs on genuine originality and modernity in favour of phoney nostalgia and pastiche.

Whereas the interest in Victorian design and Art Nouveau manifested itself largely through pattern design, the revival of interest in design from the 1920s and 1930s – both Modernism and what became known as Art Deco – was initially expressed mainly through furniture, and only subsequently through textiles and wallpapers. The impact of the re-issues of Modernist furniture design classics by Mies van der Rohe, Marcel Breuer, Le Corbusier, Charlotte Perriand and Eileen Gray has already been noted. As with the rediscovery of Victorian design, the novelty factor was important. The influence of Modernist design on the new furniture of the 1960s was most evident in the re-adoption of wide-gauge chromium-plated tubular steel. An early example of what would become an increasingly common trend during the early 1970s was the luxurious Trawden range of leather-upholstered armchairs and glass-topped coffee tables designed by Bernard Holdaway for Hull Traders in 1967, the somewhat unlikely successor to the Tomotom range of the previous year. In 1968 another British firm, OMK, launched their T range of demountable furniture, made of chromium-plated bent tubular steel with leather or canvas sling seats. In addition to easy chairs, coffee tables were produced with white fibreglass tops,

above left
Cranston, an Art Nouveau revival wallpaper design, inspired by the work of Charles Rennie Mackintosh, designed by Clare Hartley Jones for the Palladio 9 collection printed by Sanderson, 1971.
above
Sikhara, a pop Art Deco revival wallpaper designed by Peter Jones for the Palladio 9 collection, printed by Sanderson, 1971.

and in 1969 the range was extended to include a dining chair and a settee. Curved chromed tubular steel used in conjunction with either perspex or glass also formed the framework of the much more blatantly Art Deco revivalist furniture made by Plush Kicker. In an article called 'Plush, Kicker and the Nostalgia of Curves' in *Design* in June 1969, Alastair Best remarked on the current craze for 1930s design:

This fickle nostalgia has its fruitful side. Collectors, stockpiling ephemera in the surefire certainty that one day it will be in demand, have made a killing. And designers have benefited most of all: on the one hand the revivals have provided them with a wealth of pictorial language of which they can have been only mistily aware; on the other it has created a market for extravagant designs.

Plush Kicker established a healthy market for their work in the USA, where the attraction of Art Deco was particularly strong. The Americans had enthusiastically embraced the style during its first incarnation, and in the skyscrapers of New York in particular, there were many potent reminders of this era of luxury and glamour. Two New York based designers whose work made reference to the glory days of the Jazz Age were John Mascheroni and Tony Palladino, although instead of using tubular steel in their furniture they employed tubular aluminium, the gauge of which was exaggeratedly wide. Their work demonstrates the way in which designers dabbled with Art Deco revivalism during the late 1960s, not seeking to make literal copies, but taking distinctive features and exaggerating them. The excesses of Art Deco were thus deliberately blown up further by designers of the late 1960s, and in this way, although indebted to the past, the style was transformed into something new. The fact that Mascheroni and Palladino's work was interpreted as being fundamentally original at the time that it was created is indicated by its selection for inclusion in the permanent collection at the Museum of Modern Art in New York.

In the field of pattern design, the firm of Warner Fabrics was among the first to produce overtly Art Deco-inspired textiles. A definitive Art Deco revival design was Archway by Eddie Squires dating from of 1968 with its stylized imagery of skyscraper and starburst motifs. Sanderson's Palladio 8 wallpaper collection of the same year included a pattern called Ziggurat by Margaret Cannon, stepped forms being one of the *leitmotifs* of the Jazz Modern style. This trend was consolidated in the Palladio 9 collection of 1971, which contained John Garnet's complementary Broadway East and Broadway West wallpapers, combining ziggurats with stylized fountains, another potent and recurrent Art Deco symbol. An even more outlandish interpretation of these motifs was reflected in Peter Jones's bold multi-coloured Sikhara wallpaper, which combined the exuberance of Art Deco with the brashness of 1950s pinball machines. Palladio 9 also contained the flamboyant Main Street wallpaper by John Wilkinson and Deco by Judith Cash, both of which drew on starburst and shooting star motifs, the latter honestly acknowledging its source of inspiration in its title. The decadence of the Art Deco era clearly appealed to Ettore Sottsass and the radical Italian design group Archizoom, both of whom used spoof Art Deco forms in their furniture and lighting: examples being the series of Art Deco-inspired beds and *chaise-longues* designed by Archizoom in 1967; Sottsass's ziggurat-shaped Tantra ceramics, 1969; and his pink plastic, wavy-rimmed, internally

lit Ultrafragola mirror manufactured by Poltronova of 1970. Thus British pattern designers and Italian furniture designers both demonstrated in their different ways the rich source of imagery they had discovered in Art Deco design.

Ethnic Sources
Clearly related to the fashion for historical revivalism, although pursued along parallel lines, was the growing interest in multicultural sources for design. The origins of this trend can be traced back to the second quarter of the 1960s, which was when pattern designers first began to cast their net wider than their traditional Eurocentric or North American frames of reference. Abstract geometric patterns, although liberating in one way, ultimately proved restrictive, and it was in response to this feeling of confinement that designers began to look further afield for alternative sources of inspiration. Even before the advent of the hippy trail to Marrakech, North African and Hispano-Moresque culture proved one of the richest sources of inspiration, although this was partly because of the natural affinity between Moorish decoration and some of the abstract geometric patterns of 'the look'. The Palladio 6 collection of 1963 contains two Moorish wallpaper patterns by Margaret Cannon called Alhambra and Valencia. Alhambra was also the name of a printed textile designed by Mary Yonge for Edinburgh Weavers, advertised in *Design* in May 1964, while in the same year John Line produced a wallpaper called Malaga, described as 'Moresque' in style. Malaga was also the name of a textile by Shelagh Wakely for Edinburgh Weavers in 1965. According to the designer this jacquard woven textile resulted from a study of Moorish laceria patterns, ornamental mouldings of square and circular design, consisting of a series of rings with a rosebud in the centre, which were joined together to form an unending decorative motif. Moorish designs also proved an attraction at Heal's, where their influence was reflected in several new patterns launched in 1968, including Arabesque and Moresco by David Bartle, and Alhambra by Heather Brown dating from 1971.

The eclectic firm of Hull Traders was among the first to begin exploring non-Western sources of inspiration. Its Time Present collection dating from around 1963 included a printed furnishing fabric called Totem designed by Trevor Coleman, the pattern suggesting an African mask. This design appeared at about the same time as Susan Williams-Ellis's Totem range of relief-moulded ceramics for Portmeirion Pottery. Totem was also the name of a wallpaper in the Palladio 7 collection in 1966, confirming that designers were increasingly interested in exploring visual ideas derived from what had hitherto been considered mysterious ethnic sources. In 1965 Edinburgh Weavers demonstrated its interest in ethnography by commissioning a series of patterns inspired by mainly non-Western cultures, which were promoted as a coherent collection via a series of adverts in *House and Garden*. The series included a pattern called Jungle by Betty Middleton-Sandford, which depicted exotic flowers and plants; Sookhothai by Dennis Hawkins, which exploited the strongly calligraphic style of painting seen in Japanese art; and Zacatecas by Carola and Daniel Olsen, inspired by what the designers referred to as the 'bold vigour' of Aztec art.

From 1965 onwards the number of British textiles inspired by ethnic sources increased significantly, with a new emphasis on patterns from India and other parts of Asia.

left
Pageant, a printed cotton
furnishing fabric designed
by Jyoti Bhomik for Heal's,
1966.
below
Advert for Edinburgh
Weavers, 1965, showing a
fabric called Jungle
designed by Betty
Middleton-Sanford.

ALHAMBRA, a screen print on plain cotton by Mary Yonge. 24" repeat. 8 colourways.

EDINBURGH WEAVERS
CARLISLE AND LONDON

The Aztec heritage of Mexico

Among the fabrics surveyed by *The Ambassador* in July 1965, for example, were designs called Coptic and Indian by G P and J Baker, Casbah created by Nadia Czapla for Fidelis Furnishing Fabrics, and Kashmir by David Whitehead. In 1965 Warner Fabrics launched their Caspian Sea collection, which contained a rich and vividly coloured design called Soumak by Eddie Squires, inspired by the geometric patterns of Persian carpets. In 1966 Heal's began to produce patterns by Jyoti Bhomik, a designer who was himself of Indian origin, a factor that gave added authenticity to Heal's exploration of Indian pattern-making. Bhomik had come over to Britain in order to study at the Central School of Arts and Crafts, and his patterns represented a potent blend of traditional Indian design, British Pop and the psychedelic. One of his first patterns to enter production was Pageant, dating from 1966, a simple but powerful design printed in bright fiery colours. This was followed in 1967 by the evocative Indian Summer, and in 1968 by a design called Persian Garden. The text of an advertising leaflet produced by Heal's to promote their 1968 collection remarked on the prevalence of 'flat, stylized florals showing a predilection for the Orient'. Bhomik was also instrumental in transferring Indian-inspired pattern designs to ceramics when, like Terence Conran and Barbara Brown before him, he was commissioned to create surface patterns for Midwinter. The pattern that Bhomik designed for the Fine range in 1968 was produced in two different colourways, one called Kismet, printed in blue, brown, orange and mustard, and the other called Bengal, printed in blue, purple, green and mustard. Possibly as a result of this alliance, Midwinter's resident pattern designer, Jessie Tait, created two new patterns for Fine in 1968, one called Persia and another called Spanish Garden, the latter inspired by the pattern on a Liberty tie. Spanish Garden proved one of Midwinter's all time best sellers, and remained in production until the 1980s. Meanwhile Jyoti Bhomik carried on working for Heal's over the next few years, and the vibrant colours and patterns of his native country continued to influence his later designs, which included Insignia from 1970 and Pomona from 1971. Strong colours were also used by Donald Brothers in their Hebridean collection of 1969 to evoke a 'world of colour and texture and romance'. The names given to specific woven fabrics in this collection, however, were intended to evoke the hot dusty cities of Asia rather than the windswept Hebridean islands off the north of Scotland referred to in the collection's title. Individual designs included Kabul – 'hot, violent counterpoints of light and shade captured in fabrics' – and Samarkand – 'haunted city of dreams woven gently into cloth'.

As well as the literal and direct influence of African, Asian and South American cultures on decoration, ethnic influences sometimes extended to encompass philosophical ideas. From the mid-1960s onwards many young people in Europe and America, the Beatles included, became interested in Eastern mysticism. Just as this affected their music, so in the case of some designers, the exploration of Hindu or Buddhist philosophies affected their aesthetic output. A noteworthy example was Ettore Sottsass, although in his commentary on his Tantra ceramics in *Domus* in September 1969, Sottsass took pains to clarify that he was not jumping on the hippy bandwagon, pointing out that he was too old to be attracted by 'frenzied dancing, Oriental philosophy, wild gear, community life and marijuana cigarettes'. The designer had, however, developed a genuine interest in Tantric art after reading a book on the subject by Ajit Mookeryiee, and had become fascinated by the idea of 'the cosmos as continuous energy', an idea that he had tried to express through his Tantra ceramics. What interested Sottsass was the creative interplay between East and West and he tried, through his Tantra series, to suggest a synthesis between different cultures. Throughout the decade one of the main impulses driving his work forward was the creation of coherent designs from apparently opposing elements. Although Sottsass himself was successful in achieving a creative synthesis in his work, he was very much aware, however, that the world around him, including the design world, was rapidly fragmenting.

Crafts Movement

Having looked at the impact of historical revivalism, ethnography, Pop, Op, psychedelia and anti-design, the final ingredient in the counter-revolutionary hotpot of the late 1960s was the crafts movement. The evolution of the crafts during the twentieth century is a major topic in its own right, and it is not the purpose of this book to give a full analysis of it, except in so far as it influenced the development of mass production and industrial aesthetics. The crafts movement was just one of the many conflicting proactive and reactive forces at work during the 1960s which, during the latter part of the decade, became part of a much more explosive cocktail. After the turbulence of 1968, it was to the crafts rather than to industry that many art students began to look, choosing to become makers rather than designers. Much of the new talent that would previously have been at the service of applied art industries was instead directed towards the creation of individual objects. This, combined with the rapid decline of many traditional applied art manufacturing industries in the West during the 1970s, and their increasing reliance on historical revivalism, completely transformed the range and quality of domestic design on the market. From the point of view of the 1960s, however, a vigorous surge of interest in the crafts (whether prompted by the desire for direct artistic self-expression, or by the urge to make a philosophical statement about personal values by adopting an 'alternative' lifestyle) added a significant new dimension to the diversity of design at the end of the decade.

Whereas the fashion for Art Nouveau and Op Art can be pin-pointed to fairly specific dates, the influence of the crafts is a more nebulous and less coherent area of study. The crafts were already well established before the emergence of 'the look', for example, and lived on well after the demise of inflatable furniture and Art Deco revivalism. Also, whereas these short-lived trends spread rapidly from one country to another, the crafts movement in each country began from a different starting point. The Scandinavians, for example, were still very much rooted in the crafts at the start of the 1960s, having never actually left them behind during the 1950s, and they carried this legacy with them into the 1970s. The 'new' crafts movement of the 1960s was strongest in the USA and Eastern Europe, particularly Poland and Czechoslovakia, which gave these countries a decided head start. In Italy, by

contrast, where industry had only recently managed to break away from its handicraft roots, but where modern design now flourished, there was much less interest in the crafts *per se*. In Britain and central Europe it was not until the 1970s that the crafts movement became identifiable as a distinct entity and developed sufficient critical mass to be accepted as part of the Establishment. Nor was development within the crafts evenly distributed across the board through all media: art fabrics and studio glass were by far the two most interesting 'new' craft media during the 1960s, while, with the exception of a few outstanding individuals such as Hans Coper and Lucie Rie, less significant activity took place in studio ceramics than had occurred previously, or would happen later in the 1970s. In silver, apart from the one-off pieces by Gerald Benney, Stuart Devlin, David Mellor and Robert Welch, the most innovative work in this medium was carried out in the field of jewellery rather than domestic design.

Even before the 'new' craft movement began to emerge, one particular aesthetic derived from the crafts – textured surfaces – was already exerting a major influence on design at the start of the 1960s and would continue to have a significant impact for the remainder of the decade. The smooth surfaces and ultra-precise controlled shapes and patterns of 'the look' were complemented and counter-balanced by a parallel interest in rough uneven textures, and random forms and patterns. Sometimes there was even a crossover between the two, as in the deep-pile rugs designed by Verner Panton for Unika Vaev in 1960, which combined formal abstract geometric patterns with rugged textures. In fact, it was in the field of what were known as 'accent' rugs that the interest in textures was manifested most frequently and decisively during the early 1960s. In the 1950s there had been a revival of interest in traditional Northern Scandinavian long-pile *rya* rugs, a trend associated with Finland in particular. Because of their loose shaggy nature, these rugs provided an ideal vehicle for abstract patterns, including those inspired by Abstract Expressionism. The Italian rug designer Renata Bonfanti worked very much in this idiom during the 1950s and 1960s, and many *rya*-type rugs of this style were produced by commercial British carpet manufacturers for the Scandinavian market.

Contemporary architecture of the 1950s, with its promotion of uncarpeted hard wood floors, had generated a new interest in accent rugs, prompting an explanatory article on the source of this trend in *Design* in December 1965:
The modern rya *originates from rugs which were hand-made in Northern Scandinavia and used for floor, bench and wall coverings. The early Scandinavian* rya *had a very long pile and was usually decorated with one of a number of traditional motifs – shields, crosses, geometrical shapes, plant forms, etc. Over the years, the patterns were modified under the influence of the industrial revolution, when* ryas *began to be machine made, and trends in modern art later exerted their influence. The characteristics of the modern* rya *include luxuriant long pile, a subtle graduation of colour using many different tones, and the dramatic use of pattern.*
In Finland the revived craft was actively fostered by groups such as the Friends of Finnish Handicraft. Most designs were purely abstract, and many had geometric patterns, although on the whole this branch of the applied arts did not fall into the same neat categories of expression as other

Indian and Turkish patterns had a strong influence on British textile design during the late 1960s and early 1970s.
opposite top
Fragrance designed by Dorothy Evans for Heal's, 1971.
opposite centre left
Soumak, a textile from the Caspian Sea Collection designed by Eddie Squires for Warner Fabrics, 1965.
opposite centre right
Alhambra, a Moorish pattern designed by Mary Yonge for Edinburgh Weavers, 1964.
opposite bottom right
Zacatecas, inspired by Mexican Aztec patterns, designed by Carola and Daniel Olsen for Sanderson, 1965.

forms of textiles. The medium itself seemed to encourage independence and individual expression, and the most effective patterns were often the simplest. British carpet manufacturers such as John Crossley, Firth's, and Quayle and Tranter were quick to pick up on the new trend, especially after an exhibition of Finnish *rya* rugs held at the Victoria and Albert Museum in 1961, which attracted a lot of attention. By adapting their Axminster looms, British firms were able to mass-produce machine-made versions of *rya* rugs with Scandinavian-inspired designs, which they then successfully exported back to Scandinavia. In January 1964 *The Ambassador* illustrated the Norsk *rya* rug designed by Uve Luick for Quayle and Tranter of Kidderminster, and the following April a large group of British rugs were featured in order to demonstrate the prevailing Scandinavian influence on this field of design. Many of these had overtly Scandinavian titles, such as the Fjord rug by Bond Worth, the Dagrutta rug by Stoddard (part of their Rannock range, based on designs purchased from students in Scandinavia), the Homespun *rya* rug by Firth's (part of their Viking range), the Finlandia range by Broadloom Carpets, and the Forestal rug by Tomkinsons. According to an advert in *The Ambassador* in July 1964, Firth's Viking range was originally made purely for the Scandinavian market, but due to domestic demand was now being sold in the UK. The feature in *Design* in December 1965 drew attention to the fact that the British *rya* had become an outstandingly successful export line, and suggested that this was due in part to the competitiveness of British machine-made rugs, but also to the 'extremely close attention paid to quality, colour and design'.

Another branch of textiles in which textures played a prominent role was woven upholstery fabrics. The Stratford firm of Tibor, run by Hungarian-born Tibor Reich, had led the way during the late 1950s with its strongly textural Fotexur prints, and its subtly textured woven fabrics, ideas that were further developed during the mid-1960s via Tibor's Deep Texture upholstery fabrics. Overtly rough grainy textures became popular for upholstery fabrics, and were often produced in extremely bright colours such as orange or pink. In 1964, for example, the Scottish firm of Donald Brothers won a Design Centre Award for their Glendale fabric designed by Peter Simpson, which combined linen, rayon and cotton in its weave and was produced in twenty-one different colourways. Another much admired British textile firm which found particular favour with the design Establishment, was Sekers, a Cumbrian company. Its Kistna range, designed by Sir Nicholas Sekers in 1963, won a Design Centre Award in 1965. Although closely associated with silks, Sekers successfully expanded into the field of woven rayons for curtain fabrics. As with Donald Brothers, the reason why their work stood out was partly because of the rich textures of their weaves, and partly because of the ravishing colours in which their fabrics were dyed.

One of the most creative ways in which synthetic fibres were used during the 1960s was in woven fabrics for upholstery, where the textural potential of these fibres was exploited to the full. Among the design leaders in this field was Margo Fabrics, which achieved success in 1969 as a result of collaborating with the designer and artist Bernat Klein. Klein was an important figure in the textile world during the 1960s, having collaborated with various firms in

Scandinavia and Ireland, where his talents for exploiting colours and textures were fully appreciated. In 1967 Klein was appointed as design consultant for the Newcastle-based firm of Margo Fabrics, for which he created a range of acrylic-backed fabrics, each with a unique fibre composition based on different proportions of natural and synthetic fibres, viscose in particular. The resulting textiles looked natural, but had the toughness and resilience of synthetic fabrics, and they were dyed in a range of stunning colours. According to Klein, however, although colour was important: 'designing begins with selecting the right raw material, for the use of thick or thin or rough or smooth yarns can make all the difference to the final fabric.'

Textural abstract patterns had been an important feature of both printed textiles and wallpaper designs during the late 1950s and early 1960s, in part inspired by the still novel technique of screen-printing, which made the reproduction of painterly, grainy and textural patterns possible for the first time. The Palladio 4 wallpaper collection produced in 1960 was dominated by patterns of this type, such as Impasto by Audrey Levy and Wattle by Edward Veevers, the titles of which both reflect their textural qualities. The Palladio 5 collection of 1961 included a grainy pattern called Gradua by Peter Hall, while Palladio 6, which appeared two years later, contained another overtly textural pattern by the same designer called Textura. Over the next few years, however, the fashion shifted from simulated textures to wall coverings that were actually textured, a trend mirrored in other branches of the applied arts such as ceramics and glass. Several new textural materials were introduced during the 1960s that made a significant impact on interior design of the period. In 1963, for example, Sanderson advertised a range of textural Japanese wall coverings, including grass cloths, paper-backed silks and metallic papers. Another popular new wallcovering was hessian fabric, which began to be actively promoted in the mid-1960s. In 1966 an advert appeared in the *Architectural Review* for a Swedish-made hessian wall covering called the Comfort Range, by a Gothenburg-based firm called Galon. From this date onwards hessian became one of the most ubiquitous fabric-based wall coverings, particularly for exhibition and display purposes. Other products which came on the market at this date included vinyl-coated fabrics, such as Arlan Mural Texturide manufactured by Arlington Plastics, which was coated with Tedlar, the trade name for a new extra-tough polyvinyl fluoride film developed by Du Pont. According to an eyecatching advert in the *Architectural Review* in March 1967, Arlan was produced in 'a palette of with-it colours from soft through to scintillating, in subtle textures and exciting designs'.

Not all firms chose to go down the road of using bright colours. Heal Fabrics imported undyed linen sheers from Belgium, while Edinburgh Weavers advertised their own range of natural open weaves in the *Architectural Review* in March 1963, with evocative names such as Skelbo, Skene and Screel highlighting their Celtic associations. Also at the muted end of the spectrum were the furnishing textiles of Tamesa Fabrics, a company that specialized in natural colours, which, according to *Design* in February 1965 provided a 'refreshing relief from the strident colours of many modern furnishing fabrics'. Tamesa Fabrics was established in the mid-1960s by the designer Isabel Tisdall, who had formerly worked for Edinburgh Weavers, and the company specialized in both printed and woven fabrics. Subtle textural effects were its hallmark, a typical example being a fabric called Umbria from 1965, woven from a mixture of wool, cotton and linen, and produced in earth brown, raw sienna, oatmeal and cream. The contribution made by Tamesa was significant because it indicated the start of a reaction against exaggeratedly and artificially bright colours (the result of refinements in artificial chemical dyes), and signified the start of a preference for more natural effects, a trend closely allied with the 'back to the earth' movement. Tamesa's new fabrics met with the full approval of the architectural Establishment, which praised their 'timelessness' in the face of what the *Architectural Review* referred to in April 1965 as 'the fashion-crazed field of design activity'. Sekers and Tamesa continued to find favour with architects throughout the remainder of the decade.

Closely related to the prevailing interest in textures in the field of industrially produced furnishing fabrics was the development of what Jack Lenor Larsen was to call the 'Art Fabric'. In his landmark survey book called *Beyond Craft: The Art Fabric*, co-written with Mildred Constantine, Larsen defined the art fabric as 'a construction, individually created by an artist. It may be woven on the loom or free of the loom or may be produced by knotting, knitting, crochet, or other techniques.' Along with the studio glass movement, the art fabric was one of the most important manifestations of the crafts revival during the second half of the 1960s, and it was through textiles that the crafts movement as a whole was spearheaded, so vigorous and confident was the work being carried out in this field. This new interest in the creative potential of textiles was partly a reaction against the limitations of the purely industrial applications of textile design, and partly an assertion of the desire for greater and more direct freedom of expression. During the 1950s makers had achieved this by making handwoven tapestries and rugs. During the 1960s their aspirations rose dramatically, their work became much more sculptural and, in physical terms, it grew dramatically in size, hence the change in terminology from 'craft textiles' to 'art fabrics'. In an article in *Design* in September 1969, entitled 'Tapestry's Other Dimension', Milena Lamarova described the key features of the evolution of the art fabric during the 1960s:

Characteristic developments in modern tapestry are the destruction of flat rectangular form and traditional size; material used to interpret three-dimensional concepts; designs in which the subject is non-narrative but rather an expression of the material's structure and texture; creative invention in applying and combining different techniques; and a shift into architectonic forms which participate directly in creating the environment. The basic concern is therefore with materials and technology and has much to do with the most progressive ideas in art and architecture.

While important makers emerged in many different parts of the world during the course of the decade – Peter Collingwood and Tadek Beutlich in Britain, for example, and Moik Schiele in Switzerland – it was in Poland and the USA that the most significant and adventurous work was carried out, and where the number of accomplished textile artists was greatest. Particularly outstanding and original was the work of Magdalena Abakanowicz and Wojciech Sadley in Poland, and Sheila Hicks and Lenore Tawney in the USA.

opposite top left
This Norsk rug is a British version of the Finnish long pile *rya* rug, machine-made by Quayle and Tranter. The *rya*, decorated with simple, bold, abstract designs were very popular during the early 1960s. British firms even managed to successfully export their own versions of the rug back to Scandinavia.
opposite top right
Shadows in the Snow, a hand-made *rya* rug by the Finnish designer, Kirsti Ilvessalo, 1968.
opposite bottom
Range of textural woven upholstery textiles designed by Bernat Klein for Margo Fabrics, 1967–8, winner of a Design Centre Award in 1969. From top to bottom, Aspen, Spruce, Rowan and Larch, each one made of a different composition of wool and viscose backed with acrylic, and produced in up to ten different colourways. Klein's work was particularly admired in Scandinavia and he worked with a number of firms internationally.

Abakanowicz and Hicks were both noteworthy for the fact that they moved from two-dimensional wall-based woven works to large-scale freestanding or suspended three-dimensional textile sculptures. In fact Abakanowicz went further still with the creation of her textile 'situations' of the early 1970s which were complete environments rather than individual works. According to Jack Lenor Larsen, this departure was part of a much wider trend:

During the 1960s, about the same time environment entered the vocabulary of architecture and ecology, there developed, internationally and simultaneously, a keen awareness of the possibilities of environmental art. Although the concept has taken on several meanings, chief among them is the idea of the heightened emotional involvement of an art to be in – not to look at. In addition to such logical considerations, the environmental approach borders on mysticism and the surreal and is identified with bowers and lairs, the shrine and the womb.

Although the art fabric flowered in both Poland and the USA during the 1960s, it was for contrasting reasons. Like glass in Czechoslovakia, textiles were accepted by the Communist regime in Poland as an acceptable form of artistic expression, whereas fine art was regarded as potentially controversial. After the Second World War state support was provided for the development of native Polish handicrafts, weaving in particular. This policy was so successful that Poland was able to send an impressive group of woven hangings to the Milan Triennale in 1957 made from vegetable-dyed hand-spun wool, and from this date onwards the evolution of the Polish art fabric went from strength to strength. The American enthusiasm for the art fabric appears to have been for the opposite reason: the country's *lack* of tradition. The art fabric, being virgin territory, provided an ideal avenue for the Americans to assert their cultural identity, and for individuals to explore new uncharted areas of creative expression. It was also appealing because it could be used as a way of making grand statements, as in the tapestries created by Sheila Hicks in conjunction with Warren Platner for the Ford Foundation in New York in 1967, one of the many major art fabric commissions for public and commercial buildings during the 1960s and 1970s.

The second 'new' craft medium that the Americans co-opted during the 1960s was glass, although it is generally acknowledged that, because of their inexperience and the technical difficulties of establishing control over this material, none of their glass artists actually reached maturity until the 1970s. As with textiles, the main motivating factor behind the exploration of this new material was its use as a vehicle for direct creative expression. Hence the significance of working outside the established factory framework, in order to guarantee complete artistic freedom and the direct involvement of the artist in the making process. The key date in the evolution of the studio glass movement was 1962, when Harvey Littleton, a potter, and Dominick Labino, a glass scientist, collaborated in two seminar workshops at the Toledo Museum of Art, Ohio, to create hot glass using a small tank furnace. Although the actual objects produced were extremely crude, the seminars were recognized as a symbolic breakthrough and led to the setting up of a host of glass programmes in universities across the USA, culminating in the establishment of the famous Pilchuck School near Seattle in 1971. Littleton himself was the only artist who achieved any degree of con-

sistency in his work during the 1960s, his speciality being irregular sculptural blown vessels with applied decoration in the form of large prunts. Other important pioneers in the American studio glass movement included Marvin Lipofsky, Dale Chihuly and Sam Herman. It was Herman who brought the studio glass movement to Britain, when he came over to teach at the Royal College of Art and set up a glass-making cooperative in London called The Glasshouse. His presence influenced students emerging from the RCA during the late 1960s, including Peter Wheeler who went on to work briefly at Whitefriars Glass. In this way cross-fertilization took place with receptive factories, and fresh new ideas derived from studio glass were injected into the glass industry. At Whitefriars this new thinking was reflected in the short-run Studio ranges of 1969, through which complex, multi-layered, richly coloured vases were created. It was in the Peacock series from the Studio range that the technique of random strapping was first used, whereby trails of coloured glass were wound loosely and at random around the waist or shoulder of a vessel. Meanwhile an English designer called Michael Harris, who had taught at the RCA and had been inspired by the techniques and aesthetics of studio glass to carry out experiments of his own, moved to Malta during the mid-1960s to set up a small factory workshop called Mdina Glass. Using locally trained rather than imported labour in order to ensure the required degree of spontaneity, Mdina Glass specialized in studio-type ornamental glass, with Harris himself acting as both designer and maker. In the early 1970s Michael Harris returned to Britain where he established another firm called Isle of Wight Glass which produced glass in a similar idiom.

The two other countries most closely linked to the development of the studio glass movement were Sweden and Czechoslovakia, both of which had enjoyed long traditions of glass-making over several centuries. Although designers and glass artists in these countries continued to work within the framework of the existing glass industry during the 1960s, and it was not until the following decade that individual makers began to set up their own studios, there were nevertheless significant parallels between their work and the work of the pioneer studio glass-makers in the USA in terms of aesthetics and creative aspirations. It was in Czechoslovakia that the potential of glass as a purely artistic medium was first recognized after the war, and the Czechs made a major impression with the work they showed at the Brussels World Fair in 1958. Particularly important were the free-blown sculptural works by René Roubicek, chief artist at Borské Sklo from 1952 to 1965. He created spheres decorated with applied bulges and long spikes, which perfectly embodied the spontaneity and vigour to which the pioneer American studio glass-makers aspired. Also highly influential from the late 1940s onwards was Stanislav Libenský who subsequently worked closely with his wife, the sculptor Jaroslava Brychtová, and who exerted a major influence on Czech glass via his teaching as well as his glass-making activities. Libenský taught enamel-painting at the specialized school of glass-making at Nový Bor from 1945, before being appointed head of the glass-making school at Zelezný Brod in 1954. It was shortly after this that he began to collaborate with Brychtová, and moved on from making delicate engraved and enamelled vessels to creating monumental cast-glass sculptures. In 1958 Libenský and Brychtová made their first major

right

Prompted by the desire of independent practitioners for greater freedom and more direct hands-on involvement in the production process, the 1960s witnessed the birth of the studio glass movement. Although early creations were somewhat crude, the movement had lasting repercussions, and by the second half of the decade was starting to influence the type of glass made in some factories. It took several years before studio glassmakers could achieve works as accomplished as Dominick Labino's Immersion glass sculpture from the 1970s, with its veiled layers of coloured underlay.

below

Tortoiseshell bottle vase made by Michael Harris for Isle of Wight Glass, 1974. Harris taught at the Royal College of Art during the mid-1960s, and in 1966 pioneered the introduction of studio glass-making within the industrial glass department. Shortly afterwards he set up the Mdina glassworks on Malta, a small factory making studio glass, returning to Britain in the early 1970s to establish a similar enterprise: Isle of Wight Glass.

bottom centre

Vessel with silver oxide decoration made by Harvey Littleton, USA, 1965.

bottom right

Vase made by Sam Herman, early 1970s. Herman arrived in Britain on a Fulbright Scholarship from the USA in 1965. He exerted great influence over the development of studio glass in Britain, especially between 1969–74 when he taught at the Royal College of Art.

large-scale sculpture, a glass wall for the Brussels World Fair. In 1963 Libenský was appointed Professor at the Academy of Applied Arts in Prague, where he played a significant role for the next twenty-three years. Throughout the 1960s Libenský and Brychtová's work was very much in demand at international exhibitions, and they were commissioned to make pieces for both the Montreal Expo of 1967 (a giant 4-metre-high pyramid) and the Osaka Expo of 1970 (a huge allegorical sculpture called River of Life). Other important glass artists in Czechoslovakia during the 1960s included: Karel Vanura, who specialized in painted and engraved glass with subtle abstract designs; Pavel Hlava, who made rich use of colour, and developed a technique for making skeletal internal indentations inside his vessels; Vladimír Jelínek, who combined colour with simple optical effects; Vladimír Kopecký, who decorated his pieces with small-scale enamelled or acid-etched abstract patterns; Frantisek Vizner, who designed simple pure forms with slightly roughened matt surfaces, some produced by means of press-moulding; Jirí Harcuba, who specialized in strong deep-relief engraving, both abstract and representational; Karel Wünsch, who created quirky linear engraved patterns as well as designs combining enamelling with sgraffito; Václav Cigler, who was interested in the optical potential of cut glass in both sculpture and tableware; and Miluse Roubicková, who created unusual tall narrow vessels with raised surface spots.

Whereas Czech glass was associated from the late 1940s onwards with the work of individual artists, the identity of Swedish glass was defined first and foremost during the early post-war period by the character of particular factories. This is not to suggest that all the designers at Orrefors, for example, had a homogeneous style, but there were particular techniques associated with the factory, such as Ariel and Graal, which produced a distinctive Orrefors 'look' during the 1950s. This changed during the second half of the 1960s with the emergence of the more idiosyncratic designs of Gunnar Cyrén, whose cartoon-like enamel-painted Sweden bowls of 1967–8 – straight out of the Beatles' Yellow Submarine – and

whose vibrant psychedelic Pop goblets of 1967, were clearly part of a new trend. During the early 1960s things seemed to be going a little quiet in the Swedish glass industry after all the excitement of the previous decade. Even the token rebel, Erik Höglund at Boda, seemed less controversial ten years on. However, just when it seemed that the industry might be losing its momentum, Monica Boman reported in Form (no 9) towards the end of 1965:

A fresh wind is blowing from the Swedish province of Småland. Sporadic reports during the past year have warned that the Småland glass industry was undergoing a regeneration and rejuvenation. More and more glassworks are engaging designers, are daring to gamble on a line of their own which can give the company a special profile … In 1963 Bertil Vallien became associated with Åfors and Christer Sjögren with Lindshammar. In 1964 Monica Backström came to Boda, Erik and Margareta Hennix to Johansfors and Lars Hellsten to Skruf. The same year Ann and Göran Wärff moved from Pukeberg to Kosta. None in this group are over 40 years old, six of them are under 30. In other words, it's a new generation getting their chance, storming the citadels of Swedish glass artistry, blowing new life into the forms, giving glass new expressions.

This flood of young designers brought with them many refreshing new ideas, and what was particularly noticeable was how, as with studio glass, the personality of the designer was vitally important. Thus when a photograph appeared in Form (no 9) in 1967 showing Lars Hellsten on a motorbike with his Red Square glass sculpture balanced on the handle bars, it immediately suggested the idea of the designer as hellraiser. Although most of these designers had signed up with their respective factories before there was any widespread awareness of the birth pangs of the American studio glass movement, the same spirit of independence and iconoclasm seemed to characterize their approach. Boman's article suggested the idea of a fraternity among the 'youthquake', and implied that the designers themselves felt an affinity in their work and a sense of solidarity in their aims. Although

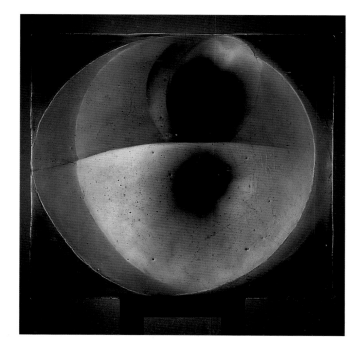

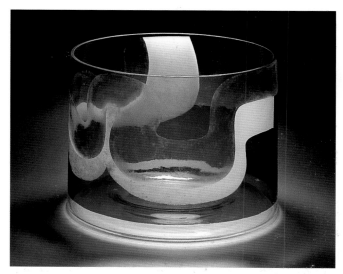

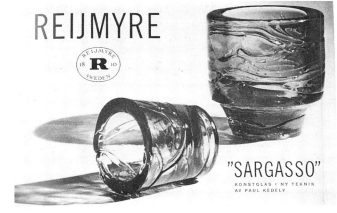

REIJMYRE

"SARGASSO"

KONSTGLAS I NY TEKNIK
AV PAUL KEDELV

each individual or couple had a distinct identity, as evidenced by the idiosyncratic imagery of Ann and Göran Wärff, and the eclecticism of Bertil Vallien, for example, there were some shared themes and techniques. One of these was the creation of vigorously textural vessels created by means of blowing glass into a still mould. In the case of Lars Hellsten at Skruf, both the shapes and the surface textures of his pieces were bursting with movement and visual excitement. Similarly vigorous and texturally rich was the Sargasso range designed by Paul Kedelv for Reijmyre, in 1964, and the Oresund range of bowls and vases designed by Björn Ramél for Kosta in 1966. The latter provided a striking contrast to the optical cut-glass vases designed by Mona Morales-Schildt for Kosta earlier in the decade, with Schildt's work embodying the clarity and precision of 'the look', and Ramél's designs reflecting the heightened roughness and spontaneity of the craft aesthetic of the later 1960s. Christer Sjögren's mould-blown designs for Lindshammar, although quieter, were equally dependent for their impact on their subtle linear and grainy textured surfaces. Had there been just one breakaway designer, as with Erik Höglund during the 1950s, that individual's work would have been in danger of being marginalized, but because they formed such a substantial group they exerted a collective impact which generated further creativity.

Monica Boman's 1965 article, 'Happenings in Glass' was followed two years later in *Form* (no 3) in 1967 by Katarina Dunér's feature entitled 'How Free?', its title referring to the challenging way in which young designers were treating glass as a material, and the increasing emphasis on individual expression and spontaneity. The illustrations in this article brought home how far Swedish glass had developed over the last two years. The eruption of the 'youthquake' had not only shaken things up but dramatically accelerated the pace of change. By an ironic twist, the once sophisticated forms of Bertil Vallien, and Ann and Göran Wärff were now increasingly lumpen and deformed, not by default but by design. Along with Vallien, Sjögren, Hellsten and the Wärffs, another designer whose work was discussed in this feature was the Finn, Oiva Toikka. Toikka had joined the firm of Nuutajärvi in 1963 and immediately injected a new spirit of fun into Finnish glass. Among his first studio designs, shown at an exhibition in Helsinki in 1963, were his Pickle Jars, large bowls perched on a broad stem. Also dating from 1963 were the first of his Bambu sculptures, a theme upon which he would produce a series of variations over the next few years, including engraved and coloured versions. It was in 1966 that the playful, mischievous and iconoclastic qualities in Toikka's character began to manifest themselves in his studio work, particularly in the Monsters he created for an exhibition in Helsinki in 1966, tall narrow misshapen lumpy vessels described by Ulf Hård af Segerstad as 'free-form Neo-Baroque'. As with other designers at this date, textures became all-important in Toikka's work, and uneven surfaces and skewed forms were synonymous with revolt. These ideas were developed further in the works he created for a joint exhibition with Bertil Vallien held at the Nordiska Kompaniet department store in Stockholm in February 1967, where it was acknowledged by Segerstad that although the work of these two designers could not be described as beautiful (in the conventional Scandinavian Modern sense), it was the most exciting work seen in Sweden for many years.

Throughout the decade Toikka also designed wares for mass production, many with strongly textural surfaces, such as the press-moulded Dewdrop range of 1964 with its jewel-like rings of decoration, and his mould-blown Flora tableware of 1966 decorated with cartoon-like flower power imagery. Through these highly decorative but cheap and functional tablewares he demonstrated a remarkable ability to create everyday objects, the imagery and resonance of which perfectly reflected the visual dynamism of Pop design. Finally, at the end of the decade, Toikka created a new range of studio glass for an exhibition at Heal's in London in 1969, pieces which became synonymous with Pop design. These were his Lollipops, individual and multiple flattened lollipop-shaped sculptures produced in vibrant colours, the pieces in clusters being known as Lollipop Isle. Also included in this exhibition were Toikka's playful Pom-Pom vases, vessels which had sprouted colourful leaves and pom-pom balls around the rim. More fantastical still were his Lake Palace sculptures, monumental composite forms constructed from solid blocks of glass, like paperweights, each encasing a different image – pompoms, lollipops, monsters, birds – suggesting an offbeat personal mythology.

Although Toikka was by far the most liberated and irreverent of the designers working in the Finnish glass industry during the 1960s, he was not alone in his desire to challenge the Establishment. When his work was exhibited at Heal's in 1969 it was shown alongside the latest designs of Timo Sarpaneva who, although by this date one of the elder statesmen of Finnish glass, reinvented himself in 1964 with the creation of his Finlandia range. Through the one-off pieces in this range, with their erupted forms and their cauterised surfaces, Sarpaneva defied conventional notions of beauty, and questioned the validity of good taste. Like Katarina Dunér when she raised the question 'How free?', Sarpaneva challenged the idea that Scandinavian glass was synonymous with control and restraint. Closer to the spirit of Toikka, although by no means in his image, was another Finnish designer, Nanny Still who worked with the firm of Riihimäki. A foretaste of her unconventional approach was suggested by the entertaining Harlequin tableware range of 1958, with its startling bright blue colouring and its quirky conical and spherical forms. During the early 1960s Still was one of the first designers to explore the potential of textured surfaces, work which came to fruition in her Flindari bottles of 1963, made using a part-wood, part-textured sheet-metal mould. Two years later Still created a series of pendant ribbed conical sculptures, which were displayed in a large cluster in an installation called *Bluebeard* in Paris in 1965. The culmination of her exploration of textured surfaces and irregular forms came in 1967 when she designed a range of sculptural vessels called Fantasma, the moulds for which were lined with copper nails, the pieces themselves being blown from lugubrious deep colours such as dark green and violet. Coincidentally in Britain at this date Geoffrey Baxter employed a similar method at Whitefriars Glass to create the pitted surfaces on his textured range. Designed in 1966 and launched in January 1967, this series, like the work of Still, Toikka and Sarpaneva, was motivated by a rebellious desire to challenge the false restrictions of conventional aesthetics and good taste. Like Sarpaneva, some of Baxter's textures were created from natural materials such as tree bark, but

other textures were derived from man-made materials, such as nail heads, gouged and chiselled wood, and stapled scrolls of copper wire. Like Sarpaneva's Finlandia range, which in fact Baxter did not actually encounter until the Heal's exhibition of 1969, Whitefriars' Textured range changed the course of British glass, paving the way for further initiatives in the field of studio glass during the 1970s.

Divergence and Fragmentation

In 1966 the American architect Robert Venturi published a manifesto called *Complexity and Contradiction in Architecture*, in which he wrote:

I like complexity and contradiction in architecture …
I like elements which are hybrid rather than pure …
I am for messy vitality over obvious unity …
I prefer 'both-and' to 'either-or' …

As this selective survey has shown, designers as well as architects were pulling in many different directions during the second half of the 1960s, and the situation was becoming increasingly complex. Although in many ways this creative tension, or 'messy vitality' as Venturi has described it, was healthy, producing a second wave of counter-revolutionary designs which were just as invigorating but even more varied than the 'obvious unity' of 'the look', inevitably there were also some negative effects. Greater diversity led to growing fragmentation, for example, and because there was no longer one clear path forward, some

manufacturers became increasingly indecisive and confused.

During the 1960s the most successful design-led firms had been those that relied on the vision and astuteness of one individual to make the right design decisions. If the management structure changed so that these decisions were taken out of their hands, this could rapidly alter the direction of a company. Particularly dangerous in the commercial climate of the early 1970s was the growing influence of the sales reps and the marketing staff who, unlike the design directors, were not concerned with forecasting or setting future trends but with repeating a winning formula. Guy Busby, the design manager of the Lightbown Aspinall branch of the Wall Paper Manufacturers, and the man behind the inspired Palladio wallpaper ranges, had warned about this in an article in *Design* magazine in November 1964:

I consider that advice or information from the sales side or any market research should be valued but treated with caution, and used in a very general sense. To be wholly guided and conditioned by it would mean the end of any incentive or ability to be genuinely creative in producing a high standard of design and fresh ideas.

Such views were reiterated by John Mellor, director of design at Carpet Trades Ltd: 'One of the main dangers of market research is that it tends only to be able to tell you what has been successful in the past. It cannot predict what will be any good in the future, and therefore always tends to make you look backward to your historical predecessors rather

far left
Flindari decanters designed by Nanny Still for the Finnish firm, Riihimäki, 1963, combining bright colours and artificial textures. Like Oiva Toikka, Still challenged conventional notions of good taste. Her work presents an interesting contrast to the cool colourless glass designed by Tapio Wirkkala and Timo Sarpaneva at Iittala during the 1960s.

left and below
Vases decorated with random strapping designed by Geoffrey Baxter for Whitefriars Glass, 1972–4. From the late 1960s onwards the handmade glass produced at this factory reflected the influence of the studio glass movement.

opposite top left
Flora tableware, designed by Oiva Toikka, 1966. Toikka worked closely with the glassmakers at Nuutajärvi to create an exuberant and iconoclastic series of one-off sculptures during the 1960s. He also revolutionized glass tableware with playful moulded designs.

opposite top right
Lollipop Isle, 1969, which introduced the aesthetics of pop design into the hitherto restrained Finnish glass industry.

opposite bottom left
Lollipop, c1968. An installation of these sculptures was shown at Heal's in London in 1969.

left
Arango Residence,
Acapulco, Mexico, designed
by John Lautner, 1973. In
this house Lautner explored
the neo-organic theme in
design, and apparently
came full circle back to
organic Modernism and a
Niemeyer-esque version of
the Contemporary style.
opposite
Takara Beautilion, designed
by Kisho Kurokawa for Expo
'70 at Osaka in Japan. This
project represented a more
fully developed version of
the Plug-In City idea posited
by Archigram earlier in the
decade. The Japanese
Metabolists were interested
in biological cycles of
growth and decay, and
believed that such ideas
applied to buildings as well
as living organisms.
Kurokawa's Takara
Beautilion was composed
of a standardized steel
structure which could be
extended ad infinitum in any
direction, and into which
capsules and mechanical
services could be 'plugged'.
Unlike Moshe Safdie's
Habitat at the Montreal
Expo, the construction of
which was fraught with
unforeseen technical problems, this structure was
assembled in a week.

than forward to new solutions.' Similarly, Tom Worthington
at Heal Fabrics cautioned against relying too heavily on
market research because 'after all, it can only tell you what
is being sold now, and that doesn't concern me'. The mes-
sage from Worthington was clear: if manufacturers allowed
themselves to be guided solely by market research, progress
in design would grind to a halt, which is exactly what began
to happen during the 1970s.

Designer-retailers such as Mary Quant, Terence
Conran and Barbara Hulanicki were all revolutionaries of one
sort or another. The reason why they were successful was,
not because of their business acumen, but because of their
creative drive and personal vision. What they shared was a
genuine commitment to making something new and exciting
available to a wider public, and they recognized that in order
to retain public interest, they had to keep doing this over and
over again. This spirit of constant reinvention sustained creative momentum.

During the 1970s, however, the creative, economic
and commercial climates all changed. Suddenly people had
to come to terms with unfamiliar concepts such as recession
and unemployment. Ironically, what contributed to the collapse of the system in the end, however, was the sheer scale
of the idealism of the 1960s. Freedom led to complexity and
contradiction, and complexity and contradiction led to fragmentation and disintegration. One of these fragments, historical revivalism, although initially an exciting and positive development, ultimately exerted a damaging effect on the applied
arts as manufacturers came to rely on it instead of encouraging advances in modern design. Design lost its edge during
the 1970s as it came to be dominated more and more by
purely commercial rather than creative interests. In 1984
Olivier Mourgue commented: 'A whole form of design seems
to me to have died since the seventies. I travel, I attend exhibitions, and the showrooms are very boring. Young people
are not interested in them; they are in search of the marvellous.' By the mid-1970s few manufacturers or retailers were
still motivated by the 'marvellous' – in other words, the high-
minded ideals of the pioneering entrepreneurs of the 1960s –
and among the design fraternity, as Mourgue himself was all
too well aware, there was a gradual realization that a unique
era of creative opportunity had come to a close.

Throughout the 1960s there are interesting parallels between the career of the Beatles

and the development of international design. Like 'the look', the Beatles were a product

of the 1950s, shaped by American rhythm and blues and rock 'n' roll, but with a dis-

tinctive, new and uniquely English pop identity of their own. They recorded their first sin-

gle in 1962 – just at the time when 'the look' was taking off – and they revolutionized

the British and international pop scene with their unique combination of infectious

music and clean-cut stylish fashions. From the early to the mid-1960s the Beatles went

from strength to strength as a group, and their success parallels the commercial and

creative buoyancy of British and Italian design. They wore suits designed by Pierre

Cardin, shopped at the John Stephen boutiques on Carnaby Street, and bought furni-

ture and accessories from the revolutionary new design store, Habitat. Their success,

and the commercial success of John Stephen and Habitat, drew attention to the

London Scene and triggered off a frenzy of interest in Swinging London. After the warn-

ing signals of *Help!* which suggested that they were reaching 'maximum pressure point'

(to use a phrase from Archigram's Plug-In City), the release of 'Revolver' in 1966

marked a significant turning point for the group. Its title was a reference not only to a

gun but to records revolving on a turntable, and it suggested that the wheel had turned

and the first phase of the cultural revolution of the 1960s was now coming to an end.

For the remainder of the decade the Beatles actively experimented with different alter-

natives, both in their music and in their personal lives. The key to this second phase of

their development was their growth as individuals which, although positive in many

respects, ultimately led to the fragmentation and break-up of the group in 1970. Many

of the avenues that the Beatles chose to explore during the second half of the 1960s

correspond to developments in contemporary design. The historical revivalism of

Sergeant Pepper, for example, parallels the revival of interest in antiques and Victorian

design. The Beatles' cartoon of Yellow Submarine reflects the flat stylized imagery of

Pop design and flower power. The impact of hallucinogenic drugs in songs such as

'Lucy in the Sky with Diamonds' is mirrored in the imagery of Op patterns and psyche-

delic graphics. George Harrison's fascination with Eastern mysticism and Indian music

parallels the impact of Indian patterns on textiles and wallpapers. The back-to-basics

approach of the White Album suggests a conscious rejection of sophistication in favour

of gritty hands-on individual self-expression, crude but spontaneous, just like the crafts

movement. John Lennon's interest in performance art, such as the activities of Fluxus,

the avant-garde art movement in which Yoko Ono was a key player, parallels the emer-

gence of radical design in Italy. His decision to pose nude with Yoko on the cover of

their 1968 album Two Virgins, declaring that the couple had nothing to hide, mirrors

Quasar Khanh's philosophy of transparency; while songs such as 'All You Need Is Love'

and John and Yoko's 'Bed in' for peace parallel the interest in soft furniture and com-

munal seating pools towards the end of the decade.

opposite left
International Love Heart, a
printed textile panel
designed by Alexander
Girard for Herman Miller,
c1970, a belated tribute to
the Summer of Love
opposite right
John Lennon and Yoko Ono
in a hotel in Montreal in
1969 during their public
'Bed In' to promote world
peace.
right
Psychedelic mural by a
group of Dutch designers
called the Fool, painted on
the facade above the
Beatles' Apple shop in
London, 1967.

Individually and collectively, the Beatles played a key role in all the main cultural developments of the 1960s, and it is uncanny how often they themselves seemed to act as a catalyst for change. The extent of their desire to make creative things happen – for themselves and for others – was indicated by the setting up of their own company, Apple, in 1967, itself a reflection of the spirit of creative and commercial entrepreneurialism and idealism of the 1960s. Even the psychedelic mural painted on the wall above their ill-fated boutique reflected the latest trends in graphic design. The title of their 1968 single, 'Revolution', was particularly significant as it was the Beatles themselves who had changed the world. Revolution and counter-revolution, complexity and contradiction, divergence and fragmentation. What happened to the Beatles during the course of the 1960s, including their eventual acrimonious break-up and the eclecticism of their subsequent solo careers, provides a mirror for developments in design throughout the decade and beyond.

Select Bibliography

Twentieth-Century Design

Burney, Jan, *Ettore Sottsass*, Trefoil Publications, London, 1991

Clark, Robert Judson, (ed), *Design in America – The Cranbrook Vision*, Harry Abrams, New York, 1983

Collins, Michael, *Towards Post-Modernism – Design Since 1851*, British Museum, London, 1987

Eidelberg, Martin, (ed), *Design 1935–1965 – What Modern Was*, Abrams, New York, 1991

Erlhoff, M, *Designed in Germany since 1949*, Rat für Formgebung, Munich, 1990

Ferrari, Paolo, *Achille Castiglioni*, Electa, Milan, 1984

Grassi, A, and Anty Pansera, *Atlante del Design Italiano 1940–1980*, Milan, 1980

Gregotti, V, *Il Designo del Prodotto Industriale Italiano, Italia 1860–1980*, Electa, Milan, 1982

Hiesinger, K B, and G H Marcus, *Design Since 1945*, Philadelphia Museum of Art, Philadelphia, 1984

Jackson, Lesley, *The New Look – Design in the Fifties*, Thames and Hudson, London, 1991

Karlsen, Arne, Bent Salicath and Mogens Utzon-Frank, (eds), *Contemporary Danish Design*, The Danish Society of Arts and Crafts and Industrial Design, Copenhagen, 1960

Lindqvist, Lennart, *Design in Sweden*, The Swedish Institute, Stockholm, 1972 and 1977

Lutteman, Helena Dahlbäck, and Marianne Uggla, (eds), *The Lunning Prize*, Nationalmuseum, Stockholm, 1986

MacFadden, David Revere, (ed), *Scandinavian Modern Design*, Cooper Hewitt Museum, New York, 1982

Møller, Henrik Sten, *Danish Design*, Rhodos, Copenhagen, 1975

Moody, Ella, (ed), *Decorative Art in Modern Interiors*, Vols 50–60, Studio Vista, London, 1960–1970

Mundt, Barbara, *Produkt-Design 1900–1990 – Eine Auswahl*, Kunstgewerbemuseum, Berlin, 1991

Mundt, Barbara, *Interieur und Design in Deutschland 1945–1960*, Kunstgewerbemuseum, Berlin, 1993

Ornamo, *The Ornamo Book of Finnish Design*, Ornamo, Helsinki, 1962

Pansera, Anty, *Storia e Cronica della Triennale*, Longanesi, Milan, 1978

Piranova, C, *Compasso d'Oro 1954–1984*, Cracow, 1985

Ponti, L L, *Gio Ponti*, Thames and Hudson, London, 1990

Pulos, Arthur J, *The American Design Adventure*, MIT Press, Cambridge, MA, 1988

Radice, Barbara, *Ettore Sottsass – A Critical Biography*, Thames and Hudson, London, 1993

Segerstad, Ulf Hård Af, *Modern Finnish Design*, Weidenfeld & Nicolson, London, 1969

Sparke, Penny, *Ettore Sottsass Jnr*, Design Council, London, 1982

Sparke, Penny, *Italian Design*, Thames and Hudson, London, 1989

Staal, G, and H Walters, (eds), *Holland in Vorm, Dutch Design 1945–1987*, Stichting Holland in Vorm, The Hague, 1987

The Fine Art Society, *Austerity to Affluence – British Art and Design 1945–1962*, Merrell Holberton, London, 1997

Weston, Richard, *Modernism*, Phaidon, London, 1996

Wichmann, H, *Italien Design 1945 Bis Heute*, Neues Sammlung, Munich, 1988

Zahle, Erik, (ed), *Scandinavian Domestic Design*, Methuen, London, 1963

1960s Design and Culture

Ambasz, Emilio, (ed), *Italy – The New Domestic Landscape*, Museum of Modern Art, New York, 1972

Arquitectura Interior 1964, Aguilar S A de Ediciones, Madrid, 1964

Booker, Christopher, *The Neophiliacs – A Study of the Revolution in English Life in the Fifties and Sixties*, Collins, London, 1969

Booker, Christopher, Anthony D'Abreu, Roger McGough and Tony Palmer, (eds), *The Sixties – Sociopack*, Sociopack Publications, London, 1973

Branzi, Andrea, *The Hot House – Italian New Wave Design*, Thames and Hudson, London, 1984

Boxer, Mark, *The Trendy Ape*, Hodder and Stoughton, London, 1968

Campbell, John, John Harris, Richard Maltby, C S Nicholls, Sydney Pollard and J M Winter, (eds), *The Culture of Youth – History of the 20th Century Volume 7, 1960–1973*, Hamlyn, London, 1994

Casson, Hugh, (ed), *Inscape – The Design of Interiors*, Architectural Press, London, 1968

Caute, David, *Sixty-Eight – The Year of the Barricades*, Hamish Hamilton, London, 1988

Cawthorne, Nigel, *Sixties Source Book*, Quarto, London, 1989

Centre Georges Pompidou, *Design Français 1960–1990*, Paris, 1988

Coleridge, Nicholas, and Stephen Quinn, (eds), *The Sixties in Queen*, Ebury Press, London, 1987

Crow, Thomas, *The Rise of the Sixties – American and European Art in the Era of Dissent 1955–69*, Weidenfeld & Nicolson, London, 1996

Farber, David, (ed), *The Sixties – From Memory to History*, University of North Carolina Press, London, 1994

Fulford, Robert, *This Was Expo*, McClelland and Stewart Limited, Toronto, 1968

Garner, Philippe, *Sixties Design*, Taschen, Köln, 1996

Gevereau, Laurent, and David Mellor, (eds), *Les Sixties – Années Utopies*, Somogy Éditions d'Art, Paris, 1996

Harling, Robert, *House and Garden Book of Interiors*, Condé Nast, London, 1962

Harris, Jennifer, Sarah Hyde and Greg Smith, *1966 And All That – Design and the Consumer in Britain '1960–1969*, Trefoil Books, London, 1986

Hewison, Robert, *Too Much – Art and Society in the Sixties, 1960–75*, Methuen, London, 1986

Hine, Thomas, *Populuxe – The Look and Life of America in the '50s and '60s*, Alfred Knopf, New York, 1986

Hopkinson, Amanda, *Sixties London – Photos by Dorothy Bohm*, Lund Humphries, London, 1996

Ind, Nicholas, *Terence Conran – The Authorized Biography*, Sidgwick & Jackson, London, 1995

Kornfeld, Albert, *The Doubleday Book of Interior Decorating*, Western Publishing Company, New York, 1965

Kozinn, Allan, *The Beatles*, Phaidon, London, 1995

Magnani, Franco, (ed), *Living Spaces*, Studio Vista, London, 1978

Magnani, Franco, (ed), *One Room Interiors*, Studio Vista, London, 1979

Masters, Brian, *The Swinging Sixties*, Constable, London, 1985

McCartney, Linda, *Sixties – Portrait of an Era*, Pyramid, London, 1992

Mellor, David, *The Sixties – Art Scene in London*, Phaidon, London, 1993

Morris, Brian, *An Introduction to Mary Quant's London*, London Museum, London, 1973

Pearce, Christopher, *The Sixties – A Pictorial Review*, Blossom, London, 1991

Peel, L, and P Powell, *50's and 60's Style*, Apple Press, London, 1988

Phillips, Barty, *Conran and the Habitat Story*, Weidenfeld & Nicolson, 1984

Phillips, Derek, *Lighting*, Macdonald, London, 1966

Pichaske, David, *A Generation in Motion – Popular Music and Culture in the Sixties*, Ellis Press, Granite Falls, Minnesota, 1989

Prizeman, John, and John Vaughan, *European Interiors*, Queen Anne Press Limited, London, 1969

Rowntree, Diana, *Interior Design*, Penguin, Harmondsworth, 1964

Stern, Jane and Michael, *Sixties People*, Macmillan, London, 1990

Stine, Peter, (ed), *The Sixties*, Wayne State University Press, Detroit, Michigan, 1995

Wheen, Francis, *The Sixties – A Fresh Look at a Decade of Change*, Century Publishing, London, 1982

Whiteley, Nigel, *Pop Design – Modernism to Mod*, Design Council, London, 1987

Architecture

Aulenti, Gae, *Gae Aulenti*, Electa, Milan, 1975

Banham, Reyner, *Megastructure – Urban Futures of the Recent Past*, Thames and Hudson, London, 1976

Banham, Reyner, *Design by Choice*, Academy Editions, London, 1981

Banham, Mary, Paul Barker, Sutherland Lyall and Cedric Price, (eds), *A Critic Writes – Essays by Reyner Banham*, University of California Press, Berkeley, Los Angeles, 1996

Boyd, Robin, *Kenzo Tange*, George Braziller, New York, 1962

Collymore, Peter, *The Architecture of Ralph Erskine*, Academy Editions, London, 1994

Cook, Peter, (ed), *Archigram*, Studio Vista, London, 1977

Curtis, William J R, *Modern Architecture since 1900*, Phaidon, Oxford, 1982

Curtis, William J R, *Denys Lasdun – Architecture, City, Landscape*, Phaidon, London, 1994

Dini, Massimo, *Renzo Piano – Progetti e Architetture 1964–1983*, Electa, Milan, 1983

Donat, John, (ed) *World Architecture 1–4*, Studio Vista, London, 1964–1967

Doumato, Lamia, *Minoru Yamasaki*, Vance Bibliographies, Monticello, Illinois, 1986

Drew, Philip, *Frei Otto – Form and Substance*, Crosby Lockwood Staples, London, 1976

Drexler, Arthur, and Thomas Hine, *The Architecture of Richard Neutra – From International Style to California Modern*, Metropolitan Museum of Art, New York, 1982

Edwards, Brian, *Basil Spence 1907–76*, Rutland Press, Edinburgh, 1995

Escher, Frank, (ed) *John Lautner, Architect*, Artemis, London, 1994

Faber, Tobias, *Arne Jacobsen*, Gerd Hatje, Stuttgart, 1964

Gibberd, Frederick, *Metropolitan Cathedral of Christ the King, Liverpool*, Architectural Press, London, 1968

Goldstein, Barbara, and Esther McCoy, *Guide to US Architecture 1940–1980*, Arts and Architecture Press, Santa Monica, 1982

Jacobus, John M, *Philip Johnson*, George Brazilier, New York, 1962

Jackson, Lesley, *'Contemporary' Architecture and Interiors of the 1950s*, Phaidon, London, 1994

Jencks, Charles, *Modern Movements in Architecture*, Penguin, Harmondsworth, 1973

Joedicke, Jurgen, *Architecture Since 1945 – Sources and Directions*, Pall Mall Press, London, 1969

Johnson, Burgee, and Nony Miller, *The Buildings and Projects of Philip Johnson*, Architectural Press, London, 1980

Kassler, Elisabeth B, *Modern Gardens and the Landscape*, Museum of Modern Art, New York, 1964

Kean, John M, *Leicester University Engineering Building – James Stirling and James Gowan*, Phaidon, London, 1994

Kidder Smith, G E, *The New Architecture of Europe*, Prentice-Hall, London, 1962

Kidder Smith, G E, *The New Churches of Europe*, The Architectural Press, London, 1964

Kohn, Wendy, *Moshe Safdie*, Academy Editions, London, 1996

Kultermann, Udo, *New Architecture in the World*, Thames and Hudson, London, 1966

Landau, Royston, *New Directions in British Architecture*, Studio Vista, London, 1968

Maguire, Robert, and Keith Murray, *Modern Churches of the World*, Studio Vista, London, 1965

Maxwell, Robert, *New British Architecture*, Thames and Hudson, London, 1972

McCoy, Esther, *Craig Ellwood*, Walker and Co, New York, 1968

McCoy, Esther, *Case Study Houses 1945–1962*, 2nd edition, Hennessey and Ingalls, Los Angeles, 1977

McCoy, Esther, *The Second Generation*, Gibbs M Smith, Salt Lake City, 1984

Meller, James, (ed) *The Buckminster Fuller Reader*, Penguin, Harmondsworth, 1972

Murray, Peter, and Stephen Trombley, *Modern British Architecture Since 1945*, RIBA, London, 1984

Pawley, Martin, *Buckminster Fuller*, Trefoil, London, 1990

Pettena, Gianni, *Hans Hollein – Works 1960–1988*, Idea Books, Milan, 1988

Ponner, Heinz, *Louis I Kahn – Complete Works 1935–1974*, Birkhäuser Verlag, Basel, 1987

Price, Cedric, *Cedric Price*, Architectural Association, London, 1984

Riani, Paolo, *Kenzo Tange*, Hamlyn, Feltham, 1970

Rogers, Richard, et al, *Norman Foster, Team 4 and Foster Associates – Buildings and Projects, vol 1 1964–1973*, Watermark, Godalming, 1991

Rosa, Joseph, *A Constructed View – The Architectural Photography of Julius Shulman*, Rizzoli, New York, 1994

Rudolph, Paul, *The Architecture of Paul Rudolph*, Thames and Hudson, London, 1970

Skidmore, Owings and Merrill, *Architecture of Skidmore, Owings and Merrill 1950–62*, The Architectural Press, London, 1963

Smith, Elizabeth A T, (ed) *Blueprints for Modern Living – History and Legacy of the Case Study Houses*, MIT Press, Cambridge, Massachusetts, 1989

Smithson, Alison and Peter, *Peter and Alison Smithson*, Academy Editions, London, 1982

Spade, Rupert, *Oscar Niemeyer*, Thames and Hudson, London, 1971

Spade, Rupert, *Eero Saarinen*, Thames and Hudson, London, 1971

Steele, James, *Salk Institute – Louis I Kahn*, Phaidon, London, 1993

Stewart, David B, *Arata Isozaki – Architecture 1960–1990*, Rizzoli, New York, 1991

Stirling, James, *James Stirling – Buildings and Projects 1950–74*, Thames and Hudson, London, 1975

Tempel, Egon, *New Finnish Architecture*, The Architectural Press, London, 1968

Vaudon, Valérie, *Richard Meier*, Electa, Milan, 1986

Von Alvensleben, Rudolf, *John Lautner, Architect, Los Angeles*, Hochschule für Angewandte Kunst, Vienna, 1991

Whiting, Penelope, *New Single Storey Houses*, The Architectural Press, London, 1966

Winter, John, *Modern Buildings*, Hamlyn, London, 1969

Ceramics, Glass, Metalwork and Plastics

Arnost, Frantisek, Olga Drahotova and Antonín Langhamer, *Bohemian Glass*, Crystalex, Nový Bor, 1985

Barovier, Marina, (ed), *Art of the Barovier Glassmakers in Murano 1866–1972*, Arsenale Editrice, Venice, 1993

Barovier, Marina, Rosa Barovier Mentasti and Attilia Dorigato, *Il Vetro di Murano alle Biennali 1895–1972*, Leonardo Arte, Milan, 1995

Barovier Mentasti, Rosa, *Venetian Glass 1890–1990*, Arsenale Editrice, Venice, 1992

Beard, Geoffrey, *Modern Glass*, Studio Vista, London, 1968

Bischofberger, Bruno, (ed), *Ettore Sottsass Ceramics*, Thames and Hudson, London, 1995

Bojani, Gian Carlo, Claudio Piersanti and Rita Rava, *Gio Ponti – Ceramica e Architettura*, Centro Di, Florence, 1987

Coatts, Margot, *Robert Welch – Designer-Silversmith*, Cheltenham Art Gallery and Museums, 1995

Coatts, Margot, (ed), *Lucie Rie and Hans Coper – Potters in Parallel*, Herbert Press, London, 1997

Cooper-Willis, Euan, and Victoria Stanton, *The Story of Portmeirion Potteries 1960–1995 – A Collectors' Guide*, Portmeirion Potteries, Stoke-on-Trent, 1995

Deboni, Franco, *Venini Glass*, Society Editrice Umberto Allemandi & C, 1990

Dorigato, Attilia, *Ercole Barovier 1889–1974*, Venice, 1989

Duncan, Alastair, *Orrefors Glass*, Antique Collectors' Club, Woodbridge, Suffolk, 1995

Eatwell, Ann, *Susie Cooper Productions*, Victoria and Albert Museum, London, 1987

Hayward, Leslie, *Poole Pottery*, Richard Dennis, Somerset, 1995

Hilschenz, Helga, *Rosenthal – Hundert Jahre Porzellan*, Kestner-Museum, Hannover, 1982

Hughes, Graham, *Modern Silver Throughout the World 1880–1967*, Studio Vista, London, 1967

Iittala Glass Museum, *Iittala in the Triennales of Milan*, Iittala, 1987

Jackson, Lesley, (ed), *Whitefriars Glass – The Art of James Powell & Sons*, Richard Dennis, Somerset, 1996

Jenkins, Steven, *Midwinter Pottery – A Revolution in British Tableware*, Richard Dennis, Somerset, 1997

Katz, Sylvia, *Classic Plastics – From Bakelite to High-Tech*, Thames and Hudson, London, 1984

Koivisto, Kaisa, (ed), *European Glass in Use*, Finnish Glass Museum, Riihimäki, 1994

Koivisto, Kaisa, and Kirsi Niemistö, *The Modern Spirit – Glass from Finland*, Finnish Glass Museum, Riihimäki, 1985

Koivisto, Kaisa, and Michèle Thiry, *Nanny Still – 45 Years of Design*, Charleroi Culture, Charleroi, 1995

Kumela, Marjut, Kristiina Paatero and Kaarina Rissanen, *Arabia*, Oy Wärtsila AB, Helsinki, 1987

Larkman, Brian, *Metalwork Designs of Today*, John Murray, London, 1969

Larkman, Brian, and S H Glenister, *Contemporary Design in Metalwork*, John Murray, London, 1963

Lassen, E, and Mogens Schlüter, *Dansk Glas 1926–1985*, Arnold Busck, Copenhagen, 1987

Laurén, Uta, (ed), *Make Glass Not War*, Finnish Glass Museum, Riihimäki, 1992

Lutteman, Helena Dahlbäck, *Stig Lindberg – Formgivare*, Nationalmuseum, Stockholm, 1982

Museum Of Applied Arts, Helsinki, *Timo Sarpaneva – Sculpture in Vetro*, Museum of Applied Arts, Helsinki, 1987

Nationalmuseum, Stockholm, *Gustavsberg 150ar*, Stockholm, 1975

Olivier, Jean Luc, and Sylva Petrová (eds), *Bohemian Glass*, Flammarion, Paris, 1990

Opie, Jennifer, *Scandinavia – Ceramics and Glass in the Twentieth Century*, Victoria and Albert Museum, London, 1989

Peat, Alan, *Midwinter – A Collector's Guide*, Cameron and Hollis, Moffat, 1992

Peltonen, K, *Birger Kaipiainen*, Museum of Applied Art, Helsinki, 1989

Persson, Sigurd, *Sigurd Persson Silver*, Arne Tryckare, Stockholm, 1979

Petrová, Sylva, *Pavel Hlava*, Pavel Hlava, Prague, 1995

Poutasuo, Tuula, *Nuutajärvi – 200 Years of Finnish Glass*, Oy Hackman AB, Nuutajärvi, 1993

Reihnér, Anders, *Ingeborg Lundin*, Orrefors Glasbruk, Orrefors, 1989

Simanainen, Timo, *Oiva Toikka Glass*, Finnish Glass Museum, Riihimäki, 1988

Smålands Museum, *Erik Höglund – 30 år Med Glas och Brons*, Växjö, 1990

Sparke, Penny, (ed), *The Plastics Age – From Modernity to Post-Modernity*, Victoria and Albert Museum, London, 1990

Stennett-Willson, R, *Modern Glass*, Studio Vista, London, 1975

Suhonen, Pekka, *Tapio Wirkkala*, Finnish Society of Crafts and Design, Helsinki, 1985

Victoria and Albert Museum, *Bohemian Glass*, London, 1965

Walker, Susannah, *Queensberry Hunt – Creativity and Industry*, Fourth Estate and Wordsearch, London, 1992

Welch, Robert, *Hand and Machine*, Robert Welch, Chipping Campden, 1986

Widman, Dag, *Stig Lindberg – Swedish Artist and Designer*, Rabén & Sjögren, Stockholm, 1962

The Worshipful Company of Goldsmiths, *Modern British Silver*, Goldsmiths' Hall, London, 1963

The Worshipful Company of Goldsmiths, *The Goldsmith Today*, Goldsmiths' Hall, London, 1967

The Worshipful Company of Goldsmiths, *25 Years of Stuart Devlin in London*, Goldsmiths' Hall, London, 1983

Fashion

Carter, Ernestine, *Magic Names of Fashion*, Weidenfeld & Nicolson, London, 1980

Drake, Nick, *The Sixties – A Decade in Vogue*, Pyramid, London, 1988

Hulanicki, Barbara, *From A to Biba*, Hutchinson, London, 1983

London Museum, *Mary Quant's London,* Kensington Palace, London, 1973

Lynam, R, (ed), *Paris Fashion*, Michael Joseph, London, 1972

McDowell, Colin, *McDowell's Directory of Twentieth Century Fashion*, Frederick Muller, London, 1984

Mendes, Valerie, *Pierre Cardin – Past, Present, Future*, Dirk Nishen Publishing, London, 1990

Quant, Mary, *Quant by Quant*, Cassell, London, 1965

Ruby, Jennifer, *The 1960s and 1970s (Costume in Context)*, Batsford, London, 1989

Steele, Valerie, *Women of Fashion – Twentieth Century Designers*, Rizzoli, New York, 1991

Tyne and Wear Museums, *Biba – The Label, The Lifestyle, The Look*, Newcastle-upon-Tyne, 1993

Furniture and Lighting

Abercrombie, Stanley, *George Nelson – The Design of Modern Design*, MIT, Cambridge, Massachusetts, 1995

Baroni, Daniele, *Arflex '51 '81*, Arflex, Milan, 1981

Buttler, Laura, Carla Enbom, Leena Maunula and Jarno Peltonen, *Lisa Johansson-Pape*, Museum Of Applied Arts, Helsinki, 1986

Caplan, R, *The Design of Herman Miller*, Whitney Library of Design, New York, 1976

Casiani, Stefano, *Mobili Come Architetture – Il Disegno della Produzione Zanotta*, Arcadia Edizioni, Milan, 1984

Casiani, Stefano, *Industrial Art – Objects, Play and Thought in Danese Production*, Arcadia Edizioni, Milan, 1988

Chapoutot, Anne, *Pierre Paulin – Un Univers de Formes*, Editions du May, Paris, 1992

Cooke, Edward, Joseph Giovanni, and Taragin Davira, *Furniture by Wendell Castle*, Hudson Hills Press, New York, 1990

Dunas, Peter, Mathias Schwartz-Clauss and Alexander von Vegesack, *100 Masterpieces from the Vitra Design Museum Collection*, Vitra Design Museum, Weil am Rhein, 1996

Favata, Ignazia, *Joe Colombo and Italian Design of the Sixties*, Thames and Hudson, London, 1988

Fehrman, Cherie and Kenneth, *Postwar Interior Design 1945–1960*, Van Nostrand Reinhold, New York, 1987

Gramigna, G, *1950–1980 Repertory – Pictures and Ideas Regarding the History of Italian Furniture*, Arnoldo Mondadori, Milan, 1985

Jalk, Grete, *The Copenhagen Cabinetmakers' Guild Exhibitions*, vols 4–5, Techologisk Institut Forlag, Copenhagen, 1987

Larrabee, E, and M Vignelli, *Knoll Design*, Harry Abrams, New York, 1981

Larson, L, *Lighting and its Design*, Whitney Library of Design, New York, 1964

Lyall, Sutherland, *Hille – 75 Years of British Furniture*, Victoria and Albert Museum, London, 1984

Miestamo, Riitta, *The Form and Substance of Finnish Furniture*, Asko, Lahti, 1980

Museum of Decorative Arts, Copenhagen, *Hans J Wegner en Stolemaker*, Danish Design Centre, Copenhagen, 1989

Nelson, George, *George Nelson on Design*, Whitney Library of Design, New York, 1979

Neuhart, John and Marilyn, and Ray Eames, *Eames Design – The Work of the Office of Charles and Ray Eames*, Thames and Hudson, London, 1989

Panton, Verner, *Verner Panton*, Copenhagen, 1986

Pasca, Vanni, *Vico Magistretti – Elegance and Innovation in Postwar Italian Design*, Thames and Hudson, 1991

Piva, Antonio, *Afra e Tobia Scarpa – Architetti e Designers*, Arnoldo Mondadori, Milan, 1985

Santini, Pier Carlo, *The Years of Italian Design – A Portrait of Cesare Cassina*, Electa, Milan, 1981

Segerstad, Ulf Hård Af, *Modern Scandinavian Furniture*, Nordisk Rotogravyr, Stockholm, 1963

Sembach, Klaus-Jürgen, *Contemporary Furniture – An International Review of Modern Furniture, 1950 to the Present*, Design Council, London, 1982

Tallon, Roger, *Roger Tallon – Itinèraires d'un Designer Industriel*, Editions Centre Pompidou, Paris, 1993

Tanchis, Aldo, *Bruno Munari – From Futurism to Post-Industrial Design*, Lund Humphries, London, 1987

Tøjner, Poul Erik, and Kjeld Mindum, *Arne Jacobsen – Architect and Designer*, Danish Design Centre, Copenhagen, 1994

Vanlaethem, France, *Gaetano Pesce – Architect, Designer, Artist*, Rizzoli, New York, 1989

Whitechapel Art Gallery, *Modern Chairs 1918–1970*, London, 1970

Textiles and Wallpapers

Constantine, Mildred, and Jack Lenor Larsen, *Beyond Craft – The Art Fabric*, Van Nostrand Reinhold, New York, 1973

Hamilton, J, and C Oman, *Wallpaper – A History and Illustrated Catalogue of the Collection in the Victoria and Albert Museum*, Sotheby's, London, 1982

Harris, Jennifer, *Lucienne Day – A Career in Design*, Whitworth Art Gallery, Manchester, 1993

Hicks, David, *David Hicks on Decoration – With Fabrics*, Britwell Books, London, 1971

Hicks, David, *David Hicks on Decoration*, Britwell Books, London, 1972

Hoskins, Lesley, Mark Pinney and Mark Turner, *A Popular Art – British Wallpapers 1930–1960*, Silver Studio Archive, Middlesex Polytechnic, London, 1989

Hoskins, Lesley, (ed), *The Papered Wall – The History, Patterns and Techniques of Wallpaper*, Thames and Hudson, London, 1994

Larsen, Jack Lenor, *Jack Lenor Larsen – 30 Years of Creative Textiles*, Jack Lenor Larsen, New York, 1981

Peat, Alan, *David Whitehead Fabrics – Artist Designed Textiles 1952–1969*, Oldham Art Gallery, Oldham, 1993

Schoeser, Mary, *Fabrics and Wallpapers*, Bell & Hyman, London, 1986

Index

Picture Acknowledgements

The Advertising Archives 9l, 9r; Richard Bryant/Arcaid 23b; Richard Einzig/Arcaid 132t, 132br; Archigram Archives/Photo Dennis Crompton 179; Archivio Gio Ponti 95l, 96t; Arflex International, Milan 196c; Artemide spa, Milan/Photo Studio Ballo 118b, 161tr , 193l, 195ll; Artifort, Maastricht 155br, 189t; Asko, Lahti, Finland 171b; B&B Italia 161b, 190-191, 197t; Bernini spa 108t; Courtesy of the estate of Marc Boxer 38r; Braun AG 62tr; Brighton Museum and Art Gallery 24bl; British Architectural Library, RIBA, London 74t, 77r, 78, 81t, 100, 120tl, 124t, 130b,138b, 176tr; British Film Institute 175t, 191b, 203tl; Cassina spa/Photo Aldo Ballo 108bl; Centre d'Histoire de Montréal (Photo Francine Genest)136t,136b, (Rosengarten Collection)137t and 137b; Christo and Jeanne-Claude, © Christo 1966/Photo Carole T Hartwell 199cl; Max Clendinning 145b, 147tr, 183b; Comfort srl 182l; The Corning Museum of Glass 218bc; Robin Day 33; Richard Dennis Publications 58b, 63c, 127t ('Whitefriars Glass. The Art of James Powell & Sons', ed. Lesley Jackson), 147br ('Poole Pottery, Carter & Company and their Successors, 1873-1995', by Leslie Hayward, ed. Paul Atterbury); © Design Council Slide Collection at The Manchester Metropolitan University 20br, 24br, 36r, 47cl, 51br, 59b, 64bl, 71b, 72l, 95r, 195bl, 200bl, 210, 214tl, 218bl; Design Council Slide Collection at The Manchester Metropolitan University 3cr, 47br, 48cl © Habitat Designs, 48b, 51t, 69t © Buzas and Irvine, 72r, 94t, 101b, 104b © Keith Albarn, 138t, 139, 145t and 146 © Garnett, Cloughley, Blakemore & Associates, 184b © The Observer, 200br © Papp und Faltmöbel, 218br © Samuel J Herman; Domus/Photo Casali Domus 92tl, 93; EMAP Construct 23t, 34, 36l, 68br, 69b, 79b, 80t, 132bl, 134; Ezra Stoller © ESTO 106tl, 120tr; Fiell International Ltd/Photo P Chave 171t, 188, 200tl; Rodney Fitch 48tl; Flos, Milan 117, 118t; Galleria Marina Barovier, Venice, Italy 2l, 67, 92tr, 92b, 160l, 174; GA Photographers © Yukio Futagawa 15; Philippe Garner 31br, 35b, 42tr, 45bc, 47t, 110, 147tl, 181b, 226r, 227l; Gruppo Associati Sormani, Arosio 183r; Hackman Designor Oy Ab, Iittala Glass Museum, 14500 Iittala, Finland 28tl, 28tr, 29tl, 29tr, 64tl Photo INDAV/Timo Kauppila, 216br, Photo Gero Mylius, 222tl, 222b; Fritz Hansen A/S 19b, 24bc, 165tr; Harrods Ltd 37r, 107t; Hans Hollein, Vienna/Photo Franz Hubmann 106bl, 106br; © Angelo Hornak Library 141b, 148tl, 148b, 161tl Courtesy of V&A Museum, 218t; Hulton Getty 42bl; Illums Bolighus, Copenhagen 49; Arata Isozaki & Associates/GA Photographers © Yoshio Takase 178r; Grete Jalk 2c, 165tl, 165b; Kartell spa 71l; Keramiskt Centrum, Gustavsberg Porslin 26bl, 168tl, 168tr, 168br; Courtesy of Knoll Archives, New York 11, 155t; Balthazar Korab Ltd 82br, 101c, 102t, 148tr; Kosta Boda 167t, 167br, 220b; Kisho Kurokawa architect and associates/Photo Tomio Ohashi 225; Jack Larsen 151, 152; Nanny Still McKinney 64bc; Maguire & Co/photo John Whybrow 133b; Manchester Metropolitan University 25, 65, 73br, 80b, 109l, 115t, 119b, 127b, 150l, 150c, 150r, 155bl, 156, 159bl, 168bl, 172t, 177r, 181t, 193r, 195br, 199cr, 200tr, 220tl, 220tr; Angelo Mangiarotti 79; Milan Triennale 142b, 157l; Herman Miller Inc 124bl, 153, 228l; Courtesy of the Montreal Museum of Decorative Arts D84.111.1 – gift of Herman Miller Inc/ Photo Giles Rivest (Montreal) 59tl, D87.247.1 – gift of Eric and Nanette Brill/Photo Richard P Goodbody, New York 109r, D89.102.1-47 – The Liliane & David M Stewart Collection/Photo David Arky (New York) 216t; Museum of Art and Design, Helsinki (Taideteollisuusmuseo) 2cl, 39bl, 94b, 140, 172c, 172b, 173bl, 173bc, 173br, 214tr; Museum of Decorative Arts, Prague (Umeleckoprumyslové Muzeum)/Photo Gabriel Urbánek 64r, 142tl, 219l, 219r; Museum of Finnish Architecture (Suomen Rakennustaiteen Museo) 103b; J L Miller 162t; National Monuments Record 98; National Museum, Stockholm 168bc; Orrefors, Sweden 26br, 27, 167bl; Verner Panton 3l, 55t, 107b, 114, 115b, 186, 187t, 187b, 199t; Pentagram, London 44; Philadelphia Museum of Art 159tr, 194; Renzo Piano Building Workshop 101t; Portmeirion Potteries Ltd 61tl; Pringle Brandon/Photo Colin Westwood 129b; Private Collection/Photo David Giles 2r, 13, 18t, 18bl, 18br, 20tl, 20tr, 47bl, 54, 56t, 61tr, 61b, 63b, 83tl, 96b, 203b, 211l, 212t; Mary Quant Ltd 35t, 42tl, 42cr, 52b; Queensbury Hunt Levien 59cr; Wendy Ramshaw/Photo Bob Cramp 51bl; Rex Features Ltd 6, 38l, 39t, 41, 42br, 45cl, 45br, 52t, 175r, 176b, 177l, 226l, 227l, 228r, 229; Bridget Riley/Photo Prudence Cuming Associates Ltd 86; Rosenthal AG 29bl, 59tr, 111, 184t, 185; Saporiti Italia 195tr; Julius Shulman 12, 14, 16t, 55b, 68t, 75, 76-77, 103t, 105, 122-123, 128bl, 128br, 131b, 133t, 176tl, 224; Alison and Peter Smithson 104t; Ettore Sottsass 62l Photo Santi Caleca, 97l Photo Fioravanti, 97r, 159br, 178l; A/S Stelton 24t; The Stillman and Eastwick-Field Partnership/Photo Keith Gibson 130t; Studio Ballo 160r; Studio Joe Colombo, Milan 70, 73t, 106tr, 158, 182r; Studio Dillon/Photo Maurer 180t; Kenzo Tange Associates/Photo Osamu Murai 74b, 81b, 131t; © 1966 Time Inc, reprinted by permission/Katz Pictures Ltd 39br; V & A Picture Library 222tr; The Vintage Magazine Company Archive 37l; Vitra Design Museum Collection, Weil am Rhein 4, 17b, 163, 180b, 189b, 196b, 199bc; Von Klier Associati, Milan 57t, 57l; Vuokko Oy, Helsinki/Photo Max Petrelius 141t, 173t; Robert Welch 30l, 30r, 58l; Whitmore + Thomas + Angell 45bl; Designed by Whitmore + Thomas + Angell 45t; The Whitworth Art Gallery, The University of Manchester 56b, 83bl, 83r, 85t, 85b, 87t, 88t, 88b, 91l, 127c, 203tr, 204, 205r, 206t, 206b, 208t, 208b, 209l, 209r, 212bl; Sami Wirkkala 29br, 66, 87b; Wolff Olins 40b; The Worshipful Company of Goldsmiths 216bl, 216bc;

Front and Back Cover and Flaps

Details from illustrations courtesy of B&B Italia, British Architectural Library, RIBA, Richard Dennis Publications, Design Council Slide Collection at the Manchester Metropolitan University, Domus/Photo Casali Domus, Fiell International Ltd/Photo P Chave, Philippe Garner, Angelo Hornak Library, Manchester Metropolitan University, Herman Miller Inc, Museum of Art and Design, Helsinki, Museum of Decorative Arts, Prague, Verner Panton, Private Collection/Photo David Giles, Mary Quant Ltd, Rex Features, Rosenthal AG, Julius Shulman, V&A Picture Library, Vitra Design Museum, The Whitworth Art Gallery, The University of Manchester, Sami Wirkkala

Front Cover

Columns, from left to right, top to bottom:
Column 1: Falmer House, University of Sussex, by Sir Basil Spence, 1960; Jungle textile by Betty Middleton-Sandford for Edinburgh Weavers, 1965; Colonnade textile by Barbara Brown for Heal's, 1964.
Column 2: Mary Quant having her hair cut by Vidal Sassoon, 1964; Heart sculpture by Stanislav Libenský and Jaroslava Brychtová, 1968.
Column 3: Delphis range by Poole Pottery, late 1960s; Globe chair by Eero Aarnio for Asko, 1965; Aztec pattern on Studio shape by Tom Arnold for J & G Meakin, c1964.
Column 4: American Pavilion at the Montreal Expo by Buckminster Fuller, 1967; Visiona installation at the Cologne Furniture Fair designed by Verner Panton, 1968; Quasar and Emmanuelle Khanh, in an inflatable house on blow-up furniture, 1968; Paul McCartney and John Lennon; Metropolitan Opera House, Lincoln Center for the Performing Arts, New York, by Wallace K Harrrison, 1966; Lollipop Isle by Oiva Toikka for Nuutajärvi, 1969.
Column 5: Reiner Residence, Silvertop, Los Angeles, by John Lautner, 1963; woven textiles by Marjatta Metsovaara, 1960s; Panton chair by Verner Panton for Herman Miller, 1960.

Front Flap

Left: Pulp and Paper Pavilion, Montreal Expo, 1967; right: Koreana bowl by Tapio Wirkkala for Venini, 1968.

Back Flap

Top: Op Art interior by Gae Aulenti for the Centro-Fly department store in Milan, 1966; bottom left: printed fabric panel by Alexander Girard for Herman Miller, c1971; bottom right: Lombrico sofa by Marco Zanuso for C & B Italia, 1967.

Back Cover

Column 1: Melooni fabric by Maija Isola for Marimekko, 1963; bottle by Tapio Wirkkala, for Venini, c1966.
Column 2: Stevens Residence, Malibu, California, by John Lautner, 1968; cover of Disraeli Gears by Cream, designed by Martin Sharp, 1967.
Column 3: London Combination modular seating by Geoffrey Harcourt for Artifort, 1967; Hecuba wallpaper by David Bartle for Sanderson, 1968; Composition coffee cup by Tapio Wirkkala for Rosenthal, 1963; Ribbon chair by Pierre Paulin for Artifort, 1966 and Chimera lamp by Vico Magistretti for Artemide, 1966; stoneware vessels by Lisa Larsen for Gustavsberg, c1962.
Column 4: Cone chairs by Verner Panton for Plus-Linje, 1958; Monrepos dress by Annika Rimala for Marimekko, 1967, made from Oasis fabric, 1966.
Column 5: Girl on a moped wearing a Marimekko dress, c1966.

PAGE 2, left to right:

Contrappunto vases by Antonio da Ros for Gino Cenedese, shown at the Venice Biennale in 1960; Shadows in the Snow, a hand-made rya rug by the Finnish designer, Kirsti Ilvessalo, 1968; ribbon-like laminated oak chair by Grete Jalk for P Jeppesen, 1963.

PAGE 3, left to right

Aztec pattern on Studio shape by Tom Arnold for J & G Meakin, c1964; Visir or Moon lamp by Verner Panton for Louis Poulsen, 1960; Concord wallpaper by Michael Hatjoullis for Sanderson, 1966; American Pavilion at the Montreal Expo by Buckminster Fuller, 1967.

PAGE 4

Donna chair and footrest, UP5 and UP6 from a series by Gaetano Pesce for C & B Italia, 1969.

For Ian

Author's Acknowledgements

I would particularly like to thank Ian Fishwick for the extensive research and fact-verification that he has contributed to this book. I am grateful to Eileen Preston for her personal recollections of the Montreal Expo, and to Don Doehring for rooting out valuable information about this event. Thanks are also due to family and friends who have generously supplied me with stimulating books and objects over the years, with special thanks to Liz Broadley for the textiles insight for which I am lastingly grateful, and also to Judith and Bill Amos.

Many museum curators throughout the world have graciously sent me information about their collections and subsequently supplied images. Access to collections in storage has been invaluable for my research, and I would particularly like to thank Dr Jennifer Harris, Frances Pritchard and Christine Woods at the Whitworth Art Gallery, and the curators at the Victoria and Albert Museum, especially Judith Crouch. I would also like to thank John Davis, Gaye Smith and their colleagues at Manchester Metropolitan University, whose resources I have drawn upon. The collections of both the Museum of Decorative Arts, Prague (Umeleckoprumyslové Muzeum) and the Museum of Art and Design, Helsinki (Taideteollisuusmuseo) have also proved most fruitful. Many thanks are also due to the Twentieth Century Society for the stimulating events they have organized which have given me the opportunity to see numerous important post-war buildings at first hand.

In order to fully capture the excitement and intensity of the period, and to give an accurate and authentic representation of the ideas of the designers and entrepreneurs of the 1960s, I have quoted from contemporary sources and first-hand accounts and would like to thank those writers and practitioners whose views I have cited. Thanks are also due to Fitzroy Dearborn for allowing me to draw on some of the text I had previously written for entries in their *Encyclopedia of Interior Design* published in 1997.

Securing the range and quality of images required for this book has proved a monumental undertaking, particularly the tracking down of original photographs from the period. I would particularly like to thank my picture researcher, Christine Crawshaw, for her tireless efforts in locating all this material, ably assisted by Rebecca Teevan. Thanks are also due to all the architects, designers, artists, manufacturers and photographers around the world who have generously supplied original material and allowed their work to be illustrated, including Julius Shulman for allowing us access to a wealth of previously unpublished work and whose images are so resonant, and with special thanks to Jane Dillon for the loan of valuable periodicals.

Finally, I would like to thank Roger Sears who originally encouraged me to write this book, and Iona Baird, my project editor at Phaidon, for her patience and attention to detail in preparing it for publication.

Phaidon Press Limited
Regent's Wharf
All Saints Street
London N1 9PA

First published 1998
Reprinted 1999
Reprinted in paperback 2000
© 1998 Phaidon Press Limited

ISBN 0 7148 3963 9
A CIP Catalogue record for this book is available from the British Library

Printed in Hong Kong